The Early Church and Today

The Early Church and Today

Volume 2 · Christian Life, Scripture, and Restoration

Everett Ferguson

Abilene Christian University Press

THE EARLY CHURCH AND TODAY

Volume Two: Christian Life, Scripture, and Restoration

ACU PRESS

Copyright 2014 by Everett Ferguson

ISBN 978-0-89112-584-6
LCCN 2012025192

Printed in the United States of America

LIBRARY OF CONGRESS CATALOGING-IN-PUBLICATION DATA
Ferguson, Everett, 1933-
The early church and today / Everett Ferguson.
    p. cm.
ISBN 978-0-89112-584-6
1. Church history--Primitive and early church, ca. 30-600. I. Title.
BR165.F373 2014
270.1--dc23

2012025192

Cover design by Rick Gibson
Interior text design by Sandy Armstrong, Strong Design

For information contact:
Abilene Christian University Press
1626 Campus Court
Abilene, Texas 79601

1-877-816-4455
www.abilenechristianuniversitypress.com

14 15 16 17 18 19 / 7 6 5 4 3 2 1

To the memory of Dr. Donald Everett Lewis,
my best friend and then brother-in-law; a kind, humble, and
responsible man of integrity; learned chemist;
compassionate teacher, caring for his subject and his students;
loving husband, father, and grandfather;
dedicated Christian and churchman.

Contents

Part IV: Restoration Movement

Part V: Religious Liberty

Part VI: Biblical Eschatology

Acknowledgments

The following journals, publishers, and institutions generously gave permission for reprinting my articles:

Abilene Christian University
Acta Patristica et Byzantina
Australian E-Journal of Theology
Baker Publishing Co.
Freed-Hardeman University
Gospel Advocate Co.
Harding University
Pepperdine University Press
Restoration Quarterly
Scottish Journal of Theology
Southern Methodist University Press
Thomas Jefferson University Press
Trinity Press International
Western Christian Foundation
Wm. B. Eerdmans Publishing Co.

Acknowledgment of the original source of publication accompanies each article.

Part I

Christian Living

Christian Living in a Pagan Society

Background

Pagan morality in the early centuries of Christianity presents a mixed picture. The pagan satirists Horace and Juvenal give evidence of much immorality in Roman society at the beginning of the Christian era. But there were pagans who lived morally upright lives. These same satirists and moralists are themselves evidence of codes of acceptable moral conduct, or else they would not have made their criticisms or received a hearing. In the New Testament Paul's devastating critique in Romans 1:18–32 must be balanced by his recognition in 2:14–16 of another side to Gentile conduct.

Ethics was the primary concern of the philosophical schools in the Hellenistic age. Platonists, Aristotelians, and especially Stoics developed high standards and provided moral guidance for many people. Religion for Gentiles had to do with sacrifices, ceremonies, and ritual purity; otherwise it had very little to do with one's conduct. For moral guidance one turned to the poets (who were the center of the educational curriculum), playwrights, and philosophers.

One place where similarities of pagan philosophy to Christian teaching is evident is in what are now called the household codes; that is, how one should conduct oneself in various relationships—for the man as father, husband, and slave-owner. Examples in Christian literature are Ephesians 5:21–6:9; Colossians 3:18–4:1; and more loosely Polycarp, *Philippians* 4.2–6.1.

Even where the conduct was the same, Christian motives were different—more on that later; for now, note that the difference in motives often led to differences in behavior. And the Christian approach was different, addressing the subordinate members of the relationships as well as the superiors.

The closest parallels to Christian moral teaching, as is to be expected, are in Judaism.

The Two Ways

One framework for Jewish moral teaching, itself influenced in the Hellenistic age by a motif in Greek literature and philosophy, was "the two ways." The basis in Judaism was Deuteronomy 30:15–20 on the way of life and the way of death. In the Dead Sea Scrolls the two ways are expressed as the way of light and the way of darkness (1QS III, 18–25; 1QM I, 1–10).

This scheme is set forth in the baptismal instruction at the beginning of the *Didache*, a manual of early Christian Judaism.

> There are two ways, one of life, the other of death, and between the two ways there is a great difference.
>
> Now the way of life is this: you shall love first the God who created you, then your neighbor as yourself, and do not yourself do to another what you would not want done to you.
>
> Here is the teaching from these words. Bless those who curse you and pray for your enemies, fast for those who persecute you. . . .
>
> The second commandment of the doctrine: You shall not murder. You shall not commit adultery. You shall not corrupt children. You shall not fornicate. You shall not steal. You shall

not practice magic. You shall not use the confections of a sorcerer. You shall not murder a child, whether by abortion or by killing it once it is born. You shall not covet what belongs to your neighbor. You shall not swear falsely. You shall not bear false witness. You shall not speak evil of anyone. You shall not harbor resentment. You shall not equivocate, either in what you think or in what you say.... Your word shall not be false or empty but shall be fulfilled in what you really do. You shall not be given to greed, or swindling, or hypocrisy, or malice, or pride. You shall not plot evil against your neighbor. You shall not hate anyone. (*Didache* 1.1–2.7)[1]

The *Didache* sets this expansion of the Decalogue within the framework of the teachings of Jesus.

Christian Apologists

Impressive to me is the way Christian apologists of the second and third centuries put so much emphasis on Christian living as an argument for the truth of Christianity.[2] Part of that is defensive—to answer charges of immorality against Christians and to remove suspicion about a secretive group.[3] The apologists go beyond that, however, to make a positive claim for Christianity.

Do Christian apologists do that today? Would they even be able to make a claim for the truth of Christianity from the way Christians live? One factor is that Christian ethics have had two millennia to leaven society, at times reducing the difference between what Christians teach and others accept. Nevertheless, in our post-Christian world we are returning to the situation of the early centuries. Ways of thinking and standards of the non-Christian society heavily influence church members. There is always the need to instruct church members and especially to clarify the different premises of secular and Christian conduct.

Not all Christians measured up to the conduct the apologists presented. The apologists certainly did some idealizing. Yet there must have been some basis for the claims. Otherwise, why take this approach? Philosophers took the position that they cured or healed human conduct. That which accomplished such a cure was central to philosophy's truth claims. I think there is something to that. In our day, the manner of life that results from a philosophy or religion is important in judging it. As Jesus said, "By their fruits ye shall know them" (Matt. 7:16 ASV).

Even the popular philosophers influenced for the most part only a small portion of the population. Christianity accomplished for the masses, especially the uneducated, what philosophy had not been able to do.[4]

The Christian manner of life had converting power. Justin Martyr, himself converted in part because of the influence of the way Christians faced martyrdom,[5] described how Christian examples changed the lives of others.

> [Christ] urged us through forbearance and gentleness to lead everyone out of shame and the desire for evil. This we are able to show in regard to many who were once of your way of thinking. They changed from their violent and tyrannical ways, being overcome when they observed the patient endurance of life by their neighbors or perceived the unusual forbearance of their fellow travellers when defrauded or made proof of those with whom they had business dealings. (*1 Apology* 16)

The apologists grounded Christian ethics in theology. This is evident already in the moving description of the Christian manner of life by one of the earliest apologists whose work has survived, Aristides of Athens.

> [The Christians] know and trust God . . . from whom they received commandments which they engraved upon their minds and observe in hope and expectation of the world which is to come. Wherefore they do not commit adultery nor fornication, nor bear false witness, nor embezzle what is held in pledge, nor covet what is not theirs. They honor father and mother, and show kindness to those near to them; and whenever they are judges, they judge uprightly. They do not worship idols . . . and whatsoever they would not that others should do unto them, they do not do to others. . . . They do good to their enemies. And their women are pure and virgins and do not offer their wombs; and their men exercise self-control from every unlawful union and especially from impurity; and their wives similarly exercise

self-control, for they cling to a great hope of the world to come. If they should have bondmen and bondwomen or children, they persuade them to become Christians in order that they might be friends, and when they have become such, they call them brothers and sisters without distinction. . . . They are gentle, moderate, modest, and truthful. They love one another. They do not overlook the widow, and they save the orphan. He who has ministers ungrudgingly to him who does not have. When they see strangers, they take them under their own roof and rejoice over them as true brothers, for they do not call themselves brothers according to the flesh but according to the soul. And whenever they see one of their poor has died, each one of them according to ability contributes ungrudgingly and they bury him. And if they hear that some are condemned or imprisoned on account of the name of the Lord, they contribute for those condemned and send to them what they need, and if it is possible, they redeem them. . . . They observe carefully the precepts of God and live holily and justly as the Lord their God commanded them. They give thanks to him every morning and every hour for food and drink and other good things. If any righteous person among them dies, they rejoice and offer thanks and pray concerning *after death?* that one; and they escort the body as if for one setting out on a journey. And when a child has been born to one of them, they give thanks to God; and if it should die as an infant, they give thanks the more, because it has departed life sinless. But if any one should die in sins, they weep, since that one goes to punishment. (Aristides, *Apology* 15)

We notice at the beginning of the passage that it is because Christians know and trust God and have received his commandments that they act the way they do. Then Aristides repeats the point toward the end of the chapter that Christians are careful to observe what God commands. The eschatological basis of Christian conduct is also evident. Christians live in hope and expectation of the world to come, and that hope motivates purity in sexual matters.

The Christian faith gives assurance at the death of the righteous and of small children but grief at the death of sinners who go to punishment.

Specific Differences

There are some specific practices acceptable in the Greco-Roman world that were unacceptable to Jews and Christians.

One of these practices was the exposure of unwanted children. The quotation from the *Didache* above expresses the prohibition of killing a newborn child. The occasion for the prevalent practice in the ancient Mediterranean world of abandoning unwanted babies was economic. There was the persistent problem of too many mouths to feed. Girls were more of a financial liability than boys, for the bride's family had to provide a dowry. Hence, more girl babies were exposed than boys. The legal basis of the practice was that a child was not considered a person until the father accepted the child. Therefore, exposure of the child was not considered murder but refusal to admit to society.

A related practice was abortion. Only a few pagans opposed the practice. It was mainly Jews and Christians in the ancient world who took a stand against it. The modern debate over abortion justifies a fuller statement of the historic Christian position.[6]

Abortion is forbidden in *Didache* 2.2 (above) and in the *Epistle of Barnabas* 20.1–2. The *Apocalypse of Peter* 8 puts those guilty of abortion in hell.[7]

Some writers provide the moral rationale for the prohibition of abortion.

The apologist Athenagoras, answering the slander by some pagans that Christians murdered babies and ate their flesh, says this:

> And when we say that those women who use drugs to bring on abortion commit murder and will have to give an account to God for the abortion, on what principle should we commit murder? For it does not belong to the same person to regard the very fetus in the womb as a created being, and therefore an object of God's care, and when it has passed into life to kill it; and not to expose an infant, because those who expose them are chargeable with child-murder, and on the other hand, when it has been reared to destroy it. (*Plea* 35)

Athenagoras reasons from the Christian opposition to child exposure and to abortion to show the unreasonableness of the charge that the Lord's Supper was a Thyestean banquet. He gives the moral argument that the fetus is a created person and object of God's care, so to take its life is murder.

Clement of Alexandria similarly says that "women who resort to some sort of deadly abortion drug kill not only the embryo but along with it all human kindness" (*Paedagogus* 2.10.96). He elsewhere quotes an older predecessor that "the embryo is a living thing; for that the soul entering into the womb after it has been by cleansing prepared for conception" and quotes Luke 1:41 in support (*Eclogues* 50).

Tertullian of Carthage among the early writers has the most to say:

> For us [Christians] murder is once for all forbidden; so even the child in the womb, while yet the mother's blood is still being drawn on to form the human beings, it is not lawful for us to destroy. To forbid birth is only quicker murder. It makes no difference whether one take away the life once born or destroy it as it is coming to birth. One is a human who is to be a human; the fruit is always present in the seed. (*Apology* 9.8)

His treatise *On the Soul* 27 also affirms that life begins at conception. Similar to the statement in his *Apology* he says, "To us it is no more lawful to hurt a child in the process of birth than one already born" (*Chastity* 12).

As with abortion, on the matter of homosexual conduct, my concern is not with legal aspects but the early Christian stance on the moral aspects. Homosexual relations were commonly accepted in the Greco-Roman society of the early church. Jews and Christians once more manifested a different attitude.[8]

Here the texts of the New Testament are explicit. Romans 1:26–27 is notable for expressly including female as well as male conduct in its strictures:

> For this reason [not acknowledging God as Creator] God gave them up to degrading passions. Their women exchanged natural intercourse for unnatural, and in the same way also the men, giving up natural intercourse with women, were consumed with passion for one another. Men committed shameless acts with

men and received in their own persons the due penalty for their error. (NRSV)

First Corinthians 6:9 includes the Greek words used for the passive partners (the ones penetrated—*malakoi*) and the active partners (the ones penetrating—*arsenokoitai*) in homosexual relationships in its list of those who will not "inherit the kingdom of God." First Timothy 1:10 uses the latter word in a general sense for homosexual immorality parallel with the word for heterosexual immorality (*pornois*).

Other early Christian literature repeats the prohibition. *Didache* 2.2, quoted above, puts "corrupting boys" (the common form of Greek homosexuality) alongside but distinct from fornication. Athenagoras refers to pagans "who do not abstain even from males, males with males committing shocking abominations, outraging all the noblest and comeliest bodies in all sorts of ways, so dishonoring the fair workmanship of God" (*Plea* 34).

Clement of Alexandria has the most to say on the subject of homosexual activity. Out of his larger discussion of the natural order I select this quotation:

> The clear conclusion that we must draw, then, is that we must condemn sodomy, all fruitless sowing of seed, any unnatural methods of holding intercourse and the reversal of the sexual role in intercourse. (*Instructor* 2.10.87)

In another passage he mentions lesbianism along with prostitution and male homosexuality:

> Women live in brothels, there offering their own bodies for sale to satisfy lustful pleasure, and boys are taught to renounce their own natures and play the role of women. Self-indulgence has turned everything upside down. . . . It seeks everything, it attempts everything, it forces everything, it violates even nature. Men have become the passive mate in sexual relations, and women act as men; contrary to nature, women now are both wives and husbands. (*Instructor* 3.3.21; cf. 3.3.23)

These texts deal with homosexual acts, not "sexual orientation," just as texts on fornication and adultery concern practices. Modern efforts to limit the application of the texts (the New Testament especially) to pederasty or explain them as related to pagan temple prostitutes and idolatry find no support in the texts themselves. To discount them as belonging to an age that did not know modern views on sexual orientation likewise misses their import.

Conclusion

Christian morality is at odds with modern lifestyles as much as it was with pagan life in antiquity. As the modern western world moves to an increasingly post-Christian, post-modern situation, Christian living may be informed by the ancient Christian understanding.

* Adapted from an unpublished lecture given at Carey Baptist College, Auckland, New Zealand, March 14, 2003, and at the University of Melbourne, Australia, April 4, 2003.

Chapter 1 Endnotes

1 The comparable material in the *Epistle of Barnabas* 18–20 is framed as the way of light and the way of darkness.

2 Everett Ferguson, *Early Christians Speak*, 3rd ed. (Abilene: ACU Press, 1999), 189–202.

3 Athenagoras, *Plea* 3.

4 Origen, *Against Celsus* 7.41, 44.

5 Justin Martyr, *2 Apology* 12.

6 A fuller collection of passages can be found in M. J. Gorman, *Abortion and the Early Church: Christian, Jewish, and Pagan Attitudes in the Greco-Roman World* (Downers Grove: InterVarsity, 1982).

7 Patrick Gray, "Abortion, Infanticide, and the Social Rhetoric of the *Apocalypse of Peter*," *Journal of Early Christian Studies* 9, no. 3 (Fall 2001): 313–337.

8 D. F. Wright, "Homosexuals or Prostitutes? The Meaning of *arsenokoitai* (1 Cor. 6:9; 1 Tim. 1:10)," *Vigiliae Christianae* 38 (1984): 125–153; Wright, "Early Christian Attitudes to Homosexuality," *Studia Patristica* 18.2 (1989): 291–300; B. J. Brooten, *Love between Women: Early Christian Responses to Female Homoeroticism* (Chicago: University of Chicago Press, 1996).

Love of Enemies and Nonretaliation in the Second Century

G eorge Williams has a marvelous capacity to place things in a grand perspective and show their wider relationships. To listen to his lectures and to read his writings is to attend the Mind Extension University. Taking notes on his lectures was the despair of students. Every sentence was a paragraph set in such a large context with numerous parallels and so many nuances and qualifications that lesser minds soon suffered information overload.

One characteristic of George Williams's work that has impressed me the most is the sense of the wholeness of church history that he conveyed. I have not been able to follow him in carrying on original research across the whole length and breadth of Christian history, but he gave me a conception of the whole that I trust has continued to inform and give perspective to my teaching, editing, and writing. In his presentations Catholic and Orthodox, Protestant and Free Church, all have their place as expressions of the Christian faith and as providing different facets of the wholeness of Christian teaching.

If we may liken the study of Church History to riding on the MBTA (Metropolitan Boston Transit Authority), George Williams commuted daily—one day getting off at the sixteenth century, another day at the twelfth century, or the fourth, or the second. He knows those neighborhoods, as well as all others, exceedingly well. We students had a saying, "George Williams does not lecture on church history; he reminisces."

The American Society of Church History, of which George Williams was president, has a prize in ecumenical church history (the Albert C. Outler Prize). George Williams was practicing ecumenical church history long before there was a name for it. This study takes a tiny slice, topically and chronologically, out of Christian history. Its modest proportions, reflecting only a quite small measure of my indebtedness to Professor Williams, nonetheless point to some of his central moral concerns and to a core of early Christian moral teachings.

Some New Testament scholars have suggested that the repetition of the command "Do not repay evil for evil" in the paraenetic sections of different New Testament letters indicates a catechetical tradition also reflected in Matthew 5 and Luke 6.[1] I propose to follow that suggestion through some of the second-century Christian literature.[2] The influence of the Sermon on the Mount/Sermon on the Plain in the early church has been the subject of other studies.[3] This influence, I am persuaded, is due in part to the use of some of this material in the instruction of new converts. My purpose here will be limited to the teaching in common between Matt. 5:21–48 and Luke 6:27–38 on love for enemies and nonretaliation.

The love of enemies was not unique to Christian teaching.[4] The frequency with which Christians taught it[5] and the insistence that Christians actually lived by it, however, did make it distinctive of Christianity.

Perhaps the earliest reflection in noncanonical literature of this theme of doing good to those who have wronged you is *1 Clement* 13.2, which calls on the readers to "remember the words of the Lord Jesus":

> Be merciful in order that you may receive mercy; forgive in order
> you may be forgiven; as you do, so it will be done to you; as you

give, so it will be given to you; as you judge so you will be judged; as you show kindness, so kindness will be shown to you; with what measure you measure, by the same you will be measured.[6]

This passage comes near the beginning of Clement's discussion of humility. In a typical sequence, he opens with a quotation of an Old Testament text (Jer. 9:23–24) followed by the words of Jesus that I have quoted; he then proceeds with examples of humility from Christ and Old Testament heroes. Clement thus sees these words of Jesus as requiring a humble attitude, and this attitude he felt was needed by the Corinthian Christians in resolving their internal conflict.

Clement has a fondness for groupings of seven sayings and seven examples, so it is not out of the question that this particular collection of the sayings of Jesus, although using traditional oral and written material, is his own. The statements are structurally balanced, so some care was given to their wording. Such a careful formulation, if not later than Matthew and Luke, then was independent of them, for it is to be presumed that if an author knew such an attractively constructed collection of sayings, this would be the form in which the sayings were used.[7] How early a writer quotes written Gospels and how late one quotes oral formulations parallel to or independent of written Gospels is not my concern here. Such is a worthwhile task, the solution to which has not been expressed to everyone's satisfaction.[8] I think that the variety of formulations of essentially the same teaching[9] is a reflection not of fluidity of content but rather of how common the teaching was and how frequently it was employed in different settings and for different purposes, and so of its preservation and repetition in a variety of forms.[10]

Clement could expect the Corinthian Christians to "remember" these words of Jesus because they were a part of common Christian instruction. I turn now to the *Didache*, which I consider in essentially its present form perhaps as early as *1 Clement,* but such an early date is not necessary to a claim that common catechetical usage is reflected in it. The present form of the *Didache* inserts into the contents of "The Two Ways" a description of "the way of life" that contains the closest parallels in the *Didache* to the synoptic Gospels, and those parallels pertain to the section of the Sermon on the Mount/Plain dealing with love of enemies and nonretaliation.

> Bless those who curse you and pray for your enemies; fast on behalf of those who persecute you. For what grace is it if you love those who love you? Do not the Gentiles do this? But love those who hate you, and you will not have an enemy. Abstain from fleshly and bodily lusts. If anyone gives you a blow on the right cheek, turn to him the other, and you will be perfect. If one presses you into service for one mile, go with him two. If someone takes your cloak, give to him also your undergarment. If someone takes what is yours, do not refuse, for so you are able to be perfect.[11] To everyone who asks you, give and do not refuse. . . . (*Did.* 1.3–5a)

Again we have close parallels to Matthew 5 and Luke 6, but not exact correspondence. Whether the formulation is that of the compiler of the *Didache* or is earlier, and whether it is dependent on the synoptic Gospels or on sources independent of them, remains debatable.[12] In the absence of external controls, arguments concerning literary dependence are often reversible. There are clearly seams separating 1.2b–2.1 from the present context; hence, it is usually considered that this is a later insertion into the framework of "The Two Ways." However, that the Christian material is secondary in time to the Jewish "Two Ways" does not mean that it is necessarily secondary in the compilation of the *Didache*.[13] It is possible that the Christian section could have been joined to the Jewish "Two Ways" in order to give more specific moral teaching needed by Gentile converts, and if the "evangelical section" is based on oral tradition earlier than or independent of the written Gospels, then this could have occurred quite early. The main point I want to make now is unaffected by these questions of source analysis.

What is not to be doubted is that the compiler of the *Didache* in its present form intended by his arrangement of the material to present the teachings of Jesus, the words we have quoted above, as a baptismal catechesis. They would be included in the instructions given concerning baptism in chapter 7: "Having previously said these things, baptize in the name of the Father, the Son, and the Holy Spirit." By combining the moral injunctions of "The Two Ways" with the words of Jesus he specifies some of the things involved in "love of neighbor," doing good for enemies, and not retaliating for evil. These principles, the compiler says, prohibit, among other things (2.2), taking human life ("murder"), abortion ("murder a child by abortion"),[14] and infanticide ("kill what has been born"), or in modern terms the ultimate in child abuse.[15]

Justin Martyr's liturgical information offers sufficient parallels to the *Didache* that it has been suggested that he was acquainted with the document.[16] Many of these parallels may simply be common Christian material, but it would seem that Justin knew the *Didache* or a similar baptismal practice. George Williams has devoted a study to the "Baptismal Theology and Practice in Rome as Reflected in Justin Martyr."[17] There is an indication that Justin presupposes the use of the same words from Jesus in the instruction of new converts as the *Didache* employs. If we may assume that Justin's work as a teacher in Rome[18] included preparing converts for baptism, then what he says about Christian teaching is especially pertinent. Justin introduces his account of baptism in this way: "As many as are persuaded and believe that these things taught and said by us are true and promise to be able to live accordingly are taught while fasting to pray and ask from God the forgiveness of past sins" (*1 Apol.* 61.2). He explains the name "illumination" for baptism as indicating that "the ones learning these things [Christian teachings] are illuminated in their understanding" (*1 Apol.* 61.12). The passage stresses the moral contrast between previous "bad habits and evil conduct" and the new birth of Christians (*1 Apol.* 61.4, 10).

The "things taught and said" by Christians, about which the new convert must be persuaded and according to which Christians must undertake to live, would include those details of Jesus' teaching elaborated in *1 Apology* 14–16. The conversion context of the passage is evident:

> After being *persuaded* by the word . . . those who formerly rejoiced in fornication now embrace chastity alone; . . . those desiring more than anything the acquisition of wealth and possessions now bring what they have into a common fund and share with everyone in need; those who hated and destroyed one another and on account of their customs would not share a common table with those of another race now after the coming of Christ eat together with them, and they pray for their enemies

and endeavor to persuade those who hate them unjustly to live
according to the good precepts of Christ. (*1 Apol.* 14.2–3)

Justin then proceeds in chapters 15 and 16 to quote some of the teachings
of Jesus, mostly from the Sermon on the Mount/Plain and grouped under
four headings:[19] (1) "Concerning chastity"—citing Matt. 5:28, 29, 32; 19:11–
12; (2) "Concerning love for all"—citing Matt. 5:42, 44, 46 (Luke 6:27–28,
32); 5:45, 48; 6:19–20 (Luke 6:35–36); (3) "Concerning being patient, servants all, and free from wrath"—citing Matt. 5:39–40 (Luke 6:29);[20] (4)
"Concerning not swearing at all"—citing Matt. 5:34, 37. Although Justin's
quotations are often not verbatim, and various explanations of this have been
offered,[21] there is little doubt, in contrast to the situation with the *Didache*
and *1 Clement*, that Justin is using written Gospels.[22] In fact, Bellinzoni and
Koester postulate that Justin is one step beyond using written texts and has
made his own harmony of the Gospels.[23]

In the discussion of chastity Justin claims to be able to show "from every
race" disciples who have lived celibate from childhood to the age of sixty or
seventy. That Justin can make this claim provides incidental confirmation
that he can assume in this section a common moral teaching throughout
the church. Justin elsewhere expressly connects the moral teaching by Jesus
with conversion. In his *Dialogue with Trypho* 85.7 he cites the command of
Jesus "to love even one's enemies" (Matt. 5:44) as having been previously
preached by Isaiah (66:5–11), when the prophet spoke of the "mystery of our
(re)birth."[24] We want to return to Justin for a different point later, but let us
note now another witness to the use of the Sermon on the Mount tradition
in catechesis.

I have elsewhere argued that Irenaeus's *Demonstration [Proof] of the
Apostolic Preaching* had a catechetical rather than an apologetic purpose,
indeed may have been a manual to guide catechists in their instruction of
new converts.[25] The work begins with an allusion to the two ways (chap. 1);
the way of life or light requires faith and good works (chap. 2). The "rule of
faith" is connected with baptism (chaps. 3, 6–7). Irenaeus then surveys the
biblical history of salvation (chaps. 8–42a) and gives its spiritual meaning
(chaps. 42b–97). The latter part of the work contains the moral teachings of
the new covenant (chaps. 87–97), so that one may be "well-pleasing to God

through good works and sound moral character" (chap. 98).[26] Christians have no need for the Law as a pedagogue, because Christ's teachings about the heart supersede these requirements (chap. 96). He cites several examples from Matthew 5, including the following:

> For no more shall the law say . . . : "Thou shalt not kill" to him who has put away from himself all anger and enmity . . . Nor "an eye for an eye and a tooth for a tooth," to him who counts no man his enemy but all his neighbors, and therefore cannot even put forth his hand to revenge.[27]

The catechetical use of Jesus' teaching about love for enemies and nonretaliation is set forth in the *Didache*, Justin Martyr, and Irenaeus—therefore, from the early, to the mid-, to the late second century; from Syria, to Rome, to Gaul.

Catechesis and apologetics often have a large area of overlap in content. This is reflected in the confusion about the purpose of Irenaeus's *Demonstration* and the extent to which the apologists of the second century incorporated materials from basic Christian teaching into their apologies.[28] This feature was expedited in Justin's case by his dual function as catechist and apologist. The good moral life of Christians, in fact, was one of the principal arguments used by the apologists on behalf of the truth of Christian teaching.[29] The reverse side of this was the reproach by pagans when Christians did not live accordingly. Thus *2 Clement* 13.3–4 can admonish a Christian congregation that when pagans hear the excellent and marvelous teaching about loving enemies (Luke 6:27, 32, 35; Matt. 5:46–47) but see Christians not only not loving those who hate them but not loving even those who love them, they will laugh and blaspheme the name.[30]

The appeal to the Christian moral life is often stated in terms of Jesus' teaching recorded in the Sermon on the Mount/Plain. Already in the *Apology* of Aristides, without specific citation, although he refers to "observ[ing] the Messiah's precepts carefully" (15.10) and the "writings" of Christians (16.5),[31] there is the claim that Christians "comfort those who mistreat them and make them their friends, and they are diligent to do good to their enemies" (15.5).[32]

Justin develops the moral teaching from which we have drawn above, as do other second-century apologists, in answer to charges that Christians were atheists and some had been convicted as evildoers (*1 Apol.* 5.7). Later picking up the theme of peace from this early context (12.1), he makes the same contrast as made in chapter 14 between conduct before and after conversion. After quoting Isaiah 2:3–4 ("They shall not learn war any more"), he expresses the peace commitment of Christians: "We who formerly murdered one another not only do not make war on our enemies but also, in order that we might not lie nor deceive our examiners, willingly die confessing Christ" (*1 Apol.* 39.3).[33] The *Dialogue with Trypho* similarly refers to the acceptance of martyrdom, this time expressly connected with a citation of Jesus' teaching about love of enemies and being merciful[34]: Rather than "deny the name of Christ, we choose and endure rather to be put to death." Then he explains, "This Christ taught us to pray for our enemies, saying, 'Be kind and merciful, as also your Father in heaven' [cf. Luke 6:28, 35–36]" (*Dial.* 96.2–3).[35]

Theophilus, who as bishop of Antioch would have been involved with catechetical instruction, responds like Justin to the charges against Christians by appealing to Christian moral teaching. Christians could not practice sexual promiscuity and cannibalism, he argues, because of the teaching found in the Law, the Prophets, and the Gospels (*Autol.* 3.4, 12).[36] After citing "Solomon" (Proverbs) and the "Gospel" about not looking on a woman with lust, Theophilus repeats the connection Justin (*Dial.*85.7) made between Isaiah 66:5 (LXX, modified) and Matt. 5:44 ("the Gospel"), here perhaps combined with Luke 6:28, "Love your enemies, and pray for those who mistreat you" (*Autol.* 3.13, 14).[37] He concludes that "those who teach such things" cannot be guilty of unlawful intercourse or eating human flesh, "inasmuch as it is forbidden to us even to look at the spectacles of gladiators, lest we be partners and accomplices in murders" (*Autol.* 3.15).[38]

Athenagoras was philosophically the most sophisticated of the second-century Greek apologists. His citations of Gospel material, as is the case with Theophilus, are limited to the material in the Sermon on the Mount/Plain.[39] In a format similar to Justin and Theophilus, Athenagoras includes in his response to the charges of atheism, cannibalism, and incest (*Plea* 3) an appeal to Christian moral teaching.

> What then are the words in which we are nurtured? "I say to
> you: Love your enemies, bless those who curse you; pray for

those who persecute you, in order that you may be sons of the Father in heaven." (*Plea* 11.2, combining Matt. 5:44–45 and Luke 6:27–28)[40]

He points out that Christians, instead of returning evil, positively do good to their enemies. They, Athenagoras claims, succeed where grammarians and rhetoricians have failed in producing moral excellence:

> Among us you may find uneducated persons, workmen, and old women, who if by discourse are unable to present the benefit which comes from our doctrine, by deed demonstrate the benefit which comes from this persuasion. For they do not call to mind the words, but they exhibit good works. When they are struck, they do not strike back. When robbed, they do not go to law. They give to those asking and they love their neighbors as themselves. (*Plea* 11.4, alluding to Matt. 5:39–43 and Luke 6:29–30)[41]

Christians do not limit their love to their friends (*Plea* 12.3, quoting words similar to Luke 6:32, 34, and Matt. 5:46).

Later in his work Athenagoras returns to such teachings as they applied to some of the moral issues that Christians saw in the pagan society of the second century. In the same order as Justin and Theophilus he first takes up chastity, citing Matt. 5:28 (*Plea* 32.2). As something of an aside, Athenagoras further characterizes Christians as "those to whom it is not lawful when struck not to offer themselves [for more], nor when defamed not to bless; for it does not suffice to be just . . . but it is required [of us] to be good and patient" (*Plea* 34.3). These teachings, then, are clearly in Athenagoras's mind as he makes his next argument.

Athenagoras contends against the possibility that Christians are murderers (since cannibalism requires the taking of a human life) by indicating their attitude toward the gladiatorial contests and abortion. Christians cannot endure to see a person put to death, even justly. With reference to the contests of gladiators and wild beasts, Athenagoras states: "We, considering that to see one put to death is the next thing to killing him, have renounced such spectacles. How then can we who do not even look at such sights lest we should

31

contract guilt and pollution commit murder?" (*Plea* 35.5). Athenagoras proceeds to elaborate on the *Didache's* prohibition of abortion and infanticide:

> And we who say that the women who use drugs to induce abortions commit murder and must give an account to God for the abortion, by what reason would we be murderers? For the same person would not consider the foetus in the womb a living being and on account of this an object of God's care and then kill what has entered into life, and would not expose what has been born on the grounds that those who expose such are child-murderers, nor again would kill what has been reared. (*Plea* 35.6)

Athenagoras claims to present the common Christian position in considering the fetus a living being comparable to the child that is born, so that abortion is murder, an act for which the person must give account to God.[42]

For an illustration of Christians' actually observing the teachings against revenge, as Athenagoras claims they did, note may be made of an incident in a polemical context from the apocryphal *Acts of Peter*, itself no doubt apocryphal. When the crowd in Rome was ready to have Simon Magus killed for his deceptive use of magic, Peter protested and gave as his reason that Christians had learned not "to repay evil with evil" but rather "to love their enemies" (Matt. 5:44).[43]

The legend (or remembrance?) of debates between Peter and Simon is the setting in which the *Pseudo Clementines* have Peter describe Jesus: "He loved even those who hated him, and wept over the unbelieving, and blessed those who slandered him, and prayed for those who were in enmity against him . . . He also taught his disciples to do the like" (*Hom.* 3.19.13). When such a good man reigns, Peter concludes, there is joy among those who are ruled over. Despite the use of early Jewish-Christian material, the real interest of the compiler seems to be in topics of popular philosophy. Thus, "Peter" in an exposition of philanthropy, as distinct from friendship, defines the philanthropic person as one "who does good to his enemies" (*Hom.* 12.26). The Master taught his followers not to resist and not to avenge lest "they should compel them to sin more" (*Hom.* 12.30).

> The righteous man tries also to love his enemies and to bless
> those who slander him, and even to pray for his enemies, and
> to be compassionate to those who do him wrong. Wherefore
> also he refrains from doing wrong, and blesses those who curse
> him, pardons those who strike him, and submits to those who
> persecute him, and salutes those who do not salute him, shares
> such things as he has with those who have not . . . (*Hom.* 12.32)

The teaching about "turning the other cheek" (Matt. 5:39–41; Luke 6:29)
gets cited by "Peter" in a discussion of the difference between true religion
and philosophy (*Hom.* 15.5.5).[44]

There is ample evidence, therefore, that the teachings of Jesus on love for
enemies and nonretaliation were central to early Christian moral catechesis (*Didache,* Justin, Irenaeus). The so-called Apostolic Fathers applied this
teaching to internal church problems (*1 Clement, 2 Clement,* Polycarp).[45]
The Apologists applied these teachings as an argument to refute the slanders
against Christians (Justin, Theophilus, Athenagoras) and as an explanation
for Christians' acceptance of martyrdom (Justin, Clement of Alexandria,
Tertullian). The philosophical context of early Christian apologetics then
became the basis for introducing this teaching into topics discussed by moral
philosophers (Pseudo-Clement, *Homilies*). The application of this teaching
to the basic moral life and to the practice of nonresistance highlights the
Christian opposition to the taking of human life—whether in war (Justin,
Irenaeus), as a punishment for evildoers (*Acts of Peter*), the gladiatorial games
(Theophilus, Athenagoras), or abortion (*Didache,* Athenagoras).

This feature of early Christian moral teaching reminds me of two articles by George Williams that I think may not be so well known but that
have been very significant for me: "Religious Residues and Presuppositions
in the American Debate on Abortion"[46] and "Four Modalities of Violence,
with Special Reference to the Writings of Georges Sorel."[47] His antiwar and
antiabortion activities have provoked strong opposition from opposite con-
stituencies. Nevertheless, his peace witness and stand against abortion have
an internal consistency, being united by an affirmation of life. In his role as
a historian of the universal church he has set his ethical compass for crossing

the ocean of contemporary public policy according to the historical Christian moral tradition.

Appendix: Texts on Love of Enemies and Nonretaliation

Lukea 6:27–30, 32	Matthew 5:39–42, 44, 46	Didacheb 1.3–5	Justinc 15.9–10; 16.1–2	Theophilusd 3:14	Athenagorase 11.2
1 ἀγαπᾶτε τοὺς ἐχθροὺς ὑμῶν, καλῶς ποιεῖτε τοῖς μισοῦσιν ὑμᾶς,	7. ἀγαπᾶτε τοὺς ἐχθροὺς ὑμῶν καὶ	3. ὑμεῖς δὲ φιλεῖτε τοὺς μισοῦντας ὑμᾶς, . . .	1. εὔχεσθε ὑπὲρ τῶν ἐχθρῶν ὑμῶν καὶ ἀγαπᾶτε τοὺς μισοῦντας ὑμᾶς καὶ	ἀγαπᾶτε τοὺς ἐχθροὺς ὑμῶν καὶ	ἀγαπᾶτε τοὺς ἐχθροὺς ὑμῶν
εὐλογεῖτε τοὺς καταρωμένους		1. εὐλογεῖτε τοὺς καταρωμένους	εὐλογεῖτε τοὺς καταρωμένους		εὐλογεῖτε τοὺς καταρωμένους
ὑμᾶς προσεύχεσθε περὶ τῶν ἐπηρεαζόντων ὑμᾶς.	προσεύχεσθε ὑπὲρ τῶν διωκόντων ὑμᾶς, . . . 1. μὴ ἀντιστῆναι τῷ πονηρῷ	ὑμῖν καὶ προσεύχεσθε ὑπὲρ τῶν ἐχθρῶν ὑμῶν, νηστεύετε δὲ ὑπὲρ τῶν διωκόντων ὑμᾶς	ὑμῖν καὶ εὔχεσθε ὑπὲρ τῶν ἐπηρεαζόντων ὑμᾶς.	προσεύχεσθε ὑπὲρ τῶν ἐπηρεαζόντων ὑμᾶς.	προσεύχεσθε ὑπὲρ τῶν διωκόντων ὑμᾶς
	2. ἀλλ᾽ ὅστις σε	4. ἐάν τις σοι			
2. τῷ τύπτοντί σε ἐπὶ τὴν σιαγόνα Πάρεχε καὶ τὴν ἄλλην,	ῥαπίζει εἰς τὴν δεξιὰν σιαγόνα σου στρέψον αὐτῷ καὶ τὴν ἄλλην	δῷ ῥάπισμα εἰς τὴν δεξιὰν σιαγόνα, στρέψον αὐτῷ καὶ τὴν ἄλλην, . . .	3. τῷ τύπτοντί σου τὴν σιαγόνα πάρεχε καὶ τὴν ἄλλην,		
3. καὶ ἀπὸ τοῦ αἴροντός σου τὸ ἱμάτιον καὶ τὸν χιτῶνα μὴ κωλύσῃς.	3. καὶ τῷ θέλοντί σοι κριθῆναι καὶ τὸν χιτῶνά σου λαβεῖν, ἄφες αὐτῷ καὶ τὸ ἱμάτιον·	6. ἐὰν ἄρῃ τις τὸ ἱμάτιόν σου, δὸς αὐτῷ καὶ τὸν χιτῶνα	4. καὶ τὸν αἴροντά σου τὸν χιτῶνα ἢ τὸ ἱμάτιον μὴ κωλύσῃς . . .		

	4. καὶ ὅστις σε ἀγγαρεύσει μίλιον ἕν, ὕπαγε μετ' αὐτοῦ δύο.	5. ἐὰν ἀγγαρεύσῃ σέ τις μίλιον ἕν, ὕπαγε μετ' αὐτοῦ δύο·	5. παντὶ δὲ ἀγγαρεύοντί σε μίλιον ἀκολούθησον δύο.		
		7. ἐὰν λάβῃ τις ἀπὸ σοῦ τὸ σόν, μὴ ἀπαίτει· ...			
4. παντὶ αἰτοῦντί σε δίδου,	5. τῷ αἰτοῦντί σε δός,	παντὶ τῷ αἰτοῦντί σε δίδου	2. παντὶ τῷ αἰτοῦντί δίδοτε		
καὶ ἀπὸ τοῦ αἴροντος τὰ σὰ μὴ ἀπαίτει	6. ...	καὶ μὴ ἀπαίτει· ...			
5. καὶ εἰ ἀγαπᾶτε τοὺς ἀγαπῶντας ὑμᾶς, ποία ὑμῖν χάρις ἐστίν;	8. ἐὰν γὰρ ἀγαπήσητε τοὺς ἀγαπῶντας ὑμᾶς, τίνα μισθὸν ἔχετε;	2. ποία γὰρ χάρις, ἐὰν ἀγαπᾶτε τοὺς ἀγαπῶντας ὑμᾶς;		ἐὰν γὰρ ἀγαπᾶτε τοὺς ἀγαπῶντας ὑμᾶς, ποῖον μισθὸν ἔχετε;	

a. The text of Luke and Matthew is that of Nestle-Aland, *Novum Testamentum Graece*, 27th ed. (Stuttgart: Deutsche Bibelstiftung, 2004). I have given Luke as the base text because the order of the quotation of these sayings in the second century is closer to the Lukan order: the wording, however, more often is closer to that of Matthew. The numerals before sections of text indicate the order of the sayings in the given document.

b. The text of *Didache* is that of F. X. Funk, et.al., *Die Apostolischen Väter* (Tübingen: J. C. B. Mohr [Siebeck], 1992).

c. The text of Justin is that of Βιβλιοθήκη Ἑλλήνων Πατέρων, vol. 3 (Athens: Apostolic Ministry of the Church of Greece, 1995).

d. The text of Theophilus is that of Robert M. Grant, *Theophilus of Antioch: Ad Autolycum* (Oxford: Clarendon, 1970).

e. The text of Athenagoras is that of W.R. Schoedel, *Athenagoras: Legatio and De Resurrectione* (Oxford: Clarendon, 1972).

*Originally printed in Rodney L. Petersen and Calvin Augustine Pater, eds., *The Contentious Triangle: Church, State, and University: A Festschrift in Honor of Professor George Huntson Williams* (Kirksville, MO: Thomas Jefferson University Press, 1999), 81–95.

Chapter 2 Endnotes

1. Rom. 12:17, 1 Thess. 5:15, 1 Pet. 3:9; see Victor Paul Furnish, *The Love Command in the New Testament* (London: SCM, 1973), 106; Walter Wink, *Engaging the Powers* (Minneapolis:Fortress,1993), 185–86; C. E. B. Cranfield, *The Epistle to the Romans* (ICC; Edinburgh:T & T Clark, 1979), 2.645. For the general theme in the New Testament, see Willard M. Swartley, ed., *Love of Enemy and Nonretaliation in the New Testament* (Louisville: Westminster/John Knox, 1992).

2. For the love command in general see Eric Osborn, "The Love Command in Second-Century Christian Writing," *The Second Century* 1 (1981): 223–43; discussion on love of enemies, 238–41.

3. Karlmann Beyschlag, "Zur Geschichte der Bergpredigt in der Alten Kirche," *Zeitschrift für Theologie und Kirche* 74 (1977): 291–322, esp.297, where he comments that the question of whether this teaching was fulfillable did not exist for the early church. Matt. 5:44 is the only verse he chooses for discussion that falls within my purview in this paper: 313–17. Robert M. Grant, "The Sermon on the Mount in Early Christianity," *Semeia* 12 (1978):215–31, who also states that for early Christian authors the commands of Jesus were meant to be obeyed literally: 217, 218, 223, 227.

4. John Whittaker, "Christianity and Morality in the Roman Empire," *Vigiliae Christianae* 33 (1979): 209–25, repr. in Everett Ferguson, *Studies in Early Christianity*, vol. 16: *Christian Life: Ethics, Morality, and Discipline in the Early Church* (New York: Garland/Taylor and Francis, 1993), 19–35.

5. It can be claimed as the most frequently cited logion of Jesus in the second century—William Klassen, "'Love Your Enemies': Some Reflections on the Current Status of Research," in Swartley, *The Love of Enemy*, 8, citing Helmut Koester, *Synoptische Überlieferung bei den Apostolischen Vätern* (Berlin: Akademie, 1957), 44, 76. Wayne A. Meeks, *The Origins of Christian Morality: The First Two Centuries* (New Haven: Yale, 1993), gives only passing notice of the teaching (120–21) Francis, 1993), 19–35.

It can be claimed as the most frequently cited logion of Jesus in the second century—William Klassen, "'Love Your Enemies': Some Reflections on the Current Status of Research," in Swartley, *The Love of Enemy*, 8, citing Helmut Koester, *Synoptische Überlieferung bei den Apostolischen Vätern* (Berlin: Akademie, 1957), 44, 76. Wayne A. Meeks, *The Origins of Christian Morality* because he was not concerned with the great ethical principles of the early Christians but with the ways in which they developed "a moral common sense" (11).

6. The identical quotation is found in Clement of Alexandria, *Str.* 2.18 (probably taken from his Roman namesake) in a context of showing the harmony of the law of Moses with God's universal moral requirements.

7. Edouard Massaux, in *The Influence of the Gospel of Saint Matthew on Christian Literature before Saint Irenaeus* (Macon: Mercer, 1990), 1.7–12, suggests Clement was dependent on a catechetical summary of Jesus' teaching that drew on Matthew. On the other hand, Koester, in *Synoptische Überlieferungen*, 12–16, 23, asserts Clement did not use our synoptic Gospels. We do not know Clement's source; it may be an independent written collection or perhaps a local oral catechism. See the evaluations of these studies and fresh examinations of the evidence by Arthur J. Bellinzoni, "The Gospel of Matthew in the Second Century," and Enrique Nardoni, "Interaction of Orality and Textuality: Response to Arthur J. Bellinzoni," *The Second Century* 9 (1992): 201–4, 265–68; Donald A. Hagner, *The Use of the Old and New Testaments in Clement of Rome* (Leiden: Brill, 1973), 140–51; Hagner, "The Sayings of Jesus in the Apostolic Fathers and Justin Martyr," *The Jesus Tradition outside the Gospels*, Gospel Perspectives, vol. 5, ed. D. Wenham (Sheffield: JSOT, 1984), 233–68; and Wolf-Dietrich Köhler, *Die Rezeption des Matthäusevangeliums in der Zeit vor Irenaeus* (Tübingen: J. C. B. Mohr [Siebeck], 1987), 60–72, all of whom find it improbable that *1 Clement* 13.2 derives directly from the Gospels.

8. Contrast Massaux, *Influence,* and Köhler, *Die Rezeption*, with Koester, *Synoptische Überlieferung.*

9. See the appendix to this paper.

10. Polycarp, *Phil.* 2.2–3, has an introductory formula about "remembering" that is similar to *1 Clem.* 13: it contains four of the same items but in different order and some differently formulated, and sets the teaching more explicitly in a context of nonretaliation. Cf. Polycarp, *Phil.* 12.3: "Pray for those that persecute and hate you, and for the enemies of the cross," which Kohler, *Rezeption*, 100–2, concludes is probably dependent on Matt. 5:44.

11. Following the emendation of Bentley Layton, "The Sources, Date and Transmission of *Didache* 1.3b–2.1," *Harvard Theological Review* 61 (1968): 345–49.

12. Massaux, *Influence,* 3.145–52, finds dependence on Matthew; this conclusion is supported by C. M. Tuckett, "Synoptic Tradition in the *Didache*," in *The New Testament in Early Christianity*, ed. J. M. Sevrin (Leuven: Peeters, 1989), 197–230. Koester, *Synoptische Überlieferung*, 217–41, argues that the Didachist used the same sources from which the written Gospels derived their material but that the redactor of 1.3–2.1 (who is to be distinguished from the compiler of the *Didache*) knew Matthew

and Luke as sources among others for the words of Jesus; cf. his later judgment that 1.3–5 is "certainly drawn from written gospels," found in *Ancient Christian Gospels* (Philadelphia: Trinity Press International, 1990), 17. Layton, "Sources," 343–83, similarly thinks it unlikely that the compositor of 1.3b–2.1 was the compiler of the rest of the document (380–82) and considers the section a harmonizing of earlier sources, especially Matthew (349, 357, 370–72); Jean-Paul Audet , *La Didachè: Instructions des Apôtres* (Paris: J. Gabalda, 1958), 183–86, 264, concludes that the interpolation, as a variation on a common theme in the gospel tradition, is independent of Matthew and Luke; Hagner, "Sayings of Jesus," 240–42, also favors dependence on oral tradition. Köhler, *Rezeption*, 53–56, reverses Koester's judgments by finding that the Didachist knew and used Matthew but that dependence on Matthew is improbable in 1.3b–6, being redacted by the Didachist himself from oral or written collections of Jesus' words (43–47). Clayton N. Jefford, *The Sayings of Jesus in the Teaching of the Twelve Apostles* (Leiden: Brill, 1989), although finding that most of the "sayings" material in the *Didache* was collected in the same community from which Matthew came and was earlier than Matthew, decides that 1.3b–2.1 is dependent on synoptic texts that were derived from Q and cannot be dated more closely than some time in the second century (18, 38–53, 142–45). Graham N. Stanton, "The Fourfold Gospel," *New Testament Studies* 43 (1997): 334, concludes, contrary to Koester above, that Εὐαγγέλιον in *Didache* 8.2, 11.3, and twice in 15.3–4, refers to a writing. See further the next note.

13. Tuckett, "Synoptic Tradition," 215, affirms that 1.3–2.1 is a later addition to "The Two Ways," but points out that whether it is secondary to the rest of the *Didache* is another matter. W. Rordorf, "Le problème de la transmission textuelle de *Didachè* 1.3b–2.1," Überlieferungschichtliche *Untersuchungen*, ed. F. Paschke (*Texte und Untersuchungen* 125; Berlin, 1981), 499–513, and "Does the *Didache* Contain Jesus Tradition Independently of the Synoptic Gospels?" in *Jesus and the Oral Gospel Tradition*, ed. Henry Wansbrough (Sheffield: JSOT Press, 1992), 394–423, concludes that 1.3b–2.1 is so closely connected with the rest of the document that it is from the same redactor but makes a strong argument for no direct dependence of the *Didache* on the Gospels.

14. Michael Gorman, *Abortion and the Early Church* (Downers Grove: InterVarsity, 1982), 49. With comparison to *Barnabas* 19.5.

15. Clement of Alexandria similarly conflates commands from "The Two Ways" with Jesus' words. He, as the *Didache*, expands the Ten Commandments by adding after "You shall not commit adultery," "You shall not corrupt boys" (*Prot.* 10), immediately followed by Jesus' words about loving neighbor and nonretaliation (Luke 6:27–29); *Paed.* 3.12.89, with the same words of Jesus more fully cited later in the chapter.

16. M. A. Smith, "Did Justin Know the *Didache*?" *Studia Patristica* 7 (*Texte und Untersuchungen* 92, 1966), 287–90.

17. In *The Ecumenical World of Orthodox Civilization: Essays in Honor of Georges Florovsky*, ed. Andrew Blane and Thomas E. Bird (The Hague/Paris: Mouton, 1974), 3.9–34. This is part of a larger interest in Justin: "Justin Glimpsed as Martyr among His Roman Contemporaries," in *The Context of Contemporary Theology: Essays in Honor of*

Paul Lehmann, ed. Alexander J. McKelway and E. David Willis (Atlanta: John Knox, 1974), 99–126; reprinted in Everett Ferguson, ed., *Studies in Early Christianity*, vol. l, *Personalities of the Early Church* (New York: Garland/Taylor and Francis 1993), 81–108.

18. *Acts of Justin* 3.3; 4.5.

19. I give the references in Matthew that are identical with or most nearly approximate Justin's quotations, only noting the parallels in Luke when they are especially close, which is the case with the passages cited in the appendix.

20. Here Köhler, *Rezeption,* 179, observes that Justin is closer to Luke 6:29.

21. The different approaches are summarized in Arthur J. Bellinzoni, "The Gospel of Matthew in the Second Century," *The Second Century* 9 (1992): 239–40.

22. Justin, *1 Apology 66*.3, 67.3; *Dialogue* 103.6. Stanton, "Fourfold Gospel," 329–32, argues that Justin accepted our four Gospels.

23. Arthur Bellinzoni, *The Sayings of Jesus in the Writings of Justin Martyr* (Leiden: Brill, 1967), 139–42, concludes that Justin used for catechetical purposes written sources that harmonized the parallel material in Matthew and Luke (and possibly Mark) and conflated related material in different parts of the same Gospel; this written catechism may have been prepared by Justin and his pupils (see his "The Gospel of Matthew," 240). Helmut Koester, "The Text of the Synoptic Gospels in the Second Century," in *Gospel Traditions in the Second Century,* ed. William L. Petersen (Notre Dame: University of Notre Dame Press, 1989), 30, goes further in suggesting that Justin composed a full harmony of Matthew and Luke and possibly Mark. Köhler, *Rezeption,* 166–73, confirms Justin's probable use of Matthew and says that to explain his departures from the text of our Gospels does not require a written extracanonical source. E. R. Buckley, "Justin Martyr's Quotations from the Synoptic Tradition," *Journal of Theological Studies* 36 (1935): 173–76, made an argument from the form of Justin's quotations that in *1 Apol.* 15 on love of enemies Justin did not use a harmony but drew from a now lost gospel.

24. The passage gives a message to "those who hate you" and speaks of the children to whom Zion gives birth.

25. "Irenaeus' *Proof of the Apostolic Preaching* and Early Catechetical Instruction," *Studia Patristica* 18.3 (1989): 119–40.

26. Quotations are from the translation by Joseph P. Smith, *St. Irenaeus: Proof of the Apostolic Preaching*, Ancient Christian Writers 16 (New York: Newman, 1952).

27. Irenaeus, *Adv. Haer.* 4.13.1–3; 4.16.4–5 cites the same passages, but in the anti-Gnostic context of that work he stresses that Jesus' interpretation did not abrogate the law but fulfilled and extended it. Ptolemy, from the Valentinian Gnostic side, is not that different. He identified the command "You shall not kill" with the pure legislation of God that the Savior came to fulfill in the further command not to be angry (Matt. 5:22) and the command "an eye for an eye and a tooth for a tooth" with the legislation interwoven with injustice that God's Son abolished by saying "Do not in any way resist

one who is evil" (Matt. 5:39)—Epiphanius, *Panarion* 33.5.1–63 (Bentley Layton, *The Gnostic Scriptures* [Garden City: Doubleday, 1987], 310–13).

28. Not only was catechetical material included in apologetic writings, but catechesis was in part apologetic, as indicated by Irenaeus's *Demonstration* and from a later period the heavily apologetic element in Gregory of Nyssa's *Catechetical Oration*.

29. Everett Ferguson, *Early Christians Speak*, 3rd ed. (Abilene: ACU Press, 1999), 189–202.

30. Cf. Ignatius, *Polyc.* 2.1. Koester, *Synoptische Überlieferung*, 75–77, finds the departures from the text of Luke in this quotation in *2 Clement* to be usual (in sayings collections such as *2 Clement* employed) and not to indicate the author's poor memory; Köhler, *Rezeption*, 142–43, considers it improbable that *2 Clement* 13.4 is dependent on Matthew.

31. There is a similar appeal later in Tertullian, *Apology* 31, to examine the Christian's sacred books to confirm their teaching about praying for enemies and persecutors.

32. Cf. *Ep. Diogn.* 6.5.

33. Irenaeus, *Adv. Haer.* 4.34.4, offers a parallel; after quoting Isa. 2:3–4, Irenaeus says that the word of God preached by the apostles is causing peace throughout the world so that peoples "are now unaccustomed to fighting, but when struck, offer also the other cheek."

34. The theme of nonretaliation in the face of persecution is fairly common: Clement of Alexandria, *Str.*4.14, quotes Luke 6:27–28 and Matt. 5:44–45 in reference to martyrdom; Tertullian, *Apol.* 37, insists that although Christians are ready to sacrifice their lives there is not a single case of revenge for injury from persecution; and the apology in the *Acts of Apollonius* 37 says that Jesus taught "not to turn in vengeance against those who mistreat" you but rather "to despise the penalty of death." I have developed the theme of nonresistance in relation to martyrdom in "Early Christian Martyrdom and Civil Disobedience," *Journal of Early Christian Studies* 1 (1993): 73–83.

35. The thoughts of *1 Apol.* 39.3 and *Dial.* 96.2–3 are combined in *Dial.* 110.3–4, one of the finest passages in the work: "We who were full of war, murder, and all evil have each from all the earth changed our instruments of war, 'our swords into ploughshares and our spears into pruning hooks,' and we cultivate piety, righteousness, philanthropy, faith, and hope . . . It is evident that although beheaded, crucified, thrown to wild animals, chains, fire, and all the other kinds of torture we do not abandon our confession."

36. Why does Theophilus refer to "Gospels," but then, when quoting, cite "the Gospel" according to the wording of more than one? Does he quote a variant text, a harmony or a conflated text of selected teachings used for catechesis? I would suggest that as laws give expression to the Law, and the Prophets to prophecy, so too the Gospels, even as the word does in Irenaeus (*Adv. Haer* 3.11.8), embody the one gospel.

37. Köhler, *Rezeption*, 502, says that Theophilus follows primarily Matthew.

38. Tertullian, *Spec.* 16, supports the prohibition of Christians to attend the circus by appeal to the commands "to love our enemies" and not "to curse" but "to bless."

39. See Massaux, *Influence* 3.120–25 and Köhler, *Rezeption* 494–98 on Athenagoras; on Theophilus, Massaux 3.134–38 and Köhler 500–4.

40. Köhler, *Rezeption,* 495–96, sees Matthew as the primary basis of Athenagoras's citations.

41. The citation in *Plea* 11.2 follows Matthew's wording but inserts Luke's statement about blessing those who curse you; the description in 11.4 follows Matthew in placing love for enemies after the details of nonretaliation and in presupposing a legal context for the taking of garments but follows Luke in omitting the saying about compulsory service to a Roman soldier.

42. Gorman, *Abortion,* 54.

43. *Act. Pet.* 28.

44. These passages are discussed by Leslie L. Kline in *The Sayings of Jesus in the Pseudo-Clementine Homilies* (Missoula: Scholars, 1975), 14–26, for their textual character in relation to other quotations of the teachings of Jesus.

45. Cf. Clement of Alexandria, *Str.* 7.14.85, for the application of Matt. 5:44 to the interpretation of 1 Cor. 6:1 on the true Gnostic's not going to law against a fellow Christian.

46. *Theological Studies* 31 (1970): 10–75.

47. *Journal of Church and State* 16:1 and 2 (1974): 11–30, 237–61.

Response to Robert L. Wilken,

"Free Choice, the Divine Will, and Early Christian Greek Commentaries on St. Paul"

Professor Wilken has rightly called attention to the importance of Greek philosophy as the context in which early Christians discussed the problem of free will. This is evident in the first explicit treatments of the subject in Christian literature, in the apologists of the second century. Perhaps because of the concern with rewards and punishment, they sometimes relate their statements about free will to discussions of the immortality of the soul. Denying its natural immortality, some said that the soul is neither mortal nor immortal but capable of either (Tatian 11, 13; Theophilus 2.27). Free will was a gift from God in creation (Justin, *Dialogue* 102, 141).

Lest the paper leave the impression, however, that the biblical teaching ran counter to human freedom, another source for early Christian teaching in addition to the Greek philosophical analysis of free will must be considered: the Hebrew/Jewish emphasis on human accountability before God. Jewish writers in the centuries surrounding the beginning of the Christian era were themselves influenced in their formulations by Greek thought. This is especially clear in Josephus's description of the views of the Jewish sects on providence and human responsibility (*Ant.* 13.171–73). These views are stated in the terminology of fate (*heimarmene*) and free will (*eph hemin*). Nevertheless, the teaching of the Hebrew Bible provided a distinct impulse. Deuteronomy 30:15–19 ("I have set before you life and death . . . therefore choose life") has been a basic source of the doctrine of free will in Judaism.[1] Professor Wilken notes the use of that text by Justin (*1 Apol.* 43), and it is one of the passages cited by Origen in his discussion of free will (*Princ.* 3.1.6). Philo in his basic treatment of free will (*Deus imm.* 1047ff.) also cites this passage, while making appeal to praise and blame, which Wilken observes was a customary corollary of the argument for free will. Another important text was Isaiah 1:16–20 ("If you are willing and obedient"). It too is included in Justin's and Origen's citations, and it is in Theodoret's dossier also (*Affectu* 5.5).

Discussions of free will are to be found not only in such Hellenized Jewish writers as Josephus and Philo. Among the Pseudepigrapha note the *Psalms of Solomon* 9:4: "Our works are in the choosing and power of our souls, to do right and wrong in the works of our hands, and in your righteousness you oversee human beings. The one who does what is right saves up life for himself with the Lord, and the one who does what is wrong causes his own life to be destroyed; for the Lord's righteous judgments are according to the individual and the household." And *2 Enoch* 30:15 has God say of man: "I gave him his free will and I pointed out to him the two ways—light and darkness." Even *4 Ezra*, which approximates a doctrine of original sin (7:118), yet maintains free will (3:8; 8:56). Rabbinic literature confirms Josephus's description of the Pharisees' attempt to balance fate (or providence) and free will. Rabbi Akiba (early second century) said, "Everything is foreseen, but the right of choice is granted, and the world is judged with goodness, and everything is in accordance with the preponderance of [man's] deeds" (Aboth 3.15). Hanina ben Pape, a late third-century Palestinian rabbi who was outspoken on behalf of human accountability, agreed: "Everything is in the hands of heaven except the fear of God," quoting Deuteronomy 10:12 (Niddah 16b). This same rabbi reversed normal expectations in assigning a greater reward to actions in obedience to God's commands than to the same actions when not commanded (Abodah Zara 3a). The point seems to be that the moral act has greater merit when done in obedience to the command of God, for that provides the only sure basis for conduct. The rabbis closely approximated the teaching of some church fathers that God's grace helps the person who is trying to do right: "All who draw near to God, God draws near to him" (*Sifre Num.* 78, f. 20b). Although the rabbis had a realistic awareness of the power of sin in human life, they expected a person to be able to do right. The midrash to Genesis 4:7 affirms the power in human beings to rule over the evil impulse (*yetzer*) in their nature (*Gen. R.* 22.6). The discussion in the midrash of the hardening of Pharaoh's heart, such a crux in the biblical teaching about free will, has interesting parallels to some Christian treatments. It is noted that the text of Exodus says five times that Pharaoh hardened his heart before it says that God hardened his heart. Only when Pharaoh had rejected God's words five times did God close Pharaoh's heart against repentance so that he could exact vengeance for his sins (*Midrash Rabbah* Ex. 13.3; cf. 11.6). Philo too had occasion to refer to Pharaoh, and he attributes his attitude to his disposition from his earliest years (*Vita Moysis* 1.88f.).

Perhaps the most important point in Professor Wilken's paper, and what it seems he especially wants to say to us, is that the Greek Christian commentators took the biblical text seriously. In this he is surely correct. Besides the passages affirming human responsibility, there were others that seemed inconsistent with free will. In general the Greek theologians tried to incorporate all of the biblical teaching on a subject; nor did they any more than commentators in other ages simply try to explain away uncomfortable texts. I want to take the treatment of the hardening of Pharaoh's heart as a center around which to organize some additional comments.

Irenaeus has the first treatment of this as a problem, and although his context is the Gnostic controversy and not philosophical discussions about free will, he enunciates some of the points which became fairly constant in later treatments. The choice, according to Irenaeus, was Pharaoh's, and God in his foreknowledge treated him accordingly. God knows those who will not believe and gives them over to unbelief, "leaving them in the darkness which they themselves have chosen for themselves" (*Adversus haereses* 4.29.2). What wonder is it then that he gave over Pharaoh, "who never would have believed, along with those who were with him?"

Origen discussed the hardening of Pharaoh's heart not only in his *Homilies on Exodus* and *Commentary on Romans* but also in his *On First Principles,* the *Commentary on the Song of Songs,* and *On Prayer.*[2] The *Commentary on Romans* sees the hardening of Pharaoh's heart as the result of God's actions but not as caused by them. God's longsuffering wished to allow even Pharaoh to change, but the light punishments were followed by gradually increasing severity. God's treatment of Pharaoh was comparable to a slave owner who kills one of his worst slaves as an example to the others. *On First Principles* book 3 gives more explicit formulation to the view that God sent the influences and Pharaoh was responsible because he hardened his own heart to God's miracles. It is basic to Origen's defense of free will to affirm that although external influences are not in our power, how we respond to them is in our power (*Princ.* 3.1.3). After citing passages from the Bible on behalf of free will, Origen takes up Romans 9 as the first of those passages that appear to be contrary to it. He argues that acts with a kindly intent (illustrated by Hebrews 6:7f.—the land that brings forth vegetation or thorns) may have two opposite effects (3.1.10). The one operation of Moses revealed the hardness of Pharaoh's heart and the persuadability of the mixed Egyptian multitudes (3.1.11). Origen then cites Isaiah 63:17f. and Jeremiah 20:7 as other instances where God is said to "cause" what is a "result" of his actions. Origen saw clearly the effect of outside influences in inclining the will to evil. The same could apply to good. Using Psalms 127:1 and 1 Corinthians 3:6f. to illustrate that God and human beings must cooperate, Origen continues: "So, too, our perfection does not come to pass without our doing anything, and yet it is not completed as a result of our efforts, but God performs the greater part of it" (3.1.18). Origen, furthermore, began the practice of juxtaposing 2 Timothy 2:2–3 (vessels for noble and ignoble use) to Romans 9:21 in order to affirm that both God's will and the human will are involved in salvation, so there is no contradiction in the passages (3.1.24). The *Homilies on Exodus* do not give such a full treatment. There Origen appeals to Romans 2:4–5 to explain Pharaoh hardening his heart and then the Lord doing so. Romans 9:18–20 is left as a great mystery not explained; Paul silenced opposition by appealing to his apostolic authority.

Free will is basic to Gregory of Nyssa's theology.[3] I will confine my remarks here to Gregory's *Life of Moses*. This treatise discusses free will in connection with the hardening of Pharaoh's heart (II.73–88) and cites passages from Romans in the exposition but not Romans 9. Gregory seems to give two explanations for the language of hardening the heart: (1) like Origen, he says God sends the influences to which Pharaoh responds (cf. II.80f. for the same influences producing darkness among the Egyptians and light among the Hebrews): and (2) God as a physician brings hardness of heart into the open by his punishment, which is designed to be corrective (a view also anticipated by Origen). Gregory insists that free choice is the cause of evil (II. 88). On the other hand, divine activity assists the soul that has made the first moves toward virtue (II.44ff.). This might imply that the initiative for virtue lies with human beings, but Gregory was not dealing in these statements with the total picture. He does recognize the historical priority of grace in Christ, for those who receive the outstretched hands of the Lawgiver on the cross are set free from their passion (II.78), and the word of God softens resistance unless free will refuses to receive it (II.76).

John Chrysostom and Theodoret, although Antiochians, reflect some of the same concerns of Origen and Gregory. Chrysostom, as Origen before him (*Comm. Rom.*[4]), takes the "purpose" or "will" (*próthesis*) of Romans 8:28 ("those who are called according to [his] purpose") to be man's will and not God's will. "It is not the calling alone, but the purpose of those called too, that works salvation. . . . All then were called, but not all obeyed the call" (*Hom. 15 on Rom.*). So much am I a prisoner of the Western tradition of interpretation that it had never occurred to me that the will here might be the will of anyone other than God, but the common interpretation in the Greek commentators is the human will: the calling is from God, but the willing or purpose is the human person's (e.g., Theodoret and later Oecumenius). Is this interpretation a way of preserving free will, or must we nuance Wilken's point about the divine will and ask if the commentators think first of the human will? In regard to Pharaoh, Chrysostom puts the emphasis on his choices: "Pharaoh was a vessel of wrath, that is, a man who by his own hard-heartedness had kindled the wrath of God" (*Hom. 16 on Rom.*, 9:22–24). Again, "As Pharaoh became a vessel of wrath by his own lawlessness, so did [others] become vessels of mercy by their own readiness to obey. For though the more part is of God, still they also have contributed themselves some little" (ibid.). Almost echoing Origen, Chrysostom says, "The greater part was of grace, though not the whole" (*Hom. 19 on Rom.*, 11:8). "For grace, though it be grace, saves the willing, not those who will not have it" (ibid., 11:6).

Two points may be added from Theodoret's commentary on Romans in order to reinforce the continuity in the exegetical concerns. Commenting on Romans 8:30, Theodoret argues that foreknowledge is not the cause of one doing good or evil because God does not compel; otherwise he would not be just. Since he is just, he can praise the good and punish the bad. Professor Wilken notes that Justin had to defend prophecy in a similar fashion against a charge that prophecy involved determinism. Origen had to do the same in responding to Celsus (2.20): "Celsus imagines that an event, predicted through foreknowledge, comes to pass because it was predicted; but we do not grant this, maintaining that he who foretold it was not the cause of its happening because he foretold it would happen; but the future event itself, which would have taken place though not predicted, afforded the occasion to him who was endowed with foreknowledge of foretelling its occurrence." And Origen proceeded to deal with the arguments with which Greek philosophers wrestled. Theodoret on Romans 9:23f. makes another point which sounds like Origen: "God is not the maker of Pharaoh's wickedness, but he was gracious in his customary longsuffering. But Pharaoh took the longsuffering for weakness, and because of this increased his natural disobedience." The "vessels of wrath" are understood in relation to 2 Timothy 2:20f. and 1 Corinthians 3:12, as Origen had done, "teaching the free will of men." God "calls vessels of mercy those worthy of the divine love."

The phrase "those worthy" leads to another observation. Professor Wilken twice quotes without comment (pp. 133, 349 note 45) Theodore of Mopsuestia's words that God in his grace "considers some to be worthy of his election." A reader must be impressed with how often such language occurs in the Greek commentators. Gregory of Nyssa says that the guidance of the Spirit comes to "those who are worthy" (*V. M.* II.121). John Chrysostom, in dealing with Esau and Jacob and arguing that "election [is] made according to foreknowledge," stated that, spiritually speaking, children are such not by birth but by "being worthy of the father's virtue" (*Hom. 16 on Rom.*, 9:10). Theodoret similarly declares, "God only, and no man, knows those worthy of salvation" (*Interp. Rom.*, 9:23f.). To those accustomed to think of grace as contradictory to merit, or at least as the precondition of good works, such language seems impossible or erroneous. It is no wonder that many historians think that the Greek commentators have missed the radical priority of grace; but for that reason we need to probe more deeply, as Professor Wilken has done, into the actual thought world of the Greek theologians.

There is, moreover, a corresponding lack of depth in the understanding of the cause of sin, a matter where the Augustinian teaching goes beyond the Greek commentators. The Greeks appreciated the effects of external influences on the will, but they did not carry their consideration of the effects of internal dispositions on the inclination of the will as far as Augustine did. Augustine introduced another dimension into the question of sin and free will by raising the issue of the effect fallen human nature has on the power to fulfill one's choices; for him the will is free, but impotent.

With such considerations, thought is forced to move beyond the options of classical antiquity with its alternatives of fate or determinism on one hand and human free will on the other. There is implied in Professor Wilken's presentation (pp. 132ff.) a third option, which he does not explicitly formulate. That option is God's gracious will, his election/mercy as inclining the human will to faith and love. I choose this terminology in order to avoid the complication of the language of predestination. Whether we use the language of predestination, to suit Augustine and the classical Reformers, or the language of election and mercy to suit Jewish and Greek patristic terminology, the biblical and specifically Christian teaching about the active will of God and his involvement in human events introduces another perspective. It may be that, as Wilken says, Theodoret's illustration of the magnetic rock could have been used by pagan champions of free will, but Theodoret and other Christians would have said that the "grace of the divine oracles" introduced a viewpoint that goes beyond the attractive force of "laws and precepts and examples," that is, the story of divine love. As Wilken quotes Apollinaris, "the one who shows mercy is the cause" (p. 131), not a physically coercive cause but a morally compelling cause.

As Professor Wilken began with an illustration, I will move toward a conclusion by reference to two frequently recurring illustrations in the Greek commentators. Both pertain to an active divine agency, God's will. Theodoret's words about the magnetic rock refer to God as "the physician of souls." Medical analogies were staples in the drugstore of illustrations patronized by ancient rhetoricians and philosophers. Origen follows his discussion of the hardening of Pharaoh's heart by referring to the practice of physicians who consider it better to let a patient "remain in his fever and sickness for a long time in order that he may regain permanent health, rather than appear to restore him quickly to strength and afterwards to see him relapse and this quicker cure prove only temporary" (*Princ.* 3.1.13; cf. *On Prayer* 16). Similarly in the *Commentary on Exodus* (*Philoc.* 27.4–8) God as a physician intensifies Pharaoh's illness in order to cure it by repentance in the next world. This is somewhat different from Gregory of Nyssa's use of the medical analogy. In reference to the plagues on Egypt, as a result of Pharaoh's refusal to let the Israelites depart, Gregory says, "When the physician induces vomiting by his medicines, he does not become the cause of the sickness in the body, but on the contrary it is disorderly eating habits which bring it about; medical knowledge only brought it into the open. In the same way, even if one says that painful retribution comes directly from God upon those who abuse their free will, it would only be reasonable to note that such sufferings have their origin and cause in ourselves" (*V. M.* II.87). Theodoret gave a different turn to the illustration from medical practice. From Pharaoh's wickedness God prepared a medicine for others, as "physicians do not make snakes but prepare from them a useful medicine for men" (*Interp. Rom.* 9:23f.).

The effects of the sun provided another illustration to explain what happened in the case of Pharaoh. Irenaeus prepared the way. Reflecting on the hardening of Pharaoh's heart (and on Jesus' use of the parables—Matt. 13:11–16, citing Isa. 6:10), Irenaeus says: "For one and the same God that blesses others inflicts blindness upon those who do not believe . . . ; just as the sun, which is a creature of his, acts with regard to those who, by reason of any weakness of the eyes, cannot behold his light; but to those who believe in Him and follow Him, He grants a fuller and greater illumination of mind" (*Adv. haer.* 4.29). The sun brings light to those who open their eyes, but others, as

Theodoret would later say, are blind who do not want to see (*Interp. Rom.* 11:8). Origen used the illustration of the sun differently, but with the same purpose of showing that one cause can have different effects. In explaining Hebrews 6:7f., which in turn was used to illustrate the hardening of Pharaoh's heart, Origen comments: "So, too, if the sun were to utter a voice and say, 'I melt things and dry them up,' when being melted and being dried up are opposites, he would not be speaking falsely in regard to the point in question, since by the one heat wax is melted and mud dried" (*Princ.* 3.1.11). Origen's most extensive use of the analogy from the effects of the sun is found in his *Commentary on the Song of Songs* 1:6. We can quote only a brief excerpt:

> The sun is seen as having twofold power: by one it gives light, and by the other it scorches; but according to the nature of the objects and substances lying immediately under it, it either illuminates a thing with light, or darkens and hardens it with heat. Perhaps it is in this sense that God is said to have hardened the heart of Pharaoh, because the substance of his heart was obviously such as to elicit from the Sun of Justice not His illumination, but His power to harden and to scorch. . . . So with the self same rays wherewith He enlightened the People of Israel . . . the Sun of Justice hardened the heart of Pharaoh. (Bk. 2; *Philoc.* 27.13)

Gregory of Nyssa emphasized the refusal to receive the light of the sun: "It is as if someone who has not seen the sun blames it for causing him to fall into the ditch. Yet we do not hold that the luminary in anger pushes into the ditch someone who does not choose to look at it. . . . Rather, it is the failure to participate in the light that causes the person who does not see to fall into the ditch" (*V. M.* II.76).

Professor Wilken's paper began with human free will but then talked more about the will of God. Paul would have approved. Free will is maintained, but Christians have something more important to say.

---

* Robert Wilken's paper is in William S. Babcock, ed., *Paul and the Legacies of Paul* (Dallas: SMU Press, 1990), 123–140, and my references to it are to the page numbers in the printed text.

My response, March 6, 1987, was unpublished.

Chapter 3 Endnotes

1. I. Epstein, ed., *The Babylonian Talmud,* Aboth (London: Soncino, 1935), 38 (note).

2. W. J. P. Boyd, "On Pharaoh's Hardened Heart," *Studia Patristica* 7 (1966): 434–442; R. P. C. Hanson, *Allegory and Event* (Richmond: John Knox, 1959), 214ff. lists four ways in which Origen treated Pharaoh's hardening, but there is really one explanation with different illustrations. H.S. Benjamins, *Eingeordnete Freiheit: Freiheit und Vorsehung bei Origenes* (Leiden: Brill, 1994).

3. W. Jaeger, *Two Rediscovered Works of Ancient Christian Literature* (Leiden: Brill, 1954), 85–107; E. Muehlenberg, "Synergism in Gregory of Nyssa," *Zeitschrift fuer Neutestamentliche Wissenschraft* 68 (1977): 93–122.

4. P. Gorday, *Principles of Patristic Exegesis* (New York: Edwin Mellen, 1983), 75.

Early Church Penance

The early church father Origen lists seven items said to bring pardon for sins under the gospel. The seventh is this:

> The forgiveness of sins by repentance [penance], when the sinner "bathes his couch in tears" and "his tears are made his bread day and night," and when he is not ashamed to reveal his sin to a priest of the Lord and to seek a remedy.[1]

The disciplinary procedures, personal and ecclesiastical, to obtain forgiveness for serious postbaptismal sins are known as penance.[2] The sacrament of penance as now known in the Roman Catholic Church received its systematic theological formulation in the twelfth century.[3] I speak conventionally, if somewhat anachronistically, when I use "penance" for the disciplinary procedures in the early church dealing with postbaptismal sin. I agree with Roman Catholic historians that there was a continuity in the development of disciplinary practices; I disagree in some cases on how early certain interpretations should be given to these practices and thus the extent to which a sacramental understanding is appropriate. The material on this matter from the pre-Constantinian church will be presented topically, but this will not be to the neglect of a prior careful exegesis of each author, which must precede a systematic presentation.

Sins for Which Discipline Was Imposed

When was church discipline imposed? For what sins was discipline felt necessary?

Rebellion and Division in the Church

Clement of Rome at the end of the first century and Ignatius of Antioch at the beginning of the second addressed situations where division was imminent or recognized but where lines of fellowship were not drawn with finality.

> Let us intercede for those found in any transgression, that meekness and humility may be given to them, in order that they may submit, not to us, but to the will of God. Beloved, let us receive discipline, at which no one should be indignant. The admonition which we give one to another is good and exceedingly beneficial, for it joins us to the will of God. (*1 Clement* 56)

Ignatius advised:

> Abstain from evil plants, which Jesus Christ does not cultivate, because they are not the planting of the Father. As many as are of God and Jesus Christ, these are with the bishop. And as many as repent and come to the unity of the church these also will be of God, in order that they may live according to Jesus Christ. "Do not be deceived," my brothers, if any one follows a schismatic, "he will not inherit the kingdom of God." Where there are division and anger, God does not dwell. But to all who repent, the Lord forgives, if they turn in repentance to the unity of God and the council of the bishop.[4] (*Philadelphians* 3 and 8)

Apostasy

The concern here extended from persons who drifted away from the church to those who by word or act denied the faith in times of persecution. The first work to give extended discussion to the problem of postbaptismal sin, the *Shepherd of Hermas* (first half of second century), considers the problem.

> Those who denied and did not return to their Lord, . . . not cleaving to the servants of God but living alone, are destroying their own souls. . . . To these then there is repentance, if they be not found to have denied from their hearts. But if anyone be found to have denied from the heart, I do not know if he can live. . . . For those who denied in times past [opportunity for] repentance seems to remain. (Hermas, *Similitudes* 9.26)

The persecution in Lyons in 177 caused many Christians to deny their faith. The *Letter of the Churches of Lyons and Vienne* recounts how the faithful witnesses "gave grace [forgiveness] to those who did not bear witness" and won them back to make a confession of faith before the authorities. "And Christ was greatly glorified in those who formerly denied but now confessed contrary to the expectation of the pagans" (Eusebius, *Church History* 5.1.45–48, 50). The intense persecution under Decius in the mid-third century produced a major crisis for the church. The controversies over how to deal with the large number of apostates, many of whom sought readmission to the church after the persecution, caused the formation at Carthage of a laxist party favoring immediate reconciliation and at Rome of the rigorist schism following Novatian, who denied reconciliation to apostates. Most of the church followed the moderate position of Cyprian, bishop of Carthage, that adjusted the length and nature of the discipline to the circumstances of individual offenders.

False Doctrine and Heresy

The great church cut off heretical Gnosticism because its doctrines contradicted fundamental Christian affirmations. An early indication of the conflict is the words in the apocryphal *3 Corinthians*, found in the *Acts of Paul*, concerning those who denied the goodness of creation: "Turn away from them and flee from their teaching" (3.21; cf. 3.39).[5] Heresy and immorality are mentioned in a letter of Dionysius of Corinth (ca. 170) to the churches in Pontus instructing them "to receive back those converted from any backsliding, whether of conduct or heretical error" (Eusebius, *Church History* 4.23.6). Noetus was excluded from the church at Smyrna for teaching a primitive form of Modalism (Hippolytus, *Against Noetus* 1).

Sexual Sins

Hermas discusses the need for sexual purity in *Mandates* 4.1. The angel instructed him that a wife or a husband must not knowingly live with a mate guilty of adultery, but after the divorce must remain alone, so as to give an opportunity for repentance and restoration of the marriage. The repentance and receiving back here seem to be only personal, but the wording is the same as is employed elsewhere for ecclesiastical repentance and reconciliation. Clement Alexandria at the end of the second century similarly condemned equally the adulterer and the adulteress, and of the latter said: "She who has repented, being as it were born again by the change in her life, has a regeneration of life" (*Miscellanies* 2.23). Irenaeus, bishop of Lyons in the late second century, told how the wife of a deacon who was "corrupted in mind and body" by the Gnostic Marcus "spent all her time in confession, weeping and lamenting the defilement which she suffered" (*Against Heresies* 1.13.5).

The rigorist Tertullian, in his Montanist period (early third century), took strong exception to a bishop (Callistus of Rome or Agrippina of Carthage) who claimed to "remit the sins of adultery and fornication to those who have performed penance" (*On Modesty* 1). Tertullian at that stage of his life did not approve, but he is a witness to what was being done. Cyprian, bishop of Carthage in the mid-third century, knew of bishops who "thought that peace was not to be granted to adulterers and wholly closed the gate of repentance against adultery." Yet, unlike Hippolytus in Rome and the Montanists generally, "They did not withdraw from the assembly of their co-bishops, nor break the unity of the Catholic Church by that persistency of their severity or censure" (*Epistle* 51.21).[6]

Robbery

Clement of Alexandria, in order to encourage those who had fallen into sin after baptism to "take heart," because "having truly repented, there remains for you a trustworthy hope of salvation," records a story told about the apostle John. A young man, raised by an elder in the church and baptized, became the leader of an outlaw band. John went in search of him.

> The robber spoke in his defense with lamentations and baptized himself a second time with tears.... The apostle prayed, kneeled down, kissed his right hand as having been purified by repentance. He brought him back to the church and made intercession for him with profuse prayers. He struggled with him in continual fastings. With many soothing words he subdued his mind, and he did not depart before he restored him to the church.[7]

The Big Three: Idolatry, Adultery, and Murder

Tertullian understood the "Apostolic Decree" of Acts 15:28–29, according to the moral interpretation given in manuscripts of the Western text, as forbidding sacrifices to idols, fornication, and shedding blood (murder), and he regarded these sins as unforgivable (*On Modesty* 12).[8] In another passage he gives a longer list: "Homicide, idolatry, fraud, denial, blasphemy, indeed adultery and fornication, and any other violation of the temple of God" (ibid., 19), but this seems to be an elaboration of the basic three. Despite arguments by modern scholars to the contrary, it seems that Tertullian the Montanist was an innovator in making certain sins irremissible (ibid., 2, 19).[9] The distinction was maintained by other rigorist groups.

Other Sins

Although Tertullian denied reconciliation to the church for serious sins, he listed other sins subject to church discipline. These involved compromises with the pagan lifestyle, such as attendance at chariot races, gladiatorial combats, theatrical performances, and athletic contests; filling public office where idolatrous practices were involved; ambiguous words of denial or blasphemy (*On Modesty* 7). He further refers to wrath, reviling, swearing rashly, lying, and the temptations in business, in official duties, in trade, in food, in what we see, and in what we hear (ibid., 19). These latter "offenses of daily occurrence to which all of us are liable" may not have required public penance. Origen similarly distinguished serious sins requiring church penance from daily sins for which forgiveness was easier to obtain.[10]

Missing Church

As time went on, the sources become more detailed on the sins requiring discipline and more precise as to the punishment for each. For example, the Council of Elvira in Spain decreed: "If anyone who dwells in the city shall fail to come to church for three Sundays, let him be deprived [of the Eucharist] for a short time, that he may appear to have been punished" (*Can.* 21).[11]

The Imposition of Discipline

How was discipline imposed? What procedures were employed? Very little is said in the surviving sources about the way in which discipline was imposed, and it is seldom possible to be sure to what stage of the disciplinary process the statements apply.

The apocryphal *Epistle of the Apostles* 47–48, from the mid-second century, presents Jesus in a postresurrection appearance to the apostles as repeating the instructions of Matthew 18:15–17, but it omits the step about the involvement of the church in the process.[12]

Tertullian in his *Apology*, written around 200, before he became a Montanist, describes censures being given in the assembly of Christians presided over by their elders.

> In these meetings [he has referred to praying and reading the scriptures] there are also exhortations, rebukes, and divine censures. For judgment is administered with great authority, as among those in the presence of God, and it is the supreme anticipation of the judgment to come if any has so sinned that he is banished from participation in our prayer, our gatherings, and all holy fellowship. Elders who are proved men preside over us (39).

Elders are mentioned, without reference to a bishop, in other cases of discipline.[13]

We must assume that the leaders of the church took the lead in imposing discipline, and this becomes explicit in third-century sources. Origen counsels the sinner to seek out a "merciful physician" of souls to whom private confession is made, and this may be followed by a public confession:

> Look about very carefully for the person to whom you ought to confess your sin. . . . Then whatever counsel he gives, you will act on it and follow it. If he has understood and foreseen that your ailment is such as needs to be exposed and cured in the assembly of the whole church, from which others may be edified and you yourself more easily cured, this must be arranged with much deliberation and the experienced counsel of that physician. (*Homilies on Psalms* 37 2.6)

Cyprian gives the same advice about private confession in cases of sins of thought and employs the same medical imagery, but he specifies that the confession is to be made to God's priests, usually meaning bishops in Cyprian (*On the Lapsed* 28).[14]

Even prior to Cyprian, the imposition of penance was clearly in the hands of the bishop according to the instructions of the Syriac *Didascalia* (6 [2.1.16]).[15]

Nature of the Discipline

What was involved in the discipline? What did the church do? As the instructions in *Didascalia* 6 state ("put him forth . . . and keep him without the Church") and some of the other quotations already cited indicate, the ultimate discipline was separation from the fellowship of the church. This might come about by the person's own actions and lifestyle, as with the robber in the story about the apostle John, in which nothing is said about the church having taken any action to exclude him. By his conduct he excluded himself. Our concern here, however, is with indications of actions taken by the church through its members or leaders. The earliest surviving extrabiblical document, the *Didache*, commands as follows: "Reprove one another, not in wrath but in peace, as you have it in the Gospel. No one is to speak to anyone who has wronged his neighbor; he is not to hear from you until he repents" (15.3). This is a strong statement of separation from social intercourse with a fellow believer who has sinned against another believer, similar to some New Testament statements (1 Cor. 5:11; 2 John 10). More of the statements apply to exclusion from the activities of the church. Irenaeus reports that Cerdon, after alternately confessing to the church and teaching in secret, "and then again confessing and being rebuked for his evil teachings, he was separated from the assembly of the brothers" (*Against Heresies* 4.3.3).[16] Origen in an interesting passage speaks of "two ways by which men are delivered from the church into the power of the devil" (1 Cor. 5:5):

> The first way is when his fault is revealed in church and he is expelled by the priests of the church, so that "noted" (2 Thess. 3:14) by men, he may be ashamed and by conversion come [to salvation]. . . . The second way is when his sin is not revealed to men but when God, "who sees in secret" [Matt. 6:6], . . . "delivers him to Satan" [1 Cor. 5:5]. (*Homilies on Judges* 2.5)

Elsewhere Origen considers the situations of those who should have been disfellowshipped and were not, and those who were disfellowshipped and should not have been:

> Finally, when someone has been overthrown by his own sin, he also departs from the assembly and community of the saints. We take an example: Someone of the faithful sins; although he is not cast out by the judgment of the bishop, he is nevertheless cast out by the sin that he committed. However much he enters the church, he is nevertheless cast out, separated from the association and unity of the faithful. . . . On the contrary, it sometimes happens that someone may be expelled and thrust outside by an unjust judgment of those who are over the church. But he did not go out . . . because he appears to be expelled by men on an unjust judgment. And so it is that sometimes the one who is thrust outside may be inside, and the one outside appears to be retained inside. (*Homilies on Leviticus* 14.2)

These descriptions show the significance of the withdrawal of the fellowship of the church.

Exclusion from the church was, especially, exclusion from the Lord's Supper.[17] This is implied in Justin Martyr's description of the Eucharist in the mid-second century (*1 Apology* 66). Origen rebukes one who despises the judgment of God and the admonition of the church in regard to his sins with this warning: "Do you not fear to profane [or, to share in] the body of Christ by approaching the Eucharist as if you were clean and pure, as if nothing in you was unworthy?" He proceeds to apply 1 Corinthians 11:30 to the person, since such a one does not understand what it is "to have communion with the church and to approach so great and eminent mysteries" (*Homilies on the Psalms* 2.6).

There was a period of probation before the excluded sinner was restored to the fellowship of the community. Origen drew the comparison between the catechumenate as a preparation for baptism and the period of discipline before a return to the life of the church (*Against Celsus* 3.51).[18] The classification of different stages in the period of probation came later, and the fourth-century sources assign lengths of time for the exclusion from the church according to different sins.[19]

Hermas declared as a matter of revelation that there was to be only one repentance after baptism (*Mandates* 4.3.6; cf. 4.1.8). Clement of Alexandria, closely following the wording of Hermas, repeats that a return to the church is possible only once, designating this a "second repentance," that is, a second after the baptismal repentance (*Miscellanies* 2.13.55). So, too, does Tertullian, who with reluctance speaks of this one last hope after baptism (*On* Repentance 7). Origen said that "the place of repentance is conceded once only," but specifies that this was for graver sins, since "common faults" always allow repentance and forgiveness (*Homilies on Leviticus* 15.2). The limitation to one ecclesiastical penance remained normative in the Latin church up to the sixth century; thereafter private penance became common and was repeatable.[20]

Requirements for Reconciliation

As sin was an act of the will, so it could be eliminated only by another freely performed act.[21] This meant that the sin had to be given up and a submissive attitude manifested. Clement of Rome gave this command to the rebels at Corinth: "Submit to the elders and receive the discipline of repentance, bending the knees of your hearts" (*1 Clement* 57).

Repentance

Most often, as this statement and many others already cited indicate,[22] the requirement for return to fellowship was described as repentance. Several statements offer partial definitions or explanations of what repentance involved. The "angel of repentance" explained to Hermas: "He repents and no longer does evil but does good abundantly, and humbles his soul and punishes it" (*Mandates* 4.2.2). Clement of Alexandria offered this definition: "True repentance is to be no longer guilty of the same things but wholly to root out of the soul the sins for which one condemned himself to death" (*Who Is the Rich Man?* 39). Tertullian defined repentance as "cessation from sin" (*On Modesty* 10), or again, "Repentance is admission of fault" (*On the Flesh of Christ* 8).

The concern with "true repentance" is reflected already in Polycarp, bishop of Smyrna in the early second century (*Philippians* 11.4). It is expressed in the frequent phrase "to repent with the whole heart," a characteristic expression in *2 Clement* and Hermas.[23] Later authors speak of "real conversion"[24] and "complete and sincere repentance."[25] These expressions indicate that in true repentance the sinner detests sin more because it offends God than because it hurts the self.[26]

Confession

Besides "repentance" or "second repentance," the process of restoration of the sinner was known by the Greek word *exomologesis*, "confession" or "acknowledgment." If repentance was the inward turning away from sin to God, confession was the outward expression in word and deed. Tertullian, writing in Latin, says, "This second repentance ... in order that it may not be exhibited in conscience alone, but may likewise be carried out in some act ... which is most often expressed by the Greek name, is *exomologesis*, by which we confess our transgressions to the Lord" (*On Repentance* 9).

Repentance and confession are often linked together in the early sources. "After [death] we can no longer there make confession or repent" (*2 Clement* 8.3). Clement of Alexandria speaks of "those who confess with repentance" (*Miscellanies* 2.13).[27] That is a good summary of a narrative in the apocryphal *Acts of Peter* 10, from the second half of the second century. Marcellus begged Peter to pray for him, made a detailed confession of how Simon the Magician deceived him, and then declared, "I repent and resort to your prayers. . . . I believe that the Lord will have mercy on me since I repent."[28]

The *Didache* addressed the individual (singular) with the command, "In the assembly (*ekklesia*) confess your sins, and do not come to your prayer [congregational ?] with an evil conscience" (4). It is not clear whether the same confession before the congregation or a prior personal confession is intended by Chapter 14: "Each Lord's day of the Lord, come together, break bread and give thanks, after confessing your transgressions so that your sacrifice may be pure. Everyone who has a quarrel with his fellow must not meet with you until they be reconciled."[29]

Some passages already cited refer to making a public confession before the church.[30] Origen considered it possible that Psalms 56:10 (LXX) "is an exhortation to make confession of sins in church" (*Selections in Psalms*, PG 12.1472C). Not all sins required public confession. Cyprian, in dealing with private confession for sins of thought, advised: "Since they have even thought of such things, with grief and simplicity, they should confess this very thing to God's priests" (*On the Lapsed* 28).

Where the reference is to public confession, it is not clear that the confession was specific or detailed. In some cases, the sin was obvious and so did not require specifics. Actually, in usage, "confession" often referred to the acts of public humiliation by which one signified acknowledgment of sin and submission to the discipline of the church.

Expressions of Repentance and Confession

The penitent came, as it were, knocking at the door of the church (Tertullian, *On Repentance* 7). The word *exomologesis* implied public manifestations. People naturally drew back from such public, outward manifestations of remorse and shame,[31] so Tertullian reassured them that they were among "brothers and fellow-servants," who would "join with one consent in the grief and in laboring for the remedy." Moreover, "Is it better," he asks, "to be condemned in secret than absolved in public?" (ibid., 10).

The early second-century homily known as *2 Clement* refers to almsgiving, prayer, fasting, and love as rescuing from sin (16.4). It seems that these are personal activities rather than requirements imposed by the community. Similarly, some other early statements may refer to spontaneous expressions of a person's own feelings.[32] However, the move toward formalizing, or ritualizing, the expressions of repentance began early. Such arrangements grew out of the conviction expressed by the Shepherd to Hermas: "Do you suppose that the sins of those who repent are forgiven immediately? Assuredly not. Rather it is necessary for the one who repents to torture his own soul and be exceedingly humble in his every deed and to be afflicted with many different afflictions" (*Similitudes* 7.4).[33]

The account of the robber restored to the church by John may combine elements of personal remorse and church discipline. Clement of Alexandria tells the story as an example of someone who "truly repented" and refers to his weeping and fasting and the prayers said for him (*Who Is the Rich Man?* 42). Tertullian gives the most circumstantial account of the discipline required for readmission to the church. The element of spontaneous sorrow for sin is not to be discounted, but Tertullian presents the activities as required expressions:

> The *exomologesis* . . . commands with regard to the very clothes and dress to lie in sackcloth and ashes, to cover the body with soiled clothing, to lay the soul low with lamentations, to exchange severe treatment for those sins which were committed; for the rest to allow only plain food and drink, not (to be sure) for the stomach's sake but the soul's. And for the most part it commands indeed to strengthen prayers with fastings, to heave sighs, to weep, to groan day and night to your Lord God, to fall prostrate before the elders, to kneel before God's dear ones, to enjoin on all the brothers to be ambassadors on behalf of your supplications. (*On Repentance* 9)

Tertullian confirms this account in other passages in his writings.[34] Lest this be thought an instance of Tertullian's exaggeration, there are independent confirmations of this severe humiliation as a way of demonstrating repentance. From Tertullian's time, Eusebius reports the return of Natalius from Adoptionism to the Orthodox Roman church: "He put on sackcloth and sprinkled himself with ashes and with much haste and tears he fell down at the feet of Zephyrinus the bishop. Rolling at the feet of the clergy and the laity, he moved with his tears the compassionate church of the merciful Christ. [Even so] he was scarcely readmitted to fellowship" (*Church History* 5.28.12). Celsus, the pagan critic of Christianity, may have known something of the church's disciplinary practices: "The humble man humiliates himself shamelessly and improperly, prostrating himself face downward and grovelling upon his knees, clothing himself with wretched garments, and heaping dust on himself" (Origen, *Against Celsus* 6.15).

The *Didascalia* 6 refers to a time of fasting and admonition before reconciliation to the church.[35]

Cyprian emphasizes the lamentation by repentant sinners. In several passages he makes various combinations of repentance, lamentation, entreaty, tears, weeping, and mourning (*Epistles* 51.28–29; 53.1; *On the Lapsed* 30). Cyprian has many references, in fact, to the penitential discipline, including prayer, fasting, wearing penitential clothing, vigils, and almsgiving.[36]

Commodian, a Latin poet of uncertain date, perhaps third century, summarizes the disciplinary practices by referring to "prayer night and day," "confession of guilt," "to weep openly," "to put hair and beard in the dust of the earth," and "to be prostrate in sackcloth" (*Instructions* 2.8 [49]). No significance is to be put in the order in which the poet mentions these items.

Theological Meaning of Discipline

Why was discipline imposed? What was the meaning of the acts of repentance and confession to which the sinner was submitted? Some passages speak to the psychological value of the penitential discipline.[37] Our concern here will be limited to the theological interpretation given of the discipline.

Ultimately, the repentance that produces death to sin, whether the "first" or the "second" repentance, was a sharing in Christ's passion.[38] During the second and third centuries, however, there was a shift away from the biblical understanding whereby grace covers postbaptismal as well as prebaptismal sins as long as the person maintains the means by which forgiveness was received in the first place, namely, faith and repentance. That shift involved a change from an emphasis on the free forgiveness of God to becoming worthy of forgiveness. This was expressed by works of satisfaction that could be viewed as a sacrifice for sin or making recompense for the sins.[39] Schwartz observes that exclusion from the church originally was to protect the community where the Holy Spirit lived from profanation by the unworthy and was an expression of the ethical earnestness of every Christian; by the third century it was a disciplinary punishment adjusted to the sin.[40]

The background of this development is the employment of the language of recompense or compensation to describe one's repentance for sins. "While we have opportunity to be healed, let us give ourselves to God, who heals us, giving him recompense. Of what sort? Repentance from a sincere heart" (*2 Clement* 9.7–8). Hermas is sometimes cited as an early representative of a distinction between "remission" in baptism and "purgation" in penance.[41] The distinction is stated explicitly by Clement of Alexandria: "It ought to be known then that those who fall into sin after baptism are those who are subjected to discipline; for the deeds done before baptism are remitted, and those done after are purged" (*Miscellanies* 4.24.154.3). The distinction between "forgiveness" in baptism and "expiation" in penance has become a staple of Catholic interpretation.[42]

The Latin sources freely say that penitential acts "make satisfaction" to God. For example, from Tertullian's treatise *On Repentance*: "By confession satisfaction is received . . . ; by repentance God is appeased" (9.2; cf.7.14). These acts of discipline replace eternal punishments: "Consider in your heart the hell that *exomologesis* will extinguish for you" (12.1; cf. 9.5). We should be warned against reading the full medieval sense of satisfaction into Tertullian, but there is much on works and at least the beginning of statements which could be understood as saying that the disciplinary acts were not just personal expressions of repentance but were some kind of equivalent recompense.[43] The Latin translation of Origen's *Homilies on Judges* (the Greek does not survive) similarly speaks of church discipline as a satisfaction: "Humble yourself before

God himself and make satisfaction to him in the confession of repentance" (3.2). The distinction between gratuitous pardon in baptism and merited expiation through acts of penance has been invoked to bring consistency to Origen's teachings on forgiveness of sins.[44]

The language of satisfaction becomes quite common in Cyprian's penitential teaching. Passages from his treatise *On the Lapsed* will show his usage.

> Before their sins are expiated, before confession has been made of their crime, before their conscience has been purged by sacrifice and by the hand of the priest, before the offence of an angry and threatening Lord is placated. (16)
>
> The Lord must be appeased by our satisfaction. (17; cf. also 28 and 29)

Perhaps I may leave the role of historian here and be permitted a theological judgment. Although I have often followed the results of Catholic historians on the development of penitential practices, I have difficulty with their sacramental interpretation of the practices, specifically their acceptance of the theological significance given to these practices in the Latin tradition. Interpreting the expressions of repentance and confession as a compensation for sin goes well beyond the biblical "conditions" for accepting the grace of forgiveness.

Reconciliation to the Church

The acts of repentance were brought to a close by the sinner's acceptance once more into the fellowship of the church. Several early texts emphasize that reconciliation is available for "any transgression."[45] Clement of Alexandria said, "God, being very merciful, gave still another second repentance to those who, though in faith, fall into any transgression" (*Miscellanies* 2.13). Tertullian, while still in the Catholic Church, referring to the parables of Luke 15, called upon all to repent with the promise of being received back (*On Repentance* 8).[46] The Montanists and the followers of Hippolytus and Novatian, on the contrary, refused to readmit to the communion of the church those guilty of serious sins. Such persons, if repentant, were kept by the church in the category of penitents, and their eternal destiny was left in the hands of God, who alone could pardon serious transgressions.[47]

Among rigorists, those guilty of lighter sins were forgiven by the church, and among others, all sinners in principle could be forgiven. Some form of the word "receive" was the common term for welcoming back the sinner.[48] Several of the passages already cited, even when describing the penitential discipline, do not give any details of how the return to the fellowship of the church was expressed or acknowledged.[49]

One fairly circumstantial account is found in the Pseudo-Clementine *Homilies*, in a passage probably from the third century but possibly earlier:

> [Followers of Simon the Magician], falling at Peter's feet, begged that they might be pardoned for having been carried away with Simon, and on repenting, to be received. Peter, admitting those who repented and the rest of the crowd, prayed and laid his hands on them, and healing those who were sick among them, he dismissed them.[50]

The ceremony of reconciliation in the *Didascalia* included prayer by the people and imposition of hand by the bishop (7).[51]

Prayer holds a prominent place in the reconciliation. Origen refers to certain priests who claimed to forgive even idolatry, adultery, and fornication "on the ground that by means of the prayer offered for those who have committed these deeds even 'the sin unto death' is loosed" (*On Prayer* 28.10).[52]

The prayer was accompanied by the imposition of the hand of the bishop. This is especially emphasized by Cyprian, who was struggling against the martyrs and confessors in Carthage to keep control of discipline in the hands of the bishop. "By the laying on of the hand of the bishop and clergy receive the right of communion."[53] Cyprian drew a parallel between reception into the church by baptism and restoration to the church (*Epistle* 70.2) and stated that the laying of hands on those returning to the church was to bestow the Holy Spirit (ibid., 75.11; 73.5).

The parallel with baptism is elaborated in the fairly detailed instructions in *Didascalia* 10:

> [Commenting on Mt. 18:15f., the author refers to those who promise to repent and are admitted to church to hear the word but may not communicate in prayer.] And afterwards, as each

one of them repents and shows the fruits of repentance, receive him to prayer after the manner of a heathen. And as thou baptizest a heathen and then receivest him, so also lay hand upon this man, whilst all pray for him, and then bring him in and let him communicate with the Church. For the imposition of hand shall be to him in the place of baptism: for whether by the imposition of hand, or by baptism, they receive the communication of the Holy Spirit.[54]

The interpretation given by Cyprian and the *Didascalia* has led modern scholars to see the significance of the laying on of hands in the reconciliation of penitents to be the imparting of the Holy Spirit.[55] My own studies of the laying on of hands in ordination point to the earliest and primary meaning of this gesture in Christianity as the sign of blessing, of whatever nature.[56] If an imposition of hands was a part of the reconciliation to the church prior to the third century (and I consider that likely), then the meaning of the gesture as a sign of blessing in this context was the restoration of fellowship in the community of believers, and the interpretation of this act as a fresh bestowal of the Holy Spirit was a secondary development. If the gesture was introduced as part of the reconciliation of penitents only in the third century, then the association with the Holy Spirit may have accompanied its introduction.

Restoration to the fellowship of the church involved especially return to participation in the Lord's Supper.[57] Not to go through the necessary penance and rashly to partake of communion was "to do violence to the Lord's body and blood" (Cyprian, *On the Lapsed* 16).[58] There was a strong desire for penitents to partake of the Eucharist before death so that they could die in communion with the church.[59]

Restored penitents were not appointed to any office in the church or, if clergy at the time of their fall, were restored only as laymen.[60]

The Role of the Church

The discipline and the reconciliation had both personal and ecclesiastical elements. The reconciliation to which I now call attention was with the church and meant a return to its fellowship.[61]

Congregational prayer was made for those who fell into sin. Clement commended the Corinthian church for its past conduct: "With good will and pious confidence you stretched out your hands to Almighty God, beseeching him to be merciful if you sinned unwillingly. Day and night you strove on behalf of the whole brotherhood in order that the number of his elect might be saved" (*1 Clement* 2.3–4).[62] Ignatius counselled the church in Smyrna: "Pray for them, if somehow they might repent" (*Smyrnaeans* 4.1).

Indeed, there is much emphasis in the sources on the efforts, beyond prayer, to bring back those who went astray. The homily known as *2 Clement* states, "It is no small reward to return to salvation a soul that is wandering and perishing" (14). And again: "Let us then help one another and bring back to the good those who are weak, in order that we all may be saved and convert and exhort one another" (17.1–2). Irenaeus reported that the brothers "with much effort" converted a deacon's wife (*Against Heresies* 1.13.5). Clement of Alexandria prefaces his story of the diligent efforts by the apostle John to rescue the young convert from his life of crime with these words: "It is impossible immediately to eradicate inbred passions, but by the power of God, human intercession, the help of brothers, sincere repentance, and constant care, they are corrected" (*Who is the Rich Man?* 40).

There is, further, much about the role of the church in receiving back the sinner. Polycarp wrote: "Call them [Valens and his wife] back as fallible and erring members so that you may save your whole body. For in doing this you edify yourselves" (*Philippians* 11.4).[63] Tertullian encouraged participation in the public expressions of discipline with these similitudes:

> Where there is common hope, fear, joy, grief, suffering, because there is a common Spirit of a common Lord and Father, why do you think these believers to be anything other than yourself? . . . With one or two there is the church, and where is the church there indeed is Christ. When then you cast yourself at the knees of the brothers, you are handling Christ, you are entreating Christ. And when they shed tears over you, it is Christ who suffers, Christ who prays to the Father. (*On Repentance* 10)

In his Montanist period, Tertullian granted the claim of his Catholic opponents that "the church has the power of forgiving sins," but he disputed which church ("the church of the Spirit, not the church of the bishops") and the propriety of indiscriminate exercise of the right ("I will not do it, lest they commit others"—*On Modesty* 21). The whole church had to be concerned, because, as Origen says, the sin of one harms the whole people (*Homilies on Joshua* 7.6). Specific persons in the church were given a special role in reconciling sinners. Tertullian refers to those, not able to obtain peace from the church, who sought it from imprisoned martyrs (*To the Martyrs* 1.4–6). Since those who confessed the faith before the authorities were believed to have the Holy Spirit in a special way (cf. Luke 12:12), they could grant forgiveness. Their readiness to exercise this right apart from the usual structure of church discipline created serious problems for Cyprian during and after the Decian persecution.[64]

The role of the elders in the disciplinary process is met in several passages, especially in second-century sources. Polycarp instructed, "And the elders are to be compassionate, showing mercy to all, turning back those who have strayed, looking after all the weak" (*Philippians* 6.1). Tertullian's account of the public confession mentions bowing at the feet of the elders (*On Repentance* 9; cf. *On Modesty* 13), and that elders preside over the disciplinary activities of the church is implied by his *Apology* 39. Tertullian is also witness to the bishop's authority in disciplinary matters (*On Modesty* 1). Other sources from the early third century show the responsibility of the bishop in dealing with sinners. Hippolytus includes in his model prayer for the ordination of a bishop these words: "And by the high priestly Spirit he may have authority to . . . 'loose every bond' according to the authority Thou gavest to the Apostles."[65] The exercise of this authority to forgive sins by the Roman bishop Callistus, however, aroused Hippolytus' rigorist ire (*Refutation of All Heresies* 9.7 [12]). Origen testifies to the use of Matthew 16:19 by bishops of his day to support their right to bind and loose sins, but he contends that only those with the way of life of Peter may exercise the privilege (*Commentary on Matthew* 12.14). Although Cyprian included the other clergy in his policies, he was a key figure in locating the power of penance in the bishop.[66]

Reconciliation with the church was considered necessary for reconciliation with God, and reconciliation with God was necessary for reconciliation with the church. If we can avoid the efforts at juridical definition which have accompanied debates over church discipline and if we can recover the sense of wholeness that characterized early Christianity before these matters were debated, then both halves of this equation may be affirmed. The relationship with the church and the relationship with God belong together.

*Originally printed in *Restoration Quarterly* 36 (1994): 81–100.

This is a shortened version of a paper read at the Believers Church Conference on "The Rule of Christ: Matthew 18:15–20" at Goshen College, Goshen, Indiana, May 21, 1992.

Chapter 4 Endnotes

1. Origen, *Homilies on Leviticus* 2.4. In support of forgiveness by penance he cites Pss. 6:7; 41:4; 31:5; Jas. 5:14–15.

2. The basic collection of texts and discussion is B. Poschmann, *Paenitentia Secunda* (Bonn: Hanstein, 1940). A full collection of Greek and Latin texts through the mid–third century has been assembled by H. Karpp in the series "Traditio christiania" 1 with German translation in *Die Busse, Quellen zur Entstehung des altkirchlichen Busswesens* (Zurich: EVZ, 1969) and French translation in *La Pénitence* (Neuchâtel: Delachaux et Niestle, 1970). Texts in the original with English translations may be found in O. D. Watkins, *A History of Penance*, vol. 1 (London: Longmans, Green, 1920); English translations of selections are in Paul F. Palmer, *Sources of Christian Theology*, vol. 2, *Sacraments and Forgiveness* (Westminster: Newman, 1959); and more selectively E. Ferguson, *Early Christians Speak*, 3rd ed. (Abilene: ACU Press, 1999) 177–187. For the early history see R. S. T. Haslehurst, *Penitential Discipline of the Early Church* (London: SPCK, 1921); E. Schwartz, "Busstufen und Katechumenatsklassen," *Gesammelte Schriften zum Neuen Testament und zum frühen Christentum*, vol. 5 (Berlin: DeGruyter, 1963) 274–362; B. Poschmann, *Penance and the Anointing of the Sick* (London: Burns and Oates, 1964); K. Rahner, *Theological Investigations*, vol. 15, *Penance in the Early Church* (New York: Crossroad, 1982); Ingrid Goldhahn-Müller, *Die Grenze der Gemeinde: Studien zum Problem der zweiten Busse im Neuen Testament unter Berücksichtigung der Entwicklung im 2. Jh. bis Tertullian* (Göttingen: Vandenhoeck und Ruprecht, 1989). For surveys including the later history see W. Telfer, *The Forgiveness of Sins* (London: SCM, 1959) and P. Anciaux, *The Sacrament of Penance* (New York: Sheed and Ward, 1962); James Dallen, *The Reconciling Community: The Rite of Penance* (Collegeville, MN: Liturgical, 1986); A. Firey, ed., *New History of Penance* (Leiden: Brill, 2008).

3. Anciaux, *Sacrament of Penance*, 46.

4. Cf. Ignatius, *Ephesians* 7.1; 9.1.

5. Wilhelm Schneemelcher, *New Testament Apocrypha*, vol. 2, R. McL. Wilson, trans. and ed. (Louisville: Westminster/John Knox, 1992) 255–56. Cf. Tertullian, *Prescription of Heretics* 30 for Marcion and Valentinus expelled from the church.

6. See Rahner, *Penance*, 176, on the different sins which Cyprian considered serious enough to require church penance.

7. Clement of Alexandria, *Who Is the Rich Man That Is Saved?*, 39–42.

8. Cf. 5, where he objects to the inconsistency of the church forgiving sexual sins but not idolatry and homicide.

9. Poschmann, *Penance and the Anointing*, 44, followed by Rahner, *Penance*, 127, argues that the division between remissible and irremissible sins was new with Tertullian. So also G. H. Joyce, "Private Penance in the Early Church," *Journal of Theological Studies* 42 (1991): 18–42. For the contrary view, see Watkins, *History of Penance*, 101–142, 467–469. Goldhahn-Müller, *Grenze der Gemeinde*, 372, says that what was new for Tertullian was in not specifying that certain sins were irremissible but attempting to identify which sins these were (but he did not have a fixed list, even of three).

10. *Homilies on Leviticus* 15.2; *Commentary on John* 19.14; *Commentary on Matthew* 13.30. See Poschmann, *Penance and the Anointing*, 66–73, and Rahner, *Penance*, 252–266. They reject the conclusion of Watkins in *History of Penance*, 133–134, 137–138 that Origen had a third class of sins, those unforgivable.

11. Palmer, *Sacraments*, 67.

12. Wilhelm Schneemelcher, ed., *New Testament Apocrypha*, vol. 1, *Gospels and Related Writings*, R. McL. Wilson, trans. and ed. (Louisville: Westminster/John Knox, 1991) 276–277.

13. Polycarp, *Philippians* 6; Hippolytus, *Against Noetus* 1; cf. Tertullian, *On Repentance* 9.

14. Rahner, *Penance*, 275, points out the difference that, for Cyprian, healing is an image for punishment, but in Origen punishment is an image for healing.

15. R. Hugh Connolly, *Didascalia Apostolorum* (Oxford: Clarendon, 1929), 52.

16. Cf. Irenaeus, *Against Heresies* 4.26.4, about keeping apart from heretics, schismatics, and hypocrites (4.26.2) and adhering to those who hold to the doctrine of the apostles.

17. Rahner, *Penance*, 62; W. Elert, *Eucharist and Church Fellowship in the First Four Centuries* (St. Louis: Concordia, 1966). Cf. *Acts of Peter 2*; *Didascalia 10*; Tertullian, *On Modesty* 3.5, 7.22.

18. For the working out of this comparison in the fourth century, see Schwartz, *Gesammelte Schriften*, vol. 5, 308–310, 338–352.

19. Ibid., 308–352; cf. Watkins, *History of Penance*, 239–246, and chapters 6 and 7.

20. Anciaux, *Sacrament of Penance*, 46.

21. Ibid., 90.

22. Hermas, *Mandates* 4.1.5; 7, 8, 10; Ignatius, *Philadelphians* 3; 8; Eusebius, *Church History* 5.1.46; Clement of Alexandria, *Miscellanies* 2.13, 2.23, *Who Is the Rich Man?* 42; Tertullian, *On Repentance* 7; Origen, *Homilies on Leviticus* 2.4, 15.2; *Didascalia* 6 [2.12].

23. *2 Clement* 8.2; 9.8; 17.1; 19.1; cf. "with the soul" in 13.1; Hermas, *Visions* 1.3.2; 2.2.4; 3.13.4; 4.2.5; *Mandates* 5.1.7; 12.6.2; *Similitudes* 7.4; 8.11.3.

24. Origen, *Against Celsus* 3.51.

25. Cyprian, *Letters* 51.18.

26. Anciaux, *Sacrament of Penance*, 97–104.

27. Cf. Origen, *Selections in Psalms* 24:6 (LXX), "repent and confess."

28. Schneemelcher, *New Testament Apocrypha*, 292–297.

29. E. Kreider, "Let the Faithful Greet Each Other: The Kiss of Peace," *Conrad Grebel Review* 5 (1987): 35–37.

30. Irenaeus, *Against Heresies* 1.13.5 (cf. also 1.13.7 and 1.6.3); 3.4.3.

31. Ibid., 1.13.7.

32. Cf. the wife of the deacon who spent her time weeping and lamenting. Irenaeus, 1.13.5, cited above under sexual sins.

33. Although postbaptismal conversion was not yet formalized, repentance was connected with grief (*Mandate* 10.2), prayer (*Vision* 1.1.9), and confession (*Vision* 1.1.3; 3.1.5–6; *Similitudes* 9.13.4). Goldhahn-Müller, *Grenze der Gemeinde*, 281.

34. *On Modesty* 5 and 13. See Rahner, *Penance*, 130–141, on the practice of penance according to Tertullian, including evidence for two stages—asking to be admitted to penance and the actual penance itself.

35. Connolly, *Didascalia*, 52–53.

36. E.g., *On the Lapsed* 35, 36. For Cyprian's penitential teaching as a whole, see Rahner, *Penance*, 155–220, especially his analysis of the three stages: performance of works of penance, *exomologesis* before the community, and reconciliation by imposition of hands.

37. Although not the main concern, see Tertullian, *On Repentance* 8–10; Cyprian, *On the Lapsed* 30, 34–36. Rahner, 183–189.

38. Anciaux, *Sacrament of Penance*, 8.

39. L. Michael White uses the term "transactionalism" for this understanding of the penitential acts: "Transactionalism in the Penitential Thought of Gregory the Great," *Restoration Quarterly* 21 (1978): 33–51, in which he notes the background in Tertullian and Cyprian to Gregory's interpretation.

40. Schwartz, *Gesammelte Schriften* vol. 5, 29–293. He refers to Cyprian, *Epistles* 61.4.

41. *Mandates* 4.3.3. Rahner, *Penance,* 77. Hermas may simply be withholding the promise of postbaptismal repentance to present and future believers (so as not to weaken the intensity of Christian faithfulness) in contrast to the repentance offered to those who had previously fallen away. Graydon F. Snyder, *The Shepherd of Hermas*, vol. 6 of *The Apostolic Fathers*, ed. R. M. Grant (New York: Nelson, 1968) 36, 69–72. See also Poschmann, *Penance and the Anointing,* 28.

42. Anciaux, *Sacrament of Penance,* 78–83. Rahner, *Penance,* 10.

43. G. Hallonsten, *Satisfactio bei Tertullian* (Lund, 1984), argues that Tertullian does not use *satisfactio* in the sense of compensation but as equivalent to reconciliation and repentance. But the sense of works is still there. See Goldhahn-Müller, *Grenze der Gemeinde,* 358–360.

44. Poschmann, *Penance and the Anointing,* 66ff. Rahner, *Penance,* 266–279.

45. See *1 Clement* 56 and Ignatius, *Philadelphians* 8.

46. After he became a Montanist, he tried to reply to the Catholic argument that "repentance will be practiced in vain if it is without pardon" (*On Modesty* 3). The Council of Nicaea in 325, *Canon* 13, provided that anyone on the point of death, "who asks to partake of the Eucharist, let the bishop give it to him after due examination."

47. Watkins, *History,* 104–105, 112–113, 119–121, 213–218.

48. Cf. Hermas, *Mandates,* 4.1.8; Ignatius, *Smyrnaeans* 4.1; Dionysius of Corinth in Eusebius, *Church History* 4.23.6. Goldhahn-Müller, *Grenze der Gemeinde,* 331–332.

49. For instance, the submission to the presbyters at Corinth of those who had rebelled against them—*1 Clement* 57; the readmission to fellowship of Natalius at Rome—Eusebius, *Church History* 5.28.12; the robber in Clement of Alexandria, *Who Is the Rich Man?* 42.

50. Cf. *Homilies* 3.6.2; 8.19.3.

51. Connolly, *Didascalia,* 56.

52. Origen's rejection of these claims may be a rigorist rejection of forgiveness for these sins or only a rejection of forgiveness by prayer alone without the "sacrifice" of penitential discipline. Contrast the notes in J. E. L. Oulton and H. Chadwick, *Alexandrian Christianity*, Library of Christian Classics, Vol. 2 (Philadelphia: Westminster, 1954) 372–375, and Rahner, *Penance,* 306–307.

53. Cf. 10.1; 11.2; 12.1; 13.2; 14.3: 70.2; *On the Lapsed* 16, quoted above.

54. Connolly, *Didascalia,* 102–104.

55. P. Galtier, "Imposition des mains," *Dictionnaire de théologie catholique* (Paris: Letouzey et Ané), vol. 7, Col. 1398–1404; Rahner, *Penance,* 145–171, 234–237 (an imparting of the Holy Spirit, but not a confirmation).

56. E. Ferguson, "Ordination in the Ancient Church (II)," *Restoration Quarterly* 5 (1961): 134–136, 141–143; *idem,* "Laying on of Hands: Its Significance in Ordination," *Journal of Theological Studies,* ns 26 (1975): 1–12.

57. Note Cyprian, *Epistles* 9.2 and 11.2, cited above, and references in note 53.

58. Cf. *Epistles* 10.1. Superstitious ideas associated with the elements are evident in *On the Lapsed* 25–26.

59. See Dionysius of Alexandria, second half of the third century, in Eusebius, *Church History* 6.44.

60. Origen, *Against Celsus* 3.51; Cyprian, *Epistles* 71.2.

61. In Hermas, *Visions* 3.5, the stones once rejected but later placed in the tower (the church) are those who sinned but repent while the tower is still being built.

62. Cf. *1 Clement* 56.

63. For the process of discipline as edifying others, see Origen, *Homilies on the Psalms* 37.2.6.

64. E.g., Cyprian, *Epistles* 9, 10, 13, 26, 39, 50; *On the Lapsed*.

65. G. Dix, *The Apostolic Tradition of St. Hippolytus of Rome* (London: SPCK, 1968) 5–6.

66. Rahner, *Penance*, 195.

5

Wine as a Table Drink in the Ancient World

The ordinary table beverage of the Mediterranean world in Roman times was wine mixed with water. This information, well known to Classicists,[1] has not found its way into much literature dealing with the Bible and so is not so well known in religious circles. This article will adduce some of the relevant statements from Greek, Roman, Jewish, and Christian authors of the Hellenistic-Roman period and call attention to some of the possible implications in the interpretation of certain New Testament passages.

Drinking did not accompany the dinner in Greece, but in Rome a small amount of wine was taken with the meal. The amphorae in which the wine was stored were opened and the contents poured through a strainer into a large mixing bowl (*kratēr*). There the wine was mixed with water. From it the drinking bowls (*kantharos*) or cups (*kylix*) were filled. Many of these different types of containers have been recovered from excavations and may be seen at museums of classical antiquities.[2] At Greek formal banquets the guests elected a president who determined the proportions of water and wine. When the main course was finished, the libation was poured out and the symposium or "drinking party," proper began. Various forms of entertainment—from acrobatic stunts, musical performances, recitations, love making, to serious philosophical discussions—concluded the evening.[3]

The ratio of water to wine varied considerably. One of the earliest references[4] gives the most diluted mixture—twenty parts water to one part of wine (was the wine really that strong?). Other references tend to stay within less extreme proportions, but nearly always the quantity of water predominated. A strong mixture was three parts of water to two parts of wine, as in the playwright Aristophanes:

> S. Here, drink this also, mingled three and two.
> Demus. Zeus! but it's sweet and bears the three parts well.[5]

The moralist poet Hesiod spoke of a ratio of three to one.[6] But even this could be mildly stimulating, as celebrated in the fifth century BC poet Euenos:

> The best measure of wine is neither much nor very little;
> For 'tis the cause of either grief or madness.
> It pleases the wine to be the fourth, mixed with three nymphs.
> Then too 'tis most suited for the bridal chamber and love.
> But if it breathe too fiercely, it puts the Loves to flight,
> and plunges men in a sleep, neighbour to death.[7]

The fullest source of information is *The Learned Banquet* by Athenaeus, about AD 200. Book X is largely a collection of statements from earlier writers about drinking practices. A few of Athenaeus' quotations will illustrate the popular combinations.

Alexis in *The Nurse* urges a still more temperate mixture: "A. Look, here is wine. Shall I pour a 'Triton' [three parts water to one part wine-EF]? B. No, it's much better as one and four. A. Too watery, that! However, drink it up and tell me the news; let's have some conversation while we drink." And Diocles in *The Bees*: "A. How is the wine to be mixed I am to drink? B. Four and two."[8]

The poet Ion, in his work *On Chios*, says: "The seer Palamedes prophesied that the Greeks would have a speedy voyage if they drank three cups to one."

But others, who adopted a stronger mixture in their potions drank two parts of wine to five of water. [Four quotations mentioning this ratio follow.] But in Anacreon we have one cup of wine to two of water.[9]

[The lyric poet Alcaeus] says somewhere: "Pour it out, mixing it one and two." . . . Yet Anacreon requires it still stronger in the lines where he says: "Let it be poured out, five and three, in a clean cup." But Philetaerus in *Tereus* has two parts of water to three of neat [Greek, "unmixed"] wine. . . . Pherecrates in *Corianno* has two of water to four of wine. . . . Ephippus in *Circe* has the proportion three to four: "A. It's much safer for you to drink wine well diluted. B. No, by Mother Earth! rather three and four. A. Are you going to drink it so strong? Tell me. B. What have you to say to that?" Timocles in *Conisalus* makes it half and half: "I'll whack you into telling the whole truth with large cups of half and half." [Six other quotations follow mentioning the strong combination of equal parts of water and wine.][10]

Elsewhere Athenaeus quotes Mnesitheus of Athens about the relative strengths:

> The gods had revealed wine to mortals, to be the greatest blessing for those who use it aright, but for those who use it without measure, the reverse. For it gives food to them that take it and strength in mind and body. In medicine it is most beneficial; it can be mixed with liquid drugs and it brings aid to the wounded. In daily intercourse, to those who mix and drink it moderately, it gives good cheer; but if you overstep the bounds, it brings violence. Mix it half and half, and you get madness; unmixed, bodily collapse.[11]

Earlier in the second century Plutarch gives similar information:

> And so they say and sing,—Drink either five or three, but not four. For the fifth has the sesquilateral proportion, three cups of water being mingled with two of wine; the third has the double proportion, two cups of water being put to one of wine; but the fourth answers to the epitrite proportion of the three parts of water poured into one of wine. Now this last proportion be fit for some grave magistrates sitting in the council-hall, or for

logicians who pull up their brows when they are busy in watching
the unfolding of their arguments; for surely it is a mixture sober
and weak enough. As for the other twain; that medley which
carries the proportion of two for one brings in that turbulent
tone of those who are half-drunk, . . . for it suffers a man neither
to be fully sober, nor yet to drench himself so deep in wine as to
be altogether witless and past his sense; but the other, standing
upon the proportion of three to two, is of all the most musical
accord, causing a man to sleep peaceably, and forget all cares.[12]

It should be noted that the resultant beverage was still called "wine," as
Plutarch himself says, "We call a mixture 'wine' although the larger of the
component parts is water."[13] When speaking of the ordinary drinking beverage, a writer simply said "wine," for it was taken for granted that it was
mixed water and wine. Only in special circumstances was information given
on the mixture.

Latin authors also speak of the normal practice of drinking mixed
water and wine at meals. Juvenal, the late first-century satirist, refers to "the
page who has cost so many thousands [who] cannot mix a drink for a poor
man."[14] Martial writes: "A cunning taverner imposed on me lately at Ravenna.
Whereas I asked for negus [Latin, *mixtum*], he sold me wine neat."[15] The preceding epigram explains that due to the shortage of water in Ravenna water
was more expensive than wine.

The amount of alcoholic content which could be achieved by fermenta-
tion was not high when compared with what can be attained through modern
methods of distillation, unknown in the ancient world.[16] Thus the ordinary
table drink would have had a low percentage of alcohol in it. Nevertheless,
the danger of drunkenness was real, and our sources warn about it. Yet in
doing so, they significantly connect intoxication with the drinking of wine
full strength. Thus the comic playwright Menander, "Too much neat liquor
[literally, "unmixed"—EF] means too little wit."[17] Philo the Jew speaks of
"drinking copiously of the unmixed intoxicant."[18] Athenaeus quotes the epigram "The cup of unmixed wine, twice pledged in quick succession, carried
off Erasixenus, that deep wine drinker."[19] From Alexis, *The Phrygian*:

If the headache only came to us before we drink to intoxication, no one would ever indulge himself in wine immoderately. But as it is, foreseeing not that punishment for drunkenness will come, we readily give ourselves over to drinking unmixed cups.[20]

Marcus Argentarius, a poet of the Augustan age, wrote in Greek:

Dead, five feet of earth shall be yours.
You'll not look on the delights of life nor on the rays of the sun.
So take the cup of unmixed Bacchos, Cincius, and drain it
Rejoicing with your arm round your lovely mistress.[21]

But to drink wine unmixed was regarded by the Greeks of the classical age as a barbarian (Scythian) custom.[22] It is to be noted how in ordinary usage, even as "'wine" meant "wine mixed with water," so if one wanted to say straight or neat wine, it was necessary to add the adjective "unmixed."

A bizarre story was told of drugging elephants "with copious handfuls of frankincense, and abundance of unmixed wine, and then when they were maddened by the plentiful supply of drink" turning them loose on the enemy.[23] There were ways of increasing the alcoholic content of the wine[24] and of increasing its intoxicating effect through the addition of certain drugs.[25] On the other hand, Aristotle knew that boiling reduced the intoxicating effect of wine.[26]

The ancient Greeks were devoted to their water, and spring water was a valued rarity.[27] Pindar sings its praises.[28] Athenaeus records a number of famous water drinkers in Greek history.[29] One might even call the ancients "water drinkers" in view of the preponderance of water in the drink. In most cases, however, it was safer and more hygenic to drink wine. Somehow the ancients had discovered that mixing wine with water had a purifying effect on the water so that it became safe to drink.[30]

In general, abstinence from wine altogether was a mark of asceticism. Thus Philo describes the Therapeutae as abstaining from the flesh of animals and from wine, for the latter applying to their entire lives the Old Testament proscription against priests drinking wine when they sacrificed.[31] There were various efforts from time to time to regulate the drinking of wine, and philosophers in the Hellenistic world promoted the idea of temperance.[32]

Wine had various medicinal uses.[33] One of the allowable occasions for drinking of unmixed wine was on a physician's advice. Athenaeus relates, "Among the Western Locrians, if anyone drank unmixed wine without a physician's prescription to effect a cure, the penalty was death."[34] Pliny the Elder in the first century gives an extensive treatment of the medicinal use of wine in which he repeats a prescription for mixed wine:

> In cardiac disease the one hope of relief lies undoubtedly in wine. . . . The general opinion is that a satisfactory mixture is one cyathus of wine to two of water. If the stomach be disordered, should the food not pass down, the wine must be given once more.[35]

He gives a long list of poisons and ailments for which neat wine is to be given.[36]

Any early Jewish distaste for wine diluted with water[37] was overcome by Roman times. Intertestamental and Rabbinic literature allude to the custom. Second Maccabees 15:39 declares, "It is harmful to drink wine alone, or again, to drink water alone, while wine mixed with water is sweet and delicious and enhances one's enjoyment."[38] The Mishnah records the judgment of Rabbi Eliezer (ca. AD 100) that "They do not say the Benediction over the wine until water has been added to it," but reports the majority opinion as allowing the benediction even over wine without water.[39] Elsewhere in the Mishnah it seems assumed that the ratio would be one part of wine to two parts of water,[40] but later Talmudic sources refer to a one to three mixture.[41] The Talmud further refers to the medicinal use of wine: "And according to the Rabbis—for what kind of drink is undiluted wine suitable?—It is suitable for [mixing with] *karyotis*." The latter was a date used for medicinal purposes.[42]

Before the New Testament era, wine had become a normal part of the Passover ritual.[43] The account of the observance of the Passover compiled in the Mishnah in the second century of the Christian era mentions the drinking of four cups during the Passover meal. For three of these it is specifically said that they "mix him the . . . cup."[44]

Therefore, we may safely conclude that the "fruit of the vine"[45] used at the institution of the Lord's Supper (Matt. 26:27ff. and parallels) was the normal table drink of the Jews and other peoples of the Mediterranean world, namely, diluted or mixed wine.

The later Christian accounts which have occasion to refer to the contents of the "cup" at the Last Supper and in the church's celebration speak of water mixed with the wine. In Justin Martyr's description of the Eucharist, about AD 150, "bread is brought, and wine and water, and the president sends up prayers and thanksgivings."[46] Justin, as an apologist, specifically mentions the water perhaps in order to underscore the fact that Christians used the common table beverage and were not having a drunken feast.[47] About sixty-five years later Hippolytus instructed that the bishop "shall eucharistize first the bread into the representation of the Flesh of Christ; and the cup mixed with wine for the antitype of the Blood which was shed for all who have believed in Him."[48]

It seems that there was some necessity to insist on the presence of wine with the water in the cup. Cyprian about 250 argued against those who used water alone in the Lord's Supper:

> Nothing must be done by us but what the Lord first did on our behalf as that the cup which is offered in remembrance of Him should be offered mingled with wine. . . .
>
> I wonder very much whence has originated this practice, that contrary to evangelical and apostolical discipline, water is offered in some places in the Lord's cup, which water by itself cannot express the blood of Christ. . . .
>
> For because Christ bore us all, in that He also bore our sins, we see that in the water is understood the people, but in the wine is showed the blood of Christ. But when the water is mingled in the cup with wine, the people is made one with Christ, and the assembly of believers is associated and conjoined with Him on whom it believes; which association and conjunction of water and wine is so mingled in the Lord's cup, that that mixture cannot any more be separated. . . . Thus, therefore, in consecrating the cup of the Lord, water alone cannot be offered, even as wine alone cannot be offered. For if any one offer wine only the blood of Christ is dissociated from us; but if the water be alone,

> the people are dissociated from Christ. . . . Thus the cup of the
> Lord is not indeed water alone, nor wine alone, unless each be
> mingled with the other.[49]

The contrast appears not to have been the mixed cup versus pure wine; no one (who was religious) took it straight, and the mixed cup was assumed. The presence of water in the drink could be assumed. The wine could not be, for certain ascetics carried their abstinence to the Lord's Supper as well. Clement of Alexandria writes:

> The Scripture manifestly applying the terms bread and water to
> nothing else but to those heresies, which employ bread and water
> in the oblation, not according to the canon of the church. For
> there are those who celebrate the Eucharist with mere water.[50]

The heresies he would have in mind were those which looked upon the material creation as evil and so rejected meat, marriage, and wine. Later sources ascribe this abstention to the second-century Encratites of Tatian, Marcionites, and certain Gnostics.[51] Without the dualist negation of creation the Jewish Christian Ebionites also observed an ascetic Eucharist.[52]

Christian terminology continued to reflect the practice of mixing water with wine. In the early fifth century Theodoret, drawing the Melchizedek = Christ parallel, says, "Even so also having mixed the cup, he gave to his disciples."[53] In another place he states, "In the delivery of the mysteries he called the bread his body and the mixture his blood."[54]

Christian usage in a non-Eucharistic context concurs. An inscription accompanying a painting of the celestial banquet in the Catacomb of Peter and Marcellinus recalls the language of earthly banquets: "'Irene, some hot water!' 'Agape, stir it for me!' 'Agape, mix us some wine!' 'Irene, pour some hot water!'"[55] Clement of Alexandria warns against drunkenness and describes conduct at banquets. He advises abstinence, but does not insist upon it.[56] In describing the beverage he says:

> It is best for the wine to be mixed with as much water as pos-
> sible. . . . For both are works of God, and the mixing of the
> two, both of water and wine, produces health, because life is

composed of a necessary element and a useful element. To the necessary element, the water, which is in the greatest quantity, there is to be mixed in some of the useful element.[57]

The modern Greek word for wine, accordingly, is not the *oinos* of our literature but *krasi*, from *krasis* (literally "mixing").[58] And I am told that this practice still obtains in parts of southern Europe.

Origen comments on the metaphorical uses of wine in Scripture, how it may stand both for God's punishments (he cites Psalms 75:8)[59] and for his blessing (Proverbs 9:5 and the Lord's Supper). He further notes that it was not written of the cup at the Last Supper that it was mixed, for the "Lord rejoiced his disciples with unmixed joy."[60] Here Origen, as frequently, sacrificed historical accuracy for the sake of an allegorical interpretation of the text. He often takes the "unmixed cup" as an expression of punishment,[61] showing that "unmixed" had for him the meaning of "undiluted."

The fourth-century Church Fathers affirmed the goodness of wine as part of God's creation against those who took the heretical view that the material world was evil. But they recognized that the use of wine was not always expedient; the degree of abstinence recommended differed for different ages and physical conditions of individuals. Excessive use was branded as an evil in itself. Because of the dangers, one was recommended not to drink wine at all if his body would permit this degree of asceticism, but it was recognized that this was not for all.[62] Fairly typical are the words of Ambrose:

> Let us use the natural drink of temperance, and would that all were able to do so. But because all are not strong the Apostle said: "Use a little wine because of your frequent infirmities." We must drink it then not for the sake of pleasure, but because of infirmity, and therefore sparingly as a remedy, not in excess as a gratification.[63]

In the light of the evidence adduced in this paper, when Jesus is called a "wine drinker" (Matt. 11:18f.) and when he changed water into wine at the marriage feast in Cana (John 2:1ff.), we may assume that the reference is to a mixture of wine with water, which was the ordinary social beverage accompanying meals and banquets in his day. Paul's advice to Timothy, "No longer drink only water, but use a little wine for the sake of your stomach and your frequent ailments,"[64] may be seen in the light of the medicinal use of wine at the time. More particularly, in view of the ascetic context in which Timothy was working (1 Tim. 4:3), likely Timothy had been abstaining from wine altogether, and Paul counsels him to return to the normal drink, taking a little wine with his water.

Many religious people have felt a tension between the Bible's denunciations of drunkenness and strong drink and its seeming approval of wine and wine-drinking in other contexts. Perhaps the knowledge that table wine was a diluted drink will serve to relax that tension somewhat.

*Originally printed in *Restoration Quarterly* 13 (1970): 141–153.

Chapter 5 Endnotes

1. My thanks are offered to Dr. Kenneth Matthews Jr., Director of Education at the University Museum, Philadelphia, who first introduced me to this information during a lecture tour of the Greek and Roman galleries of the museum and later supplied bibliographical assistance. A fundamental study is A. Jardé, "Vinum," *Dictionnaire des antiquités grecques et Romaines*, ed. Ch. Daremberg et M. E. Saglio (Paris: Hachette, 1919), vol. 5, 921. W. Halbertsma, "Wine in Classical Antiquity," *Minerva* 7 (1996): esp. 115–17.

2. The principal styles are conveniently shown in the *Atlas of the Classical World*, ed. A. A. M. van der Heyden and H. H. Scullard (New York: Nelson, 1959), 62f., but pictures may also be found in many works on classical art and civilization.

3. The contents of the (untypical) *Symposium* of Plato and of Xenophon and the *Satyricon* of Petronius are summarized in chapters 1 and 2 of Charles Seltman, *Wine in the Ancient World* (London: Routledge & Degan Paul, 1957). One may also consult Plutarch's *Quaestionum convivalium* (Table Talk) = *Moralia* 612C–748D.

4. Homer, *Odyssey* ix.208f. Pliny, *Natural History,* xiv.vi.54 records that the wine from the same district was in the first century mixed eight to one.

5. *Knights* 1187f. Quotations from classical authors, unless otherwise noted, are from the Loeb Classical Library.

6. Hesiod, *Works and Days* 596.

7. From Seltman, *Wine*, 118. *Greek Anthology* 11.49

8. Athenaeus, *Deipnosophists* x.426c, d.

9. Ibid., 426e,f.

10. Ibid., 429f–431b.

11. Ibid., ii.36a, b.

12. Plutarch, *Symposiacs* iii.ix, quoted in A. H. Clough and W. W. Goodwin, *Plutarch's Essays and Miscellanies* (New York, 1905), Vol. iii, 283.

13. Plutarch, *Advice to Bride and Groom* 20 in *Moralia* 140f.

14. *Satire* v.60.

15. *Epigrams* iii.lvii.

16. R. J. Forbes, *Studies in Ancient Technology,* Vol. iii (Lieden: E. J. Brill, 1955), 60ff., esp. 70.

17. Fragment 779, from J. M. Edmonds, *The Fragments of Attic Comedy*, Vol. iii B (Leiden: E. J. Brill, 1961), 847. Cf. Martial, *Epigrams* i.xi and vi.lxxxix.

18. *On Husbandry* xxxvi.157; cf. *On Noah's Work as a Planter* xxxvi.147, where he calls unmixed wine a poison and also his whole treatise *On Drunkenness*, esp. xxxii.124ff.

19. Athenaeus, *Deipnosophists* X.436e. On the difference between unmixed and mixed wine, Diodorus Siculus 4.3.2–5.

20. Ibid., X.429e.

21. Seltman, *Wine*, 122.

22. Athenaeus, *Deipnosophists* X.427b; Plato, *Laws* i.637E.

23. *Third Maccabees* 5:2.

24. Cf. Forbes, *Studies*, 118.

25. See further below, note 59.

26. As we know now, the alcohol would boil away, leaving only the wine flavor— Aristotle, *Symposium* Fragment 8 in *The Works of Aristotle*, ed. David Ross, Vol. XII (Oxford, 1952), 13 from *Deipnosophists* 429c.

27. Seltman, *Wine,* chapter 5.

28. *Olympian Ode* I.I.

29. Athenaeus, *Deipnosophists* ii.44.

30. Forbes, *Studies*, vol. I, 173–175, gives various ancient methods of purifying water, of which mixing wine was the most common. Pliny, *Natural History* XXXI discusses different kinds of water. In section 40 he speaks of boiling water to purify it.

31. *The Contemplative Life* ix.73f.

32. I. W. Raymond, *The Teaching of the Early Church on the Use of Wine and Strong Drink* (New York: Columbia University Press, 1927), chapter 2.

33. R. Pique, "Le vin et la médicine dans l'antiquité," *Chimie et industrie,* special issue Sept., 1925, 552–560.

34. Athenaeus, *Deipnosophists* X.429a.

35. *Natural History* XXIII.xxv.50f.

36. Ibid., XXIII.xxiii.43. Clement of Alexandria, *To the Newly Baptized*, gives this counsel: "Be not a flesh-eater [*sarkoboros*] nor a lover of wine [*philoinos*], when no sickness leads you to this as a cure."

37. Isaiah 1:22, but the context may not suggest an ordinary mixture for table purposes.

38. The note on this verse in the *Oxford Annotated Apocrypha*, ed. Bruce M. Metzger (New York, 1965), 293, correctly states that to drink unmixed wine was a mark of a drunkard; cf. the nearly contemporary *Psalms of Solomon* 8:14, "gave them to drink a cup of undiluted wine, that they might become drunken," and the classical references above. But the statement about water alone as the drink of the poor and ascetics misses the point that "it is harmful," which is explained by the impurity of water (see at note 30). According to the supplement to the Rule of the Community, the Dead Sea Scrolls appear to refer to mixed wine in the future Messianic Meal, *IQSa* 2.18, trans. Dupont-Sommer.

39. Berakoth 7:5, Quotations from the Mishnah are from the translation by Herbert Danby (London: Oxford U. Press, 1933).

40. In Niddah 2:7 as part of a description of different colors it is said, "And 'like mixed [water and wine]' [means a colour like as] when two parts of water [are mixed] with one part of wine, or the wine of Sharon." Cf. *Midrash Rabbah Numbers* I.4 (135d) commenting on the "mingled wine" of Song of Solomon 7:3, "Wine that is mixed in the correct proportions consists of one-third of a cup of wine to two-thirds of water." English edition edited by H. Freedman and Maurice Simon (London: Soncino Press, 1939). bPesachim 108b.

41. bShabbath 77a refers to the two to one ratio but cites the opinion of Rabbah b. Abbuha (c. 300) supported by Raba (d. 352) that wine must contain one part of wine to three parts of water (and apparently not a smaller percentage of wine). Raba's view is referred to in bErubim 54a and bNedarim 55a. The translation of the Babylonian Talmud used is that edited by me. Epstein (London: Soncino Press).

42. bBerakoth 50b and the note in the Soncino edition.

43. *Jubilees* 49:6.

44. Pesachim 10:2, 4, 7.

45. The phrase occurs in Berakoth 6:1 and bBerakoth 50b.

46. *Apology*, 1, 67.5. Similarly in 65.3 and 5. The parallel of the two latter verses indicates that *krama* (literally "mixed drink") in 3 is used to mean simply "wine" (5). Cf. note 58.

47. For the pagan slander about Christian orgies, see Minucius Felix, *Octavius* ix. Tertullian also defends the soberness of the Christian love feast, *Apology* xxxix.

48. *Apostolic Tradition* xxiii.1; in 7 it is called simply "wine." Translation by Gregory Dix (London: SPCK, 1937). Irenaeus, *Against Heresies* v.ii.2 alludes to the "mingled cup" of the eucharist, as does the Epitaph of Abercius, line 16 (translated by J. Quasten, *Patrology*, vol. 1 [Utrecht: Spectrum, 1953], 172). Justin *Dial.* 70 and cf. *1 Apol.* 66 on Mithras.

49. *Epistle* lxii.2. 11, and 13. Translation in Ante-Nicene Fathers.

50. *Miscellanies* I.xix.96.I.

51. Epiphanius, *Heresies* xlvii.1.7 (cf. lxi.1.2 and Hippolytus, *Refutation of All Heresies* VIII.xiii.28); xlii.3.3. The *Acts of Thomas* has a eucharist of bread and water (ch. 121), but also speaks of a "mixed cup of water" (ch. 120)—see E. Hennecke, *New Testament Apocrypha*, ed. W. Schneemelcher, vol. 2 (London: James Clarke, 1992), 387–388.

52. Epiphanius, *Heresies* xxx.16.1. A eucharist of bread and water in otherwise orthodox circles is reported in *Acts of Peter* 2 (cf. *Acts of Paul* 7). An abstinence from wine not promoted by heretical motives is seen in Eusebius, *Ecclesiastical History* V. 3.

53. *In Psalms* 109:4 (PG 80.1772c).

54. *Eranistes* (Dialogue) 1.26 (PG 83.56).

55. Quoted from L. Hertling and E. Kirschbaum, *The Roman Catacombs* (London: Darton, Longman & Todd, 1956), 241. The inscription is number 1569 in Ernestus Diehl, *Inscriptiones latinae christianae veteres*.

56. His main discussion is in *Instructor* II.ii, but compare the passage quoted in note 36.

57. *Instructor* II.ii.23.3–24.1. An earlier reference to "the wine mixed with the water" (20.1) is in a context using eucharistic language.

58. C. D. Buck, *A Dictionary of Selected Synonyms in the Principal Indo-European Languages* (Chicago: University of Chicago Press, 1949), 390.

59. The same metaphorical language of the Psalm appears in Revelation 14:10. Although Bauer's Lexicon, ed. F. W. Danker, suggests "poured" for the *kekerasmenos* used with *akratou* (unmixed), it may still keep its usual meaning of "mixed." *Akratou* was expressed to specify undiluted wine; *Kekerasmenos* then would refer to the addition of drugs or spices to increase the potency of the unmixed wine. Such is its usage in the medical prescription of *Oxyrhynchus Papyri* VIII.1088, 53ff. The mixing of wine with drugs was common in the Near East and explains why "mixed" in such passages as Psalms 75:8 and Proverbs 23:29 (cf. Song of Solomon 8:2) means a stronger drink, contrary to classical usage. See J. F. Ross, "Wine," *Interpreter's Dictionary of the Bible* (New York: Abingdon, 1962), vol. 4, 850.

60. *Homily on Jeremiah* XII.2 on Jeremiah 13:12 in commenting on Psalms 23:5.

61. *Commentary on Psalms* 60:3.

62. See I. W. Raymond, *Teaching of the Early Church*, the summaries to chaps. 4 and 5.

63. *Epistle* LXIII.28, translation in *Nicene and Post-Nicene Fathers*, ed. Philip Schaff and Henry Wace (Grand Rapids: Wm. B. Eerdmans, 1954 reprint), vol. 10, 460.

64. 1 Timothy 5:23, RSV.

Part II

Book of Acts

The Purpose of Acts

S cholars have given much attention in recent years to *The Purpose of Luke-Acts,* to borrow the title of the important book by Robert Maddox. We must take seriously the fact that Luke and Acts are two volumes of one work; nevertheless, the following survey, superficial as it is, must be limited to Acts, except where the argument requires inclusion also of Luke. Depending heavily on Maddox, I will present a classification of some of the interpretations advanced concerning the purpose of Acts and then will offer a modest proposal of a perspective to be included in considering the intention of Luke in writing his work.

Evangelistic

Some scholars see the purpose of Acts as evangelistic. In its simplest form, this theory presents the purpose of Acts as to convert unbelievers, primarily pagans. Writers as different as F. F. Bruce and J. C. O'Neill emphasize the evangelistic nature of Acts. Bruce sees the apologetic aspects of Acts as designed to lead sympathetic Romans to an interest in Jesus. O'Neill makes a more explicit claim that Luke attempted to persuade educated Romans to become Christians. Acts demonstrated the power of the true God, opened up to educated citizens the possibility of belief, and demonstrated the innocence of Christians of any revolutionary tendencies.

Several features of Luke-Acts could serve evangelistic purposes. The Gospel presents the story of Jesus in an attractive way. The title of Leander Keck's little book *Mandate to Witness: Studies in the Book of Acts* catches the spirit of the evangelistic thrust of Acts. Many of the speeches in Acts are missionary in nature. Already in the prologue to Acts (Acts 1:1–5), Luke mentions the themes important in the book: Jesus' death and resurrection, the kingdom of God, the Holy Spirit of promise, and the mission of the apostles—in other words, basic facts of the gospel. But there are problems with this interpretation. A key question is, "Who or what was Theophilus?" The title "most excellent" would seem to indicate a government official, but he may have been the patron of the work rather than indicative of the class to whom the work was addressed. He is described as already informed in matters of the Christian faith. And certainly much of Luke-Acts seems to assume considerable knowledge of the Old Testament and not be designed for complete outsiders. Acts 21–28, the conclusion of the book, does not fit this view of the purpose.

A variation on the theme of evangelism interprets Luke's purpose in terms of the justification of the Gentile mission. According to this view, Luke is writing primarily to show that God was behind the spread of the gospel to Gentiles and that the incorporation of them into the people of God was in fulfillment of God's purposes. He may have been writing to Jewish Christians to reassure them concerning the developments that had occurred or to Gentile Christians to affirm their place in the divine scheme of redemption. Certainly much fits this interpretation: the Holy Spirit coming on the Gentiles as well as Jews, the approval of the mission of Paul by Peter and James, the space given to Paul's mission, the pattern of "to the Jews first, and also to the Gentiles." More of this theme will recur in some later points. On the other hand, so much more is found in Acts that it seems this purpose must be placed in a larger context.

Apologetic

Many scholars have called attention to the apologetic elements in Luke's work. Acts may be read as an apology for Christianity to the Roman authorities. Roman officials are shown as favorable to Christianity. Christians are presented as not politically subversive and as true to the Jewish religious heritage. Although Luke records disturbances caused by Christian preaching, the agitation is stirred up by others. Many Jews rejected the Christian message, but many did not; and Christianity is presented as the fulfillment of the Jewish Bible and Jewish hopes (and, therefore, by implication entitled to the protection enjoyed by Judaism as a recognized religion in the Roman Empire).

The content of Luke-Acts, however, proves to be somewhat ambiguous as a plea for tolerance by Rome. The relations of Christians to the state and the synagogue constitute a mixed story in Acts. Romans themselves would have been quite puzzled by most of the contents. If one were simply writing an apology for Christianity, there was more to be said, and much that was said should have been left unsaid.

A more specific version of the apologetic reading of Acts claims that the book was written as a brief for Paul's defense at his trial. A. J. Mattill has been a leading exponent of this view. Acts 21–28 certainly is preoccupied with the defense of Paul before Roman authorities against Jewish charges.

If Luke wrote immediately after Paul's two-year imprisonment in Rome, there is an explanation for the ending of the book, and an early date is consistent with the defense of Paul as its purpose. Most scholars, however, date the book in the 80s or 90s, making the defense of Paul at his trial before Caesar's court problematic for the purpose of the book. A more serious problem for this theory is the Gospel and Acts 1–12. How do they fit? They would seem to be a rather more extensive prologue than the avowed purpose called for!

Polemical

Various polemical purposes may have been served by Acts. Defending Paul is central to several scholars' views of Luke's purpose and is involved in Jacob Jervell's influential work. Paul occupies such a large place in Acts because Luke was defending his memory against the charges of Jewish Christians against him. Jervell sees Luke as concerned with establishing the Jewishness of the church; as part of this, he presents Paul as a Law-keeping Jew. Another version of the defense of Paul for polemical purposes posits that Luke was writing at a later stage in history when early Catholicism was trying to create unity out of the divergent emphases from the apostolic period. Luke's purpose, hence, was to domesticate Paul in the church of the late first or early second century by smoothing over differences between him and Peter and James, between his version of Gentile Christianity and the Jewish Christianity that strongly opposed him.

The Jewishness of Paul is a point well taken and can be supported from his letters. These views, on the other hand, do not give much attention to the Gospel and hardly account for the total content of Acts. They also depend, especially in the latter form, on a late date for Acts.

Instead of looking in the direction of Jewish Christianity, Charles H. Talbert argues for an opposite polemical direction. Luke-Acts was written, he claims, for an express anti-Gnostic purpose. Much of the material in Acts could be used against Gnosticism, but that was true of much of the deposit of apostolic teaching. A deliberate opposition to Gnosticism is not readily apparent in the text, and this theory requires either a later date for Luke-Acts or an earlier date for Gnosticism than seems likely.

Theological

Some scholars state the purpose of Acts as more expressly theological. They develop Luke's theology especially in terms of eschatology (the second coming of Christ) and ecclesiology (the place of the church in the plan of redemption).

Hans Conzelmann has been largely responsible for the recent interest in Luke as a theologian. He set forth the purpose of Luke as an attempt to solve an alleged crisis of faith in the church caused by the delay of the Parousia. The time of Jesus is the midpoint in time between the old order of Judaism and the new order of the church. In his theory, Luke redirected Jesus' message about an imminent end of the world to an indefinite future, and the Holy Spirit became the substitute for the delayed eschatological fulfillment. It is now generally agreed that Conzelmann was wrong in saying that Luke wrote to deal with the problem of the delay of the Parousia. Luke did not consistently remove the final consummation into the distant future, and the theory overlooks the theme in Luke-Acts that eschatology has already begun to be fulfilled.

Helmut Flender takes a more promising direction in the writing of *St. Luke: Theologian of Redemptive History,* and this aspect will enter into some further comments below. According to Flender, Luke did not just transmit traditions, but interpreted them for his own time; he was a theologian of the post-apostolic age. The place given to the church as the community where the divine work of salvation continues is a welcome contribution. Yet Flender makes Luke too much of a theologian and too little of a historian. As I. Howard Marshall phrases it, the author was *Luke: Historian and Theologian.* If an earlier age neglected the theological aspects of Luke's work, many modern works neglect the historical. But the emphasis on Luke's theology reminds us that he was not writing simply history. Luke wrote a historical monograph shaped by theological concerns.

Pastoral

Robert Maddox, on whom this presentation is so dependent, in his own view gives to Luke primarily a pastoral purpose. Noting the importance of the words "fulfilled" ("accomplished") and "certainty" ("reliability') in the preface to Luke, he defines Luke's purpose as being to reassure fellow Christians about the truth of the message and about the faith which was theirs. Luke's work was a confirmation of the gospel. I have no particular quarrel with Maddox's conclusion, and it indeed rests on a well-argued case. Nevertheless, I wonder if his formulation is too narrowly defined. Reassurance may have been a specific motivation for Luke, but other concerns have their place too.

Historical

Some scholars still reaffirm the historical purpose of Acts. A recent work has enlarged the field of comparison for the category of historical writing.

Richard I. Pervo has called attention to another dimension in Acts by comparing it with the historical novels of the Hellenistic world. These pseudo-histories have their closest counterpart in Christian literature in the apocryphal acts of individual apostles written with great enthusiasm in the second century. Luke does have an eye for the entertaining, and certainly he was writing for edification. A travel narrative occupies a prominent place in Acts. Nonetheless, it is stretching genre classifications beyond recognition to put Acts in the same bag with Hellenistic novels. The reader need only compare the contents of Acts with the contents of the Greek novels, the apocryphal acts, and the Pseudo-Clementine literature in order to see the differences. It is better to compare Luke with Hellenistic historians. He did not write history, however, simply to be telling a story for its own sake.

The best comparison for Luke as a historian is not in the Greek world, or at least not exclusively so. I would propose that more attention needs to be given to Luke's background in Old Testament history. Revelation and redemption are presented in the framework of history in the Pentateuch and Former Prophets (historical books) of the Old Testament. Luke tells his story in continuity with this history as the further unfolding of God's saving acts. What began in the people of Israel was climaxed in the ministry of Jesus and continued in the church. Luke consciously wrote in "biblical Greek" in the early chapters of the Gospel and of Acts. This is but one of the indications that it will be fruitful to see Luke as choosing the same medium as employed in the Old Testament revelation for his presentation of the climactic revelatory and redemptive events associated with Jesus and the church.

Conclusion

All of the theories noted above perhaps have some truth in them, some more than others. It is difficult to reduce such a complex and richly varied work as Luke-Acts to a single or limited statement of purpose. As we try to evaluate the work of the theological historian and historical theologian Luke, I would suggest that we include the perspective provided by biblical history as not only influencing his style but also motivating him to write. As long as we have Acts, Christianity, like Judaism, will remain a religion anchored in history. Luke-Acts has done for the new covenant what the first seventeen books of the Bible did for the old covenant.

*Originally printed in *Acts: The Spreading Flame,* Harding University Lectureship (Searcy: Harding University, 1989), 660–666.

Chapter 6 Bibliography

Alexander, Loveday. *Acts in its Ancient Literary Context: A Classicist Looks at the Acts of the Apostles*. London: T & T Clark, 2005.

Bruce, F. F. *The Book of the Acts*. The New International Commentary on the New Testament. Grand Rapids, MI: Wm. B. Eerdmans Publishing Co., 1954.

Conzelmann, Hans. *The Theology of St. Luke*. Philadelphia, PA: Fortress Press, 1982.

Evans, Craig A. "The Pseudepigrapha and the New Testament: The Case of the Acts of the Apostles." In *Jewish and Christian Scriptures: The Function of "Canonical" and "non-Canonical" Religious Texts*, edited by James H. Charlesworth and Lee Martin McDonald, 131–45. London: T & T Clark, 2010.

Flender, Helmut. *St. Luke: Theologian of Redemptive History*. Translated by Reginald H. and Ilse Fuller. London: S. P. C. K., 1967

Gasque, W. Ward. "A Fruitful Field: Recent Study of the Acts of the Apostles." *Interpretation* 42 (1988): 117–31.

Haenchen, Ernst. *The Acts of the Apostles: A Commentary*. Philadelphia, PA: Westminster Press, 1971.

Jervell, Jacob. *Luke and the People of God: A Look at Luke-Acts*. Minneapolis, MN: Augsburg, 1972.

—————. "The Future of the Past: Luke's Vision of Salvation History and Its Bearing on His Writing of History." In *History, Literature, and Society in the Book of Acts*, edited by B. Witherington, 104–26. Cambridge: Cambridge University Press, 1996.

—————. *The Theology of the Acts of the Apostles*. Cambridge: Cambridge University Press, 1996.

Johnson, Luke Timothy. *The Acts of the Apostles*. Collegeville, MN: Liturgical Press, 1992.

Keck, Leander. *Mandate to Witness: Studies in the Book of Acts*. Valley Forge, PA: Judson Press, 1964.

Maddox, Robert. *The Purpose of Luke-Acts*. Edinburgh, Scotland: T. & T. Clark, 1982.

Marguerat, Daniel. *The First Christian Historian: Writing 'the Acts of the Apostles.'* Cambridge: Cambridge University Press, 2002.

Marshall, I. Howard, *Luke: Historian and Theologian*. Grand Rapids, MI: Zondervan, 1971.

Mattill, A. J. "Naherwartung, Fernerwartung and the Purpose of Luke-Acts: Weymouth Reconsidered." *Catholic Biblical Quarterly* 34 (1972): 276–93.

O'Neill, J. C. *The Theology of Acts in Its Historical Setting*. London: S. P. C. K., 1961.

Pao, D. W. *Acts and the Isaianic New Exodus*. Grand Rapids, MI: Baker, 2000.

Pervo, Richard I. *Profit with Delight: The Literary Genre of the Acts of the Apostles*. Philadelphia, PA: Fortress Press, 1987.

Schneider, G. "Der Zweck des lukanischen Doppelwerkes." *Biblische Zeitschrift* 21 (1977): 45–66.

Sterling, Gregory E. *Historiography and Self Definition: Josephos, Luke-Acts and Apologetic Historiography.* Leiden: Brill, 1992.

Talbert, Charles H. *Luke and the Gnostics.* Nashville, TN: Abingdon Press, 1966.

7

Theological Themes in Acts

Luke, it seems, did not give a title to his second book "to Theophilus," but the earliest citations of the book by name from the second century and all the major manuscripts give it the title "Acts of the Apostles." It has been suggested the book might also be called "Acts of the Holy Spirit." Since Luke's "first book" was about "all that Jesus began to do and teach" (Acts 1:1), he might have called his second volume "Further Acts of Jesus Christ."

Luke sets the theme of the apostolic preaching with Peter's climactic declaration, "God has made this Jesus both Lord and Christ" (2:36; translation my own; those not my own in this chapter are from the NRSV). The titles given to Jesus in Acts show his exaltation. Christ, or Messiah, presents Jesus as God's Anointed (or Chosen) One of Jewish expectation. The burden of much of the early preaching was the Messiahship of Jesus (3:20; 5:42; 9:22; 17:3; 18:5, 28). His anointing was not the literal anointing with oil that kings and priests received but an anointing with the Holy Spirit (4:27; 10:38). Related to the Messiahship of Jesus are the titles Servant (3:13, 26; 4:27, 30) and Leader (3:15; 5:31). The Jews knew that preaching Jesus as Christ made him a king (17:7). As Messiah, Jesus was designated the "Holy and Righteous One" (3:14; cf. 2:27; 4:27, 30; 7:52; 13:35). His role could also be interpreted as the Prophet like Moses (3:22–26; 7:37).

Jesus was also declared to be Lord. This designation of God in the Old Testament (1:24; 2:39; 3:22) most often in Acts refers to Jesus (to cite only the verses using "Lord Jesus": 1:21; 4:33; 7:59; 11:17, 20; 15:11, 26; 16:31; 19:5, 13; 17:24, 35; 21:13; 28:31). He is declared to be "Lord of all" (10:36). Jesus does the things in Acts that God does in the Old Testament: acting through the Spirit (2:33); giving visionary experiences (9:5; 18:9–10; 22:17; 23:11); and caring for, protecting, and guiding his people (7:55–56, 59; 18:9–10). God gave the function of Judge to Jesus (10:42; cf. 17:31). Accordingly, Jesus is named "Son of God" (9:20).

The "name of Jesus" functions in the same way as "name of the Lord" (God) does in the Old Testament (of God in Acts only in 15:14, 17). Acts uses "name" in reference to Jesus' deity thirty-two times. "In the name of" means "with reference to," "in respect of"; "to call upon the name" is to worship or acknowledge the person. In the name of Jesus, preaching was done (4:17–18; 5:28, 40; 9:15, 27–28); baptism was performed (2:38; 8:16; 10:48; 19:5; 22:16); healing was done (3:6, 16; 4:7, 10, 30); demons were expelled (16:18; 19:13); and suffering was endured (5:41; 9:16; 15:26; 21:13). Jesus' name was invoked in worship (9:14, 21; 22:16) and was praised (19:17)—another appropriation of Old Testament language about God, for to call on his name was to worship him and pray to him. Salvation is in Jesus' name (4:12; 8:12; 10:43), whereas in the Old Testament God alone was Savior (Isa. 43:11). A title of Jesus is Savior (5:31; 13:23). As in Old Testament usage, the name of Jesus stood for the person and presence of Jesus.

According to Peter's sermon in Acts 2, what made Jesus Lord and Christ was his crucifixion and resurrection (2:22–24, 32, 36). The prologue connects Acts with the Gospel of Luke by referring to Jesus' sufferings and resurrection appearances (1:3). The death and resurrection are the consistent theme of the evangelistic preaching in Acts (3:14–15; 5:30; 10:39–50; 13:28¬36; 17:3). It is stated succinctly in 4:10, "Jesus Christ of Nazareth, whom you crucified, whom God raised from the dead." Much more is said about the resurrection of Jesus (4:33; 17:32; 26:8, 23), which was a guarantee of the general resurrection (4:2) and of judgment (17:30).

The resurrection of Jesus was followed by his ascension (1:11, 22; 2:34). The ascension in turn led to Jesus' being seated at the right hand of God (3:21; 5:31; 7:55–56). Being raised and being seated at the throne of God means Jesus is now ruling over his kingdom. This is the import of the argument from Psalms 16:8–11 in 2:25–35 (cf. 13:32–37). The resurrected Jesus, as he had done in his ministry, spoke about the kingdom of God (1:3), and Paul continued to preach about this (19:8; 20:25). In Acts, the kingdom of God is now related to the name of Jesus Christ (8:12; 28:23, 31). Acts includes a future dimension also to the kingdom, for Paul encouraged the disciples that through persecutions they would enter the kingdom of God (14:22).

The resurrected Jesus poured out the Holy Spirit (2:33) and continued his ministry through the Holy Spirit, so the Holy Spirit is connected with Christ and does not act independently from him. He is the "Spirit of Jesus" (16:7). His work, announced in the prologue (1:2, 45), is associated with power (1:8: 10:38). His powerful presence marked the beginning of the new age (2:24, 17–19; 10:44–47; 11:15). The Spirit had been active before, especially in inspiring Scripture (1:16; 4:25; 28:25), and his presence had empowered the ministry of Jesus (10:38). Now he gave revelation through prophets (11:28; 20:23; 21:11), directed the church in sending out missionaries (13:2, 4), then at times directed their travels (16:6–7; 19:21), directed policy deliberations (15:28), and comforted the church (9:31).

The Holy Spirit was promised to those baptized in the name of Jesus Christ (2:38); receiving the Spirit was conditioned upon obedience (5:31). Various individuals were said to be filled with the Spirit, apparently at times to an unusual extent: Peter (4:8), Stephen (6:5; 7:55), Paul (9:17; 13:9), Barnabas (11:24), and the disciples (13:52). To be full of the Spirit (like being full of wisdom, joy, and faith) was apparently exceptional only in degree rather than in the kind of working by the Holy Spirit. This filling with the Spirit was often associated with speaking (4:31). The coming of the Spirit equipped the disciples to be witnesses (1:8). The Spirit for Luke enables the proclamation of the word, but the word, not the Spirit directly, produces faith (8:12; 14:1; 15:7; 16:32; 17:11–12; 18:8).

Special manifestations of the Spirit occurred at significant moments in the progress of the gospel: the beginning of the church at Pentecost (2:1–21), the conversion of Samaritans (8:4–18), the conversion of Gentiles (10:44–48; 11:16), and the incorporation of disciples of John the Baptist into the church (19:17). These manifestations that could be discerned by the senses, specified in three of the cases as speaking in tongues, functioned to verify that God was at work and to sanction the incorporation of the groups into his people. The tongues in Acts 2 and 10 were a sign of the universalism of the gospel, which was for all people and was to be spoken in their own languages (2:11), but we never find the gift used as a missionary tool. In no case were conditions beyond conversion met before receiving the Holy Spirit. In Acts 8:16 it is implied that the Spirit was expected at baptism, so there was something unusual here. That Samaritans too were Christians needed to be authenticated in the presence of apostles, so the coming of the Spirit was delayed in this instance. In view of the close connection of John's ministry with Christ's and of his baptism with Christian baptism, there was a need to differentiate clearly the status of his disciples from Jesus' disciples (19:1–6).

The Spirit came only to believers (Acts 10 is only a partial exception). The number of references to the Spirit decreases toward the end of Acts, perhaps an indication that the special manifestations of the Spirit belonged to the time of beginnings and that from Luke's day forward the Spirit would work in other ways.

For all the attention to Christ and the Holy Spirit, we should not overlook that Acts is a very God-centered book. God's plan is behind all the themes in Acts, and the action of God is present in all the events narrated. The kingdom is God's (1:3). God brought a Savior to Israel (13:23). God anointed Jesus (4:27), and Jesus did what he did because God was at work through him (2:22) and "was with him" (10:38; cf.3:26). What happened to Jesus was according to the plan of God (2:23). God raised Jesus from the dead (2:32; 3:15; 4:10; 5:30; 10:40; 17:31). God spoke by the Holy Spirit (4:25) and gives the Holy Spirit (5:32). Indeed most of the important doctrinal topics in Acts are related to what God is said to do.

In addition to the words "God" and "Lord," the word "Father" identifies God (1:4, 7; 2:33). He is addressed in prayer as the "Sovereign Lord who made" all things (4:24), the one who "knows the heart of everyone" (1:28; 15:8). He is not only the creator and the "living God," but his providence in nature and history also continues to bear witness to him (14:15–17; 17:23¬26). He ordained the plan of salvation (2:23; 4:28; 11:18; cf. 20:27), having been behind the Old Testament preparation (7:2, 25). He was at work in the apostles' ministry (14:27) and miracles (19:11), and their message was "the word of God" (4:29, 31; 13:46). God took the initiative and human action followed, but providence did not remove human freedom. God was present in the words of his messengers, only rarely in a direct manner.

The theme of Acts might be expressed by the description the people on Pentecost gave to the things they heard the apostles speaking: "the great things" or "mighty deeds" of God (2:11). What God does is characterized by grace (14:26). His word is the "word of his grace" (14:3; 20:32), and the ministry of the apostles is "to testify to the gospel [the good news] of God's grace" (20:24). Hence, to become believers came about through grace (18:27). The turning of great numbers to the Lord was a manifestation of the grace of God (11:21, 23). Those interested in the message of the gospel were urged to "continue in the grace of God" (13:43). To be commended to God's grace was to be entrusted to his providential care (14:26; 15:40). Once more, what is done by God is also done by Jesus, for salvation comes about "through the grace of the Lord Jesus" (15:11).

Some have suggested that the unifying theme of Acts is salvation (Marshall, 92). If the purpose of the Gospel was to show the saving activity of Jesus, then Acts shows how the church continued to proclaim and confirm this salvation (Marshall, 93). The plan of God is to bring humanity to salvation through Jesus Christ, and the Holy Spirit empowered God's messengers to bring this message to all humanity. Salvation is announced at the beginning and end of the first sermon. It is the result of the outpouring of the Holy Spirit (2:21), and Peter's closing exhortation is "save yourselves from this corrupt generation" (2:40). The content of salvation includes the "forgiveness of sins" (2:38; 5:31; 10:43; 13:38; cf. 3:19). Salvation is for all people, reaching "to the ends of the earth" (13:47), and is from God (28:28). It is only in Christ (4:12), and this way of salvation (16:17) is communicated by words (11:14; 13:26). The Spirit (8:29; 10:19–20; 11:12) or the Lord (9:46) might intervene to get a preacher and a convert together, but the saving words (11:14) were always spoken by human messengers. The hearing of the word was essential for salvation (2:37; 4:4; 8:6; 10:33; 13:12, 44, 48; 16:14; 17:11; 18:8; 19:5, 10).

Humans do not achieve salvation; they receive it. Response to the "message of salvation" (13:26) is described in several ways. Luke speaks in general of conversion, or turning (3:19, 26; 9:35; 11:21; 14:15; 15:3, 19; 26:18, 20; 28:27). He also refers to specific responses, but often used in a broader sense to stand for the whole process of conversion. Many times persons are said to respond to the word by believing (4:4; 5:14; 8:13; 9:42; 11:17, 21; 13:12, 48; 14:1, 23; 16:34; 17:12, 34; 18:8; 19:18), or they are commanded to believe (16:31; implied in 20:21), or believing is stated as a condition of God's promises (10:43; 13:39). Faith cleanses the heart (15:9). The message itself can be described as "the faith" (13:8), which was something to be obeyed (6:7).

Closely related to conversion is repentance. Since Jews already believed in God, faith for them was directed "toward our Lord Jesus"; for them repentance might also be necessary, as it certainly was for Gentiles, who did not know God (20:21). Repentance was a gift to both Jews and Gentiles from God, perhaps in the sense of God giving the inducements or the opportunity for repentance (5:31; 11:18). The command to repent is stated expressly to those who had not accepted Jesus (2:38; 3:19; 17:30), and to one who had come to faith and baptism but then sinned (8:22).

Baptism is often mentioned as part of conversion. It was included in the preaching about Jesus (8:35–39). Baptism is commanded (2:38; 10:47–48; 22:16) and is stated as included in the response to the gospel (8:13, 16; 16:15, 33; 18:8).

The Lord brought together those being saved (2:47), thus forming a church. As God had a people, a community, in Old Testament times, so his saving work in Christ was not simply with individuals but to create a people. Salvation involves incorporation into the community of God's people in Christ. Their community life is described in 2:41–47 and 4:32–35. Their identity with Jesus was so close that to persecute them was to persecute Jesus himself (9:45). Acts is concerned to show that this new people includes all races, not only Jews but also Samaritans and Gentiles (8:4–25; 10:1–11:18), and those who were outcasts from the Jewish perspective (8:26–39). The basis of this people was not race, but the grace of God.

An early name for Christian teaching was "the way" (19:9, 23; 22:4, 14, 22), and Christians are those "who belonged to the way" (9:2). Those who followed this way formed a community designated "the church." The word means "assembly" and could be used of God's people who followed Moses in the wilderness (7:38) or a political assembly (19:32, 39, 41). Most often in Acts it refers to God's people in Christ (5:11; 8:3; 11:26; 12:1, 5; 14:27; 15:3, 4, 22; 18:22), identified as "the church of God" in 20:28. A church might be located by a geographical designation such as Jerusalem (8:1; 11:22), Judaea (9:31), Antioch (13:1); and so individual churches (or meetings) are specified by use of the plural (15:41; 16:5). There were elders appointed in "each church" (14:23; cf. 20:17).

Various names are given to those who make up this people. They are "believers" (e.g. 2:44; 15:5, 7; 16:1, 15; 18:27; 21:20, 25; 22:19). Most often they are "brothers" (inclusive of sisters; 1:15; 6:3; 9:30; 10:23; 11:1, 12, 29; 12:17; 14.2; 15:1, 3, 7, 13, 22, 23, 32, 33, 36, 40; 16:2, 40; 17:6, 10, 14; 18:18, 27; 21:7, 17, 20; 28:14, 15). Another common name is "disciples" (6:1, 2, 7; 9:1, 10, 19, 25, 26, 38; 11:26, 29; 13:52; 14:20, 22, 28; 15:10; 16:1; 18:23, 27; 19:1, 9, 30; 20:1, 30; 21:4, 16). A few times they are designated "saints" (9:13, 32, 41; 26:10). Acts contains two of the three occurrences in the New Testament of "Christians," those who identified with Christ, followed him, and belonged to his party (11:26; 26:28).

*Originally printed in David Lipe, ed., *Opening Our Eyes to Jesus: From Darkness to Light in Acts,* Freed-Hardeman University Lectures (Henderson, TN: Freed-Hardeman University, 2004), 129–146.

For Further Reading

Jervell, Jacob. *The Theology of the Acts of the Apostles*. Cambridge: Cambridge University Press, 1996.

Marguerat, Daniel. *The First Christian Historian: Writing 'the Acts of the Apostles'*. Cambridge: Cambridge University Press, 2002.

Marshall, I. Howard. *Luke: Historian and Theologian*. 3rd ed. Downers Grove: InterVarsity, 1988.

Marshall, I. Howard, and David Peterson, eds. *Witness to the Gospel: The Theology of Acts*. Grand Rapids: Eerdmans, 1998.

8

Literary Themes in Acts

Inscribing a dedication to a work was a way of publishing it, making it public, in the Greco-Roman world. The dedications to Theophilus in Luke and Acts are an indication that they were addressing a literate audience.

The main themes were often in the prologues to a work. The prologue to the Gospel of Luke (Lk. 1:1–4) would cover the book of Acts as well. Both books concerned "the events fulfilled among us," which were "handed on to us" by those with two qualifications. They were "eyewitnesses," and they were "ministers of the word." Luke presents his account as carefully researched ("followed closely from the beginning") so as to be written "accurately" and "orderly." The purpose was to give "certainty" concerning Christian instruction. The prologue to Acts (1:1–5) is a retrospective summary of the Gospel as relevant to the present volume: the continuation of the story of Jesus, his sufferings and the convincing proof of his resurrection, his instructions to the (chosen) apostles, given through the Holy Spirit, concerning the kingdom of God, his exaltation, and the importance of Jerusalem, where they would receive the promised Holy Spirit.

Acts 1:8 provides a summary outline of the book: Jerusalem (1:6–8:1), Judaea and Samaria (8:1–12:25), and to the end of the earth (13:1–28:31). Since Rome was not "the end of the earth" in the terminology of the time, the conclusion of Acts is an open-ended ending, "proclaiming the kingdom of God and teaching about the Lord Jesus Christ with all boldness and without hindrance" (28:31). Perhaps Luke ended Acts where he did for his readers to complete by carrying on the task with which his writing concludes. The spread of the word of the Lord is the main story line in Acts. There are many summary statements of the expansion of the gospel and of the numbers who responded to it (2:41, 47; 4:4; 6:7; 8:25, 40, 46; 9:31; 11:1, 18, 19, 21, 24; 12:24; 13:49; 14:1, 21, 27; 16:5; 17:4; 18:8; 19:10, 20; 28:30–31). God is given credit for this growth.

Another division of the book takes chapter 15 as the midpoint of the narrative. Acts 2:22–15:12 may be taken as a narrative commentary on Joel 2:28–32, quoted in Acts 2:17–21. Similarly, Acts 15:13–28:28 is a narrative commentary on Amos 9:11–12, quoted in Acts 15:16–17 (Marshall and Peterson, 443–52). Acts 2:22 and 15:12 are linked by the "wonders and signs" which God did first through Jesus among the Jews and then through Paul and Barnabas among the Gentiles. In 15:13 James calls on the Jews to "hear" him; in 15:28 Paul says "the Gentiles will hear." The quotations from Joel and Amos are linked by the word "call"; quoting Joel, "everyone who calls on the name of the Lord will be saved" (2:21), and the Amos quote refers to "all the Gentiles upon whom my name has been called" (15:17). Luke takes the events of Acts 15 as the official determination that divine election extends to Gentiles as well as Jews.

Luke employs repetition to indicate the importance of certain events. The story of the conversion of Paul occurs three times, once in narrative (9:1–19) and twice in Paul's speeches (22:3–16 to Jews and 26:4–18 to political authorities). Properly speaking, the point of these accounts is not Paul's conversion, although that was necessarily involved, but his call as apostle to the nations (9:15–16; 22:14–15; 26:16–18). The experience of Paul is not presented as a model of conversion but as a unique calling of the apostle to the Gentiles, comparable to the call of the twelve as apostles to the Jews (Gal. 1:1; 2:9). This calling is important in Acts because the book is the narrative of the spread of the gospel from Jews to non-Jews, and Paul is key to this story: himself Jewish and the chosen instrument for bringing the Jewish hope to the nations.

Another story told three times is the conversion of Cornelius: first in narrative (10:1–48) and twice in Peter's speeches (11:1–18 in defense of what he had done and briefly in 15:7–9 against imposing circumcision on Gentiles). The episode might almost be described as the conversion of Peter, not his conversion to Jesus, but his conversion of attitude toward Gentiles and the necessity of their observance of the Law. This event too is crucial to Luke's purpose. The conversion of Cornelius's household was the test case for the terms under which Gentiles would be included in the new people of God. No requirements from the Law, notably circumcision, were imposed on their acceptance into the church. The few conditions required for their later conduct, mentioned three times (15:20 in the decision by the apostles and elders; 15:29 in their letter about the decision; 21:25 reaffirming the position against pressures for a stricter policy), were those that would make table fellowship possible for Gentiles with Jews of tender conscience.

Acts demonstrates Luke's skill as a writer. He could adapt his style to his material and to his audience. He employs quotations from and allusions to classical literature. For instance, the widely known poem of Aratus, *Phaenomena* 5, provides the source for Paul's use to the Athenians of the Stoic commonplace, "We are also his offspring" (17:28). Paul's account of his conversion before the Hellenized ruler Agrippa includes allusion to a famous incident in Greek literature of a ruler's resistance to divine will, "It is hard for you to kick against the goads" (26:14; Euripides, *Bacchae* 794). When Luke quotes letters, they are in the proper form of Greek letters (15:23–29; 23:26–30).

Luke was very much influenced by the vocabulary and style of the Greek translation of the Old Testament, especially in chapters 1 through 15. One may count thirty-five quotations from the Old Testament in Acts, and there are many allusions besides. The employment from the Greek Old Testament of language, themes, models, literary techniques, and theological understanding of history suggests that Luke thought of himself as continuing Old Testament history and perhaps as consciously writing Scripture.

What was Luke's literary purpose? We will discuss four aspects: Acts as history, as apology, as proclamation, and as confirmation. As a historian Luke compares well with contemporary Greek, Roman, and Jewish authors. Luke wrote with religious interests and gave a theological interpretation to the history: he pointed to God behind the events. Yet he did not invent the history nor write to historicize his theology.

Some compare Acts to other genres of literature with similarities to history. One of these is the Hellenistic novel. Acts does share some motifs with novels: miracle stories, trial narratives, travel adventures, biographical sequences, desire to give pleasure, and religious interests. But these features were also present in histories from the time. Luke does know an entertaining story when he finds it (19:13–16). However, the characteristic features of novels are not present in Acts: their principal characters are fictional, but Acts' main characters are historical; pirates and brigandage or war and romantic love are absent from Acts. The apocryphal Acts of the second century are much more like the novels, except that they are more biographical than the novels. There are similarities in Acts to travel writings. There are elements in common, such as the realism of the journey and geographical precision, but Acts does not match any of the types of travel writings in the ancient world. The Gospels fit into the category of biography better than into any other literary genre. And Luke's biographical interest continued in Acts, notably with regard to Paul, but in contrast to his Gospel, where the interest in Jesus is for his own sake, the interest in Paul is not for the sake of Paul. Paul is important for what he represents (the loyal Jew who was apostle to Gentiles) more than for himself.

Acts manifests apologetic concerns, announced already in the prologue, "many proofs" (1:3). By connecting Christianity with the Old Testament and Judaism, Luke demonstrates that Christianity was not new and deserved to be treated under the law as entitled to the privileges and protections that Jews enjoyed. Both apologetic and evangelistic is Acts' emphasis that God vindicated Jesus by raising him from the dead (2:22–24; 3:13–14; 4:10; 13:32–33). The last part of Acts is largely given over to making the case for the innocence of Paul (21:17–28:31). In regard to both Jesus and Paul there is the concern to show that Christianity is not a threat to Rome, so Roman officials and local authorities are shown as, if not favorable, at least indifferent to Christianity in its disputes with Jews (13:7, 12; 16:38–39; 18:12–17; 19:35–41; 22:27–29; 23:23–24; 24:22–23; 26:30–32; 27:42–43).

Among the arguments for the truth of Christianity are its miracles and the fulfillment of prophecy. "Powers," wonders," and "signs" are the words for miraculous deeds, and these words occur frequently, usually in combination (2:19, 22, 43; 4:30; 5:12; 6:8; 8:6, 13; 14:3; 15:12; 19:11). There is a great attention in Acts to events happening in accordance with Scripture (1:16: 2:16–21; 13:29, 33; 15:15–18), and this fits a larger emphasis on the theme of fulfillment in the new age inaugurated by Jesus (3:18; 13:27).

Corresponding to the apologetic theme is the heavy usage in Acts of the family of words for "witness." Luke uses this word group primarily in the sense of "eyewitnesses" (cf. another word in Lk. 1:2), hence it applies especially to the twelve and particularly to their witness to the resurrection (1:8, 22; 2:32; 3:15; 4:33; 5:32; 10:39, 41, 42; 13:31). Paul was called to be a witness in the same sense (22:14–15). The purpose of miracles was that God through them bore witness to his messengers (Christ in 2:22, the name of Christ in 4:30), their message (14:3), and his plan (15:8). The prophets also gave witness to Jesus (10:43). Thus the word group can be used with the broader meaning of "testifying" in the sense of declaring (2:40; 8:25; 18:5; 20:21). Their witness was to the death and resurrection of Jesus and the offer of forgiveness of sins, all according to Scripture. The readers do not become witnesses, but pass on the word of the witnesses. Some have thought the word "witness" has its later technical meaning of "martyr" in reference to Stephen (22:20), but it likely only indicates the kind of circumstances that led to this technical usage.

Acts clearly has as a central theme the proclamation of the gospel. We have taken note of the prominence of "the word" in Acts. The phrase "word of God" occurs twelve times; "word of the Lord" ten times; "the word" ten times; "the word of his grace" two times; and "the word of the gospel" and "the word of this salvation" once each.

The theme of proclamation is explicit in the speeches included in Acts. Some modern historians have argued that the practice of ancient historians in rewriting speeches means that no historical confidence can be placed in the speeches in Acts. Rhetoricians prescribed exercises for their students of writing speeches of a given person and adapting them to different audiences. However, the practice of ancient historians was not uniform, and some took the need for truthfulness seriously. Although ancient historians sometimes invented speeches and always rewrote them, in part to show the author's rhetorical ability, there was in general a concern for accuracy and for faithfulness to what was appropriate for the speaker and the occasion. The form of the speeches in Acts is Hellenistic, but the content is the Christian message, presented as in the Greek Bible and Hellenistic Jewish literature for a religious purpose and with a theological interpretation. Luke summarizes and rewrites the speeches in his style and for his purposes, but the content and individual characteristics of each speech fit the different speakers and circumstances with great verisimilitude, so that many modern studies stress the faithfulness with which Luke records the speeches.

Luke's presentation of the apostolic preaching proclaims the gospel, but the speeches are more theocentric than christocentric, for they emphasize what God has done now in Christ. One count gives thirty-six speeches or partial speeches in Acts, including those by non-Christians (Soards, 21–22). Acts 2 is programmatic for the rest of the book. It is the fullest presentation of an evangelistic sermon and response to it, details selectively employed in later accounts. Besides the evangelistic or missionary sermons to Jews and godfearers (2:14–40; 3:12–26; 4:8–12; 5:29–32; 10:34–43; 13:16–41); and to Gentiles (14:15–17; 17:22–31) there is a speech to the leaders of the church (20:18–35), and there are deliberative speeches (1:16–22; 15:7–11, 13–21), speeches of defense to Jews (7:2–53; 22:3–21) and forensic speeches in a formal trial setting (24:28; 24:10–21; 26:2–23).

The dedication of Luke to Theophilus indicated that it was written to show the "certainty" of Christian teaching (Lk. 1:3). Acts shares this purpose of confirmation. It offers a confirmation of what God did in Christ as recorded in the Gospel. Acts provides Christians with a self definition through history. Modern literary critics and sociologists note the importance of the story in shaping the identity of families and communities. Acts gives the Christian story.

Acts, moreover, is a work of encouragement for believers, a work of edification. The book is realistic. There are setbacks: many reject the gospel (6:9;

7:54; 13:8, 44–45; 14:2, 4; 17:45, 32; 18:6; 19:23–27) and cause persecution (4:13; 6:11–14; 7:58–8:3; 9:23–24, 29; 12:14; 13:50; 14:5, 19; 16:19–20; 17:6; 18:12–13; 21:30–31; 22:22). But in the midst of these troubles there are many statements of the growth in the number of believers or growth of the word (cited above), many occurring after a crisis. Hence, there is reassurance because of the triumph of the word through suffering.

*Originally printed in David Lipe, ed., *Opening Our Eyes to Jesus: From Darkness to Light in Acts,* Freed-Hardeman University Lectures (Henderson, TN: Freed-Hardeman University, 2004), 129–146.

For Further Reading

Alexander, Loveday. *The Preface to Luke's Gospel: Literary Convention and Social Context in Luke 1:1–4 and Acts 1:1.* Cambridge: Cambridge University Press, 1993.

_____. *Acts in its Ancient Literary Context: A Classicist Looks at the Acts of the Apostles.* London: T & T Clark, 2005.

Marshall, I. Howard, and David Peterson, eds. *Witness to the Gospel: The Theology of Acts.* Grand Rapids: Eerdmans, 1998.

Soards, Marion L. *The Speeches in Acts: Their Content, Context and Concerns.* Louisville: Westminster/John Knox, 1994.

Sterling, Gregory E. *Historiography and Self-Definition: Josephus, Luke-Acts and Apologetic Historiography.* Leiden: Brill, 1992.

Winter, Bruce W., and Andrew D. Clarke, eds. *Ancient Literary Setting.* The Book of Acts in Its First Century Setting, vol. 1. Grand Rapids: Eerdmans, 1993.

Witherington, Ben, III. *History, Literature, and Society in the Book of Acts.* Cambridge: Cambridge University Press, 1996.

Historical Themes in Acts

As part of my doctoral program at Harvard I took a course in the History of the Roman Empire taught by a visiting professor from Oxford. One of the required readings was the book of Acts. The professor explained that it was the most vivid and revealing source for life in the first century in the eastern Roman provinces.

We have noted that Luke, in the prologue to his Gospel, offered his account as based on research into the reports from eyewitnesses and ministers of the word and being written in an accurate and orderly manner (Lk. 1:2–3). Despite this profession, many New Testament critics have been quite negative about the historical value of Acts.

Luke's history must be evaluated by the historiography of his time, not by modern standards of history writing. Greco-Roman historians stated their concern with the truthfulness of their narratives, saw themselves as interpreting as well as recording events (the latter would be a chronicle, not a history), recorded what would be profitable (useful) to others, and wrote in a style that would please their readers. We may quote some of their statements about their intentions:

> It is only indeed by study of the interconnection of all the particulars and differences that we are enabled, at least, to make a general survey and thus derive both benefit and pleasure from history. The historian should simply record what really happened and what really was said, however commonplace. . . . For the historian it is the truth that takes precedence, the purpose being to confer benefit on learners. (Polybius, *Histories* 1.4.11; 2.56.1013)

> History cannot admit a lie, even a tiny one. . . . Historians' concern is different from that of the orators. What historians have to relate is fact and it will speak for itself, for it has already happened: what is required is arrangement and exposition. So, they must look not for what to say, but how to say it. (Lucian, *How to Write History* 7, 50)

Luke compares quite favorably with other historians of his time, especially with Josephus, who was less restrained and more rhetorical and tendentious. Luke sought to get the facts straight. He wrote in order to instruct, encourage, and edify his readers. And he wrote according to the literary and rhetorical conventions of the time. In one important respect, he was more like his Old Testament predecessors than like Greek and Roman historians. The latter sought to establish the plausibility of events: the Old Testament writers pointed to the truth of the God who rules the world. Luke, like the Old Testament historians, affirms divine activity in history.

Luke was writing history, but he was not recording history for its own sake. He had theological and practical purposes, but he grounded those purposes in a reliable history. He wrote for the benefit of his readers according to the needs of his time. But that history has remained instructive and edifying to Christians through the subsequent ages.

One of the major historical themes in Acts is the gospel's relation to Judaism. Jerusalem and the temple are central to the early chapters of Acts. The apostolic witness was to begin in Jerusalem (1:8), and the events of chapters 1–7 and subsequently 11, 12, 15, and 21–23 are located in Jerusalem. The temple was a center of activity by the early disciples (2:46; 3:1).

Themes of importance to Jews are included in the narrative, such as covenant (3:25) and the Law and the Prophets (13:15; 24:14). Jewish institutions figure prominently, like the priesthood (4:1, 23; 5:17, 21, 24, 27; 6:7; 7:1; 9:1, 14, 21; 22:14, 45; 25:2, 15; 26:10, 12), the elders (4:5, 8; 22:5; 23:14; 24:1), and the Sanhedrin (council) (4:15; 5:21, 27, 41; 6:12, 15; 22:30, 23:1, 20, 28). The Christian message is linked to persons of importance in Jewish history: Abraham (3:25; 7:2, 17; 13:26), Moses (3:22; 26:22), and David (1:16; 2:25–30; 4:25; 13:22–23, 34; 15:16). Reference is made to persons of importance in Judaism at the time: Annas and Caiaphas (4:6), Ananias (23:2; 24:1), and Gamaliel (5:34–39). Jewish history is recounted (7:2–53; 13:17–41), as well as more recent events (5:36–37).

Acts often mentions the synagogues. The precise sense is often uncertain, but some references seem to be to the organized community (6:9; 9:2; 17:1, 10; 22:19; 26:11), some to its actual meetings (9:20; 13:5, 14–15, 43; 18:4, 26), and some to its place of meeting (17:17; 18:7; 19:8; 24:12). The book is an important source for the synagogue's organization and services. There were "rulers of the synagogue" (18:8, 17), who were responsible for the service (13:15). The service centered on a reading of the Law and the Prophets followed by a "word of exhortation" if someone qualified was present (13:15, 27; 15:21). Some have argued that before AD 70 the synagogue functioned as a community center and place of instruction and not of worship. One of the common names for the synagogue was "place of prayer" (16:13, 16); it would be strange to give this name to the place of meetings if prayer was not part of the meetings!

Acts mentions proselytes (Gentile converts to Judaism; 2:10; 6:5; 13:43) and gives prominent notice to "godfearers" (10:2, 22; 13:16, 26) and "worshippers of God" ("devout"; 13:50; 16:14; 17:4, 17; 18:–7, 13). Some have questioned whether such existed as a distinct category of pious Gentiles attached to Jewish communities who did not take the step of full conversion by submitting to circumcision. Inscriptions seem to have undercut the basis for doubt, and at any rate there may have been the reality of such persons without a technical term for them. There is plenty of evidence that many

Gentiles were attracted to Judaism, accepted some of its practices, and in varying degrees identified with Jewish communities.

It is stressed in Acts that the gospel was for the Jews first (3:26; 11:19; 13:5, 46; 14:1; 17:1, 10; 18:5–6; 28:17, 28). However, it was the Jews who stirred up opposition to Christian teaching, particularly against Paul (9:23; 12:3; 13:45, 50; 14:2, 4; 17:5; 18:6, 12; 20:3, 19; 21:11, 27). A note of the separation that had occurred between Christians and Jews by Luke's time of writing is perhaps indicated by the use of the third person pronoun "their" rulers (4:5). Gentiles do not replace Jews as God's people; rather they are incorporated into God's people, and a mission continues to Jews as well as Gentiles. Although the Jews collectively rejected Jesus, individual Jews continued to be receptive (28:24). Luke is aware of a periodization of the Law: forgiveness is available in Jesus that was not possible under the Law (13:39).

Acts begins in Jerusalem and ends in Rome. The goal of Luke's story was the spread of the gospel in the person of the apostle Paul to Rome, where there were already disciples when the apostle to the Gentiles arrived (28:14–15). The narrative in Acts intersects the Roman Empire at many points.

On detail after detail, where Acts can be checked against topographical, inscriptional, and numismatic evidence, its accuracy is vindicated. For instance, Luke uses the correct terminology for local political officials: "proconsul" for Sergius Paulus as governor of the senatorial province of Cyprus with his headquarters at Paphos (13:67); the general term "rulers" (16:19) specified as "magistrates" (16:22, 36), attested in Greek for the *duoviri*, who were the chief officials of a Roman colony, as was Philippi, and were assisted by *lictores* ("rod bearers," 16:35); "politarchs" or "city authorities" in Thessalonica (17:6); the court of the "Areopagus" at Athens (17:22, 33–34); Asiarchs for the province of Asia in Ephesus (19:31); "town clerk" for the city's chief executive magistrate (19:35); and "regular (literally 'legal') assembly" for the meeting of its citizens (19:39). The same is true for references to the Roman legal system: members of the public as accusers (22:30; 24:1), right to meet accusers face to face (25:16), a citizen's protection against flogging (16:37–38; 22:24–29), trial before a governor or other magistrate seated on his tribunal (18:12) and assisted by his council (25:6, 12; 26:30), a rhetorician to plead one's case (24:12), and a citizen's right of appeal to Rome (25:10–12; 26:32).

Correct terminology is used for military troops and their officers, who appear in a favorable light (10:1; 21:31–34; 23:23).

One of the duties of provincial councils was to supervise the imperial cult, so the notice of the "Asiarchs" (19:31) is a reminder of the practice of giving divine honors to rulers. Acts does not confront directly the giving of these honors to the emperor, but it does implicitly render judgment on an expression of the ruler cult in regard to Herod Agrippa I (12:21–23).

One purpose of Acts may have been to make the case that Christianity was not subversive. The charges against Christians were in part those that continued to be leveled later: Christians were politically dangerous for preaching another king, Jesus (17:7), and offering a new set of customs (16:21); Christians were socially disruptive, for rioting accompanied their preaching (13:50; 14:19; 17:6, 13; 18:12); and the Christian message could be economically damaging when it attacked pagan superstitions and religious practices (16:16–23; 19:23–34). We noticed in the previous lesson that Acts generally gives a favorable picture of representatives of Roman rule. This approval was not uncritical, however, for Luke can note instances of shading the truth (23:27) and corrupt practices (22:28; 24:26).

There are historical problems in Acts. In Gamaliel's speech to the Sanhedrin, reference is made to insurrections by Theudas and after him Judas the Galilean (5:36–37). The problem is twofold: Josephus mentions a Theudas after Judas and places him in the period 44–46, that is after the time of Gamaliel's speech (*Antiquities* 20.5.1). I do not know why Josephus is so often assumed to be correct and Luke to be in error, when Josephus's accuracy is not as well attested as Luke's. Josephus may have had the time relationship confused. Or, it is possible that Luke was making the point from his own period in time and taking liberty with the specific instances cited by Gamaliel. Another possibility is that Gamaliel is referring to another Theudas than the one in Josephus, since the name was common and there were many insurrections around the beginning of the Christian era.

Some of the apparent historical discrepancies cluster in Stephen's speech in Acts 7. In view of Luke's practice of editing and rewriting speeches, it will not do to claim he was quoting Stephen even when Stephen was in error, but other explanations are possible. Genesis 11:31–12:3 appears to put the words of Acts 7:23 after Abraham moved to Haran rather than before. That, however, may not be the way to read Genesis, where God's command for Abraham to leave his country may be introduced after the first stage of his sojourn as the explanation for it. Or, there may have been a divine communication to Abraham before as well as after the move to Haran, for both Philo and Josephus indicate such a Jewish interpretation, which Stephen may have followed. Another problem comes in Acts 7:16, where the tomb bought by Abraham is said to have been in Shechem and bought from Hamor, whereas Abraham bought his burial cave from Ephron at Hebron (Gen. 23:16–20; 49:29–31; 50:13) and Jacob bought a plot of land from Hamor in Shechem (Gen. 33:19; Josh. 24:32). I have no satisfactory answer to this problem. The best I have heard are that somehow Abraham stands for the patriarchs, so that what was done by his descendants could be ascribed to him, or, since Jacob was buried at Hebron and Joseph at Shechem, in this abbreviated treatment there was a telescoping of two events into one.

A different kind of historical problem concerns the relation of Acts to the letters of Paul. Luke's picture of Paul is different from the picture one gets from Paul's letters. These differences, however, can easily be exaggerated. The question is, "Are they irreconcilable?" That question will be answered according to the critic's predispositions. It is usually assumed, to the disadvantage of Acts, that Paul's firsthand testimony about his controversies with Jews and Judaizers is to be given preference. On a purely human level, however, this assumption is questionable. Often a third party has a more objective view than the participants in a controversy. But may not Paul and Luke both be right? They are viewing matters from different perspectives and writing for different purposes, and taken together their information gives us a richer and fuller understanding. Ancient literature provides examples of biographical material about someone from whom we also have their own writings, a situation comparable to that of Acts and the letters of Paul; in these cases a sympathetic onlooker's view, and the person's own expression of how he wished to be seen, prove to be complementary and not contradictory (Hillard et al. in Winter and Clarke, 183–213).

The place of the cross is not as prominent in Acts as it is in Paul's writings, but it is not correct to say that the atoning death of Jesus has no place in

Luke's theology (8:32–33; 20:28). Acts speaks as clearly as Paul that the Law does not justify (13:39; 15:10) and that justification is by grace through faith (13:43; 15:9, 11; 26:18). A basic discrepancy is often urged between Luke's record in Acts 15 of the "apostolic council" and Paul's account in Galatians 2.The two accounts can be reconciled as each recording distinct aspects of the meeting, but if Paul was referring to his visit to Jerusalem in Acts 11:29–30, for which a good case can be made, then the discrepancies vanish (Wenham in Winter and Clarke, 226–43).

Acts is primarily a history of the beginnings of the church. We have observed that a main theme is the spread of the word that produced the growth of the church. Acts gives some information on Christian meetings (2:42, 46–47; 4:23–31; 20:7–12) and on the church's organization (11:30; 15:2, 6, 22; 20:17, 28), including the selection of leaders and ministers (1:15–26; 6:16; 13:13; 14:23). There are indications of the importance of women in the church (2:17–18; 9:36–41; 18:26; 21:9). One of the passages noting the presence of women (1:14) also specifies that the apostles were to be "men" (1:21), and so were the seven chosen to oversee the distribution of food to widows (6:3). As in Luke's Gospel, prayer is a prominent interest (1:14, 24; 2:42; 4:24–30; 6:4, 6; 9:11; 10:2, 4, 9; 12:5, 12; 13:3; 20:38). There is a great deal said in Acts about benevolence (2:45; 4:32, 34–37; 6:16; 9:36; 10:2, 4; 20:35; 24:17). Also, unity is stressed (1:14; 2:46; 4:32; 5:12).

Luke is the first Christian historian, indeed the first historian in antiquity to present a new religious movement in a historical manner. The special concern of Acts is to show the church as both Jewish and Gentile (26:23). Luke and Acts have the distinction of being perhaps the most pro-Jewish books in the New Testament and at the same time the most universalistic. The church, according to Acts, maintains its Jewish roots and Jewish ties but welcomes those of all races and social classes. Acts leaves us with a picture of the church rooted in the Old Testament, continuing the sayings and deeds of Jesus, proclaiming the kingdom of God and teaching about the Lord Jesus Christ, and looking expectantly for the glorious return of Jesus from heaven.

*Originally printed in David Lipe, ed., *Opening Our Eyes to Jesus: From Darkness to Light in Acts,* Freed-Hardeman University Lectures (Henderson, TN: Freed-Hardeman University, 2004), 129–146.

For Further Reading

Bauckham, Richard, ed. *The Book of Acts in Its Palestinian Setting.* The Book of Acts in Its First Century Setting, vol. 4. Grand Rapids: Eerdmans, 1995.

Cadbury, Henry J. *The Book of Acts in History.* New York: Harper, 1955.

Gill, W. J., and Conrad Gempf, eds. *The Book of Acts in Its Graeco-Roman Setting.* The Book of Acts in Its First Century Setting, vol. 2. Grand Rapids: Eerdmans, 1994.

Hemer, Colin J. *The Book of Acts in the Setting of Hellenistic History.* Tubingen: Mohr, 1989.

Levinskaya, Irina. *The Book of Acts in Its Diaspora Setting.* The Book of Acts in Its First Century Setting, vol. 5. Grand Rapids: Eerdmans, 1996.

Rapske, Brian. *The Book of Acts and Paul in Roman Custody.* The Book of Acts in Its First Century Setting, vol. 3. Grand Rapids: Eerdmans, 1994.

Winter, Bruce W., and Andrew D. Clarke, eds. *Ancient Literary Setting.* The Book of Acts in Its First Century Setting, vol. l. Grand Rapids: Eerdmans, 1993.

Part III

Biblical Interpretation

10

The Lord's Supper and Biblical Hermeneutics

The question of the day and frequency for observing the Lord's Supper will serve to illustrate a method of dealing with disputed questions. I employed this method in my book *A Cappella Music in the Public Worship of the Church*. I first developed the approach in studying the subject at hand—the day of the Christian assembly. There is nothing particularly original, certainly nothing revolutionary, in this approach. It is simply the application of historical and theological context to hermeneutics. This approach involves three steps: (1) assembling the New Testament passages on the subject under discussion; (2) examining the testimony of early Christian history for the extracanonical evidence on Christian belief and practice—this is done as a control against an unhistorical understanding or an individualistic peculiarity in interpretation; (3) consideration of the doctrinal significance in order to determine if the practice has any real significance or is only a cultural or accidental phenomenon.

For people committed to biblical authority, the first importance obviously attaches to the biblical data. Hence, as we consider the time for the observance of the Lord's Supper, the first task is to examine the New Testament evidence in order to determine if one day had special meaning and significance for Christians in New Testament times. I will not attempt to go through and examine all the passages or consider all the issues. Rather, I will present the results of the study by organizing the evidence according to the conclusion reached.

The New Testament gives special significance to the first day of the week, our Sunday:

(1) Jesus arose from the dead on the first day of the week. The resurrection narratives in the Gospels all begin with a time designation. "And when the Sabbath was past . . . and very early on the first day of the week they went to the tomb when the sun had risen" (Mark 16:1). "But on the first day of the week, at early dawn, they went to the tomb" (Luke 23:1). "That very day" (v. 13) occurred the appearance to the disciples on the road to Emmaus and other appearances (vv. 33–35), and the resurrection is affirmed as having occurred on that day (vv. 21, 46). "Now on the first day of the week Mary Magdalene came to the tomb early, while it was still dark" (John 20:1). I list these before Matthew because there has been some question about the translation of Matthew 28:1, but it seems clear to me that the Revised Standard Version gives the correct translation: "Now after the sabbath, toward the dawn of the first day of the week." Therefore, on the first day of the week Jesus was declared to be the Son of God with power (Rom. 1:4).

(2) Christ met with his disciples after the resurrection on the first day of the week. John especially makes this prominent. After telling about the discovery of the empty tomb in the morning, he says, "On the evening of that day, the first day of the week . . . Jesus came and stood among them" (v. 19). Thomas was not present at that gathering. Thus we read in verse 26, "Eight days later [i.e., the next Sunday] his disciples were again in the house, and Thomas was with them." And Jesus appeared again. The post-resurrection meals of Jesus with his disciples thus occurred on the first day of the week. Notice the eucharistic language in the description of the meal at Emmaus in Luke 24:30, 35.

(3) Pentecost came on the first day of the week (Lev. 23:15f.). There were different calendars in first-century Judaism, but I assume that Luke follows the official reckoning by the Sadducees, which put Pentecost on the first day of the week. That means that all of the events of the second chapter of Acts took place on the first day of the week: the coming of the Holy Spirit, the first gospel sermon, the three thousand converted, the birthday of the church, and observe especially the beginning of the corporate life together of the new community: "And they devoted themselves to the apostles' teaching and fellowship, to the breaking of bread and the prayers" (Acts 2:42). Notice that those activities began on the first day of the week.

(4) The New Testament church assembled on the first day of the week. In Acts 20:6–7, "We came to them at Troas, where we stayed for seven days. On the first day of the week, when we were gathered together to break bread, Paul talked with them." There seems to be some reason for the stay of seven days, namely the gathering on the first day. "On the first day of the week, each of you is to put something aside" (1 Cor. 16:2). This verse says nothing specifically about an assembly and it has its difficulty in interpretation, but I would call attention to its position, after chapter fifteen's discussion of the resurrection, which occurred on the first day of the week. And, however the putting something aside was handled, "store it up" is literally "to put in a treasury." But what concerns me here is that the first day of the week had some special significance to the Christian communities (in Galatia as well as Corinth). The natural thought is that this was the occasion when the Christians were accustomed to being together. Otherwise, the specification of the day is unintelligible.

(5) The Lord's Supper was observed on the first day of the week. The disciples were commanded to partake (Matt. 26:26–28; Luke 22:19). Christians were commanded to assemble (Heb. 10:25). There were assemblies for the purpose of eating the supper (1 Cor. 11:20–33). Notice 1 Corinthians 11:20, "When you meet together, it is not the Lord's supper that you eat," indicating that it should be the Lord's Supper that is eaten when they assemble. And verse 33, "when you come together to eat." The first day of the week is the only day identified as the time when there was a coming together for the purpose

of eating the supper: Acts 20:7, "on the first day of the week, when we were gathered together to break bread."

Negatively, the New Testament is silent on Sabbath observance by Christians as part of their distinctively Christian activities. Space forbids an examination of the Sabbath question, but suffice it to say that the Sabbath would be the only serious contender for a day given special meaning, yet there is no evidence that the Sabbath was the day for Christians to assemble or to observe the Lord's Supper.

This arrangement of the material points to one conclusion—so much so that most Christians have considered the case to be persuasive. On the other hand, I think that we must honestly say that the evidence is not so conclusive as we might want it to be. Any case which depends on a certain arrangement of texts and a chain of reasoning is subject to error by the person doing the arranging and reasoning. Certainly there are many subjects on which the New Testament is much more explicit and complete in its teaching. Therefore, we must ask the question: Is this arranging of the evidence correct?

The case for weekly communion on Sunday, as presented above, does not rest on Acts 20:7 alone, but that is the key text. Is it referring to a one-time event? Is it a casual reference not to be given great importance? Or does it reflect common, normal practice? In other words, have we read the New Testament aright? Or have we made it say something it did not intend to say? Have we forced our logic and our schemes on the contents?

One way of checking ourselves is by post-New Testament Christian history. Was the practice of the early church in harmony with the interpretation given above to the New Testament? If our conclusions about New Testament practice are correct, they should receive some confirmation from the testimony of church history. If something is not present in the early history of the church, there is grave doubt even about its presence, much more so about its importance, in apostolic teaching. On the other hand, something abundantly testified to in the early Christian literature has good claims to being a part of apostolic practice, and we should be very certain that we have good grounds for finding the New Testament teaching different.

This is not to say that history becomes our authority. It is to say that history is an important witness that deserves to be heard in the court of hermeneutics. We appeal to church history as we do to any other nonbiblical information—to help us understand Scripture better. Scripture remains the judge. But where the question concerns the decision of the judge, we should examine the testimony of all the witnesses.

It so happens that on the question of the day of Christian assembly the witnesses from the early church are numerous, unanimous, and unambiguous. Several of the important statements from the second century about the assembly on the first day of the week include a reference to the Lord's Supper. *Didache* 14:1 says, "Come together each Lord's day of the Lord, break bread, and give thanks." Notice three things in this passage: there is a weekly assembly; it is on the day called the Lord's day; and it is characterized by the breaking of bread.

Barnabas 15 does not specifically mention the Lord's Supper: "We [Christians] keep the eighth day [i.e., the first day of the week; the Sabbath was the seventh] for joy, on which also Jesus arose from the dead and when he appeared ascended into heaven."

Justin Martyr, *Apology* I, 67 tells us that "On the day called Sunday there is a gathering together in the same place of all who live in a city or rural district." There follows an account of a service of Scripture reading, preaching, and prayer; and Justin continues, "When we cease from our prayer, bread is presented and wine mixed with water. The president of the brethren in the same manner sends up prayers and thanksgivings according to his ability, and the people sing out their assent saying the 'Amen.' A distribution and participation of the elements for which thanks have been given is made to each person." A contribution is collected, and then, Justin explains, "We all make our assembly in common on the day of the Sun, since it is the first day, on which God changed the darkness and matter and made the world, and Jesus Christ our Savior arose from the dead on the same day."

The apocryphal *Acts of John* 106–10 says that "since it was the Lord's day and all the brethren were assembled, John began to say to them." After a discourse and prayer, the text continues, "And he asked for bread and gave thanks . . . and he broke bread and gave to us all, praying for each of the brethren to be worthy of the Lord's grace."

Bardesanes, in *On Fate*, explains, "On one day, the first day of the week, we assemble ourselves together." And Eusebius (*Church History* III. xxvii. 5) says of early Jewish Christians that they "were accustomed to observe the sabbath and other Jewish customs but on the Lord's days to celebrate the same practices as we [Gentile Christians] in remembrance of the resurrection of the Savior." (A fuller listing of passages with commentary may be found in my book *Early Christians Speak*.)

Note that these texts from early Christian literature stress that Christians observe the first day because it is the day of the resurrection. They observe the day with an assembly, and in that assembly they take the supper. The testimony of church history shows that we have not misread the New Testament. The apostolic practice was a weekly communion on the first day of the week. If this was not the apostolic practice, then one has the difficult job of explaining how all the churches came to adopt the same custom. The conclusion to be drawn from the historical testimony is that Acts 20:7 is not an accidental reference but reflects the general practice of New Testament churches.

The hermeneutical quest, however, cannot stop here. Something may have been a general practice yet not have any lasting significance for Christians. Was the observance of the first day of the week culturally conditioned, because of the importance of the day of the sun to pagans, or a matter of custom to distinguish Christians from Jews? These factors were present, and many others. Can the observance of the first day be accounted for by these factors, and are they the only significance of the first day of the week? I think not, but in order to deal with these questions we must turn to the doctrinal significance of the first day of the week.

The doctrinal meaning of a practice is what really wraps the question up. Does a given practice have a doctrinal significance in the New Testament? The question is not, is there a doctrinal meaning we can impart to it? but, is there a meaning arising out of the thing itself? Is the New Testament evidence accidental, or incidental, or does it really mean something? Does it mean something for Christians of all time? Here there can be no doubt about the meaning of the first day of the week for early Christians, modern Christians, all Christians.

Before drawing out that meaning, permit me a digression in regard to the significance of the Sabbath. This treatment will allow us to eliminate the principal competitor to the first day of the week and also sharpen the doctrinal significance of the latter. That the old covenant was abolished, and the Sabbath as part of it, is taught in many New Testament passages (Rom. 7:1–7; Gal. 3:23–25; Col. 2:16f.). Hence, Christians are not to be judged by it. The Sabbath itself had significance for Jews, and for Jews only: "Observe the sabbath day, to keep it holy. . . . You shall remember that you were a servant in the land of Egypt, and the LORD your God brought you out thence with a mighty hand and an outstretched arm; *therefore* the LORD your God commanded you to keep the sabbath day" (Deut. 5:12–15 RSV, emphasis mine).

It is true that Exodus 20:11 connects the Sabbath with God's rest at creation. If we were to reconcile the two passages, we would say that God's rest day was the reason for selecting the seventh day rather than some other day. But the reason for having a special observance at all was the remembrance of the exodus. The Sabbath had a doctrinal purpose for Israel. Its significance was a remembrance of the day of deliverance from Egypt. As such a remembrance, the Sabbath was given to the Jews only and had significance to Jews only—"God brought you out . . . therefore God commanded you to keep the sabbath." The Sabbath has no significance to Gentiles, who did not come out of bondage in Egypt and become the chosen nation at Sinai. The Sabbath carries no doctrinal significance to Gentile Christians today.

On the other hand, the first day of the week does have doctrinal significance for Christians. It is the day of our deliverance. It is a remembrance of the resurrection of Jesus, the great act by which we were delivered from sin and made God's people. This day is of foundational significance for the church. We meet on the first day because we are conscious of Christ's presence in our midst on the day of the resurrection; the day on which the Spirit came and the church had its beginning as a gathered people. The first day of the week is connected with the reason why there is a church (the resurrection) and with its actual coming into being as a distinctive community (the events of Acts 2). For these reasons the church observes Sunday with an assembly.

The Lord's Supper belongs in the complex of ideas because of its association with the redemption accomplished by the death and resurrection and its association with the nature of the church. It continues not only the last supper but also the resurrection meals of Jesus with his disciples. Moreover, by its very nature, the supper is a corporate act. This corporate nature of the supper is clearly seen in 1 Corinthians 10–11. Thus the supper belongs on the special day when the church shows itself as church by gathering together. As a community activity, the supper must be observed at the time of assembly.

It is perhaps significant (although I would not press the point) that the adjective "of the Lord" or "Lord's"—that which pertains to the Lord—occurs only twice in the New Testament: once for the supper (1 Cor. 11:20), and once for the Lord's day (Rev. 1:10). These two things are peculiarly the Lord's and they belong together: his day and his supper.

I find this approach much more persuasive than simply quoting Acts 20:7. This method ties the observance of the Lord's Supper more closely with the redemptive events of which it is the commemoration. It shows that the first day of the week was chosen not for incidental reasons. But it is a day with meaning, because of its importance in the history of salvation.

The Lord's Supper on any day other than Sunday weakens its doctrinal meaning. Many will know the book *Sunday: The History of the Day of Rest and Worship in the Earliest Centuries of the Christian Church*, by my friend Willy Rordorf. His conclusion includes the pungent words: "No Lord's supper without Sunday and no Sunday without the Lord's supper."

The methodology illustrated above will not provide everyone with a satisfactory solution to the problem. Some will no doubt be dissatisfied with the question chosen for discussion. I would plead nevertheless that the hermeneutical question on any issue be pursued with reference to relevant historical and doctrinal considerations and that we not attempt to interpret the Bible without these contexts.

*Originally printed in *Mission* (September, 1976), 11–14.

Christian Use of the Old Testament

There has often been an ambiguity, if not tension, in the attitude of Christians toward the Old Testament. It is in their Bible, they read it, and they employ it for various purposes; but at the same time they recognize in it much which does not measure up to the standards of Jesus' teaching, and they feel its institutions and regulations are not binding for their lives. What, then, is the authority of the Old Testament for the Christian? What is the proper use to be made of the Old Testament by Christians? This article will consider the views of the Old Testament expressed by early Christian authors, then will present aspects of the New Testament use of the Old Testament: the removal of the Mosaic system of religion, the values found in the Old Testament, and problems in the New Testament use of the Old.

Early Christian Viewpoints

The Christian's relation to the Old Testament has been a recurring problem in Christian history. In the century and a half after the writing of the New Testament, many different viewpoints toward the Old Testament were expressed. These represent, often in extreme forms, the range of alternatives which have been explored in later periods of Christian history.

Marcion, in the middle of the second century, rejected entirely the Old Testament from his Bible. Marcion's own writings are lost, but we know his viewpoint from Tertullian's five-book refutation, *Against Marcion*, written in the early third century. Setting the Law and the gospel against each other in his book entitled *Antitheses,* Marcion concluded that the God of the Old Testament could not be the God of the New.

> Marcion's special and principal work is the separation of the law and the gospel. . . . These are Marcion's *Antitheses,* or contradictory propositions, which aim at committing the gospel to a variance with the law, in order that from the diversity of the two documents which contain them, they may contend for a diversity of gods also. (Tertullian *Against Marcion* I.19)

> For it is certain that the whole aim at which he has strenuously labored, even in the drawing up of his *Antitheses,* centers in this, that he may establish a diversity between the Old and the New Testaments, so that his own Christ may be separate from the Creator . . . and as alien from the law and the prophets. (Tertullian *Against Marcion* IV.6)

Marcion saw the Old Testament God as a God of justice; the Christ he prophesied was the warrior Messiah expected by the Jews. Jesus, on the other hand, revealed the Father who is love and grace and was previously unknown to human beings. Marcion "devised different dispensations for two Gods" (*Against Marcion* III.15). His Christ came not to fulfill but to destroy the law. The consequence of this radical separation was a total rejection of the Old Testament in favor of the New on the view that the two were so incompatible that they must come from different Gods and could not both be espoused by Christians. "The whole of the Old Testament, the heretic, to the best of my belief, holds in derision" (ibid., V.5). Tertullian admits a difference and declares a superiority of the gospel to the Law, but he denies Marcion's explanations and conclusions. "It is the office of Christ's gospel to call men from the law to grace, not from the Creator to another god" (ibid., V.2). The differences are not so great as Marcion makes out, for there is law in the New Testament and grace in the Old. Moreover, book III of Tertullian's refutation presents Old Testament predictions of Jesus and argues the connection of Jesus Christ with the Creator God of the Old Testament. So, although the old dispensation has been abolished by something superior, even this was predicted by the Old Testament, and the differences are consistent with the same God having planned the whole (ibid., IV.1). Marcion represents an extreme solution to the problem of the New Testament's relation to the Old. Few have followed him, but his very extremes help us to recognize tendencies which have recurred in Christian history.

The second-century Gnostics generally shared Marcion's negative evaluation of the Old Testament, but there was a variety of positions. An interesting, and individual, view is that of the Valentinian Gnostic Ptolemy (about AD 160). His *Letter to Flora* (preserved in Epiphanius, *Panarion* XXXIII.3–7) presents an early example of "source criticism" applied to the Old Testament. There are those, Ptolemy says, who teach that the Law was ordained by God the Father (the Orthodox Christians) and those who teach that it was given by the devil (Gnostics more extreme than Ptolemy). By way of contrast he takes a middle position that the Law was given by the creator of the world (the Demiurge), who is different from the perfect God. Not all of the Law, however, comes from this creator. The New Testament attributes some parts of the Old Testament to God, some to Moses (not what was given by God through him but as legislating from his own understanding), and some to the elders of the people. The legislation of Moses and of the elders is without lasting authority. Even that part which came from the creator God may be divided into three parts. There is the pure legislation, free from evil, which the Savior "came not to destroy but to fulfill," identified by Ptolemy as the Ten Commandments. There is a second part bound up with wrongdoing and concerned with vengeance (such as "an eye for an eye and a tooth for a tooth"), which the Savior abrogated as alien to his nature. Finally, there is the typical and symbolical part (such as the Sabbath, circumcision, sacrifices) which the Savior transformed from material and bodily things into spiritual (abstaining from evil, circumcising the heart, praise and thanksgiving).

So two parts of the Old Testament did not come from God, and of the part that did some is still valid; some has been abolished; and some has been transformed. Ptolemy shows his Gnostic bias in distinguishing the Creator from the Father of Christ and not allowing any of the Old Testament to be derived from the Father. (Against the Gnostics the Orthodox Church writers emphasized the continuity between the Old and the New as both given by the same God.) Otherwise, Ptolemy's view is highly original; it is nonetheless similar to other (later) efforts to make levels or distinctions within the Old Testament, some of which are valid for Christians and some of which are not.

Another view which made distinctions within the Old Testament, but from the very opposite premises, was that of the second-century Jewish Christians known as Ebionites. They represent a survival of those Jewish Christians who were "zealous for the law" and opposed Paul (Acts 15:1, 5; 21:20; Gal. 2:4–5). In contrast to Marcion, the Ebionites impressed the mainstream of the church with their adherence to the law. Irenaeus (ca. AD 180) says of them:

> They use the Gospel according to Matthew only, and repudiate the Apostle Paul, maintaining that he was an apostate from the law. As to the prophetical writings they endeavor to expound them in a peculiar manner. They practice circumcision, preserve in the observance of those customs which are enjoined by the law, and are so Judaic in their style of life, that they even adore Jerusalem as if it were the house of God. (*Against Heresies* I.xxvi.1)

Actually the Ebionites made distinctions within the Old Testament, for not all of the Law was considered binding. Their views in detail must be reconstructed from their teachings included in the Pseudo-Clementine *Homilies* and *Recognitions*. Jesus appears as the teacher of a kind of "reform Judaism." Some passages now found in the Torah are not original but are later falsifications (*Homilies* III.47). Jesus as the True Prophet restored the proper law of God. Among the things rejected were "the sacrifices, the monarchy, and the female [false] prophecy and other such things" (*Homilies* III.52). The real point of Jesus' mission was annulling the sacrificial Law (*Recognitions* I.35ff.). The bloodshed of war seems to have been a principal reason for rejecting the monarchy, but there was Old Testament basis for not considering it a divine ordinance. For reasons which seem complicated now, prophecy was disparaged or even rejected. Finally, offensive passages in Scripture (anthropomorphisms about God and immoral deeds recorded of Old Testament heroes—the very things which Marcion and the Gnostics used against the Old Testament) were rejected as false, later additions to the Scriptures. On the other hand, following and going beyond Jesus, the Ebionites intensified certain features of the law: prohibiting meat, emphasizing poverty, and increasing the purification ceremonies (ritual immersion-baths).

Jewish Christians took varying attitudes toward Gentile observance of the Law: some (Ebionites proper) insisting that their Law was binding on Gentiles and others saying that Jews must continue to keep it while exempting Gentiles from its ritual requirements (Justin, *Dialogue with Trypho* 47).The effort to be both Jews and Christians is reflected in the statement included in Eusebius' description of the Ebionites: "Like the Jews they used to observe the sabbath and the rest of the Jewish ceremonial, but on Sundays celebrated rites like ours in commemoration of the Saviour's resurrection" (*Church History* III.xxvii.5). Their view was largely lost to the church, as it became overwhelmingly Gentile in membership and considered such combinations heretical. After the Ebionites died out, few Jews who were converted kept the Law. Conversion to Christianity meant a break with the Jewish lifestyle, something which was not true for the majority of Jewish Christians in the early days of the church.

The unknown author of the so-called *Epistle of Barnabas* (ca. 135, but possibly much earlier) also claimed the Old Testament as the Christians' Bible but in a radically different way from the Ebionites. In one sense he is the very opposite of Marcion: the Old Testament is altogether Christian. In another sense he accomplished what Marcion did without severing the church's ties with its Old Testament heritage: the Old Testament is not to be taken literally but only spiritually. The author used the Old Testament against its own requirements, for example in quoting Isaiah 1:11–14, Jeremiah 7:22–23, and Psalm 51:19 to argue that God did not intend the animal sacrifices but desired a sacrifice of the heart and in quoting Isaiah 58:4–10 to argue that God did not want literal fasting but service to others.

There were those who were saying that "the covenant is both theirs [Jews] and ours [Christians]." "Barnabas" replies with an emphatic, "It is ours." The covenant was offered to Israel, but the sin of the golden calf represented Israel's rejection of the covenant (Exod. 32). The covenant then was given to Christians. Moses broke the tablets of stone, "and their covenant was broken, in order that the covenant of Jesus the Beloved should be sealed in our hearts" (*Ep. Barnabas* 4:6–9; cf. 13–14). The renewed statement of the covenant given to Moses was never intended to be kept literally, not even by Jews. God intended it to be understood spiritually, and in that way it is observed by Christians. Most of the *Epistle of Barnabas* is a spiritual or allegorical interpretation of the characteristic features of the Mosaic religion. The ritual of the atonement was fulfilled in the sacrifice of Christ (chs. 5–8); fleshly circumcision is abolished and the real circumcision is that of the heart and ears (ch. 9); the food laws refer to types of men whose immorality is to be avoided (ch. 10); the ceremonial washings of the Old Testament have been replaced by baptism (ch. 11); the Sabbath of the Jews is displeasing to God, and Christians keep Sunday (ch. 15); the temple was in vain, for God truly dwells in the Christian people whose sin he forgives (ch. 16). "Barnabas" seems not to have had direct heirs to his novel and extreme interpretations, but the idea of reading the Old Testament spiritually as an allegory of the Christian dispensation and preserving it as a Christian book in this way was a widely influential approach in the ancient church.

It was especially the school of interpretation associated with the great city and center of learning in Egypt, Alexandria, where the allegorical interpretation of the Old Testament flourished. The earliest Orthodox writer at Alexandria from whom extensive writings survive is Clement (died before AD 215). Clement of Alexandria reflects a common early Christian teaching that the Law "was only temporary" (*Instructor* I.7; cf. *Miscellanies* VI. 5–7, 17). Its purposes were to "show sin" (*Miscellanies* II.7), to "train in piety, prescribe what is to be done, and restrain from sins by imposing penalties" (ibid., I.27). It prepared the chosen people for Christ's teaching (ibid., II.18). The "Mosaic philosophy" contains four parts: history, legislation (these two constituting ethics), sacrifice (knowledge of the physical world), and theology (metaphysics). The Law has three meanings of value to the Christian: "exhibiting a symbol, or laying down a precept for right conduct, or as uttering a prophecy" (ibid., I.28). The symbols of the Old Testament have three purposes: to arouse curiosity so men will study, to hide true doctrine from the profane, to make it possible to speak of God who is incomprehensible in his nature (ibid., VI.15). Clement shows especially the influence of Philo, the first-century Jewish philosopher from Alexandria, in finding allegories of the moral life and of the physical universe in the Old Testament. Instructive is his treatment of the Ten Commandments in *Miscellanies* VI.16. The Sabbath meant a rest from evil (not an uncommon interpretation in the early church); honor father and mother refers to God the Father and the divine knowledge and wisdom; adultery is abandoning the true knowledge of God; murder is extirpating true doctrine of God in order to introduce falsehood. The tabernacle was allegorized as the universe, for instance, the seven-branched lampstand representing the seven planets, but this Philonic interpretation is Christianized at several points, as in referring the lamp also to Christ, who gives light to the world (ibid., V.6).

Origen (185–253) systematized the Alexandrian interpretation of the Bible and carried through a massive amount of work in application of his methods. Origen found a triple sense in Scripture: the literal or historical sense, a moral or spiritual sense applying to the soul, and a mystical or typical sense referring to Christ, the church and the faith, or sometimes eternal life (*On First Princples* IV.xi.xxiii). Each passage may have all of these meanings, and every passage has a spiritual meaning even if no literal meaning.

Origen applies the scheme to the New Testament as well as to the Old. He relates the two testaments to each other as letter and spirit. Both are necessary, because one would not have the spirit without the letter, but the more important is the spirit which gives the true meaning. So it is Jesus who interprets the Law to the church (*In Joshua, Homily* ix.8). After Christ the historical has passed, and Scripture has now acquired its spiritual sense. The law itself has a literal and a spiritual element. It is always impossible to keep according to the letter—Origen cites the Sabbath command as his illustration—but spiritual obedience gives life (*Commentary on Romans* vi.12). Origen appeals to Paul as a justification for his spiritual reading of the Old Testament, for example, his use of the Exodus in 1 Corinthians 10:1ff. (*In Exodus, Homily* v.l). There is the difference, however, that for Paul the basis is a similar situation between Israel in the wilderness and the Corinthian Christians (see the treatment below), whereas for Origen the real meaning of the Old Testament text is the spiritual reference.

Whereas some, especially at Antioch, explained what were, from the Christian standpoint, imperfections in the Old Testament by God's accommodations to the needs and capacities of man in preparation for a truly spiritual religion, Origen is one of the purest advocates of allegorism as the way of overcoming the imperfections while holding onto the Old Testament as a sacred book. Origen reflects many of the common interpretations of the Old Testament to be found in the early church which are not allegorical and on occasion can use the Old Testament as ecclesiastical law in the manner of Cyprian (see below). His own preference, however, was obviously for the form of exegesis that interpreted Scripture with reference to the inner life. This became the distinctive mark of the Alexandrian school—to put the stress on the spiritual and mystical side. Thus Origen, in interpreting the tabernacle, can refer to the older interpretation that the tabernacle is the world, but he develops an allegory first in reference to the church, and then in keeping with his primary interest he passes to the soul. "Each may construct in his own soul a tabernacle to God" (*In Exodus, Homily* ix.4). This way of dealing with the Old Testament may be seen in the widely influential treatment of the stations in Israel's wilderness wandering as an allegory of the journey of the Christian soul towards perfection. An allegory of the religious life is combined with a statement of his principle of interpretation in the comment on the sweetening of the bitter waters of Marah, "The bitterness of the letter of the law is changed into the sweetness of spiritual understanding" (*In Exodus, Homily* vii.1). That is what Origen sought to do in his interpretation of the Bible.

By way of contrast with the Alexandrian way of using the Old Testament allegorically as teaching spiritual lessons for the Christian life, Latin authors read the Old Testament more literally and found in it legal requirements for

Christians. The animal sacrifices were replaced by the non-bloody (spiritual) sacrifice of the Eucharist, the Levitical priesthood was replaced by Christian ministers, the Sabbath was replaced by Sunday, the tabernacle was replaced by the church, and so through all of the institutions of the Old Testament, but the regulations stated for the Mosaical institutions could be applied to their Christian equivalent. The earliest expression of this tendency may be found in Clement of Rome (ca. AD 96), who used the Old Testament regulations about who offered sacrifice, when, and where as an argument for the need of similar good order in the church (*Epistle to the Corinthians* 40, 41).

Tertullian reflects the two sides of the Christian attitude toward the Old Testament when in his *Answer to the Jews* he affirms the contrast, "the old law has ceased [he has specifically mentioned circumcision, the Sabbath, and sacrifices] and . . . the promised new law is now in operation" (ch. 6), but in his polemic *Against Marcion* he can affirm the continuity, "the whole Mosaic system was a figure of Christ, of whom the Jews indeed were ignorant, but who is known to us Christians" (V.11). Most of Tertullian's discussion of Old Testament passages occurs in answers to Marcion's criticisms of them. There are hints of the legalistic reading of the Old Testament that was to give a very Jewish cast to the developing Catholic Church. Thus Tertullian can cite Deuteronomy's prohibition of "the reception of the Ammonites and the Moabites into the church" [the Jewish church—the use of the Christian term is significant] as supporting the gospel's command to shake the dust of the feet off against a disobedient people (*Against Marcion* IV.24). Or again, since no idolater was found in the ark, the type of the church, "let not that be in the church which was not in the ark" (*On Idolatry* xxiv).

A clearer reflection in the early centuries of the move in the direction of the use of the Old Testament as a legal guide for Christian institutions is to be found in the writings of Cyprian, bishop of Carthage (248–258). He argues that the clergy should not engage in secular work. His basis is that the Levites did not share in the division of the land of Canaan and so (which is incorrect) were not compelled to transact secular business, but received tithes from the other tribes. This "plan and rule is now maintained in respect of the clergy, that they who are promoted by clerical ordination in the church of the Lord may be distracted in no respect from the divine administration" but are supported by the contributions of the brethren (*Epistle* i.1).In a similar vein, on the basis of Numbers 20:25–26, where the appointment of Aaron as priest was made "in the presence of all the assembly," Cyprian concludes:

> God commands a [Christian] priest to be appointed in the presence of all the assembly; that is, he instructs and shows that the ordination of priests ought not to be solemnized except with the knowledge of the people standing near, . . . and the ordination . . . may be just and legitimate. (*Epistle* lxvii.4)

Many examples of this type of argument can be found in Western writers, as when bishop Callistus of Rome (217–222) justified his laxer policies on church discipline with the argument that the ark of Noah, the symbol of the church, contained both unclean and clean animals (to the horror of Hippolytus, who supplies the information, *Refutation of All Heresies* IX.7).

The allegorical and legalistic interpretations were not the only alternatives within the mainstream of the ancient church. Tertullian spoke of the Law "as preparatory to the gospel," training men gradually by stages for the "perfect light of the Christian discipline" (*Against Marcion* IV.17). He, Cyprian, Clement, and Origen all employ prophecies and types from the Old Testament as pointing toward the New. The typological, in contrast to allegorical, use of the Old Testament, in which events in the Old Testament foreshadowed the New Testament, became in the fourth century characteristic of the interpretation practiced at Antioch, whose scholars were rivals in the Greek Church to those at Alexandria. The conventional distinction between the interpretive methods at Alexandria and Antioch as allegory versus typology is recognized now to be an artificial oversimplification. The Alexandrians, Antiochians, and Latins all acknowledged the literal meaning as the starting point of interpretation, a place for nonliteral interpretations, and the necessity to find teachings that nourished the spiritual life. This historical way of looking at the Bible in terms of successive covenants and progressive revelation had important roots in the early days of the church.

Justin Martyr, in his debate with the Jew Trypho about AD 150, gave expression to the covenantal or dispensational way of looking at biblical history:

> As, then, circumcision began with Abraham, and the sabbath and sacrifices and offerings and feasts with Moses, and it has been proved they were enjoined on account of the hardness of your people's heart, so it was necessary, in accordance with the Father's will, that they should have an end in him who was born of a virgin . . . who was proclaimed as about to come to all the world, to be the everlasting law and the everlasting covenant. (*Dialogue with Trypho* 43 [cf. also 23])

Justin also says, "Some injunctions were laid on [the Jews] in reference to the worship of God and practice of righteousness; but some injunctions and acts were likewise mentioned in reference to the mystery of Christ" (*Dialogue with Trypho* 44). Because the Old Testament comes from the Father of Jesus Christ and because of their prophecies of him, Justin can argue from what is contained in "your [Jewish] Scriptures, or rather not yours, but ours" (ibid., 29). "The law promulgated on Horeb is now old, and belongs to [Jews] alone," but Jesus is "the new law and the new covenant" and his law "is for all universally," so that Christians are "the true spiritual Israel" (ibid., 11).

Irenaeus (ca. 180) gives the fullest exposition to this view, which allows full historical validity to the Old Testament, but sees it as fulfilled in Christ and superseded in the Christian age. Apart from specific interpretations of prophecies, his doctrine of the history of revelation has perhaps more to commend itself to modern views than anything found in other postapostolic authors. Irenaeus suggests that there "were four principal covenants given to the human race": those under Adam, Noah, Moses, and Christ (*Against Heresies* III.xi.8). More frequently he speaks simply of two covenants, the Law and the gospel (ibid., IV.ix.1; xxxii.2). The Mosaic Law and the grace of the New Covenant were fitted for the times; they are different, but (against Marcion) they have unity and harmony because they come from one and the same God (ibid., III.xii.12; cf. IV.ix–x). God first gave the natural law (enshrined in the Decalogue), then the Mosaic Law to discipline the Jews and by means of types to teach them the real service of God; and Christ has now fulfilled, extended, and given fuller scope to the Law (ibid., IV.xiii–xv). Christians have no need for the Law as a pedagogue, for they have a new covenant in the Spirit (*Demonstration of the Apostolic Preaching* 87; 89; 90; 96).

Irenaeus makes much of the prophecies of the Old Testament, but he insists that they can be understood only from the standpoint of their fulfillment in the Christian age (*Against Heresies* IV.xxvi.1).

With this review of the varied attitudes toward the relation of the Old and New Testaments in the postapostolic period as a background, we will now examine the New Testament attitude toward the Jewish Bible in both its negative and positive aspects.

Old Covenant Removed

No teaching is written more plainly across the pages of the New Testament than that the Old Covenant as a system of religion has been removed. A brief examination of particular passages demonstrates this teaching.

The whole argument of Galatians 3–5 is germane. Judaizing teachers, themselves perhaps Gentiles, were insisting that Gentile converts to Jesus Christ must receive circumcision in order to become a part of God's covenant people and so heirs to the salvation promised in Abraham. The issue was this: Who are the sons of Abraham and the heirs of the promises? Paul argues the case on the level of competing systems of religion—works of Law versus faith in Christ.

Paul gives three arguments in Galatians 3:1–14: (1) The argument from the religious experience of the Galatian converts—whether they received the Holy Spirit by doing the works of the Law of Moses or through faith in the preaching of the gospel (3:1–5); (2) The scriptural argument from the case of Abraham—faith was what made Abraham acceptable to God and faith marks his sons, not fleshly descent or a fleshly sign (3:6–9); and (3) the argument from the nature of the Law itself—condemnation for not keeping its demands and life by keeping them (Deut. 27:26; Lev. 18:5)—in contrast to another principle of justification, namely, life by faith (Gal. 3:10–14; cf. Hab. 2:4). Verses 13 and 14 sum up in reverse order the three arguments: "the curse of the law," "the blessing of Abraham," and "the promise of the Spirit," climaxing with the key concept of this section—faith. "In Christ Jesus" the curse is removed and the blessings come upon the Gentiles.

Paul then illustrates the promise of God to Abraham by a will (Gal. 3:15–18). The basis of the illustration is the double meaning of the Greek word *diathēkē*. The ordinary secular meaning of the word was a man's last will or "testament." The Greek translation of the Old Testament used the word to translate the Hebrew *berith,* "covenant." Since the word which might have been expected, *sunthēkē,* implied an agreement between equals, the Jews preferred *diathēkē,* which preserved the idea of God's determination of the stipulations in the covenant. The giving of the Law "four hundred thirty years" later did not annul the earlier promises (testament) to Abraham.

Paul's arguments and illustration required him to consider the objection "Why then the Law?"; the answer is that it was added because of human sins (Gal. 3:19–22). It was a moral guide and disciplinarian ("custodian" or "pedagogue"). The Law was temporary. Now that Christ has overcome sin, the Law is obsolete (3:23–25). For the purposes of this study these verses are explicit. Now that Christ has come, now that a faith system has been instituted, the Law has served its function. The Christian is "no longer under" the Law. He is "in Christ" (3:26–27). The question about the recipients of the promise is answered. Christians are the offspring of Abraham, but not the fleshly offspring. Christ and all those who are in Christ—whether Jew or Gentile—are the spiritual seed of Abraham (3:28–29). The word for "offspring" in Galatians 3:16 (cf. Gen 12:7; 15:5; 17:7, 10; 22:17, 18) is a collective noun but grammatically singular, so Paul can interpret it literally of Christ, but he brings in the collective feature at the end (3:29).

In Galatians 4 Paul continues the theme of sonship from chapter 3, employing it now as an illustration (4:1–11). The essential doctrinal argument having been made, Paul turns to a personal appeal (4:12–19). Then he seeks to clinch his case for his readers by an allegory drawn from the Law (4:21–31). It probably carried much weight with his readers but has only illustrative value to modern readers. The doctrinal position which is being illustrated, however, does have substantive value for the study at hand. When we remember that the issue with Judaizers concerned identifying the true sons of Abraham, or in other words, how one received the promises given to him, the story is aptly chosen and the allegory pointedly made. Abraham had children by two women, Hagar the slave and Sarah the free wife. Ishmael was born according to the ordinary course of nature. Isaac was the child of promise, born by the power of God long after Abraham and Sarah had passed the normal age of conception. There was a real hook for the Jews in Paul's application. The Arabs were descendants of Ishmael. If one wanted to make the promises depend on physical descent, then Arabs would have to be included. Moreover, Mount Sinai, where the Law was given, was in the territory of the Arabs. But the true sons of God are those born according to promise, not according to the flesh. Once this is recognized, there is no objection to including uncircumcised Christians among the sons of Abraham. Paul draws several parallels between the relations of Ishmael with Isaac and the relations of Jews with Christians. For the present purposes, however, note the forceful conclusion: "Cast out the slave [the covenant at Sinai]."

The practical conclusion of the arguments in relation to the issue at hand is stated in Galatians 5:1–12. To accept circumcision as a religious rite is to obligate one's self to keep the whole Law of which it was an integral part (5:3). And that is to cut one's self off from Christ (5:2, 4). To seek to be justified by the Law is to depart from and reject the system of grace. Circumcision is nothing; the Law is nothing; to be in Christ is everything (5:6). The rejection of the Law as a system of religion might seem to leave men without the moral guidance which the Law provided. Paul offers an alternative basis for ethics (5:13–25). The removal of the Law does not mean that any kind of conduct is acceptable. The choice is not between law and following the desires of the flesh. There is a third kind of life, that lived under the direction of the Holy Spirit. The personal activity of the Holy Spirit in the whole Christian people is frequently seen in the New Testament as the distinctive advance of the New Covenant over the Old (Acts 2:38f.; Heb. 6:4).

The New Covenant in Christ, therefore, is founded on the promise to Abraham, not on the Old Covenant through Moses. Behind Paul's argument for justification by faith instead of by law is his universalism. Only in Galatians and Romans, where Judaizing was a problem, does Paul make much of justification by faith. The Law was given to Jews, and one was born into relation with it. There had to be another principle of justification, available to all persons, in the new age that welcomed Gentiles. The answer was a spiritual principle: the faith principle, not the flesh principle. Under the Christian Age one has the privilege "to choose his own ancestors." He can become a part of the people of Abraham, Isaac, Jacob, et al.

Other passages may now be examined more summarily. Romans 7:1–7 declares the Christian's freedom from the Law. Paul employs an illustration from marriage (vv. 2–3). As often happens in an illustration, not every point matches what is being illustrated, but that does not weaken the force of the illustration. In the present illustration the woman's husband dies, so she is free from his law and may marry another man. In the application (vv. 4–6) the person himself dies and so is free from the Law and marries Christ. The parallel to the marriage illustration is kept to an extent in the allusion of verse 4 to the death of Christ as the means through which the Christian dies to the Law. The point is that death frees one from law (vs. 1—a good rabbinic principle), so it does not matter who is said to die. Paul may be influenced in the way he words his application by his teaching in chapter 6 that baptism is a death (vv. 1ff.). As the Christian is dead to sin (6:11), so he is dead to law (7:4, 6). The law to which the Christian died is specifically the Mosaic Law, centered in the Ten Commandments. This is clear from verse 7, "You shall not covet," as part of the Law under consideration. Freedom from sin (Rom. 6) and freedom from law (Rom. 7) do not mean freedom from moral guidance but (as in Galatians) is followed by freedom in the Spirit (Rom. 8; note especially verse 2). With the coming of the Messiah and the gift of his Spirit the Law is rendered inoperative (cf. Rom. 10:4).

The contrast between the written code of the Law and the Spirit in the Christian dispensation is stated strongly in 2 Corinthians 3:6–18. The written code kills, but the Spirit gives life (vs. 6). The theme of the New Covenant comes to the fore. The Old Covenant was a "ministry of death." This is strong language, but there is no doubt what is intended, for it was "carved in letters of stone" (v. 7). Nevertheless it came with splendor, and Paul's following verses are a commentary on Exodus 34:29–35 with its account of the glory which surrounded Moses when he came down from the mount of the giving of the Law. For our purposes we note the contrasts which Paul makes: dispensation of death and dispensation of the Spirit; dispensation of condemnation and dispensation of righteousness; what faded and what is permanent. No wonder the splendor of the New Covenant far surpasses that of the Old. The glory of the old was fading, transitory (vv. 7, 12). Paul interprets the veil which Moses put over his face as hiding the fact that the glory was fading, so Paul the preacher of the New Covenant does not veil himself as did Moses, the giver of the Old Covenant (v. 13). The veil on Moses was seen by Paul as symbolic of a veil which lay over the Law and over the Jews when they read the Law (vv. 14–15). According to the Exodus narrative, when Moses turned to the Lord, he removed the veil. Similarly when one turns to the Lord (Christ) now, the veil is removed and he can understand the Old Testament properly (v. 16). Some have understood verse 14 as saying that in Christ the Old Covenant is "taken away" or "made inoperative." The Revised Standard Version takes the "it" which is removed as the veil. The verb for "taken away" is the same as that translated "faded away" in verses 11 and 13 and "fading" in verse 7, and it is possible that the reference here also is to the splendor of the Old that fades away in Christ. That the Old Covenant itself is removed is correct to the passage as a whole. Such is implicit in the reference to a New Covenant (v. 6) and to the fading glory of the Old (v. 7) and is explicit in the declaration that the New abides but the Old is abolished or "fading away" (v. 11). Moreover, the word for "taken away" is that used in other passages for the abolition of the Law (Rom. 7:2; Gal. 5:4; Eph. 2:15).

Colossians 2:13–17 employs the forgiveness by God and new life in Christ as the basis for rejecting ritualistic and ascetic practices advocated by certain false teachers. There are difficulties in interpreting the details of the passage, but the application which is made by Paul is clear. God "cancelled" or erased the "bond" or debt of sin owed by humanity (v. 14). That "bond" consists in "legal demands" or decrees, a word which suggests some connection with the Law (cf. Eph. 2:15—"ordinances"), although the metaphor is wider in its application. Not only did God cancel the debt, but he also won a victory over "principalities and powers" in the death of Christ (v. 15). The guilt and power of sin are destroyed. The conclusion which Paul draws shows that one of the things from which man is freed by the death of Christ is the legal requirements of the Mosaic Law (human regulations as well are included—vv. 20–21). No one is to judge the Christian in the matter of the annual festivals, monthly new moon, and weekly Sabbath prescribed in the Law (v. 16; 1 Chron. 23:31; 2 Chron. 2:4; Ezek. 45:17; Hos. 2:11). These laws were a "shadow"; the reality is Christ. When one has the reality, he does not follow the shadow. The connection of thought may be something like this:

Law is the result of sin (Gal. 3:19); by reason of it one is in bondage to principalities and powers (cf. Gal. 4:8–9); when sin is cancelled and the powers overcome, law is no longer binding. Legal demands are set aside, and one is not to be judged by them.

Ephesians 2:11–18 utilizes the abolition of the Law to confirm the uniting of Jews and Gentiles in one new people of God. The religious condition of the Gentile world in relation to the Jews is painted in somber tones in verses 11 and 12. The change accomplished by the coming of Jesus is boldly stated in verse 13. What he did is elaborated in verses 14–18, developed around the theme of peace replacing hostility. Note especially verse 15. Jesus abolished the "law of commandments" in the ordinances of the Old Testament. The language employs the terminology which is normal in the Bible for the Old Testament laws. The Jewish Law was a barrier between Jews and Gentiles. It had to be removed, not only in order to open the blessings of salvation to all (as noted in the above texts), but also in order to create a new spiritual community (vv. 19–22).

The most comprehensive statement of the superiority of the New Covenant over the Old is Hebrews 7:1–10:18. The whole section is pertinent, but "of these things we cannot now speak in detail" (9:5) but can only sketch some of the main points. The superiority of the priesthood of Christ to the Levitical priesthood is emphasized in chapter 7. Christ was of the tribe of Judah, but the priests of the Old Testament were drawn from the tribe of Levi (v. 14). Christ's priesthood, therefore, must be of a different order (vv. 11, 15–17). A change in priesthood has occurred, "For when there is a change in the priesthood, there is necessarily a change in the law as well" (v. 12). No Christian rejects the high priesthood of Christ or seeks to continue the literal Levitical priesthood. Yet so integral was the priesthood to the Law that if one accepts the priesthood of Christ he must reject the Law. If one is to keep the Law, he must keep the Levitical priesthood.

Connected with the priesthood are the covenant, sanctuary, and sacrifice (Heb. 8:1–6). The discussion of these is interwoven in chapters 8–10. The change in priesthood necessitated a change in the Law on which it was predicated and to which it was central. A change in law meant a change in covenant (8:6–13). The New Covenant is better because it contains better promises

(8:6). Jeremiah's prophecy of a New Covenant (Jer. 31:31–34, quoted in Heb. 8:8–12) implied the deficiency of the Old (8:7) and the replacement of the Old, and the author can declare that Old Covenant in his time ready to vanish away (8:13).

The better promises of this better covenant are due to the superior sacrifice of the new priest. This priest offers his sacrifice in a different sanctuary—heavenly rather than earthly (Heb. 9:1–12, 23–25). Employing the double meaning of the word *diathēkē*—covenant and will—the author connects the beginning of the New Covenant with the death of Christ (9:15–17). This death is the sacrifice offered by Christ, both priest and victim (9:12–14, 26–27). The sacrifices of the Old were imperfect because they could not touch the conscience (9:9), had to be repeated (9:25), and brought a reminder of sins rather than taking them away (10:14). The sacrifice of Christ does purify the conscience, was once for all (9:26–28; 10:10), and effects an eternal redemption (9:12, 14, 15; 10:12, 14, 18). The first sacrifices are abolished by the perfect sacrifice of Christ (10:5–10). The themes of priesthood, sanctuary, sacrifice, and covenant are caught up in a summary of the whole argument in 10:11–18. Therefore, the Law was a shadow (10:1), not the substance, a rough outline without details. It has been replaced by the Christian reality.

The truth of the matter is that no one follows the Old Testament completely, or even tries to do so. Christians who appeal to the Old Testament do so when they cannot find New Testament authority for what they want to do. They employ a pick-and-choose method. On that basis almost anything can be legitimatized from the Old Testament, for all stages of human religious history are reflected in it. But the method is illegitimate. As Galatians 5:3, Colossians 2:16, and Hebrews 7:12 indicate, it is all or nothing. There are two different covenants, two different systems of religion. If one takes Christ, he has chosen a different kind of relationship with God.

Values of the Old Testament

The above passages may seem very negative. They do make a strong case. But they are not the whole story. There is a very positive assessment made of the Old Testament by New Testament writers. The Old Testament is not binding upon Christians. As a system of religion it has been superseded. Nevertheless, that does not mean that the Old Testament is valueless or can be dispensed with by Christians. Let us notice the positive values of the Old Testament for Christians.

Points to Christ

"You search the scriptures, because you think that in them you have eternal life; and it is they that bear witness to me" (John 5:39). The Old Testament points to Christ. It continues to bear witness to him (5:46–47). This is the reason that Christians can never give it up and the reason that it is not authoritative. As road signs are very valuable in directing a person to his destination but are passed by when the destination is reached (cf. Gal. 3:24–25), so the Old Testament provides road signs pointing to Christ. But Christ is the goal and the authority. One no longer depends on the witnesses when he has the object of their testimony to examine. The Jews studied the Law as an end in itself, but instead of being life-giving in itself it points away from itself.

The New Testament and early Christian authors found Christ everywhere in the Old Testament. The Gospel of John itself shows this, when it understands the heavenly vision of Isaiah 6:1ff. as referring to the glory of Christ (John 12:41). Another example is Hebrews 2:11–15, which quotes three different passages from the Psalms as words of Jesus himself. Christian preachers preached Jesus from the Old Testament, as Philip did to the Ethiopian in Acts 8:27–35.

This interpretation of the Old Testament is precisely the issue between Jews and Christians. Do the prophecies speak of Jesus, point to another yet to come, or refer to the Jewish people itself? The decision on this question is the decision of faith and is a part of the total response to the Christian message.

Shows the Unfolding Purpose of God

> The prophets who prophesied of the grace that was to be yours searched and inquired about this salvation; they inquired what person or time was indicated by the Spirit of Christ within them when predicting the sufferings of Christ and the subsequent glory. It was revealed to them that they were serving

> not themselves but you, in the things which have now been
> announced to you by those who preached the good news to you
> through the Holy Spirit sent from heaven. (1 Pet. 1:10–12 RSV)

The Old Testament gives the grand sweep of the history of salvation. Without it Jesus would seem to have come suddenly. The Christian, in looking at the Old Testament, has an advantage over the Jews, or even the prophets themselves. There is a meaning and pattern in the Old Testament that can be seen in the light of the New Testament fulfillment which could not previously be seen. The prophets spoke of the grace of salvation which now has come in Christ and is proclaimed in the gospel (Rom. 1:2; 16:26). They were able to do so because the Spirit which inspired them was the very Spirit of Christ. But they did not know of what they were speaking. They were seeking and searching concerning a truth still hidden to them. They did not know the person or the time and circumstances to which their words referred. Especially perplexing was the paradox of suffering and glory to which they testified. Their words had special reference to Christ. Thus the prophets minister to Christians. They have received the gospel through the same Spirit that had spoken through the prophets. The Spirit of Christ spoke in Old Testament prophets and in Christian evangelists. Both have words of salvation for Christians. God all along had a purpose and a plan; there was a fuller meaning in prophetic messages which can be discerned only from the standpoint of the gospel of Christ. Of this, more later.

Instructs in Salvation

With the viewpoint of the above verses, even bolder claims for the Christian value of the Old Testament can be understood:

> From childhood you have been acquainted with the sacred writings which are able to instruct you for salvation through faith in Christ Jesus. All scripture is inspired by God and profitable for teaching, for reproof, for correction, and for training in righteousness, that the man of God may be complete, equipped for every good work. (2 Tim. 3:15–17 RSV)

Whatever wider reference the passage may have, the "sacred writings" in this context refer to the Old Testament. They are able to make one wise to salvation when accompanied by faith in Jesus Christ. The Scriptures instruct one for or toward salvation. The salvation itself is by means of faith, but not any kind of faith—the faith which is placed in Christ. Once more, there is the implication that Christian faith gives a fuller meaning to the Old Testament Scriptures. Whether the statement in 2 Timothy 3:16 means that every passage of Scripture or Scripture as a whole is God breathed is much debated but inconsequential for its statement of the value of the Old Testament. The Scriptures can be used profitably for instruction or teaching, for refuting error, for correcting behavior, and for discipline or training in right conduct. They equip the preacher or teacher for every good work.

This bold statement reminds us that "the Bible" of the early church was the Old Testament. It was the basis of preaching and teaching, understood in the light of the coming of Christ and supplemented by his teaching and that of his apostles. We now have that supplement and interpretation in the New Testament Scriptures. They form the norm of Christian faith and practice.

But they rest upon the foundation of the Old Testament, which, taken along with faith in Christ, instructed men and women in salvation. Although we now ordinarily come to the Bible by way of the New Testament, the Old Testament can still serve these valuable functions for us. We hold in common with the early disciples that the Christian faith is the key and standard for understanding the old Scriptures.

Provides Examples of Righteousness

A specific illustration of the way in which the Old Testament instructs in salvation may be seen in the way the New Testament appeals to examples of virtuous living in the Old Testament. Hebrews 11 and 12 may serve to document the point. Hebrews 11 is an imposing roll call of men and women whose faithfulness commended them to God. Faith enabled them to do the things for which they are remembered:

> Therefore, since we are surrounded by so great a cloud of witnesses, let us lay aside every weight, and sin which clings so

> closely, and let us run with perseverance the race that is set before us. (Heb. 12:1 RSV)

And so much the more so because God has better promises reserved for the Christian (Heb. 11:40). The person who looks to Jesus has every reason for steadfastness in the struggle against sin (Heb. 12:2, 4ff.). The Old Testament heroes of faith remain a perennial source of encouragement to God's people. The most interesting study in the world is people. The characteristics of being human come out clearly in the Old Testament narratives. The customs may be different, but in the attitudes and behavior we can see ourselves and our acquaintances in the marvelously told stories of the Old Testament. The narratives may in fact have first taken shape as separate stories told and repeated in the oral tradition of the Hebrews. Perhaps that is why the stories of the Old Testament remain favorites with children. But they have a power for persons of every age because of their reflection of human nature. A respected psychology professor in a state university in his introduction course to psychology includes a lecture on "Why I Believe the Bible." The point of the lecture has to do with the way in which the Bible is true to human nature. All great literature would partake of this quality to some degree. But the Bible is especially effective in bringing out human motives, faults, and moments of greatness. When such persons "of like nature with ourselves" demonstrate loyalty to God, it helps us to do the same in our circumstances.

Warns of Disobedience

The same book of Hebrews, which appeals to the examples of righteousness in the Old Testament, also uses its examples of disobedience as a warning to Christians:

> Therefore we must pay the closer attention to what we have heard, lest we drift away from it. For if the message declared by angels was valid and every transgression or disobedience received a just retribution, how shall we escape if we neglect such a great salvation? It was declared at first by the Lord, and it was attested to us by those who heard him, while God also bore witness by

> signs and wonders and various miracles and by gifts of the Holy
> Spirit distributed according to his own will. (Heb. 2:1–4 RSV)

The author has demonstrated the superiority of the Son of God to angels (Heb. 1:4–14). They minister to those who receive salvation, but the Son brings salvation. Angels mediated the Old Testament revelation, as several passages affirm (Gal. 3:19; Acts 7:53; cf. Deut. 33:2). This partial revelation (Heb. 1:1) is inferior to the complete revelation brought by God's Son (1:2; 2:3). Yet disobedience to God in Old Testament times was severely punished. The Old Testament is replete with instances of human transgression and its consequences. How much more careful, then, must one be who has the benefit of a message spoken by the Son himself, confirmed by those who heard him and approved by God's miraculous gifts (cf. 1 Pet. 1:12).

Specific instances of retribution for transgression are cited in 1 Corinthians 10:1–11. The Israelites of the exodus generation knew a great salvation in their deliverance from Egyptian bondage. They had counterparts of a baptism and a Lord's Supper. Yet they fell into sin. They were guilty of idolatry, fornication, testing the Lord, and grumbling. Hence, God was not pleased with them and destroyed them in the wilderness. "Now these things are warnings for us" (1 Cor. 10:6). The word translated "warnings" is literally "types," which makes the connection between Israel's history and Christian experience even closer. The Christians at Corinth were faced with temptations to the same sins. They seemed to trust in the power of sacraments to save them regardless of what they did. The experience of Israel could serve as a warning of what might happen to them: "Now these things happened to them as a warning [typically], but they were written down for our instruction, upon whom the end of the ages has come" (1 Cor. 10:11). The fulfillment of the Old Testament has come upon Christians. They live in the overlap of the present evil age (Gal. 1:4) and the powers of the age to come (Heb. 6:5). So, although living in the last dispensation, Christians still profit from experiences of men in their dealings with God in earlier dispensations. Indeed those experiences were written down specifically for their instruction (1 Cor. 10:11). The principles of God's dealings with human beings remain the same, and so not only the Christians at Corinth but Christians of all time need to take heed to the Old Testament Scriptures and the lessons they teach.

Gives Hope

"For whatever was written in former days was written for our instruction, that by steadfastness and by the encouragement of the scriptures we might have hope" (Rom. 15:4). Paul has referred in the preceding verse to Christ as an example of self-giving love which, rather than pleasing self, accepts others in their weaknesses. He cites Psalm 69:9 as the words of Christ, as is also done in John 2:17. In a parenthetical statement Paul enlarges on his citation to affirm that all of the old Scriptures were written for Christian instruction. The Scriptures serve Christians, as our preceding citations have also affirmed. God is a God of steadfastness and encouragement, a God of hope (15:13); and, if Christians have the self-effacing and forbearing attitude of Christ, this God will enable them to live and worship together in unity (15:5–6). God has endowed his Scriptures with the same qualities which he possesses— steadfastness and encouragement. Because God and his word are faithful and consoling, his people may have hope. Biblical religion is a religion of hope. I well remember a fellow graduate student who had grown up in Burma as the son of missionaries describing the gloomier outlook among people who did not have a Bible background. Although its modern offshoot in the Western world is a secularized version, the progressive attitude toward the future is in no small measure due to the Judeo-Christian heritage. The Old Testament is character-ized by the note of hope, yet biblical religion is quite realistic about the world and life. Few (if any) peoples have suffered as did Israel. Nonetheless, there is a positive, forward-looking emphasis in the Old Testament.

Hope, in the Bible, does not refer to what one wishes for or only desires. It involves the idea of expectation and is associated with the words for endurance and faith. What gives the character of expectation to the anticipations for the future is the nature of the God who is served. His control of the world and history gives certainty about the outcome of the human processes.

Reveals the Nature of God

What was true in Old Testament times is true now. There is much biblical doctrine—about God, creation, covenant, etc.—which is simply taken for granted or assumed without being detailed again in the New Testament. Revelation of the nature of God did not have to be repeated. It is the God revealed in the Old Testament and proclaimed in the New, whose Son Jesus is. There are many references in the New Testament to God, but most of these depend on the Old Testament for their content. There are new emphases and corrections of misunderstandings, but the premises about God remain the same. The Christian doctrine of God goes beyond the Old Testament but does not contradict its teaching. Certainly more is known about God now; the Christian knows God primarily as he sees him in Jesus. The coming of Jesus has brought a new revelation of God's love. The Old Testament too had declared God's love (Deut. 7:7–8, 13). But the depth and extent of that love have been shown most fully in Jesus—his coming, life, teachings, actions, and especially his death (John 3:16; 1 John 3:16; 4:7–10). The Christian God is the God of Abraham, Isaac, and Jacob, now better known because of Jesus.

Provides a Philosophy of History and Nature

There is a biblical philosophy of history. It is not stated as such, nor is it presented as modern philosophy of history might be. Because of the longer time span covered and the special nature of the Old Testament contents, this biblical understanding of human events may best be seen from the Old Testament. Those who have cut themselves off from the Old Testament (as the ancient Gnostics) have lost a historical perspective. Briefly stated, the biblical view of history is that God is active in human affairs, that he ultimately is in control, and that he accomplishes his purposes through human processes. Persons and nations preserve their freedom, but God can still overrule and use their free choices for his larger designs. All human history is potentially open to God. He is not necessarily present in all events and in all nations, at least not to an equal degree. But all nations and all events are within his perception and providence. And he is particularly active at certain times among certain peoples. This does not violate the human and "secular" character of history. It is only by revelation on the one side and by faith on the other that God's actions in history may be known by people.

Human and world history had a point of beginning—creation. The biblical view of history is based on the doctrine of creation. The God who overrules history is the God who started the whole process in the first place. The Christian view of the natural order finds its fullest exposition in the doctrine of creation in the Old Testament. God made the world, and all the earth is his (Ps. 24:1 and elsewhere, frequently). God has given dominion over the created order to human beings (Gen. 1:28). There is therefore full scriptural warrant for the scientific enterprise. Since the world remains the Lord's, human dominion is that of a steward. Hence, there is no excuse for abuse or misuse of the natural order. Human beings are accountable to the Creator for what they do with the natural world.

Shows the Pattern of God's Revelatory Activity

There is a "pattern of correspondence" in God's revelations and saving activities. Because it is the same God acting in the arena of his own history and for the persons whom he has created, there are similarities running through the two Testaments. One of the recurring motifs of the Bible is that of the exodus (Exod. 12–15; Ps. 106:6–12, 47; Isa. 43:16–21; 63:7–64:7; Matt. 2:15; Rev. 15–16). Another common pattern is that of suffering followed by exaltation (1 Pet. 1:11; Isa. 52:13–53:12). The scope of Old Testament history once more gives one the possibility of discerning recurring correlations.

The New Testament attaches itself firmly to the hopes and expectations of the Old Testament. Perhaps one of the best ways of expressing the relationship between the Old and the New is in terms of promise and fulfillment. The Old Testament is incomplete by itself. It is looking in promise to the future. Where does one find the completeness which fulfills the Old Testament? The Talmud or the Gospels? The Jews, realizing the incompleteness of the Old Testament, have sought to make the Law applicable to ever-new situations through the accumulated rabbinic traditions of interpretation. Jesus stepped into the prophetic tradition of the Old Testament, and Christians have attached themselves primarily to the prophets and Psalms. This has continued the note of hope and given the further sense of fulfillment which characterizes Christianity.

Problems in the New Testament Use of the Old Testament

According to one count, there are 239 acknowledged quotations of the Old Testament, introduced by some kind of formula, in the New Testament; there are 198 quotations not introduced by any formula; there are 1,167 instances of Old Testament passages reworded or directly mentioned. This makes a total of 1,604 New Testament citations of 1,776 different Old Testament passages. There are many more allusions to the Old Testament and borrowings of its phrases. Most of these passages represent a straightforward, literary use of the Old Testament. The New Testament uses the Old in many ways: for vocabulary and phraseology to express its own ideas, for illustration, for proof of its statements, for moral instruction, for predictions of the new situation. Each of these and other uses could be discussed, but suffice it to say that problems in the New Testament use of the Old should not obscure the tremendous indebtedness of the later canon to the older, nor should they make that entire usage more problematic than it is.

An adequate treatment of the problems would involve looking at all the passages about which questions are raised, a task which must be left to the commentaries. Some of the principles applicable to a solution, however, may be seen by looking at three different types of problems: quotations in the New which do not agree with the Old Testament text, statements in the Gospels of the fulfillment of Old Testament passages which in their context have another meaning, and arguments drawn by Paul from the Old Testament.

Variant text forms of the Old Testament circulated in the first century, both in the Hebrew texts and in the various translations into other languages. Differences between the wording of Old Testament verses and their quotations in the New Testament are often due to the latter's following a different version from that which later became standardized by the Jews. The New Testament authors, writing in Greek for Greek-speaking readers, most often quote the Old Testament according to the existing Greek translation of the Old Testament (the Septuagint) rather than making their own translation direct from the Hebrew. Usually the Greek translation is so close to the Hebrew in meaning that the English reader is not aware of any difference. Sometimes, however, the Greek version gives a different nuance to the text (as in the Matt. 3:3 quotation of Isa. 40:3). Variations from the Hebrew Old Testament in the New Testament quotations are often, therefore, due to the use of the form of the text with which the author and his readers were familiar.

A few times a New Testament writer appears to follow the Aramaic paraphrases of the Old Testament (the Targums) in use in the Jewish synagogues (as appears to be the case with the Eph. 4:8 use of Ps. 68:18). Christianity inherited not only a Bible, but an interpreted Bible, from Judaism. When an existing interpretation of a text fits the purposes of the author, he employs it. Sometimes the New Testament writers make their own interpretations of the Old Testament and cite it according to its meaning (an interpretative quotation) rather than according to its exact wording (such may be the case in the Rom. 11:26–27 departures from Isa. 59:20–21). Or variations may simply be due in part to a free rendering as well as to an interpretive purpose (as in the Mark 7:6–7 use of Isa. 29:13). The interpretation may be effected by combining two texts from different places in the Old Testament according to a common key word or according to a common subject matter. Thus Mark 1:2–3 quotes as from Isaiah a conflation of Malachi 3:1 and Isaiah 40:3. The explanation for Matthew 27:9–10, where a passage which seems to be closest to Zechariah 11:12–13 is ascribed to Jeremiah, may be that the quotation is a composite of ideas drawn from Jeremiah (cf. Jer. 18:1–3; 32:6–15). Although not covering all the problems, these practices provide an explanation for most of the instances where some have thought that the New Testament "misquotes" the Old Testament.

Not all New Testament quotations of ancient writings are from the Old Testament, and such quotation does not confer authority on anything beyond the idea quoted with approval (as Paul's quotation of Aratus in Acts 17:28 and the quotation of Enoch in Jude 14). The source of some quotations is unknown (James 4:5), and for the explanation to some problems we must simply confess our ignorance and await further information.

A different kind of problem is presented when a New Testament author assigns a different meaning to an Old Testament text from what it apparently had in its context. The more that is learned about the exegetical practices of Jews in New Testament times, however, the more understandable the New Testament interpretation of the Old Testament becomes. The Jewish interpretations of their Scriptures are known from the apocryphal and pseudepigraphical writings, rabbinic literature, the Targums, the Dead Sea Scrolls, and the writings of Josephus and Philo. The types of interpretation practiced in these sources were varied: literal, legal and edifying reapplication, pro-phetic-fulfillment, and allegorical. The New Testament authors' use of the Old is often parallel to the kinds of interpretation to be found in the Dead Sea Scrolls (especially in the "this is that" understanding of prophecy) and in the rabbinic literature (reinterpretation of Old Testament texts for new situations, especially notable in Paul). Rarely, if ever, does the Hellenistic type of allegory represented by Philo enter into the New Testament. These various Jewish methods of treating the Old Testament text supplied the tech-niques for the Christian writers in their exegesis of the Old Testament. Such were a part of the Bible study and the communication process of the time. It would be far beyond the scope of this chapter, both in technicality and space required, to discuss these methods, but the bibliography will direct the interested reader to fuller treatments. It is sufficient for the present purpose to note that what may seem strange to the modern reader is often not so strange, or even is right at home, in the setting of first-century Jewish interpretation.

If Jewish exegesis supplied the methods, Jesus Christ supplied the formal principle for Christian interpretation of the Old Testament. His coming and his work were seen as the key which unlocked the secrets of the Old Testament. The problem of the New Testament interpreting the Old Testament in a new sense occurs frequently in citations of events as fulfilling "prophecy." It is in these situations particularly that the revelation of Jesus Christ became nor-mative for the Christian reading of the Old Testament. Various theories have been put forward to explain the phenomenon: typology (an Old Testament practice or event foreshadowed the New Testament counterpart), the "fuller sense" of Scripture (God had in mind a meaning or reference beyond what was described at the time), or "double fulfillment" (the prophet spoke of an immediate event which fulfilled his words, but a later event also fulfilled them). More important than labeling an explanation is to describe the reality. One passage may be selected to illustrate the nature of the problem and to suggest principles which may be helpful in a solution.

Matthew 2:13–15 says that the flight of Joseph and Mary with the infant Jesus to Egypt and their residence there until the death of Herod occurred in order "to fulfil what the Lord had spoken by the prophet, 'Out of Egypt have I called my son.'" The quotation is from Hosea 11:1. There is no element of prediction in the Hosea passage. It is a historical reference to the exodus of the nation of Israel, God's "first-born son," from Egypt (Exod. 4:22–23). One looks in vain for anything in Hosea's context which would suggest the life of Jesus or a prophecy of his time. A superficial view, therefore, might dismiss Matthew's statement as a misuse of Scripture, a pulling of a statement out of context and making it mean something which apparently was not intended. A deeper look, however, would suggest that this is a premature judgment. Matthew presents Jesus as the founder of the new Israel. His characteristic title for Jesus is "Son of God." Whether it be viewed as typology or "fuller sense" or whatever, there is a correspondence presented between what happened to the old Israel and the new salvation accomplished by Jesus. On this deeper level, the exodus of salvation for Israel found its counterpart in the experience of God's true Son. Jesus embodied and personified the nation, the true Israel; as such he was the beginning point of a new people of God. Jesus as the "beloved Son of God" "fulfilled" the experience of the people who were "typically" called God's "sons." In such a situation, instead of understanding "fulfilled" to refer to a prediction which comes to pass at a later time in history, we should think in terms of "this is the way God acts," "this is the pattern which is now accomplished," or "in this way the covenant promises are completely realized." When a Christian of the first century read the Old Testament in the light of Christ's coming and activities, he could not help seeing parallels (patterns of correspondence) and so understand the Old Testament in the light of the new developments. Very often, then, the presumed difficulties are of our own making when we impose our thought forms, or what we think ought to be the meaning, on the biblical texts. When we come to the Bible on its own terms and let the intentions and thought forms of the writer (which may be alien to us) determine his language and usage, then the problems or "discrepancies" either vanish or at least appear in a more understandable light.

Yet another way in which different (enlarged) meanings of the Old Testament are found may be seen in the way Paul argues from it. Galatians 3–4, surveyed above, well illustrates the complex of freedom and faithfulness with which Paul dealt with the Old Testament. There is a freedom that seems at times almost to abuse, if not ignore, the meaning of the Old Testament, which on closer look is seen to be an obedient freedom derived from the standpoint of the coming of Christ. Looking at the Law through Christ can mean a faithfulness to the Law that at times makes him a stickler for literalism. Thus he insists on the grammatical singular of "offspring" instead of the proper meaning of the word (Gal. 3:16). He gives a literal application to Christ of the curse upon one who hangs on a tree (Deut. 21:23; Gal. 3:13). On a closer look, however, Paul's use is faithfulness on a deeper level to the spiritual intent of the Old Testament. It points to faith and a life of faith (Gal. 3:7, 9); it points to Christ (Gal. 3:22, 26).

The tension between an attentive listening to the text of the Old Testament combined with a sovereign freedom in its use exemplified in the New Testament authors has remained a creative source of Christian theology throughout history. Maintaining the proper balance in the use of the Old Testament remains important for the Christian today.

*Originally printed in John Willis, ed., *World and Literature of the Old Testament,* Living Word Commentary on the Old Testament (Austin: Sweet, 1979), 346–378.

Chapter 11 Bibliography

Beale, G. K. *Commentary on New Testament Use of the Old Testament.* Grand Rapids: Baker Academic, 2007.

Bruce, F.F. *New Testament Development of Old Testament Themes.* Grand Rapids: Wm. B. Eerdmans, 1968.

Daley, Brian. "Is Patristic Exegesis Still Usable? Some Reflections on Early Christian Interpretation." In *The Art of Reading Scripture,* edited by E. F. Davis and R. B. Hays. Grand Rapids: Eerdmans, 2003.

Dodd, C. H. *According to the Scriptures.* New York: Scribner's, 1953.

Ellis, E. Earle. *Paul's Use of the Old Testament.* Edinburgh: Oliver and Boyd, 1957.

—————. *The Old Testament in Early Christianity.* Grand Rapids: Baker, 1991.

Grant, Robert M., with David Tracy. *The Bible in the Church: A Short History of Interpretation,* rev. ed. Minneapolis: Fortress, 1984.

Hall, Christopher A. *Reading Scripture with the Church Fathers.* Downers Grove: InterVarsity, 1998.

Hanson, R. P. C. *Allegory and Event*. Richmond, VA: John Knox Press, 1959. (Although primarily devoted to Origen's interpretation of the Bible, the first part of this book is a thorough study of the history of interpretation before his time.)

Hauser, Alan J., and Duane F. Watson, eds. *A History of Biblical Interpretation*. Vol. 1, *The Ancient Period*. Grand Rapids: Eerdmans, 2002.

Hays, Richard B. *Echoes of Scripture in the Letters of Paul*. New Haven: Yale University Press, 1989.

——————. *The Conversion of the Imagination: Paul's Interpretation of Scripture*. Grand Rapids: Eerdmans, 2005.

—————— and Joel B. Green. "The Use of the Old Testament by New Testament Writers." In *Hearing the New Testament*, edited by Joel B. Green. Grand Rapids: Eerdmans, 2010.

Longenecker, Richard. *Biblical Exegesis in the Apostolic Period*. Grand Rapids: Eerdmans, 1975.

Stuhlmacher, Peter. *Vom Verstehen des Neuen Testaments*. Goettingen: Vandenhoeck and Ruprecht, 1979.

Thompson, John Lee. *Reading the Bible with the Dead: What You Can Learn from the History of Exegesis that You Can't Learn from Exegesis Alone*. Grand Rapids: Eerdmans, 2007.

Von Campenhausen, Hans. *The Formation of the Christian Bible*. Philadelphia: Fortress Press, 1972. (The first part of this study of the canon considers in depth the place of the Old Testament in the church.)

Using Historical Foreground in New Testament Interpretation

If the relevant Roman, Greek, and Jewish literature, history, and customs may be labeled the "background" to the New Testament, then early Christian literature, history and practices may appropriately be termed the "foreground" of the New Testament. The use of historical background materials in the interpretation of the Bible is generally accepted and is at the foundation of the historical-grammatical approach to the Bible. Not so generally recognized is the value of early church history as an aid to the interpretation of the New Testament. What Christianity became in its early history was largely shaped by the New Testament documents, although not by these exclusively, of course. This development also deserves to be considered in attaining a proper historical perspective on the meaning of the text itself.

Two aspects of the Christian material are to be considered: (1) the actual interpretation of New Testament passages, sometimes expressed consciously and explicitly but at other times expressed only allusively or implicitly (especially in the earliest writings outside the text); (2) the faith and practice of early Christianity, which reflect the understanding of the apostolic message and often preserve early customs, presuppositions, and structures of thought. Both aspects are in view in the following discussion but are not sharply distinguished in some of the comments.

Value of Church-History Materials in Interpreting the Bible

Let it be noted that the point being made is that although early Christian materials are valuable for the interpretation of the New Testament, they are not themselves the authority. The author has no desire to substitute church tradition for Scripture as the standard for Christian faith and life, nor even to supplement Scripture as a norm with ecclesiastical tradition. The plea here, rather, is that church history may give information helpful for understanding what the Scriptures meant, or in other words, may aid one to understand and interpret correctly the biblical standard.

A knowledge of church history is essential for grasping the total historical context of the New Testament. Consideration of the background gives only half of that historical context. It tells what went before. Church history tells what came after the New Testament. Both are necessary to complete the picture that provides the proper setting for the texts.[1] It is essential to see the New Testament in its historical context. This principle has long been recognized in the study of the Bible, but the principle is imperfectly applied if the church historical foreground is neglected. The New Testament is part of a continuity from its background to its foreground. The student can more clearly define the meaning of the text and sharpen its message by seeing it against both what preceded and what followed. The New Testament is part of a historical continuum, and this total context is necessary if one is to avoid taking the Bible in a vacuum or leaving it floating in airy unreality.

The historical background and foreground set the boundaries of possible meanings for the New Testament texts. They may not tell precisely what a given text meant, but they will tell certain things that it cannot have meant and will set the range of most likely meanings. Some interpretations are historically impossible; others are historically possible. Background and foreground together determine these parameters. To give an absurd illustration, a text in the first century could not be giving a strategy for nuclear warfare, for such was unknown. Similarly, although not equally impossible, a mid-twentieth-century manual of warfare would not include a lengthy section on the use of a troop of archers. These are far-fetched ideas but may serve to demonstrate that exegesis has to do with what is historically possible. History, customs, and literature surrounding the New Testament make known what was historically possible. Even more so, they make known what was historically likely or probable in a given situation.

Even those developments in the early church that one may judge on a biblical or doctrinal basis to be erroneous may still contribute positively to a correct understanding of the text. Historical continuity requires that even error must have been derivable in some way from the apostolic setting, either as a direct line of development (but into an area outside the bounds of New Testament authorization) or as a reaction to an apostolic teaching. Thus the later developments in church history have to be accounted for from the historical circumstances that gave them rise, and these circumstances include the beginnings of the Christian movement. A scholar's understanding of early Christianity must be such as will explain the later ecclesiastical developments, even if he considers these wrong or simply unfortunate. In this regard, many have taken an unhistorical view of Christian origins or Christian teachings. (A specific illustration will be given below.) Again, it is a matter of what is possible or likely in a given historical setting: even "error" must have been of a kind derivable from what is determined to have been the "truth."

Early Christian authors, such as the Apostolic Fathers, the second-century apologists, the early theologians and anti-heretical writers, were nearer in time and place to the New Testament church than either modern scholars or even the "background" sources cited. They were therefore in a good position to preserve and transmit authentic information. They understood the customs, spoke the same language, and lived in the same tradition of faith and nearly the same historical context in which the New Testament was written. They were in a good position to preserve the original sense of a passage or intention of a teaching. They most certainly were not always right. A stream may become contaminated quite near its source, but it is much less likely to become so until farther away from its origins.

Moving from such general considerations to some things more specific, consider the meaning of words, which is determined by usage. The usage of biblical words by the early Christians and the meanings they gave to those words are important data to be considered along with other evidence in deciding the meaning to be given to a word in a given passage.[2] For instance, *cheirotoneō* became the ecclesiastical word "ordain." That meaning must be considered in deciding the meaning of a passage such as Acts 14:23. Even if not settling the meaning in a given text,[3] the direction in which the usage of a word was moving makes it possible to plot the course of development of its meaning and so helps to locate a text in that development. Sometimes the immediate background and foreground make the meaning of a word in the New Testament virtually certain.[4]

Another specific value of church-history materials to an understanding of the New Testament is in the interpretation of the Old Testament. The types of Old Testament interpretation practiced by early Christian writers would not be allowed now and there should be no desire to return to such uncritical "unhistorical" approaches. However, the kind of interpretation employed in literature close in time to the New Testament makes more intelligible the use made of the Old Testament by New Testament writers.[5] The latter were simply approaching their Bible according to the ways in which sacred literature was employed in their time. A modern scholar should not expect them to study the text the way he or she does, nor should their methods dictate today's exegesis, however theologically normative their interpretations are for Christians of all ages. In fact, New Testament interpretations of the Old Testament may seem quite sober and restrained in contrast to what some early Christian authors later did. However, even allowing for extremes, the evidence of church history allows one to see that meanings possibly strange to us were not arbitrary but were arrived at in accord with recognized practices.

Dangers to Be Avoided

Along with the plea on behalf of the values to be found in considering the historical foreground to the New Testament, certain cautions are in order. There are pitfalls that have not been avoided in the past and into which the student rushing into this area may fall.

Replacing Scriptural Authority by Tradition

This danger has already been mentioned: taking the early church, not Scripture, as authority. Some churches that accept tradition as well as Scripture as normative do this on principle. They are often as arbitrary in what they accept out of early Christian tradition as others are about what they select out of Scripture to follow. To listen attentively to the early Christian development as a testimony to the meaning of the Bible is not the same as making that development normative for present Christian practice. Nonetheless, one may unintentionally allow that development to usurp a position of authority belonging only to God's Word.

Reliance on Reverse Chronology

Another danger is perhaps closely related to the preceding: reading later positions back into the New Testament. Even someone who does not accept the authority of the early church may do this. It is often an instructive technique to take a fully developed doctrine or institution and trace it back from its fullest formulation to its roots in the New Testament.[6] This reverse historical process often reveals connections unexpected or unnoticed in the usual order of study. The person approaching the question in this way has to be especially conscious of the danger of allowing the development that did occur to control his thinking about what was true at the beginning or about what the development should have been or, under the circumstances, might have been. There were many changes in Christian practice, some occurring quite early. There were fundamental changes in the structure of thinking as the church moved from its matrix in Judaism to become predominantly Greek and Roman in membership. This shift profoundly altered the understanding of certain biblical teachings. Although this essay has argued that one should pay attention to the later Christian development, there is other evidence and other principles of exegesis (as discussed elsewhere in this volume) to serve as controls over a one-sided dependence on the Christian historical development. After all, the church's early history is to aid, not determine, the interpretation of the New Testament.

Overgeneralization

The next danger to be mentioned is of a different order. The student may take an isolated or individual view out of the historical testimony and consider it to be the general position. Of course, a single writer or source may preserve the correct understanding over against the majority position. The amateur is particularly likely to seize on an isolated quotation and attribute to it a significance it does not deserve. Such an "amateur" may be a perfectly competent scholar in some other area but not knowledgeable in church history or patristics. Here the quantity of material is important. It is more likely for an individual writer or church in a certain region to go astray than for such a thing to happen to the church over a broader territory. Given enough time, of course, this consideration diminishes in force. It is important to determine if there is a uniform testimony of many witnesses so as to establish a definite tradition of teaching. The earlier and more extensive such a consensus can be established, the stronger and more persuasive it becomes as traceable to earliest Christian times or resting on something other than individual innovation. Still, the opposite caution is also in order: a majority does not necessarily establish truth.

Missing the Writer's Purpose

The earliest Christian writers outside the New Testament text were living in a creative time. The apostolic writings were authoritative, but they were not yet collected and identified as an exclusive "canon."[7] Early second-century authors did not treat the New Testament writings as later authors did, because there was not yet an entity known as the "New Testament." Therefore, the reader has to be careful about identifying use of a given passage found in our present New Testament as a conscious interpretation of what that passage meant in its original context. Polycarp, bishop of Smyrna in the early second century, is a good example of an author who was thoroughly imbued with the language of the New Testament (especially Paul, but also John and Peter) but did not use it in a way helpful to the modern exegete. He uses the language of the text allusively and to provide a vocabulary to express his own ideas, not in order to explain the ideas of the New Testament author. The new meanings and contexts that he gives to certain passages were not misunderstandings on Polycarp's part, still less any effort to deceive. However, if one takes him as a guide to the meaning of the passages he cites, one misunderstands both Polycarp and the authors he uses. Hence, a student must be careful to determine what kind of use is being made by any early Christian author in order to assess the significance to be given to that usage in adducing it as a testimony to the meaning of a New Testament text.

To summarize, church history—that is, the historical foreground to the New Testament—is not the judge that decides the meaning of the text. Rather it is a witness in the exegete's court of inquiry. The testimony of this witness is evidence that deserves consideration and needs to be heard.

Some Examples

1. We read in 1 Corinthians 14:16 that the person who does not know the "tongue" in which another says thanks cannot say amen to that prayer because he does not understand what has been said. Both the background information about the practice in the Jewish synagogue and the foreground information about early Christian assemblies provide a precise explanation for Paul's reference. Jews and Christians alike responded to prayer in a corporate, unison "Amen,"[8] meaning "May it be so." It served as a ratification of the prayer, a way by which the whole congregation gave its endorsement to a prayer spoken by the leader and so made that prayer its own. A person who did not understand what was spoken, however, could not meaningfully join in this congregational acclamation. (It should be remembered that Paul's instructions in 1 Corinthians 14 have as their context the assembly of the church.)

The background and foreground information give an explanation of what exactly was meant by the passage. The statement does not refer to a private agreement with what was said, but rather to participation in a corporate act that was a regular part of the assembly of early Christians. The historical context confirms that Paul referred to a real "speaking" when he said, "How shall he *say* the 'Amen'?"

2. Another example of the way historical foreground gives clarity and specificity to the understanding of a New Testament text is provided by 1 Timothy 2:8. The reader might take the phrase "lifting up holy hands" to be a symbolic expression for purity of motives and life. That would be included,

but the historical context explains that something more specific provides the point of reference. Arms outstretched and hands turned up represented the symbol of prayer in the ancient world. Both literary texts and early Christian art confirm that the normal Christian posture in congregational prayer was standing with hands extended.[9] Paul was referring to this posture in prayer in these instructions (once more the Christian assembly is the context for the practice). The thrust, of course, is that these hands are to be "holy" and not engaged in wicked deeds; but the reference is still to what was actually done with the hands in the approach to God in prayer.

3. The confirmation of the correct understanding of a passage whose interpretation has been disputed in modern times may be illustrated in regard to John 3:5. The modern evangelical Protestant interpretation that "born of the water" refers to natural birth revives the ancient Gnostic effort to remove the necessity of water baptism from the plan of salvation. The uniform testimony of church history for many centuries, however, is that John 3:5 was referring to baptism.[10] In fact, one could claim that this passage was the favorite baptismal text of the early church. Only some Gnostics—and that on the doctrinal basis that material elements were bad and so could not be part of the design of the spiritual Father—denied the baptismal reference in this text. The interpretation of John 3:5 in the early church indeed provides a good illustration of the principle stated earlier that in historical development even error must be derivable in some way from truth. The emphasis on the statement that "Except one be born of water . . . he cannot enter the kingdom of heaven" led to a teaching that put the saving efficacy of baptism in the water, instead of in the accompanying response of faith. It also led to the practice of infant baptism as necessary for salvation.[11]

These developments were departures from the New Testament gospel and its emphases, yet they were possible from an isolated and exaggerated interpretation of John 3:5—but those who would dehydrate this text have no convincing way to explain these developments. If baptism had not been related positively to the forgiveness of sins and salvation in the apostolic teaching, it becomes all but impossible to account for the development of sacramental doctrine in the post-apostolic church. It is similarly all but impossible to give a historical explanation of how there was such a total misunderstanding of

John 3:5 and other teaching on baptism and salvation throughout Orthodox Christian literature in the second century. The historical foreground is a powerful argument for uniting water and the Spirit in one's understanding of baptism.

Resources and Tools

The interpreter who wants to use the Christian foreground material in understanding the New Testament is advised to obtain a working knowledge of early church history. For his course on ancient church history the author used as the textbook J. G. Davies, *The Early Christian Church*, paperback reprint (Grand Rapids: Baker, 1980) and has now written his own textbook *Church History*, vol. 1: *From Christ to Pre-Reformation* (Grand Rapids: Zondervan, 2005). For an earlier evaluation of books that would give a good survey of the field, see "A Review Article: Histories of the Early Church" in *Restoration Quarterly* 14 (1971): 205–14. There are also good surveys of early Christian literature that will give a student a working knowledge of what is available in this field: E. J. Goodspeed and R. M. Grant, *A History of Early Christian Literature* (Chicago: University of Chicago, 1966); and F. L. Cross, *The Early Christian Fathers* (London: Duckworth, 1960). More comprehensive treatments are found in the patrologies. Particularly recommended are those of J. Quasten, *Patrology*, 4 vols. (Westminster, MD: Christian Classics, 1950–86); S. Doepp and W. Geerlings, eds., *Dictionary of Early Christian Literature* (New York: Crossroad, 2000); H. R. Drobner, *The Fathers of the Church* (Peabody, MA: Hendrickson; repr. Grand Rapids: Baker, 2007).

The interpreter who wishes to make use of early Christian literature in his exposition of the biblical text now has available an excellent timesaving aid. The *Biblia Patristica*,[12] is a computer-aided publication (prepared by the *Centre d'analyse et de documentation patristiques,* published by the *Editions centre national de la recherche scientifique*). For each verse of the Bible, the *Biblia Patristica* lists the author and reference for every known citation in early Christian literature. A caution must be offered to users of these lists of references, since no effort was made to evaluate the quality of the references. If an editor of the patristic text thought he saw an allusion to the biblical text and listed it in his edition, the reference is repeated in the *Biblia Patristica*.

An allusion may or may not have relevance for understanding the biblical text, and what someone saw as an allusion to a text may not have been intended by the original author in the first place.

There are also indexes to biblical quotations in the Ante-Nicene Fathers (see below) and in most individual editions of works from early Christian literature. These may be consulted to locate references to the text being studied, although the indexes are not complete and not every patristic work is included in any set. The ordinary student will therefore have to accept that his exploration will not be comprehensive.

For detailed technical work, the student will want to consult patristic works in their original language. The latest or best editions of an author's works may be found by consulting one of the standard patrologies mentioned above or the *Clavis Patrum Graecorum*.[13] Where only the general sense of a passage is sufficient (and for most persons this is adequate), a good English translation suffices. Often the best English translation is to be found in an individual work devoted to a single treatise or to a single author, and these may be found in the standard reference works. Most often, however, the student will want to go to one of the sets of collected works. Perhaps most widely used is the *Ante-Nicene Fathers* and *Post-Nicene Fathers*.[14] It remains the most nearly complete and most accessible series, but the language and style is Victorian, more recently discovered documents are not included, and homiletic and commentary writings are for the most part not included. The highest quality of translation is most consistently maintained in *Ancient Christian Writers*.[15] The volumes in this series provide copious notes, but with a few exceptions it has aimed "to fill the gaps" by translating works not otherwise available or in need of more adequate treatment. The most comprehensive of the newer sets is *Fathers of the Church*,[16] although some of the early volumes are of indifferent quality, and the series has been more frankly Roman Catholic in orientation.

There is now in progress at the University of Laval at Sainte Foy, Quebec, Canada, a project to put on computer tape bibliographical information on all patristic literature. The project is named *Banque d'information bibliographique en patristique* (Bibliographic Information Base in Patristics). One item to be included is a listing of major treatments of biblical texts in patristic works studied in the articles included in the database. (The site is available at http://www4.bibl.ulaval.ca/bd/bibp/english.html; however, it can only be searched in French, as of now.)

An important new source for early Christian history is the Nag Hammadi Library. This is a collection of codices written in Coptic in the fourth century, but the works themselves are translations of earlier Greek writings. Most of the works are Gnostic; some were only used by Gnostics. They are being much exploited now in the interpretation of the New Testament and for understanding early Christian history. Gnosticism was previously known almost exclusively from the writings of its more orthodox opponents. Gnosticism presented a rival interpretation of the Christian message, and this material adds a new dimension to understanding the early Christian period. Many translations have appeared, notably Marvin Meyer and James M. Robinson, *The Nag Hammadi Scriptures,* revised and updated translation (San Francisco: Harper One, 2008).

The most accessible source now is the *Ancient Christian Commentary on Scripture,* edited by Thomas Oden and published by InterVarsity Press (Downers Grove, IL, 1998–), covering the whole Bible. Of higher quality but limited to selected books is *The Church's Bible,* edited by Robert Wilken and published by Eerdmans (Grand Rapids, 2003–).

*Originally printed in F. Furman Kearley, et al., eds., *Biblical Interpretation: Principles and Practices: Studies in Honor of Jack Pearl Lewis* (Grand Rapids: Baker, 1986), 254–63.

Chapter 12 Endnotes

1. J. P. Lewis, *A Study of the Interpretation of Noah and the Flood in Jewish and Christian Literature* (Leiden: Brill, 1966) provides an example by its comprehensive collection of background and foreground materials surrounding the New Testament references to the flood.

2. Unfortunately G. Kittel, *Theological Dictionary of the New Testament,* 9 vols., trans. G. Bromiley (Grand Rapids: Eerdmans, 1964–74), generally gives very brief notice to the post-New Testament usage of words. W. Bauer, *A Greek English Lexicon of the New Testament and Other Early Christian Literature,* trans. W. F. Arndt and F. W. Gingrich, 2nd ed. revised by F. W. Gingrich and F. W. Danker (Chicago: University of Chicago, 1979), now 3rd ed. by F. W. Danker (Chicago: University of Chicago,

2000) gives full attention to the Apostolic Fathers but does not include later authors, for which one must consult G. W. H. Lampe, *A Patristic Greek Lexicon* (Oxford: Clarendon, 1961).

3. See E. Ferguson, "Ordination in the Ancient Church (IV)," *Restoration Quarterly* 5 (1961): 137–139.

4. E. Ferguson, *A Cappella Music in the Public Worship of the Church,* rev. ed. (Abilene: Biblical Research Press, 1972), 1–27 on *psallō;* now 4th ed. (Abilene: Desert Willow, 2013), 9–37.

5. See E. Ferguson, "Christian Use of the Old Testament," in *The World and Literature of the Old Testament,* ed. J. T. Willis, The Living Word Commentary on the Old Testament, vol. 1 (Austin, TX: Sweet, 1979), 346–357.

6. This method is followed in E. Ferguson, "Ordination in the Ancient Church," 4 parts, *Restoration Quarterly* 4 (1960): 117–138, 5 (1961): 17–32, 67–82, 130–46.

7. For some reflections on this development see E. Ferguson's works: "Lectures on the New Testament Canon," *The Seminary Review* 24 (1978): 113–43; "The Biblical Canons," in *The Transforming Word,* ed. Mark W. Hamilton, et al. (Abilene: ACU Press, 2009), 25–32; *Early Christians Speak*, vol. 2 (Abilene: ACU Press, 2002), 1–99.

8. For some of the church history evidence see E. Ferguson, *Early Christians Speak,* 3rd ed. (Abilene: ACU Press, 1981), 80, 92, 99, 140.

9. Ibid., 137–38, esp. nn. 16–17 for some of the evidence.

10. Ibid., 34; E. Ferguson, "Baptismal Motifs in the Ancient Church," *Restoration Quarterly* 7 (1963): 211.

11. See E. Ferguson, "Inscriptions and the Origin of Infant Baptism," *Journal of Theological Studies,* New Series 30 (1979): 37–46.

12. J. Allenbach et al., ed., *Biblia Patristica: Index des Citations et allusions bibliques dans Ia litterature patristique* (Paris, 1975–).

13. Edited for Corpus Christianorum by M. Geerard, 4 vols. (Turnhout: Brepols. 1974–). One may also consult F. L. Cross and E. A. Livingstone, *The Oxford Dictionary of the Christian Church,* 3rd ed. revised (London: Oxford University, 2005).

14. A. Roberts and J. Donaldson, ed. *The Ante-Nicene Fathers,* repr. of the American Edition, 10 vols. (Grand Rapids: Eerdmans, 1951); P. Schaff and H. Wace, *A Select Library of Nicene and Post Nicene Fathers,* First Series, 14 vols.; Second Series, 14 vols., repr. (Grand Rapids: Eerdmans, 1956–1966).

15. New York: Newman Press, 1946–.

16. Washington: Catholic University of America, 1947–.

13

Jesus and Roman Coinage

The Roman Empire provided the governmental, legal, and larger social context of the New Testament. There was one aspect of Roman rule that affected nearly everyone—Roman coinage. Nearly everyone uses money. Roman rule meant that Roman coins were the standard currency for most business transactions. Various denominations of money are often mentioned in the Gospel accounts of the ministry of Jesus.

The denarius was the basic silver coin of the Roman Empire. Its Greek equivalent was the drachma. The denarius, or the drachma, was the average pay for a day laborer. The workers in the vineyard in Matthew 20:1–16 contracted to work for a denarius a day. There is other evidence that this was typical pay. In the book of Tobit, in the Old Testament Apocrypha, a companion was paid a drachma a day to accompany Tobias on a journey (5:14). The Roman historian Tacitus reports that in the late first century a Roman soldier's pay was 300 denarii a year, a little less than a denarius a day (*Annals* 1.17).

This information is more meaningful than trying to translate denarius by an equivalent in modern currency. The Authorized Version translated it "a penny"; the Revised Standard Version has a footnote that a denarius equals twenty cents; Goodspeed translated it a "dollar." Inflation and other factors make all efforts at translation into modern currency problematic. Buying power is the important thing. A denarius a day was enough for one to live on—not well, but enough for the necessities of life.

I select three lessons Jesus taught using Roman currency for illustration.

1. Government

Perhaps the best known lesson of Jesus concerning a coin was a lesson about government.

> Then they sent to him some Pharisees and some Herodians to trap him in what he said. . . . "Teacher, . . . Is it lawful to pay taxes to the emperor, or not? Should we pay them, or should we not?" But knowing their hypocrisy, he said to them, "Why are you putting me to the test? Bring me a denarius and let me see it." And they brought one. Then he said to them, "Whose head is this, and whose title?" They answered, "The emperor's." Jesus said to them, "Give to the emperor the things that are the emperor's, and to God the things that are God's." (Mark 12:13–17 NRSV)

Jewish law forbade images, and the Jews resented the loss of independence and subjection to Roman rule. Therefore, some Jews said that they should not pay taxes to Rome.

The question was a trap question. The Herodians, the supporters of the family of Herod, and so Roman collaborators, joined the Pharisees, the most scrupulous interpreters of the Mosaic Law, in asking the question. If Jesus said no to paying taxes, he could be accused before the Romans of inciting rebellion. If Jesus said yes, he would lose favor with many of his people.

It intrigues me that Jesus did not have the coin, but his questioners did. They produced a denarius. It bore the image and inscription of Emperor Tiberius.

Jesus' answer was, "Give to the emperor the things that are the emperor's, and to God the things that are God's." In other words, the coin belongs to the emperor. If you use the emperor's money, then pay his taxes. But do not avoid your duties to God.

This story teaches some lessons about government:

(1) Christians are to obey their government and not be rebellious. Christians in the early centuries did not rebel against Rome, in spite of frequent persecution. To pay taxes does not mean an endorsement of whatever the government does with the tax money.

(2) Nor do Christians deify the State. Governments of the ancient world had a sacral character. The biblical teaching desacralized the State. Rulers are not divine, even though Roman emperors were given divine honors, and the State does not have ultimate authority.

(3) Jesus' lesson on government is to pay taxes, obey it, but give ultimate loyalty to God. Some suggest that there is implicit in this story the biblical teaching that human beings are in the image of God and so belong to him.

2. Generosity in Giving

Another well known teaching of Jesus involving coins is a lesson on generosity in giving.

> He sat down opposite the treasury, and watched the crowd putting money into the treasury. Many rich people put in large sums. A poor widow came and put in two small copper coins, which are a penny. Then he called his disciples and said to them, "Truly I tell you, this poor widow has put in more than all those who are contributing to the treasury. For all of them have contributed out of their abundance; but she out of her poverty has put in everything she had, all she had to live on." (Mark 12:41–44 NRSV)

Chests were set up in the court of the temple for worshipers to make contributions.

The poor widow's gift was exceedingly small. The two coins she put in were the Greek coins least in value. Together they equaled the coin of least value in Roman currency, the quadrans. The quadrans was one-fourth of an assarion. According to Matthew 10:29 two sparrows were sold for an assarion. So, one sparrow was equal to two quadrans. According to Luke 12:6, five sparrows sold for two assarion; apparently if you bought four, a fifth was thrown in extra—the ancients too knew promotional advertising and bargain selling. A sparrow by itself sold for two quadrans. The woman's gift was one quadrans. Her two lepta had the value of only one-half a sparrow.

That information emphasizes the meager monetary value of her gift. Yet she gave more than the wealthy, if one measures what she had left.

This story presents some important lessons on generosity.

Some measure giving by the amount given.

Some measure giving by the percentage of income given. The Old Testament commanded one-tenth. Some Christians observe this standard of giving, known as tithing. It would seem that under the New Covenant one-tenth should be a floor under our giving, not a ceiling.

Jesus measures giving by the amount left after giving. A wealthy person might give 90 percent and still have more left than I do after giving 10 percent. We can be generous because God cares for his people. We can trust in him and should do so, and not trust in our possessions.

We are God's, and he wants our all. Money paid in taxes and spent on the family's needs are part of a Christian's stewardship. But the Christian looks upon all possessions as belonging to God, and himself or herself as a steward or manager of what is God's.

3. Grace

A very powerful lesson in which Jesus refers to sums of money concerns grace. This lesson is found in a parable where knowledge of the monetary values adds powerfully to the meaning.

> The kingdom of heaven may be compared to a king who wished to settle accounts with his slaves. When he began the reckoning, one who owed him ten thousand talents was brought to him; and as he could not pay, his lord ordered him to be sold, together with his wife and children and all his possessions, and payment to be made. So the slave fell on his knees before him, saying, "Have

patience with me, and I will pay you everything." And out of pity for him, the lord of that slave released him and forgave him the debt. But that same slave, as he went out, came upon one of his fellow slaves who owed him a hundred denarii; and seizing him by the throat, he said, "Pay what you owe." Then his fellow slave fell down and pleaded with him, "Have patience with me, and I will pay you." But he refused; then he went and threw him into prison until he would pay the debt. When his fellow slaves saw what had happened, they were greatly distressed, and they went and reported to their lord all that had taken place. Then his lord summoned him and said to him, "You wicked slave! I forgave you all that debt because you pleaded with me. Should you not have had mercy on your fellow slave, as I had mercy on you?" And in anger his lord handed him over to be tortured until he would pay his entire debt. So my heavenly Father will also do to every one of you, if you do not forgive your brother or sister from your heart. (Matt. 18:23–35 NRSV)

The understanding of this parable turns on the meaning of two monetary terms. The denarius, as noted above, was the basic coin in the Roman Empire, the average daily wage for an ordinary unskilled worker. The second slave had a debt of one hundred denarii. One hundred denarii was one hundred days' wages or one-third of a year's salary at something like minimum wage, or the ancient world's equivalent of a minimum wage. This was a manageable debt—what you might obtain from the bank for household repairs or a used car.

The talent was not a coin, but a sum of money. We talk about a million dollars, but you cannot go to the bank for a million dollar bill. It is a sum of money, as was the talent. A talent was equal to 6,000 denarii. A debt of 10,000 talents requires the services of a certified public accountant to calculate. It was the equivalent of 60 million denarii. A Roman soldier, paid 300 denarii a year, would require two hundred thousand years of his wages to pay a 10,000-talent debt. Jesus was engaging in hyperbole, exaggeration not intended to deceive. This was a favorite device in his teaching—for example, "strain out a gnat and swallow a camel"; a person cannot do that, but one surely remembers what Jesus said! The point of this sum of money is this was an impossible debt. The only thing I know to compare it to is the US national debt. To put this figure of 10,000 talents in perspective, Josephus tells us that the annual tribute collected by Herod Antipas, ruler of Galilee during Jesus' ministry was 200 talents. The annual tribute collected by Philip, Antipas's brother, was one hundred talents. Archelaus, the ruler of Judea after Jesus' birth, fared better; he received 600 talents a year.[1] In other words, there was no way a slave could have accumulated a debt of 10,000 talents, and no way he could have repaid it. But Jesus was not giving a lesson in economics.

The parable is a lesson on grace. This is a lesson on God's forgiveness. Our "debt" to God is like the 10,000-talent debt.

This parable is a lesson also on our response to grace. How foolish it is for us to be unforgiving of the offenses (no matter how great they seem to us) committed by others against us.

The parable needs no "interpretation"; we only need to know how it sounded in Jesus' time and the point is obvious.

Jesus used Roman money to teach some of his important lessons: on government, on giving, and on grace. We belong to God—he has first claim on our lives, our loyalty, our obedience—not to civil government. All we have comes from him; generosity in giving to God is returning to him what he has given us. God offers forgiveness of sins to us; knowing and receiving God's grace in forgiveness enables us to be forgiving to others.

*Unpublished lecture given at Southwestern Baptist Theological Seminary, March 13, 1991.

Chapter 13 Endnote

1. Josephus, *Antiquities* 17.318–20.

14

Response to Robert L. Wilken,
"Something Greater Than the Temple"

Robert Wilken's essay "Something Greater Than the Temple" sets the topic of anti-Judaism and the Gospels in the context of Christian rethinking in the aftermath of the Holocaust and the establishment of the state of Israel. Historical scholarship, no less than theology, is influenced by societal attitudes and cultural issues.

It is good that at the outset he distinguishes between the terms "anti-Judaism" and "anti-Semitism," the latter being a term that was never well chosen. As a friend of mine who lived for a number of years in the Arab world once observed, "I am not anti-Semitic; I like the Arabs." Well, I like the Jews whom I have been privileged to know; but our topic is not about racial matters.

Wilken focuses his essay on interpretations in the second century (expanded to include Origen) of selected passages in the Gospels. These interpretations are sufficient to surface three principal issues between Christians and Jews in the early history of Christianity and today.

The first is the status of the Law. Wilken is surely right that the anti-Law perspective of Christians is the important distinction. This different starting point determined the Christian stance. "Christianity," says Wilken, "is not anti-Jewish, but it is anti-halachic."[1]

A second issue is the meaning of the death of Jesus. Wilken here develops the correlation that later Christian writers (represented by Origen) made between the death of Jesus and the destruction of the Jerusalem Temple some forty years later.

A third issue is raised by the destruction of the Temple: the meaning of worship. Here, Wilken finds in Origen positive assessments of the Jewish heritage: "Salvation comes from the Jews." Indeed, on many Christian attitudes, there were significant antecedents in Judaism.

Among the many things Christians inherited from the Jews were precedents for the very attitudes now found to be objectionable or problematic. Wilken's paper provides striking examples. For instance, I found very instructive the parallel that Jon Levenson drew between the characterization of the Canaanites in the Hebrew Bible and the characterization of the Jews in patristic literature. Likewise, Josephus's correlation of the execution of John the Baptist with the defeat of Herod (as well as the prophets' interpretations of the misfortunes of the people) is parallel to Origen's treatment of the relation between the death of Jesus and the destruction of Jerusalem. In a positive vein, Origen recognized what Second Temple Jewish literature attests, that Jews too exalted a spiritual worship.

There are two ways, broadly speaking, in which Christian scholars have sought to deflect, or at least to ameliorate, the charge of anti-Judaism against early Christian literature. One approach is to argue, accurately I think, that the negative statements in the early period of the church about Jews and Jewish institutions represent a family quarrel. Similar, if not worse, negative judgments were given by Jews about Samaritans, by Pharisees about Sadducees, by Essenes about Pharisees, and so on. In our human families we say things about other family members that would infuriate us if an outsider said them. For Jewish believers in Jesus' day to say certain things about their compatriots was different from Gentiles later saying these same things. Also, it is pointed out that these negative words sounded one way when Christians were a minority struggling for survival and recognition, and another way when said many years later in a context of Christianity as the dominant religion. The situation of an intra-family quarrel has a bearing on what Wilken has described as "the dialectic that is built into Christianity's relation to Judaism"[2] (about which more in a moment).

A second approach to the "anti-Jewish" texts in early Christian literature is to present them as theological constructs. They were part of early Christianity's efforts at self-definition. It was not so much contemporary Jews and contemporary Jewish institutions that were described negatively, as it was a certain interpretation of the biblical materials. Again, at a later period, these negative judgments could reinforce negative personal feelings with unfortunate consequences, but that was not the purpose of these texts originally.

The first approach is more relevant to the New Testament period, before the separation between church and synagogue became definitive; the second approach is more applicable, although not exclusively, to the development in the second century and beyond. This second approach, the theological construct, is particularly pertinent to Wilken's discussion of Irenaeus, who was not discussing Judaism directly but Gnostics and Marcionites. Melito's sermon "On Pascha" in particular is an example of a theological construct, as Wilken portrays it. I think he is right, but it is appropriate to note, as he does, that there was a large and influential Jewish community in Sardis, a fact that surely has something to do with Melito's rhetoric.[3]

Wilken, rejecting the term "anti-Judaism" as at best a one-sided way of describing the situation, offers a third way of looking at the texts that are troublesome to modern readers within the recent historical climate. His approach is to recognize the "dialectic" inherent in the Christian position. The most that can be said for "anti-Judaism" is that it is only one part of the dialectic. Christians could never give up the Old Testament and with it the Jews, who were its recipients and preservers. It was at once the answer to the pagan charge of novelty and the verification (through its prophecies) of the Christian truth claims. The presence of living, practicing Jews, however, was an embarrassment. If the Scriptures were given to the Jews, why didn't the Jews understand them the way Christians did? The Jew Trypho could ask Justin why Christians, "professing to be pious . . . do not obey [the] commandments" pertaining to festivals, Sabbaths, and circumcision.[4] Similarly, the pagan Celsus assumes the role of a Jew to press the charge that Jewish converts to Christianity "have forsaken the law of their fathers." How is it that Christians take the beginning of their system from Judaism and then treat it with disrespect?[5] Christians were both "for" and "against" Judaism, and to dissolve the dialectic in either direction was to cease to be what they were. As Wilken's essay reminds us, everything comes down to an interpretation of Scripture. And this interpretation must be done, as Irenaeus did it, in the light of the whole of Scripture.

Wilken notes, "Once Christians dispensed with the authority of the Law, it was inevitable that Jews, who continued to live by the Law, would be the object of criticism."[6] It worked the other way too: It was inevitable that Law-observant Jews would be hostile to Christians. We should remember that in the pre-Constantinian period we have to reckon with a Jewish "anti-Christianity."[7] However, Wilken has rendered a valuable service to our discussion by lifting up the positive assessments of Jews and Judaism in Origen's comments.

The literature of the second century for the most part does not permit us to look behind the literary polemics to glimpse the actual living contact between individual Christians and individual Jews. There may have been more of this than we are explicitly told. It seems to me that the *Epistle of Barnabas* reflects real contacts and discussions.[8] Likewise, although Justin's *Dialogue with Trypho* is a literary construct, Justin's familiarity with Judaism and Jewish arguments suggests more than a bookish knowledge, so that the literary work probably reflects some actual discussions.[9] Origen had many contacts with Jews, including a "Hebrew teacher,"[10] something that may explain his favorable notices of Judaism. The theological constructs of "Judaism" may not have corresponded to what the living contacts were. My personal example comes from growing up in a strongly Catholic community in South Texas. The teaching I got in my church was strongly anti-Catholic. Yet many of my best friends in childhood were Catholic. It was as if the theological teachings and the personal relationships were two different compartments that seldom if ever met. There may have been some of that in the experience of Christians in the second century.

If we broaden our subject from the explicit exegesis of Gospel texts, we see that there were various options considered by Christians in the second century concerning their relationship to the Jewish heritage.[11] Wilken has reminded us of Marcion's total rejection of that heritage. On the opposite extreme, but with a similar result, was the *Epistle of Barnabas's* total appropriation of the Bible and its covenant for Christians with the consequence of disinheriting the Jews. Other thinkers made various distinctions within the Bible. Thus the Valentinian Gnostic Ptolemy distinguished those parts of the Law coming from God, from Moses, and from the elders.[12] The Jewish Christians known as Ebionites remained the closest to Judaism, but they claimed there were "false pericopes" that had been introduced into the Scriptures; in this way they maintained their loyalty to a Jewish way of life while rejecting large parts of the Old Testament.[13] The third-century Syriac *Didascalia,* contemporary with Origen, addressed a community in close contact with Jews. The author, perhaps himself of a Jewish background, argued that the moral law (the Decalogue) is eternal, but the ceremonial law (the "second law," in his terminology) was temporary.[14] Irenaeus developed more fully the perspective of Justin Martyr, that there were successive covenants in God's dealings with humanity so the eternal covenant in Jesus Christ has replaced the "old covenant" given through Moses.[15] This view is perhaps represented in Ignatius and drew on the statements of Paul and the author of the Epistle to the Hebrews.

As Christian self-consciousness became more sharply defined in the second century, several apologists spoke of three or four "races" of people. Their analysis closely corresponds to Origen's distinction between pagans, who worship material objects, Jews, who worship the one God with material offerings, and Christians, who worship God spiritually. The *Preaching of Peter* says, "Worship God, not as the Greeks. . . . Neither shall you worship as do the Jews. . . . Worship God in a new way through Christ. . . . We after a new manner, as a third race, worship God as Christians."[16] In a similar manner, the *Epistle to Diognetus* rejects the gods of the Greeks, credits the Jews with worshiping the one God but rejects their "superstitions"—material sacrifices, Sabbath observance, circumcision, fasts, and feasts—and praises the manner of life of Christians, who have learned the truth. The *Apology* of Aristides

(Syriac) says that there are four classes of people in this world: Barbarians, Greeks, Jews, and Christians. The detailed description of each gives superiority over Barbarians and Greeks to Jews for their confession of one God and their imitation of him in philanthropy but faults them in comparison to Christians for their observance of Sabbaths, the feast of unleavened bread, great fast, circumcision, and distinction of meats.[17] These similar arguments from second-century apologists accord with what Wilken has presented from a different group of texts: the superiority of Judaism over paganism but its inferiority to Christianity. That, historically speaking, is the "anti-Judaism" of the second-century understanding of Christianity.

*Originally printed in William R. Farmer, ed., *Anti-Judaism and the Gospels* (Harrisburg: Trinity Press International, 1999), 203–208.

Chapter 14 Endnotes

1. Robert L. Wilken, "Something Greater Than the Temple," *Anti-Judaism and the Gospels*, ed. William R. Farmer (Harrisburg, PA: Trinity Press International, 1999), 187.

2. Ibid., 179.

3. For another interpretation, Marianne Palmer Bonz, "The Jewish Community of Ancient Sardis: A Reassessment of Its Rise to Prominence," *Harvard Studies in Classical Philology* 93 (1990): 343–58; Lynn Cohick, "Melito of Sardis's *Peri Pascha* and Its 'Israel,'" *Harvard Theological Review* 91 (1998): 351–72.

4. Justin Martyr, *Dialogue with Trypho* 10.

5. Origen, *Against Celsus* 2.1, 4.

6. Wilken, "Something Greater," 187.

7. *Martyrdom of Polycarp* 13; 17; Tertullian, *Scorpiace* 10. A cautionary word on the latter is offered by David M. Scholer, "Tertullian on Jewish Persecution of Christians," *Studia Patristica* 17, no. 2 (1982): 821–28.

8. See S. Lowy, "The Confutation of Judaism in the Epistle of Barnabas," *Journal of Jewish Studies* 11(1960): 1–33; reprinted in Everett Ferguson, ed., with David M. Scholer and Paul Corby Finney, *Early Christianity and Judaism,* Studies in Early Christianity 6 (New York: Garland, 1993), 303–35.

9. See A. Lukyn Williams, *Adversus Judaeos: A Bird's-Eye View of Christian Apologiae until the Renaissance* (Cambridge: Cambridge University Press, 1935), iv.

10. See N. R. M. Lange, *Origen and the Jews: Studies in Jewish-Christian Relations in Third-Century Palestine* (Cambridge, Cambridge University Press, 1976); Paul M. Blowers, "Origen, the Rabbis, and the Bible: Toward a Picture of Judaism and Christianity in Third-Century Caesarea," in *Origen of Alexandria: His World and His Legacy*, ed. Charles Kannengiesser and William L. Petersen (Notre Dame: University of Notre Dame Press, 1988), 96–116.

11. E. Ferguson, "Justin Martyr on Jews, Christians, and the Covenant," in *Early Christianity in Context: Monuments and Documents*, eds. F. Manns and E. Alliata (Jerusalem: Franciscan Press, 1993), 395–405, discusses the topic in terms of the treatment of the Jewish Bible; see 398–402.

12. Epiphanius, *Panarion* 33.3–7.

13. Pseudo-Clement, *Homilies* 2.38; 3.52; *Recognitions* 1.35ff.

14. *Didascalia* 26.

15. Irenaeus, *Adversus Haereses* 4.32–34.

16. Clement of Alexandria, *Stromateis* 6.5.30, 41.

17. *Epistle to Diognetus* 1–4; Aristides, *Apology* 2–14.

Part IV

Restoration Movement

15

The Appeal to Apostolic Authority in the Early Centuries

The appeal to apostolic Christianity as the standard for the church in the modern Restoration Movement is comparable to the appeal to apostolic authority in the early centuries of the church. The Restoration plea was for a return to the apostolic teaching as authority for the church's faith and practice. That recognition of the teachings of the apostles as the standard for the church's life is evident also in the early centuries of church history.[1] The apostles were regarded as the persons through whom the authority of the Lord was mediated to his later disciples and as the channel through which his teachings were delivered to them.

Some General Statements about the Apostles

Eusebius summed up the view of the early church when he recorded that the Savior, "not long after the beginning of his ministry, called the twelve apostles, and these alone of all his disciples he affirmed apostles, as a special honor."[2] Paul's position was unique, but sometimes the number of the apostles was given as thirteen.[3] The church had its origin from the apostles.[4] They formed its "twelve pillared foundation."[5] With reference to Ephesians 2:20, Origen affirms that the church was built on the foundation of the apostles and prophets.[6]

The apostles were endowed with a divine power that enabled them, without the benefit of learning or eloquence, to persuade people to adopt Christianity.[7] Their mission was universal: the Lord called all nations and all languages through the apostles.[8] The teachings of the apostles converted people from impiety, stirred them to piety and faith in Christ, and enlightened souls.[9]

Moreover, the apostles govern the church: "The apostles are rulers of the church appointed by God."[10] Christ's authority is exercised through them. "In the Lord's apostles we possess our authority; for even they did not of themselves choose to introduce anything, but faithfully delivered to the nations the discipline that they had received from Christ."[11] The apostles are teachers in the church; unlike human rulers, who are in power only while alive and rule only their own people, the apostles' commands "extend to every part of the world," and their laws remain in force "also after their death."[12]

According to Justin Martyr, Christians "believed God's voice spoken by the apostles of Christ."[13] This was so because the apostles were inspired by the Holy Spirit. On Pentecost they received power from on high when they were filled with the Holy Spirit and received perfect knowledge.[14] "Christ after his ascension into heaven spoke in his apostles."[15] The oracles of God are found in the "Law and Prophets, in Gospels and Apostles" (Origen's classification of the four parts of his biblical canon), so that one who is instructed in these writings has God as a teacher.[16] Cyril of Jerusalem cited as the basis for Christians' freedom from the "legal and typical ordinances" of the Old Testament, the letter of the apostles, which showed that "though the writing was by the hands of human apostles, yet the decree is universal from the Holy Spirit" (Acts 15:23, 28–29).[17] The apostles received the Spirit and imparted it to tens of thousands.[18]

Ignatius in the early second century instructed Christians to be "inseparable from . . . Jesus Christ . . . and from the ordinances of the apostles."[19] What then were some specifics included in the appeal to apostolic authority?

An Apostolic Ministry and Church Order

The divine chain of authority and apostolic appointment of church leaders was expressed by one of the earliest post-apostolic writings, the "Letter of the Church at Rome to the Church at Corinth," known as *1 Clement*.

> The apostles were delivered the gospel for us from the Lord Jesus Christ; Jesus Christ was sent from God. Christ therefore is from God and the apostles are from Christ. . . . When they received his commands and were fully convinced by the resurrection of our Lord Jesus Christ and had full faith in the word of God, they went forth in the confidence that the Holy Spirit gives, preaching the gospel that the kingdom of God is about to come.
>
> They preached district by district and city by city and appointed their first converts, after testing them by the Spirit, as bishops and deacons of those who were going to believe. . . .
>
> Our apostles knew through our Lord Jesus Christ that there would be strife concerning the name of the episcopate. For this cause and having perfect foreknowledge, they appointed those we mentioned above and afterward gave the rule that if they died other tested men should succeed to their ministry. The men therefore who have been appointed by the apostles and afterward by other eminent men with the consent of the whole church and who have ministered unblameably to the flock of Christ humbly, quietly, and unselfishly, men who have been well testified to for many years by all, these men we do not consider it just to expel from their ministry. (42, 44)[20]

Clement of Rome here affirms as part of the divine order of preaching the gospel of the resurrected Christ and gathering churches that there was apostolic appointment of bishops and deacons for the first believers and apostolic provision for these functions to be continued in the succeeding periods of time.

We may contrast the way Ignatius of Antioch a few years later grounds his view of a threefold ministry of one bishop, presbyters, and deacons. Instead of appealing to apostolic institution of the offices, he portrays "the bishop presiding in the place of God and the presbyters in the place of the council of the apostles, and the deacons . . . entrusted with the ministry of Jesus Christ."[21] One bishop is like the one God the Father, the plurality of presbyters is like the college of apostles, and the deacons are like Christ in continuing his serving ministry. Ignatius recognized that his authority as a bishop was not the same as that of the apostles, for he could not give orders as they did.[22] As we will see below, the views of Clement and Ignatius eventually merged in the understanding that the single bishop succeeded to the place of the apostles in the church.

In the early church many manuals of church order were produced.[23] This literature about the organization, worship, and life of the church claimed an apostolic basis.[24] The earliest of these documents is the *Didache,* substantially from the late first or early second century. Its full title is "The Teaching of the Lord through the Twelve Apostles to the Nations." The claim was, like *1 Clement's* view of the basis of church organization, that its contents summarized the teaching the Lord gave through the apostles to the peoples. Its contents cover Christian living, becoming a Christian (baptism), worship (Lord's Supper), treatment of ministers (apostles, prophets, and teachers), organization of the local church (bishops and deacons chosen by the church), and the second coming of Christ.

A statue in the Vatican said to represent Hippolytus (early third century) contains a list of writings that includes the title *Apostolic Tradition.* That work has been identified with a reconstructed document formerly known as the *Egyptian Church Order.*[25] There was a tendency in the early church to make the purported author, Hippolytus, an "apostolic" figure, that is, an associate of the apostles.[26] Whether by Hippolytus, by someone else, or a "community document" that was considerably modified in transmission, the prologue (preserved in Latin) of the *Apostolic Tradition* declares that it is setting down the "tradition which has remained up to now" so that "those who preside over the church ought to hand on and preserve all things." The conclusion (according to the Sahidic version) affirms, "If everyone follows the traditions of the apostles, these things that they heard and kept, no heretic will be able to lead them astray" (43). The contents cover the appointment and duties of various functionaries in the church, the Eucharist, the initiation of new converts, community meals, and prayer.

One of the textual witnesses to the *Apostolic Tradition* is the *Canons of Hippolytus* from Egypt, now dated to the fourth century. Its preface states, "Here are the canons and precepts of the church which Hippolytus, head of bishops of Rome, wrote according to the commands of the apostles from the Holy Spirit which were spoken by him."

The Didascalia, preserved in entirety in Syriac, has as its full title *The Catholic Didascalia,* that is teaching, *of the Twelve Holy Apostles and Disciples of our Savior.* Going beyond presenting its contents as summarizing apostolic directives, the *Didascalia* claims direct apostolic authorship. Its opening contains the exhortation (preserved also in Latin, which I translate): "You who long for his promise, hear the sacred teaching given by the command of the Savior and in agreement with his glorious utterances." There is an elaborate setting of the scene of authorship of the document by the apostles when gathered in Jerusalem at the council described in Acts 15 (chap. 24–25). "We" (apostles) gave our teaching and practice "in every city throughout the whole world"; "we gave [our] testimony and left this catholic teaching worthily and justly to the catholic church for a memorial for the confirmation of the faithful" (25). The contents include sexual purity, the office of the bishop, lawsuits among Christians, worship, widows, deacons and deaconesses, orphans and bringing up children, martyrs, the Paschal fast, the danger of heresies and schisms, and the relation of Christianity to the ceremonial legislation of the Old Testament.

The *Apostolic Church Order,* perhaps around 300 in Egypt, declares itself the canons of the apostles for the direction of the church. It takes the fiction of apostolic authorship further and distributes each of its directives among the individual apostles. They are named in a peculiar order, and the number twelve is achieved by listing Peter and Cephas separately and substituting Nathaniel for Thaddaeus. The contents give a version of the two ways of life and death very close to the *Didache* and directions for the appointment of a bishop, presbyters, reader, deacons, and widows, while excluding women from the ministry of sacrificing the body and blood.

The *Apostolic Constitutions* and the appended *Apostolic Canons* come from the late fourth century in Syria or Asia Minor. Book 8 continues the practice of assigning separate regulations to the individual apostles, including Paul and James, the Lord's brother. The setting is indicated by the opening words, borrowed from Acts 15:23, "The apostles and elders to all those who from among the Gentiles have believed in the Lord Jesus Christ" (1 preface). Later the document says that the twelve apostles were joined by Paul, "chosen vessel and fellow-apostle"; James the bishop; the rest of the presbyters; and the seven deacons (in Jerusalem) "to give charge those divine constitutions concerning every ecclesiastical form."[27] The final text of the work claims to come through the hand of Clement of Rome.[28] The *Apostolic Canons* have as their title "The Ecclesiastical Canons of the Same Holy Apostles," continuing the claim that the apostles legislated the future order of the church. The *Apostolic Constitutions* is a compilation and rewriting of the *Didache, Didascalia,* and *Apostolic Tradition,* and incorporates other material as well. Its contents concern the laity, ecclesiastical offices, widows, orphans, martyrs, schisms, Christian morality, initiation into the church, spiritual gifts, the Eucharist, ordination, and discipline.

The *Testament of the Lord,* from Syria or Asia Minor in the fourth or fifth century, is preserved in Syriac, Arabic, and Ethiopic. It asserts more authority than the other church orders by presenting itself as Jesus' instructions to his disciples during the time between his resurrection and ascension, but these regulations are delivered through the apostles. The work contains an apocalypse at the beginning (cf. the conclusion of the *Didache*). The church order proper covers such things as the various ministers of the church, ordination, Christian initiation, Eucharist, daily prayer, church architecture, and the liturgical year.

A distinctive document is the Syriac *The Teachings of the Apostles,* known from a manuscript of the fifth/sixth century. It expresses the characteristic Syriac concern with the transmission of the priesthood, saying that the Lord at his ascension gave to the eleven disciples "the right hand of priesthood of the house of Moses and Aaron."[29] On Pentecost, the apostles, by the same gift of the Spirit they received on that day, appointed ordinances and laws regarding days of worship, worship activities, and church ministers. The document includes a listing of the countries to which the different apostles went to preach.

"One truth was preached by them all, that one Spirit spake in them all from one God.... Everything, therefore, which had been spoken by our Lord by the hand of the apostles, and the apostles had delivered to their disciples, was believed and received in every country."[30] With the emphasis that the apostles provided the directions for the church, it is understandable that when a clause on the church was included in the Nicaeno-Constantinopolitan Creed, the description was "one, holy, catholic, and apostolic church."

The extensive church order literature, widely used and translated, shows how uninformed was A. T. DeGroot's contention that the early church had no interest in a pattern of external forms.[31] It is true that these forms evolved through the early centuries, but what is significant is that compilers of these writings did not justify the developments as indifferent options but clothed them with the mantle of apostolic institution and viewed their decrees as applying in great detail to all aspects of the whole church. It is notable that the church orders represent themselves as presenting the instructions of all the apostles; even when the directions are distributed among the individual apostles, the composite is set forth as agreed on by all. With the changes that took place in the church's organization and practices, the instructions were updated but were still claimed to represent what the apostles had delivered to the churches. It would have been better to go back to what the apostles had actually established in the churches instead of ascribing apostolic authority to the changes, but the churches did not want to admit that their practices were anything other than apostolic. This approach led to the Roman Catholic and Greek Orthodox claim to represent the apostolic church and to have continuity with the early church, but at best this is a bare historical sequence, not a true continuity in maintaining the same organization and practice.

Part of the apostolic claim was to give greater prominence to churches of apostolic foundation. Often the prominence rested on other grounds as well, but significant for the important churches was their connection with a founding apostle or apostolic figure. Thus the church at Rome was honored as having been founded by Paul and Peter.[32] The church at Antioch looked back to Peter as the one who laid its foundation and ministered there as priest (bishop).[33] The church at Alexandria claimed Mark as its founder and first bishop.[34] The church at Ephesus had the burial place of John.[35] Constantinople was a later foundation, but an apostolic connection was established by bringing the relics of Andrew there in 357.[36] Tertullian, while giving prominence to churches founded by apostles, affirmed that other churches derived from them were also apostolic if they shared the same faith:

> [The apostles] founded churches in every city, from which all the other churches, one after another, derived the tradition of the faith and the seeds of doctrine, and are every day deriving them that they may become churches. Indeed, it is on this account only that they will be able to deem themselves apostolic, as being the offspring of apostolic churches. . . . Therefore the churches, although they are so many and so great, comprise but the one primitive church, founded by the apostles, from which they all derive. In this way all are primitive and all are apostolic.[37]

A special form of the association of churches with the apostles was the doctrine of the apostolic succession of bishops.[38] The doctrine was developed in order to counter claims by heretics that their teachings were derived through a succession of teachers going back to the apostles. Thus Basilides claimed as his teacher Glaucias, the interpreter of Peter, and Valentinus was said to have been a hearer of Theudas, a pupil of Paul.[39] Valentinus's student Ptolemy promised a special knowledge to Flora if she is "deemed worthy of the apostolic tradition which we too have received from a succession."[40] In Irenaeus's response on behalf of the Orthodox, the succession of true teaching was that preserved by the holders of the teaching chairs in the churches of apostolic foundation, including their presbyters as well as bishops.[41] What was originally a succession *from* the apostles became a succession *of* the apostles so that the bishops were regarded as fulfilling something of the same place in the church as the apostles had.[42] In the fourth and fifth centuries, apostolic succession became the succession from ordainer to ordained.

An Apostolic Worship

The church orders contain various regulations pertaining to worship—observance of the Eucharist, arrangements for the assembly, times and wording for prayers, love feasts, and fasts. The fullest of the liturgies contained in the church orders is found in *Apostolic Constitutions* 8.4–15. It is sometimes called the Clementine Liturgy because Clement of Rome was the purported transmitter of these pseudo-apostolic regulations for the church, but it likely comes from the region of Antioch. Although carrying a weighty claim and containing some early elements, this liturgy may never have actually been used.

When full liturgies that were in actual use came to be written in the fourth and fifth centuries, they were ascribed to the apostolic circles and apostolic times if not to an actual apostle. The liturgy of Jerusalem, known as the *Liturgy of James,* carries the title "The Divine Liturgy of James, the Holy Apostle and Brother of the Lord."[43] The title of the liturgy of Alexandria, the *Liturgy of Mark,* is "The Divine Liturgy of the Holy Apostle and Evangelist Mark, Disciple of the Holy Peter." At the end of the long Eucharistic prayer (the Anaphora), the same language occurs: "Remember . . . our holy father Mark, the apostle and evangelist who made known to us the way of salvation."[44] An early Syriac text still in use with elaborations, the *Liturgy of Addai and Mari,* carries the title "The Liturgy of the Blessed Apostles Composed by St. Adaeus [Thaddaeus] and St. Maris [his pupil], Teachers of the Easterns." The apostle Thaddaeus and his follower Mari (sometimes included among the seventy of Luke 10:1) were the traditional founders of the church at Edessa.

The liturgies of Constantinople, the Byzantine rite, acknowledged a later origin by carrying the names of Basil the Great (the liturgy for special festival days) and John Chrysostom (the ordinary liturgy). The service presented in these liturgies was in two parts: that to which all could attend and that which was reserved for the faithful (the Eucharist). By the length of the accounts and the details given, it is evident that the Eucharist was the center and substance of the Sunday assembly.

An Apostolic Faith

In opposing ideas judged to be heretical, church leaders appealed to the teaching of the apostles. Thus Ignatius resisted those who followed Jewish practices with the command, "Give diligence to be confirmed in the decrees of the Lord and the apostles,"[45] and those who denied the reality of Jesus' flesh and passion (Docetists) with the instruction, "All of you should follow the bishop as Jesus Christ follows the Father, and follow the presbytery as the apostles."[46]

The principal objection against Montanism was that its ecstatic manner of prophesying did not accord with the manner of prophesying in the Old Testament and New Testament, but the practice of the apostles was also brought into the argument. An unidentified source from the second or third century quoted extensively by Epiphanius in the fourth century concluded that the Montanist prophetesses Priscilla and Maximilla did not prophesy "after the prophecies which were approved by the holy apostles in the holy church." Again he asserted, "The holy prophets and the holy apostles prophesied in a manner similar to one another."[47]

Tertullian opposed Marcion's teachings of two gods by appealing to the faith in the Creator by the churches of apostolic origin.[48] His *Prescription against Heretics* (Marcion and Gnostics) makes repeated appeal to the apostles (some of what he argued is referred to above). Against the claims by heretics to a connection with the apostles, he asked, "Do we prove the faith by the persons, or the persons by the faith?"[49] His subsequent argument shows that, although the faith was first delivered by the human intermediaries, by his time the faith itself judged teachers. Against the heretics' misuse of the text, "Seek and you shall find" (Matt 7:7), Tertullian replied that "our instruction" comes by the apostles, "who were appointed to be teachers of the nations" and had for their teacher the Holy Spirit.[50] Hence, it is necessary to agree with the apostles' teaching, for Christ gave his revelation of the Father to no others than the apostles whom he sent forth to preach. That teaching is found, Tertullian argued, in the churches founded in person by the apostles, whether by spoken word or later in writings, for these churches "received [it] from the apostles, the apostles from Christ, Christ from God," and anything contrary "to the truth of the churches and apostles of Christ and God" must be judged false.[51] Later teachings that "had no existence in the time of the apostles could not possibly have had any connection with the apostles."[52]

Several early Christian writers set forth summaries of the apostolic preaching,[53] known as the "canon [or standard] of truth"[54] or "rule of faith."[55]

Irenaeus declared that "the church, although dispersed throughout the whole world . . . received from the apostles and their disciples the faith in one God the Father Almighty . . . , in one Christ Jesus the Son of God . . . , and in the Holy Spirit."[56] Origen echoed the thought: "The holy apostles, when preaching the faith of Christ, took certain doctrines, those namely which they believed to be necessary ones, and delivered them in the plainest terms to all believers."[57] He continues by summarizing the doctrines delivered by the apostles and to be believed through their teaching: the one God, Christ Jesus, the Holy Spirit, the soul, free will, devil and his angels, destruction of the world, and inspiration of the Scriptures.[58]

This faith came to be used as the confession at baptism and was called the Apostles' Creed, or Apostles' Symbol.[59] The baptismal confession of faith took the form of three questions (arranged according to Father, Son, and Holy Spirit); to each the candidate responded "I believe." This practice led in the fourth century to putting the content of the questions in declaratory form, and this positive statement was delivered to the candidates for baptism as a summary of the Christian faith that they were expected to memorize and recite before their baptism.

The name "Creed" or "Symbol" referred to a summary of the faith and was called apostolic, indicating that this faith went back to what the apostles had taught and delivered to the church. Comparable to the way in which there was a move from a presentation of the order the apostles had left for the church to a claim of direct delivery of specific instructions, the title Apostles Creed came to be taken literally to refer to a composition by the apostles and not simply a summary of the faith they had taught.[60] About the same time that the prescriptions in regard to church order were distributed among the individual apostles in the late fourth century, the parts of the Apostles Creed were assigned to individual apostles.

About 404 Rufinus of Aquileia wrote a *Commentary on the Apostles' Creed*. He refers to a tradition that before the apostles left Jerusalem to go to different countries to preach the word of God, they met to draw up a short summary of their preaching:

> When they were on the point of taking leave of each other, they first settled on a common form for their future preaching, so

that they might not find themselves, widely dispersed as they would be, delivering divergent messages to the people they were persuading to believe in Christ. So they all assembled in one spot and, being filled with the Holy Spirit, drafted this short summary . . . each contributing the clause he judged fitting; and they decreed that it should be handed out as standard teaching to converts.[61]

Rufinus's suggestion that each of the Twelve contributed one clause was elaborated by dividing the Creed into twelve articles, each assigned to one of the apostles.[62]

Creeds by the third and fourth centuries began to be used as tests of Orthodoxy. A decisive development in this usage occurred at the ecumenical council of Nicaea in 325. The creed adopted there was likely a local baptismal confession reworded to counter the teachings of Arius about the Son of God. Athanasius reports that the debate at Nicaea revolved around the interpretation of Scripture, and when the Arians gave their own interpretation of the wording of Scripture, it became necessary to employ terminology from outside Scripture to make its meaning clear.[63] The Nicene Creed, after a half century of continued controversy, came to be accepted as enshrining the apostolic faith. In the words of Epiphanius: "This holy faith of the catholic church, as the holy and only virgin of God received it from the holy apostles of the Lord as a trust to be preserved" and after quoting the creed, "This faith was handed down from the holy apostles."[64]

An Apostolic Scripture

By the latter part of the second century, even for someone such as Irenaeus, who was only the second generation removed from an apostle, the apostolic teaching was transmitted primarily, if not exclusively, in writing. Irenaeus identifies the four Gospels as the "Gospels of the apostles," "handed down from the apostles."[65] Clement of Alexandria, during the same period, uses the terms "prophets" and "apostles" as a shorthand for the two parts of Scripture.[66]

Tertullian, writing *Against Marcion* at the beginning of the third century, stated, "The evangelical Testament has apostles for its authors, to whom was assigned by the Lord himself this office of publishing the gospel" (4.2).

Tertullian was using "apostle" in a broad sense, for a little later in the passage he identified John and Matthew as apostles and Luke and Mark as "apostolic men." Throughout his polemical and ethical treatises Tertullian argued his points from the Scriptures, especially those of the New Testament.[67]

The name of an apostle attached to a writing gave an acceptance to it. Thus when bishop Serapion of Antioch was introduced to the *Gospel of Peter,* he initially allowed it to be read. On closer examination he found it suspect of Docetism. He pronounced this judgment: "We receive both Peter and the other apostles as Christ, but the writings which falsely bear their names we reject, as men of experience, knowing that such were not handed down to us."[68]

An apostolic name was not sufficient by itself to secure acceptance of a writing, for its teaching must also be correct and the work must have been handed down, thus not a newly discovered writing. Peter's was the most popular name to be assigned to apocryphal works; in addition to the *Gospel* there were *Acts of Peter, Apocalypse of Peter,* and an apologetic work *Preaching of Peter.* The apocryphal literature of the early church often claimed a connection with an apostle: *Gospel of Thomas, Gospel of Philip, Epistle of the Apostles, Apocalypse (or Vision) of Paul.* The fascination with the apostles is especially evident in the apocryphal Acts: *Acts of Paul, Acts of Peter, Acts of John, Acts of Thomas, Acts of Andrew*—to name only the earliest representatives. Since many of these works advanced ideas of doubtful orthodoxy, this phenomenon of attaching the name of an individual apostle to certain works may be a factor in the emphasis on the involvement of all the apostles in the production of the church orders and the Apostles' Creed.

Such tests as Serapion came to apply to the *Gospel of Peter* are often called criteria of canonicity. They might be applied to a writing previously unknown, but for the most part they were not standards invoked in a process of settling the canon. The apocryphal and other non-apostolic writings were not "excluded" from the canon, for they never were in it to be excluded. The criteria of canonicity were mainly expressed after the fact, that is to identify the characteristics of the books received because they had been handed down in the church from its early days.[69] How this functioned may be seen in the *Muratorian Canon.*

In explaining the acceptance of certain writings and the rejection of others, the unknown compiler of the *Muratorian Canon* appeals to the inspiration by the Spirit of the four Gospels, the applicability of Paul's letters and Revelation to the whole church, the lack of agreement with received teaching by the letters to the Laodiceans and to the Alexandrians, and public reading in the assembly (*The Shepherd of Hermas* was not to be read). Among these criteria was apostolicity, or origin in the circle of an apostle. The author emphasizes that Mark, John, and the author of Acts were eyewitnesses. All the apostles are said to have certified the Fourth Gospel. On the basis of antiquity, *The Shepherd of Hermas* was rejected because it was written "quite recently."

The criterion of apostolicity was flexible, for actual authorship by an apostle was not a necessary requirement, but a writing had to come from an associate of an apostle and be accepted by an apostle.

Conclusion

This collection of evidence is not intended as an acceptance of the historical accuracy or of the theology of all the claims made in regard to the apostles in early Christian literature. Rather, I seek to demonstrate the general recognition of the authority of the apostles in matters of church order as well as of doctrine and of the Scriptures as the primary depository of apostolic teaching. My case is indeed made even more convincingly by the invocation of the apostles where there was little or no basis for the claims. The early church could more easily have justified its position on other grounds had it not felt compelled theologically to base its faith and practice on apostolic teaching and example. That would seem to be the proper position for Christians today.

Again today, as in the early centuries, there is a question of where one finds the correct picture of Jesus and of authentic Christian faith.[70] Orthodox Christianity, in contrast to heretical versions ancient and modern, answers, "In the teaching and practice of the apostles." Where is that to be found? Tradition as well as Scripture says in the Scriptures:

> For we have learned the plan of our salvation through no others than those [the apostles] through whom the gospel came to us. They did at one time proclaim it and later truly by the will of

God they delivered it to us in the Scriptures, the foundation and support of the faith of us who came later.[71]

We have as the source of teaching the Lord through the Prophets, through the Gospel, and through the blessed Apostles "in many and various ways" [Heb. 1:1] . . . The person who is faithful to the Lord's Scripture and voice that are made effective by the Lord for the benefit of human beings is properly considered a believer. . . . We give a complete demonstration concerning the Scriptures from the Scriptures themselves.[72]

[The church in Rome (but representative here of all churches)] combines in one volume the Law and Prophets with the Writings of evangelists and apostles, from which she drinks in her faith. . . . From the Scriptures we have our being.[73]

*Originally printed in *Restoration Quarterly* 50 (2008): 49–62.

Chapter 15 Endnotes

1. Several articles in A. Hilhorst, ed., *The Apostolic Age in Patristic Thought* (Leiden: Brill, 2004), are relevant to the topics discussed below.

2. Eusebius, *Church History* 1.10.5(7).

3. *Apostolic Constitutions* 8.46. More typical is Athanasius, *Discourses against the Arians* 2.27, "Twelve apostles and Paul."

4. Irenaeus, *Against Heresies* 3.12.7.

5. Ibid., 4.21.3. Cf. Origen, *Against Celsus* 3.28 for the apostles as the foundation of Christianity.

6. Origen, *Commentary on John* 10.39.228; cf. 268.

7. Origen, *Against Celsus* 1.62; 8.47.

8. Hippolytus, *Commentary on Daniel* 4.9.2.

9. Methodius, *On Things Created* 1.

10. John Chrysostom, *Homilies on the Beginning of Acts* 3.4.

11. Tertullian, *Prescription against Heretics* 6.

12. John Chrysostom, *Commentary on Psalms* 45 (44).16.

13. Justin, *Dialogue with Trypho* 199.6.

14. Irenaeus, *Against Heresies* 3.1.1.

15. Origen, *On First Principles* preface 1; cf. 3.3.4, for the prophets and apostles attending to the divine oracles.

16. Origen, *Homilies on Jeremiah* 10:1; he continues saying that the Father teaches either by himself, through Christ, in the Holy Spirit, or through Paul, Peter, or one of the other saints, "provided only that the Spirit of God and the Word of God dwell and teach."

17. Cyril of Jerusalem, *Catechetical Lectures* 17.29.

18. John Chrysostom, *Homilies on John* 51.2.

19. Ignatius, *Trallians* 7.1; cf. *Magnesians* 13.1 quoted at n. 44.

20. Translation from Everett Ferguson, *Early Christians Speak*, 3rd ed. (Abilene: ACU Press, 1999), 163–64, and discussion (167–69). Older interpretations of the passage are discussed in my "Church Order in the Sub-Apostolic Period: A Survey of Interpretations," *Restoration Quarterly* 11 (1968): 225–48. Important articles on the development of ideas in regard to the ministry and organization of the early church are collected in Everett Ferguson, ed., *Church, Ministry, and Organization in the Early Church Era,* Studies in Early Christianity 13 (New York: Garland/Taylor and Francis, 1993).

21. Ignatius, *Magnesians* 6.1; cf. *Trallians* 3.1; and *Smyrnaeans* 8.1. The apostles are called the "presbytery of the church" in *Philadelphians* 5.1.

22. Ignatius, *Romans* 4:3; *Trallians* 3.3.

23. Joseph G. Mueller, "The Ancient Church Order Literature: Genre or Tradition?" *JECS* 15 (2007): 337–80, argues that the description "church orders" as a literary genre is inappropriate (he would place these writings in a tradition of ecclesiological Old Testament exegesis that developed into a doctrine of community life), but the labels placed on the works I mention do not affect the argument of this paper (although a tradition parallel to Jewish halakha and Haggadah would account for how something claiming to be "apostolic" was capable of revision to adapt to new situations).

24. A. F. Walls, "A Note on the Apostolic Claim in the Church Order Literature," *Studia Patristica* 2 (1957): 83–92.

25. For a history of scholarship on the work and the complicated literary relations of the witnesses to the text, see the introduction in Paul F. Bradshaw, Maxwell E. Johnson, and L. Edward Phillips, *The Apostolic Tradition*, Hermeneia: A Critical & Historical Commentary on the Bible (Minneapolis: Fortress, 2002), 1–17.

26. Allen Brent, *Hippolytus and the Roman Church in the Third Century*, *VC* Supp. 31 (Leiden: Brill, 1995), 183.

27. *Apostolic Constitutions* 8.4.1.

28. *Apostolic Constitutions* 8.46; *Apostolic Canons* 85.

29. Translation by W. Cureton, *Ancient Syriac Documents* (London, 1864; repr. Amsterdam: Oriental Press, 1967), 24; also by B. P. Pratten in *Ante-Nicene Fathers* (repr. Peabody: Hendrickson, 1994), 8.667.

30. Cureton, *Ancient Syriac Documents,* 32.

31. Alfred T. DeGroot, *The Restoration Principle* (St. Louis: Bethany, 1960), 25–75.

32. Irenaeus, *Against Heresies* 3.3.2.

33. Cureton, *The Teaching of the Apostles in Ancient Syriac Documents,* 33. Leo the Great, writing to Maximus, bishop of Antioch, recalled that Peter laid the foundation of the church by his teaching in Antioch and Rome (*Letter* 119.2).

34. Eusebius, *Church History* 2.16.1; 2.24.

35. Ibid., 3.1.1.

36. From the seventh century he was regarded as the founder of the church of Constantinople (George D. Dragas, "Andrew," in Everett Ferguson et al., eds., *Encyclopedia of Early Christianity*, 2nd ed. [New York: Garland/Taylor and Francis, 1997], 1.50–51). The Syriac *The Teaching of the Apostles* (n. 27) assigns the foundation of the church there to Luke.

37. Tertullian, *Prescription against Heretics* 20.

38. Everett Ferguson, *From Christ to Pre-Reformation*, Church History, vol. 1: (Grand Rapids: Zondervan, 2005), 107–9.

39. Clement of Alexandria, *Miscellanies* 7.17.

40. Quoted by Epiphanius, *Panarion* 33.7.

41. Irenaeus, *Against Heresies* 3.2.2; 3.3.1–3; 4.26.2, 5. Note 3.3.1, where the apostles appoint as bishops those to whom they would have imparted any secrets, if they had any such secret teachings to give.

42. Hippolytus (?), *Refutation of All Heresies,* pref.; Cyprian, *Letters* 64.3; 66.4.

43. Greek texts of the liturgies and English translation of liturgies in eastern languages in F. E. Brightman, *Liturgies Eastern and Western* (vol. 1 in *Eastern Liturgies;* Oxford: Clarendon, 1896).

44. Brightman, *Liturgies,* 128, ll.27–29.

45. Ignatius, *Magnesians* 13.1.

46. *Smyrnaeans* 8.1.

47. Epiphanius, *Panarion* 48.2.1–2; 48.8.1.

48. Tertullian, *Against Marcion* 1.21.

49. Tertullian, *Prescription against Heretics* 3.

50. Ibid., 8; cf. 20 for the twelve apostles appointed to be the teachers of the nations and receiving the power of the Holy Spirit.

51. Ibid., 2.1. Cf. 37 for the truth "which the church has handed down from the apostles, the apostles from Christ, and Christ from God."

52. Ibid., 34.

53. Some of these are translated in Ferguson, *Early Christians Speak,* 19–22.

54. The phrase is in Irenaeus, *Against Heresies* 2.27.1 in a context discussing the right interpretation of the "sacred Scriptures." Valdemar Ammundsen, "The Rule of Truth in Irenaeus," *Journal of Theological Studies* 13 (1912): 574–80; repr. in Ferguson, *Orthodoxy, Heresy, and Schism in Early Christianity,* Studies in Early Christianity 4 (New York: Garland 1993), 138–44, where the "canon of truth" means truth itself as the standard. The phrase is also in Clement of Alexandria, *Miscellanies* 6.15.124–25 for explaining the Scriptures.

55. Tertullian, *Prescription against Heretics* 12–13 for this rule taught by Christ and 14 for the "records of the faith" being the Scriptures; *Against Praxeas* 2 for this rule coming down from the beginning of the gospel; *On the Veiling of Virgins* 1.

56. Irenaeus, *Against Heresies* 1.10.1; Ferguson, *Early Christians Speak,* 20, for the whole passage. Similar statements in Irenaeus, *Proof of the Apostolic Preaching* 6 and *Against Heresies* 4.33.7, which is followed by the statement that "true knowledge is the doctrine of the apostles and the ancient constitution of the church throughout the world" (4.33.8).

57. Origen, *On First Principles* 1, preface 3–8. Albert C. Outler, "Origen and the *Regulae fidei,*" *Church History* 8 (1939): 212–21.

58. Ibid.

59. For bibliography see my survey of recent study of the Apostles Creed in "Creeds, Councils, and Canons," in Susan Ashbrook Harvey and David Hunter, eds., *The Oxford Handbook of Early Christians Studies* (Oxford: Oxford University Press, 2008), 427–45.

60. *Apostolic Constitutions* 6.14 includes a summary of the catholic doctrine written by the twelve apostles (named), James, and Paul, beginning with "only one God Almighty . . . that you must worship and adore through Jesus Christ our Lord, in the most Holy Spirit." The term "Apostles' Creed" occurs first in Ambrose, *Letter* 42.5.

61. Translation by J. N. D. Kelly, *Rufinus: A Commentary on the Apostles' Creed,* Ancient Christian Writers 20 (Westminister, MD: Newman, 1955), 29–30.

62. Pseudo-Augustine, *Sermon on the Symbol* (sixth century).

63. Athanasius, *Defense of the Nicene Definition,* especially 19–21; cf. *Letters to the Bishops of Africa* 5–6.

64. Epiphanius, *Ancoratus* 118–19. See J. N. D. Kelly, *Early Christian Creeds,* 2nd ed. (London: Longmans, 1960), 318–20, for the argument that the creed quoted by Epiphanius was originally the Nicene Creed and not the Nicaeno-Constantinopolitan Creed of 381.

65. Irenaeus, *Against Heresies* 3.11.8–9. For the language of "handed down to us" as standard terminology, see Everett Ferguson, "Factors Leading to the Selection and Closure of the New Testament Canon: A Survey of Some Recent Studies," in *The Canon Debate,* eds. Lee Martin McDonald and James A. Sanders (Peabody, MA: Hendrickson, 2002), 295–320 (295).

66. Clement of Alexandria, *Miscellanies* 1.1. For other examples of this usage, see Ferguson, "Factors," 306–7.

67. For the terminology of "New Testament" for writings in Tertullian and others, see Everett Ferguson, "The Covenant Idea in the Second Century," in *Texts and Testaments: Critical Essays on the Bible and Early Christian Fathers*, ed. W. Eugene March (San Antonio: Trinity University Press, 1980), 135–62 (148–51 on Tertullian); Wolfram Kinzig, "*Kainē Diathēkē*. The Title of the New Testament in the Second and Third Centuries," *Journal of Theological Studies*, n.s. 45 (1994): 519–44; repr. in Everett Ferguson, ed., *Norms of Faith and Life,* Recent Studies in Early Christianity 3 (New York: Garland, 1999), 59–84.

68. Quoted by Eusebius, *Church History* 6.12.3.

69. Everett Ferguson, *Early Christians Speak,* vol. 2 (Abilene: ACU Press, 2002), 72–76.

70. Richard Bauckham, *Jesus and the Eyewitnesses: The Gospels as Eyewitness Testimony* (Grand Rapids: Eerdmans, 2006) for a defense of the four Gospels as the source of authentic testimony.

71. Irenaeus, *Against Heresies* 3.1.1. On this and the subsequent quotations, see the discussion on the relation of Scripture to tradition in Ferguson, *Early Christians Speak,* 2.10–12.

72. Clement of Alexandria, *Miscellanies* 7.16. Clement by "Prophets," "Gospel," and "Apostles" is referring to his threefold classification of authoritative written texts, his three-part Bible.

73. Tertullian, *Prescription against Heretics* 36, 38. The Law, Prophets, Gospels, and Apostles are his fourfold classification of the Scriptures.

Alexander Campbell's "Sermon on the Law"
A Historical and Theological Examination

Alexander Campbell's "Sermon on the Law" has been generally regarded by historians as a significant episode in the emergence of the Restoration Movement.[1] Campbell himself assigned to this event a great importance for his own participation in the Movement.

> This unfortunate sermon afterward involved members of [the Redstone] Association, and became a matter of much debate. I found at last, however, that there was a principle at work in the plotters of said crusade, which Stephen assigns as the cause of the misfortune of Joseph.
>
> It is, therefore, highly probable to my mind, that but for the persecution begun on the alleged heresy of this sermon, whether the present reformation had ever been advocated by me.[2]

The Sermon has been treated as one of the foundation documents of the Restoration Movement, as indicated by its frequent reprinting.[3] Its historical importance has perhaps been more assumed than demonstrated, and it has seldom been subjected to theological analysis, in print at least.[4]

The Brush Run Church, in which the Campbells were guiding spirits, had been organized in 1811 and in 1815 admitted to the Redstone Baptist Association.[5] The annual meeting of the association for 1816 was held at the Cross Creek Church, three miles north of Wellsburg. Alexander Campbell's name had been submitted as a speaker at the association, but the pastor at Cross Creek (Elder Pritchard) objected that preference should be given to speakers from some distance. There was a popular protest against the decision to omit Campbell, and his replacement had a timely illness. With two hours' notice, Campbell filled the pulpit as the second of the three preachers on that Lord's Day, September 1, 1816.[6]

Although Campbell had this short time to make specific preparation for the sermon, it seems evident that these were ideas he had been thinking about for some time and had clearly formulated in his mind.[7] The sermon was not transcribed, and Campbell had only his hurriedly made notes. The ideas in the address created such a furor that Campbell wrote out the sermon as he remembered it and had it printed the same year in Steubenville, Ohio. It is in this retrospective form that the Sermon is known.

The text of the Sermon is Romans 8:3, "For what the law could not do, in that it was weak through the flesh, God, sending his own Son, in the likeness of sinful flesh, and for sin, condemned sin in the flesh."

Campbell began by defining the Law as "the whole legal or Mosaic dispensation."[8] He emphasized that he did not recognize the division of the Law into the three classifications of moral, ceremonial, and judicial. This division was characteristic of Reformed Protestantism and had been elaborated from John Calvin's distinction between moral and ceremonial Law.[9] On this view the ceremonial Law was typical of Christian practices and although superseded could be used to explicate Christian practices; the judicial Law guided Israel as a civil commonwealth and, although not binding, could also be used as a guide for civil law in a Christian commonwealth; and the moral Law was still binding (especially as summed up in the Ten Commandments).

Campbell failed to find that the Bible made such a distinction between parts of the Law and insisted on following the scriptural usage of applying the "Law" to the total Mosaic dispensation.

Campbell himself, however, made an important distinction or reservation of his own. He excluded the two great commands—"Thou shalt love the Lord thy God with all thy heart, soul, mind, and strength, and thy neighbor as thyself"—from his strictures on the Law of Moses. These commands are, he said, "of universal and immutable obligation" (273) and belong to the fundamental natural law written on every human heart, which is the basis of both the Law and the gospel. (We must return to this point.)

After these definitions and clarifications, the second part of the Sermon took up what the Law could not accomplish. According to Galatians 3:21 the Law could not give righteousness and life. Moreover, the Law could not exhibit the extent of the malignity of sin and the vastness of its demerit. Campbell does not cite a verse here but probably had his text verse in mind: God sent his Son to condemn sin in the flesh. A third limitation of the Law was that in this imperfect state it was not a suitable rule for all mankind. It was given to the Jewish nation only, as the preface to the giving of the Law in Exodus 19–20 indicates; Gentiles were never under it. Campbell returns to this point later in the Sermon.

Having considered what the Law could not accomplish, Campbell turned in the third major division of his discourse to demonstrate why the Law could not accomplish these objects. Here he restated his text verse. The defects were due to human weakness. The Law in some of its parts was too high and holy for fallen men; other parts by being carnal were too low.

Part four of the Sermon developed the means by which God remedied the defects of the Law. The coming of Jesus Christ accomplished what the Law could not. In the first place, righteousness and life, which the Law could not give, are the gifts of Jesus Christ (Rom. 6:23; 1:16–17). Secondly, the full exhibition of the demerit of sin is seen in the death of Christ; God condemned sin through him. Thirdly, as example is a more powerful teacher than precept, so Jesus Christ provides a more suitable rule of life. The law and the prophets served until John, but "then they gave place to a greater prophet and a more glorious law" (282).

The last and most extensive section of the address deduced five conclusions from the premises laid down. *First,* there is an essential difference between the Law and the gospel, the Old Testament and the New. This is shown by the different designations of the two in 2 Corinthians 3. *Second,* there is no condemnation to those in Christ (Rom. 8:1). Christians are "not under the law but under grace" (Rom. 6:15), but that does not leave them in antinomianism. Here Campbell launched into a digression dealing with the theological position which he was concerned to refute. That position qualified the statement "Ye are not under the law" by saying "not under the law as a covenant of works, but as a rule of life" (286). This was the common view of Reformed theology in that day, particularly of the Calvinistic Baptists whom Campbell was addressing. (To that position we shall return.) The reason for proposing the Law as a rule of life for Christians, Campbell states, was the fear of antinomianism. This objection had been brought against Paul's gospel (Rom. 6), and it should be dealt with as he did, not by bringing in extrinsic safeguards. Moreover, the Apostle never addressed the Gentiles as being under the Law of Moses. What is sublimest in the Law has been repromulgated by Christ. This no more makes the Law binding on Christians than the reenactment of part of the British law by the US Congress makes the British law a rule of our political life. Paul did not accuse the Gentiles of Sabbath breaking or of transgressing any peculiarity of the Jewish Law. Rather they were accused of being sinners because they failed to follow the light of nature and did what the natural conscience testified was wrong (290). Returning to his main point, Campbell reaffirmed that the Law is not a rule of life for the Christian, for Christians are under no law that can condemn them. The *third* conclusion is that there is no need to preach the Law in order to prepare persons for receiving the gospel. This was a standard understanding of the relation of the Law and the gospel since the Reformation. The gospel itself is the best means of convicting hearers of sin. At this point in the Sermon Campbell answered objections or possible objections to his position and used further Scriptures to enforce the conclusion that Christians are not under the Law, including the moral Law (Rom. 7 and Gal. 3:24). Nor is the natural law, as such, to be preached. The conscience is fitted to hear the voice of God, and preachers are to speak to their hearers' consciences. *Fourth,* all arguments and motives drawn from the Old Testament for infant baptism, tithes, holy days, Sabbath, national covenants, and establishment of religion by civil law are "inconclusive, repugnant to Christianity, and . . . ineffectual" (303). *Fifth*, we are taught by all of this to venerate Christ in the highest degree. He is far superior to Moses.

The main thrust of the "Sermon on the Law" may seem commonplace to us as successors or followers of Campbell today, but that was not the situation in the Redstone Association in 1816. There were a number of disturbances and interruptions during the delivery of the Sermon. At its conclusion some of the preachers considered an immediate refutation, but it was counseled, "That would create too much excitement, and would injure us more than Mr. Campbell. It is better to let it pass and let the people judge for themselves."[10] There was a move at the next meeting of the Association to try Campbell on a charge of heresy, but according to Campbell's later report the Association decided it had no jurisdiction and left "everyone to form his own opinion" of the Sermon.[11] The minutes of the Redstone Baptist Association have been found in the Carnegie Library, Pittsburgh, Pennsylvania.[12] Those minutes for 1817 state:

> Having received several charges and complaints against the doctrines maintained by the church of Brush Run, and more especially against a sermon preached before the last Association by Alexander Campbell, one of their elders, Resolved that having heard a written declaration of their faith as well as verbal explanations relative to the charges made against him, we are fully satisfied with the declarations of said church.

The minutes show the prominent place taken by both Thomas and Alexander Campbell in the affairs of the Association between 1815 and 1824. Both men at various times after the disturbances of 1816 filled the position of Moderator, wrote the corresponding (circular) letters, and preached at the annual meetings; and Alexander was several times the Clerk of the Association.

The minutes do not contain the particulars of the separation between the Association and the Campbell churches but do contain much information. Each church was required to submit an annual letter affirming its adherence to the doctrinal standards of the Association. The minutes for 1824 note that "the representatives of the church at Brush Run, not being able to give satisfactory reasons for the informality of their letter were objected to" and that the Association resolved to "have no fellowship with the Brush Run Church." A retrospective explanation in the minutes for 1830 mentions the following points of difference: the Trinity, nature of faith, Christian experience, and the direct operation of the Holy Spirit in conversion. Alexander Campbell and some thirty members of the Brush Run Church had already, in 1823, withdrawn to form a new congregation at Wellsburg, which united with the Mahoning Association and so was not under the jurisdiction of the Redstone Association at the time Brush Run was excluded.

The minutes of the Redstone Association do not give the specifics to which its members objected in the "Sermon on the Law." Nevertheless, it is possible to reconstruct the doctrinal grounds of objection to Campbell's Sermon, whatever personal animosities may have fueled those objections. The doctrinal standard of the Redstone Association was the *Philadelphia Confession of Faith,* adopted in 1742. This Confession, except for the addition of two articles, was an exact copy of the *Assembly Confession* of 1689, adopted by messengers of Baptist churches from England and Wales meeting in London. It in turn was but a new edition of a Baptist revision made in 1677 of the *Westminster Confession* of 1647.[13] Subscription to the *Philadelphia Confession* was required of every church seeking admission to the Redstone Association. Brush Run and some other churches had entered without making this subscription, and that fact was to be a repeated basis for seeking their exclusion. Indeed the Cross Creek Church, where the Association met in 1816, continued to be a center of the opposition to Campbell.

The *Philadelphia Confession* states in chapter 19:

> The same Law that was first written in the heart of man, continued to be a perfect rule of Righteousness after the fall; and was delivered by God upon Mount Sinai, in Ten Commandments....
>
> Besides this law commonly called moral, God was pleased to give to the people *Israel* Ceremonial Laws . . . all which Ceremonial Laws being appointed only to the time of reformation, are by Jesus Christ . . . abrogate and taken away.

> To them also he gave sundry judicial Laws, which expired together with the state of that people, . . . their general equity only, being of moral use.
>
> The moral Law doth for ever bind all, as well justified persons as others . . .: Neither doth *Christ* in the Gospel any way dissolve but much strengthen this obligation.
>
> Although true *Believers* be not under the Law, as a Covenant of *Works,* to be thereby Justified or condemned; yet it is of great use to them as well as to others: in that, as a Rule of *Life,* informing them of the Will of *God,* and their Duty, it directs and binds them, to walk accordingly. . . .[14]

These words are familiar to us from Campbell's objections, and they would be the stance from which his opponents attacked him. The *Philadelphia Confession,* and its parent *Westminster Confession,* faithfully reflected the Covenant or Federal Theology, which was especially developed by the Dutch theologian Cocceius (d. 1669) but had earlier been expounded for English Puritanism by William Ames (d. 1633). According to this theology a distinction is made between the covenant of works and the covenant of grace. Adam was under the covenant of works; after man's fall into sin, God had to deal with men according to grace and no longer according to works. The covenant of grace is essentially one but has operated under different dispensations—the patriarchal, Mosaic, and Christian.[15] These different administrations of the one covenant of grace was the basis for reading the Old Testament as a Christian book.

Campbell received part of his early theological training under the influence of the covenant theologians, and the Covenant Theology has been seen as a major tributary of his theology.[16] However, he carried its viewpoints further and in so doing arrived at a position which represents another strand of Christian thought. The sharp distinction between the old and new covenants was found in the early church as represented by Ignatius, Justin, and Irenaeus.[17] In the Reformation the Anabaptists were the most consistent advocates of this approach to the Bible, and it provided the basis for their different ecclesiology from that of the mainline Reformers.[18] More directly in Campbell's intellectual heritage were the Scotch independents (e.g., John

Glass), who in their program for the church used the distinction between Old and New Testaments.[19]

The most immediate antecedent for Campbell's position in the "Sermon on the Law," at least in its practical import, was his father, Thomas Campbell. The *Declaration and Address* had in 1809 announced the distinction between the Old and New Testaments as far as the practices of the church were concerned:[20]

> That although the Scriptures of the Old and New Testaments are inseparably connected, making together but one perfect and entire revelation of the Divine will, for the edification and salvation of the Church, and therefore in that respect cannot be separated; yet as to what directly and properly belongs to their immediate object, the New Testament is as perfect a constitution for the worship, discipline, and government of the New Testament Church, and as perfect a rule for the particular duties of its members, as the Old Testament was for the worship, discipline, and government of the Old Testament Church, and the particular duties of its members.[21]

It has also been noted that there is a great similarity between this fourth proposition of Thomas Campbell and the fourth point in Rice Haggard's proposal for Christian Unity, to be found in his "Address to the Different Religious Societies" in 1804:[22]

> Let us have one form of discipline, and government, and let this be the New Testament. The Old Testament is necessary as a guide to our faith: for by it we are led to those things we find accomplished in the new, and which we are to believe. But for the constitution of a christian church; its conduct when constituted; the reception of its members and upon what principles; the manner of expelling and for what, we have sufficient guide in the New Testament, independent of every other Book, in the world.[23]

Alexander was twenty-eight at the time of the delivery of the "Sermon on the Law." He later characterized it as a "youthful performance."[24] It was not delivered totally impromptu; four years before he had stated essentially the same position in a communication to his father:

> How many disciples of Moses are yet to be found in the professed school of Jesus Christ! and how few among the teachers of the *New Testament* seem to know that Christ's ministers are not able ministers of the *Old Testament,* but of the *New*? Do they not, like scholars to their teacher, run to Moses to prove forms of worship, ordinances, discipline, and government in the Christian Church, when asked to account for their practice? On this subject, I think we may rest satisfied, that since the great Prophet has come, . . . that all worship and forms of worship, ordinances, discipline, and government belonging to the Christian Church, must be learned exclusively from the *New Testament.* And every appeal made to Moses or the prophets to confirm any form of worship, ordinance, or any part of the Christian discipline or government is sending Christ the *Son* to Moses the *servant* to be instructed.[25]

The viewpoint on the distinction of the covenants as the framework of biblical revelation was to receive from him more elaborate and systematic treatment in a series in the *Christian Baptist.*[26] It is also expounded in *Christian Baptism*[27] and *The Christian System.*[28] It underlies the argument in the debates with Walker (which in its published form contains an appendix on the covenants)[29] and McCalla.[30] This perspective also occupies a prominent position in the debate with Owen.[31] When Campbell later reprinted the "Sermon on the Law" in *Millennial Harbinger,* he endorsed it with, "The intelligent reader will discover in it the elements of things which have characterized all our writing on the subject of modern Christianity from that day to the present."[32] So there is justification for seeing the standpoint of the "Sermon on the Law" as in some sense programmatic for the restoration efforts of Alexander Campbell. According to W. E. Garrison, the distinction between the covenants "was perhaps his most important exegetical principle."[33]

The "Sermon on the Law" clearly, therefore, does not stand alone, and it would be claiming too much for it to see it as alone shaping the thought of the heirs of Campbell on the Old Testament. B. F. Hall a few years later, in 1824, independently discovered the distinction of the covenants and had the same experience of the idea being considered "heresy" by the preachers of the Baptist churches among whom he was working in Tennessee and northern Alabama.[34] So there were other influences besides Campbell's working in this direction in the Restoration Movement. Nevertheless, the importance of the ideas enunciated in the Sermon for the Restoration Movement justifies a careful scrutiny of what it says, what it does not say, and what its context (in history and in Campbell's thought) was.

Campbell refers in three different places in the Sermon to the concept of natural law and conscience as the framework for his thought on the covenants.[35] He does so, first, when he exempts the two great commands of love for God and love for neighbor from the Law of Moses, which was abrogated by the Christian covenant. He may not be fully consistent here, but he does have the authority of Jesus for putting these commands in a special category. It might have been more consistent if he had seen these commands as examples of items from the Law of Moses repromulgated by Christ. Campbell himself, however, would say that any repromulgation was due to these commands being statements of principles antedating even the Law of Moses. There is a moral law which underlies both the Mosaic dispensation and the Christian. The great commandments are binding not because they are in the Law but because they are right.[36] Campbell identified the two great commandments with the fundamental natural law to which the human conscience answers. It is in that context that his views need to be examined.

What Campbell meant by this natural law was the moral order or moral sense of the human race. Such a moral law or natural law underlying both dispensations has a long history in Christian apologetics. From the early church one would note especially Justin Martyr[37] and Eusebius.[38] During the Middle Ages Thomas Aquinas made a clear distinction between natural law discerned by human reason and positive law supernaturally revealed by God.[39] By way of Richard Hooker and John Locke this perspective passed on to Campbell.[40] It should be noted, however, that Campbell did not grant the premise of the advocates of natural religion in his day that unaided human reason could establish the "truths" of natural religion. Even the fundamental moral law was for him the product of an original revelation.[41]

Modern theological thought, on the other hand, is not too congenial to any idea of natural law or that Paul in Romans 1–2 was referring to such.[42]

There are also difficulties with the concept of conscience. Campbell defines the conscience as the "sense of right and wrong, which all men possess, in different degrees" (301). If one stays with the idea of a moral sense or capacity, and awareness of moral accountability, to which the word of God can be addressed, one has a defensible position. When one tries to put a content into the judgments of the conscience, then one is in a morass of uncertainty.

Campbell has something to say here to his followers, or to many of them, in his approach to the alien sinner. He does not condemn man as a sinner on the basis of disobedience to the new covenant of Christ. He notes that this was not Paul's approach in Romans 1–2. Paul convicted pagans of his time as guilty before the natural law and accused by their own conscience, and Campbell makes the same point about unbelievers in his own day. The unbelieving American, he affirms, is condemned by the same law as condemned the unbelieving Roman before Christ came, that is, the law of the natural conscience, the law written in the heart (291). Campbell, therefore, adheres strictly to the understanding of a covenant as descriptive of a relationship, an agreement, the conditions of which do not apply to someone not a party to that covenant.[43]

The view of a natural moral law seems to have had something of the same function in his thought as the category of moral law as part of the Mosaic Law had in the thought of his antagonists. Campbell would have drawn the lines more narrowly on its content and of course arrived at it differently, but in terms of function—convicting of sin, defining responsibility, antecedent to the Christian gospel—there is considerable similarity. The need to convict of sin was recognized by Campbell, but he denied that preaching the Law of Moses was the way to do it. He does not say it this way, but preaching the love of God in Christ will bring repentance as readily as, or more readily than, convicting one of transgressing the Law.

Campbell in the "Sermon on the Law" works only with Paul, primarily Romans (from which he took his text) and secondarily Galatians and

2 Corinthians. He could have appealed also to Hebrews. One must remember that Paul had a special problem in mind, namely Judaizers who were binding parts of the Law of Moses on Gentile Christians as conditions of salvation, and, in applying Paul's teaching, this context must be kept in mind. On the question of the Law in particular, Campbell does not in the Sermon deal with the rather different estimate of the Law to be found in Matthew. The tension is eased when it is remembered that Campbell had Gentile Christians, exclusively, in mind. In assessing the "Sermon on the Law" and its significance one must keep this narrow textual base in view.

Furthermore, Campbell in this sermon offers no objection to the theology or doctrinal teaching of the Old Testament. That was not at issue in the context in which he spoke. Presumably what was true in the Old Testament about the nature of God, the nature of man, and the way God deals with man is true now. The biblical doctrines of God, of creation, of history, of sin, of hope, and of many other things get their meaning from and fullest exposition in the Old Testament. Campbell was not taking exception to these, and apparently would not.[44] This can be confirmed by examining his approach elsewhere and considering the whole range of his thought.

Campbell's heirs have been accused of not believing in the Old Testament; a more accurate assessment would be that they have neglected the Old Testament. That disregard for the Old Testament may be due to the "Sermon on the Law"; more likely it is due to the total influence of Campbell and of those who learned from him the perspective which found an early formulation in the "Sermon on the Law." In that sense the influence of the Sermon itself was great, however much other factors contributed to the attitude. The "Sermon on the Law," and Campbell's other writings to the same import, should be taken in context of his own practice.[45]

One of the places where the "Sermon on the Law" is reprinted is in W. T. Moore's edition of Campbell's *Familiar Lectures on the Pentateuch,* delivered daily to his students at Bethany College. In these lectures he treats the Bible as data for the development of a moral science. The Old Testament contains eternally valid principles about God and man. Those who are inclined to ignore the Old Testament on the basis that Christians are not under the

Mosaic covenant should read the *Familiar Lectures on the Pentateuch* to see how Campbell actually used the Old Testament to instruct Christians.[46]

The consideration calls for another look at what Campbell was actually concerned about in the "Sermon on the Law" and other statements of the distinction between the covenants. Just as one keeps Paul's context in mind, so must he keep Campbell's in mind. His criticism was of the use of the Law of Moses as a "rule of life" for Christians (i.e., the moral law of the Old Testament) and implicitly of Old Testament institutions (i.e., the judicial and ceremonial laws—a criticism made explicitly elsewhere in his writings).[47] The illustrations of the improper use of the Old Testament, which he notes briefly without developing them here as he did in other places, had to do with circumcision as the basis for infant baptism, tithing, holy days, Sabbath, national covenants, and civil law to support religion.

This points to the basis for the emphasis on the New Testament alone as the law for the church. Christ's "will published in the New Testament is the sole law of the church."[48] Campbell's positive task became the "restoration of the ancient order of things."[49] He held that when one came to the practical decisions of how to organize churches, how to worship, how to guide moral conduct, how to exercise discipline, how to do the work of the church, then it was important to have a clear standard, to know where to go to find instruction in these matters. Since the church of Jesus Christ is a New Testament institution, the New Testament alone was the place to go to find these practical directions.

The strictures on the law arose in a polemical context. They are directed at the way the *Philadelphia Confession of Faith* was understood and followed in the Baptist churches of western Virginia and Pennsylvania. It is a common occurrence in Christian history to extract a position from a polemical context and absolutize it. That seems to have occurred in Restoration churches in regard to the Old Testament.

For Campbell himself there was a positive side along with the negative polemic. It would be fair to say that for him the reader of the apostolic writings is supposed to have read or learned from Moses and the Prophets.

> Every one, then, who would accurately understand the Christian institution must approach it through the Mosaic; and he

that would be a proficient in the Jewish must make Paul his commentator.[50]

The gospel presupposes the law.[51]

By way of summary, Campbell rejected the distinction between the covenant of works and covenant of grace as formulated in the Reformed theology of his day. His basic distinction is between the Mosaic and Christian covenants. However, his division of the three dispensations—patriarchal, Mosaic, and Christian—parallels Reformed theology's dispensations of the covenant of grace. Campbell rejected the division of the Law of Moses into moral, ceremonial, and judicial. Natural law, however, functioned in his thought in a similar way to the moral Law in the thought of his opponents; and that to which he objected in the Old Testament closely corresponded to items in the ceremonial and judicial Laws treated by his opponents as superseded. Campbell drew the lines at different places, and he had a different basis for keeping what he did from the Old Testament—what was repromulgated by Christ and what corresponded to the natural law.

*This paper was read at the Christian Scholars Conference, Abilene Christian University, July 1982, and subsequently accepted by Dr. Tom Olbricht for publication in *Restoration Quarterly* 29 (1987): 71–85.

Chapter 16 Endnotes

1. Earl Irvin West, *The Search for the Ancient Order*, vol. 1 (Nashville: Gospel Advocate, 1949), 62–63; B. J. Humble, *The Story of the Restoration* (Austin: Firm Foundation, 1969), 26; James DeForest Murch, *Christians Only* (Cincinnati: Standard Publishing, 1962), 62–65; W. E. Garrison and A. T. DeGroot, *The Disciples of Christ: A History* (St. Louis: Bethany Press, 1958), 163–67.

2. *Millennial Harbinger* 3, no. 3 (September 1846): 493.

3. Ibid., 495–531; Alexander Campbell, *Familiar Lectures on the Pentateuch*, ed. W. T. Moore (St. Louis: Christian Publishing, 1867), 266–304; W. A. Morris, *The Writings of Alexander Campbell* (Austin: Eugene Von Boeckmann, 1896), 27–60; *Christian Standard* 67, no. 26 (June 25, 1932): 611ff. and continued in subsequent issues; C. A. Young, *Historical Documents Advocating Christian Unity* (Chicago: Christian Century, 1904), 217–82; an abridged version in *Christian Evangelist* (1938): 993ff.

4. There is Bert Louis Mercer, "A Rhetorical Study of Alexander Campbell's Sermon on the Law" (master's thesis, Abilene Christian University, 1960). Richard Elmer Prout, "Alexander Campbell's Attitude toward and Use of the Old Testament" (master's thesis, Pepperdine University, 1962), considers the "Sermon on the Law" in relation to Campbell's general use of the Old Testament but does not try to put that use in a larger historical or theological context. He summarizes the sermon and its main doctrinal points in "Alexander Campbell and the Old Testament," *Restoration Quarterly* 6 (1962): 131–42.

5. The minutes of the Redstone Baptist Association give the date of admission as 1815. These minutes have been photocopied (but with poor quality) in a limited edition by M. F. Cottrell. What pertains to the Campbells may most conveniently be read in W. H. Hanna, "The Campbells and the Redstone Baptist Association," *Christian Standard* 75, no. 31 (August 3, 1940): 739ff. and 75, no. 32 (August 10, 1940): 774–75. Alexander Campbell gave the date as 1813 in *Christian Baptist*, vol. 2 (1824), 37 (92). Is this the date when the decision was reached to enter the Association or was Campbell's memory in error?

6. Robert Richardson, *Memoirs of Alexander Campbell,* vol. 1 (Cincinnati: Standard Publishing, 1897), 469, gives the date August 30 for the convening of the Association, which was on a Friday, but the Sermon was delivered the following Sunday, September 1, again as the minutes of the Association make clear.

7. Lester G. McAllister and William E. Tucker, *Journey in Faith* (St. Louis: Bethany, 1975), 122, note evidence that Campbell preached a sermon on the same theme as early as 1813. The reference is presumably to Campbell's Sermon 332, item 17 in Bethany College file collection, which gives an outline of a sermon for June 6, 1813, to be preached at Cadiz (Ohio) on Romans 8:3, using the same points as the Sermon on the Law; but Campbell's note at the end says he did not preach it but preached from John 8:31f. The sermon based on Rom 10:5 (which is item 18) for June 9, 1813, at a home in Wheeling, has some of the same themes but a different outline. (I am indebted to David Brooker for this information from the materials collected by Hiram Lister.)

8. Quotations are taken from the edition by W. T. Moore (note 3) with reference to the page numbers in that edition; in this case, 268.

9. Ford L. Battles, trans., *Institutes of the Christian Religion* 2, Library of Christian Classics 20 (Philadelphia: Westminster, 1960), vii–xi.

10. Richardson, *Memoirs*, vol. 1, 472.

11. *Millennial Harbinger* 3, no. 3 (1846): 494. Is this the source of Richardson's words (note 6) transposed by him to an earlier occasion?

12. See note 5. Quotations from the minutes are taken from the transcription in the *Christian Standard*.

13. W. J. McGlothlin, *Baptist Confessions of Faith* (Philadelphia: American Baptist Publication Society, 1911), 293–99; 215–19.

14. Ibid., 255–56. The wording closely approximates that of the *Westminster Confession,* chap. 19; see Philip Schaff, *The Creeds of Christendom,* vol. 3 (New York: Harper & Brothers, 1877), 640–42.

15. This view is more fully stated in the *Westminster Confession,* chapter 7; more briefly in the *Philadelphia Confession* 7 and 20. The literature on Covenant Theology is extensive and growing. For a recent assessment of the origins of the Puritan doctrine see Michael McGiffert, "Grace and Works: The Rise and Division of Covenant Divinity in Elizabethan Puritanism," *Harvard Theological Review* 75 (1982): 463–502. The interest in the theme of covenant has sparked the publication of the *Covenant Letter,* John Kincaid, ed. (Department of Political Science, North Texas State University, Denton, TX), which encompasses the political and other ramifications of the concept.

16. Winfred Ernest Garrison, *Alexander Campbell's Theology: Its Sources and Historical Setting* (St. Louis: Christian Publishing, 1900), 117–58; Hiram van Kirk, *The Rise of the Current Reformation* (St. Louis: Christian Publishing, 1907), 30–51, but he fails to show Campbell's differences from the typical Covenant Theology scheme.

17. Everett Ferguson, "Christian Use of the Old Testament," *The World and Literature of the Old Testament,* ed. John T. Willis (Austin: Sweet Publishing, 1979), 346–57; Everett Ferguson, "The Covenant Idea in the Second Century," *Texts and Testaments: Critical Essays on the Bible and Early Church Fathers,* ed. W. Eugene March (San Antonio: Trinity University Press, 1980), 135–62.

18. See the special issue of *The Mennonite Quarterly Review* 40 (April 1966) on Anabaptist interpretation of the Scriptures.

19. Van Kirk, *Rise of the Current Reformation,* 75.

20. Mercer, "Rhetorical Study," 49.

21. Quoted from the edition introduced by F. D. Kershner and published by Mission Messenger, St. Louis, MO, 1972, 45.

22. John W. Neth, "Sermon on the Law," *Christian Standard* 101, no. 36 (September 3, 1966): 591–92.

23. Quoted from the edition in *Footnotes to Disciple History,* no. 4 (Nashville: Disciples of Christ Historical Society, 1954), 26.

24. *Millennial Harbinger* 3, no. 3 (1846): 493.

25. Richardson, *Memoirs,* vol. 1, 448.

26. "Essays on Man in his Primitive State and Under the Patriarchal, Jewish, and Christian Dispensations," *Christian Baptist* 6 (August 4, 1828): 7 (463) through 7 (July 5, 1830): 287ff. (655ff.), sixteen essays in all.

27. *Christian Baptism with Its Antecedents and Consequents* (St. Louis: Christian Board of Publication, 1882 reprint), 89–115.

28. *The Christian System* (Nashville: Gospel Advocate, 1970 reprint), 107–52.

29. *Debate on Christian Baptism between Mr. John Walker . . . and Alexander Campbell* (Pittsburgh: Eichbaum & Johnston, 1822), 153–74.

30. W. L. McCalla and Alexander Campbell, *Public Debate on Christian Baptism* (London: Simpkin & Marshall, 1842; reprint Kansas City: Old Paths Book Club, 1948).

31. Robert Owen and Alexander Campbell, *The Evidences of Christianity: A Debate* (Cincinnati: Jethro Jackson, 1852), 358ff.

32. *Millennial Harbinger* 3, no. 3 (1846): 493. Prout, "Alexander Campbell's Attitude" (see note 4), 49, 74–75, notes that Campbell in the *Christian Baptist* 7 (July 5, 1830): 287–88. (655–56), makes a contrast between the Law as precept and the teachings of Christ as principle and good judgment, which is not found in the Sermon.

33. Garrison, *Alexander Campbell's Theology,* 204–5. Cf. the second of Campbell's seven rules of interpretation in *Christian System*, 4. Cloyd Goodnight called the "base line" of the Sermon "a distinctive mark of all the restorers' teaching and preaching," in his article "Alexander Campbell's Sermon on the Law," *Christian Evangelist* (1925): 656.

34. R. L. Roberts has called my attention to 51–52 of the typescript of "The Autobiography of B. F. Hall," unpublished. See also Roberts's comments in "B. F. Hall: Pioneer Evangelist and Herald of Hope," *Restoration Quarterly* 8 (1965): 250–51.

35. Robert Frederick West, *Alexander Campbell and Natural Religion* (New Haven: Yale University Press, 1948), centers his study on the debate with Robert Owen and has a different interest from that which I have termed "natural law." See 150–53, 170–76 for discussion pertinent to the themes of this paper.

36. J. R. Kellems, *Alexander Campbell and the Disciples* (New York: Richard R. Smith, 1930), 151.

37. *Dialogue with Trypho* 10–47.

38. *Preparation for the Gospel* 7. 1–12.

39. Thomas Gilby, *St. Thomas Aquinas: Philosophical Texts* (London: Oxford University Press, 1951), 29–35.

40. Garrison, *Alexander Campbell's Theology,* 77–114.

41. West, *Alexander Campbell and Natural Religion,* 90–112.

42. William C. Martin, "The Bible and Natural Law," *Restoration Quarterly* 17 (1974): 193–221.

43. *Christian Baptism,* 91–115.

44. Cf. the position of John Bright, *The Authority of the Old Testament* (London: SCM Press, 1967), 140–60, that the theology of the Old Testament is still normative but its forms, institutions, and laws are not.

45. Prout "Alexander Campbell's Attitude," 76–134, amply documents Campbell's abundant use of the Old Testament.

46. Campbell recognized "many communications from God to men of immense importance to us Christians" in the Old Testament, *Millennial Harbinger* 2, no. 1 (January 3, 1831): 15.

47. Note the statement that "the Old Dispensation has passed away, and with it all institutions, ordinances, and obligations, not resanctioned by the New Testament," *Christian Baptist* 4 (September 7, 1826): 32 (268).

48. *Christian Baptist* 1 (November 3, 1823): 72 (25f.).

49. See the series by this title in *Christian Baptist* 2 (February 7, 1825): 132ff. (126ff.) and subsequent issues.

50. *Christian System,* 118. cf. *Millennial Harbinger* 2, no. 5 (May 1831): 201. [No one can] "as fully understand the New Testament, or as firmly believe in the mission of Jesus as he who is well versed in these ancient writings."

51. Kellems, *Alexander Campbell and the Disciples,* 151.

17

The Doctrine of the Church in the Writings of Alexander Campbell[1]

The emphases of Mr. Campbell and the Restoration Movement of which he was the leading figure in the first half of the nineteenth century have been stated according to a traditional classification: the ultimate principle was the conversion of the world to Christ; the material principle for achieving this goal was the union of all Christians; and the formal principle for attaining this union was the restoration of primitive Christianity as set forth in the New Testament.[2] From the beginning of the movement two emphases have been in tension the one with the other—unionism and restorationism.

The emphasis upon Christian unity in the writings of Alexander Campbell is readily apparent. He found a real and visible unity described in the Scriptures. The following statement from the *Millennial Harbinger* is representative of many:

> There is but one real Kingdom of Christ in the world, and that is equivalent to affirming that there is but one Church of Christ in

the world. As to an invisible church in a visible world, schoolmen may debate about it till doom's day, but we know nothing of an invisible church in our portion of creation.[3]

In the same context it is stated that "it is, then, a fixed fact of Christianity, that Jesus Christ has but one church, or kingdom, in this world, and that this church is composed of all the communities properly called the church of Christ."

The restoration of New Testament Christianity was the method advocated by Campbell to achieve unity. His use of the Bible in this regard represented his distinctive contribution. The following quotation from one of the historians of the Disciples will make Campbell's method clear:

> Attempts had been made, to be sure, to deduce from the Scriptures complete systems of theology, and to make these the bases of successive reformations of the church. But his own movement differed from these in seeking for the authoritatively given conditions of salvation and making these alone, as the essentials of Christianity, the basis of the unity of the church. There may be differences of theory about the facts of the Gospel, but the facts themselves are sure. There may be differences of interpretation in regard to many doctrines taught in the Bible, but, when all prejudices and preconceived opinions have been set aside, there is little room for differences in regard to the few simple commands, obedience to which was the only condition of entrance to the church in the days of the apostles.
>
> Stated in a word, his method of effecting the reconciliation between the liberty of the individual and the unity of the whole body, was a return to authority for essentials and the admission of individual differences in non-essentials.[4]

Others, too, had sought a distinction between essentials and nonessentials. Campbell said men must let the New Testament determine what constitutes the essentials. The preaching of the apostles of Christ makes clear that these are the conditions of salvation.[5]

Some have felt that there was an inconsistency between Campbell's attack on theology and his own elaboration of a system of doctrine, between his attack on creeds and his teaching that immersion was a condition of admission to the kingdom.[6] However, Campbell's theology was intended to remain *his* theology, and not become the theology of a denomination nor the basis of Christian union. Furthermore, in a movement for reunion on the basis of the original conditions of fellowship it was not felt inconsistent to grant the Christian name to others even if they were not admissible as members of a movement to unite the church on the basis indicated.[7]

When Campbell's movement took organized form, he looked to the biblical doctrine of the church as a norm and a practical basis of polity. In surveying some of his teachings on the subject of the church this paper will show the result of the application of his brilliant capacity for generalization and illustration to the fruits of biblical exegesis. It is proposed to examine Campbell's doctrine of the church under the three heads of the nature, organization, and functions of the church.

The nature of the church is presented in relation to the kingdom of God, in terms of its membership, and as a divine creation.

"In the systematizing of Mr. Campbell's doctrinal ideas, the central place must be given to his idea of the Kingdom of God."[8] The doctrine of the Church must be placed in this larger context, for it is always defined in relation to the kingdom of God.[9] God has always had and always will have a kingdom. The kingdom of God in Old Testament days was the Jewish theocracy. Coming to the New Testament, Campbell thought Matthew's preference for "kingdom of heaven" instead of "kingdom of God" was meant to contrast the institution which Jesus was going to set up with the earthly kingdom of God of which the Jews were so long in possession.[10] The kingdom was not to be, in any sense of the term, an earthly reign of Christ, but rather a wonderful new spiritual institution, His own divine creation. The distinction between church and kingdom is to be found in the fact that kingdom is a wider term, including God's government in all ages and those who were subject to it—patriarchs, faithful Jews, Christians, and infants.

> The communities collected and set in order by the Apostles were called the *congregations of Christ,* and these taken together are

sometimes called *the Kingdom of God*. But the phrases *"church of God,"* or "congregation of Christ," and the phrases "Kingdom of Heaven," or "Kingdom of God," do not always nor exactly represent the same thing. The elements of the Kingdom of Heaven, it will be remembered, are not simply its subjects, and therefore not simply the congregation of disciples of Christ. But as these communities possess the oracles of God, are under the laws and institutions of the King, and therefore enjoy the blessings of the present salvation, they are in the records of the Kingdom regarded as the only constitutional citizens of the Kingdom of Heaven; and to them exclusively belongs *the present salvation*.[11]

The essential elements of a kingdom as existing among men are stated to be five, namely: "King, Constitution, Subjects, Laws, and Territory."[12] Since the "Church" designates those who are now subject to the institutions of Christ, the terms *church* and *kingdom* became practically interchangeable for the Christian age, and it is under the figure of a kingdom that Mr. Campbell most frequently sets forth the essential characteristics of the Christian Dispensation. It is in terms of membership that the church coincides with the effective kingdom of God, as executed through Christ, in the present day, and to this topic we must return. The Lordship of a King is frequently emphasized by Campbell, particularly in the context of organization. At this point, one general statement about the subjects and their King in the kingdom of heaven is offered, in anticipation of the fuller statements later.

> The Christian brotherhood or community is set forth under the figure of a body, a family, a nation, or kingdom. Under all these figures Christ is the head and his people are his body, his family, his kingdom. They indeed are not contemplated without him, nor him without them, under any figure (1 Cor. 12:12ff.; Eph. 1:23; Rom. 12:5; Eph. 2:21; 4:4). All, then, who are of the one faith, under the one Lord, and subjects of the one baptism, animated by the one Spirit and hope, make but one body or church.[13]

Those bound to Christ by no other bond than personal allegiance live within a Constitutional Kingdom, founded upon the New Covenant of Jesus Christ, which was delivered to men through the preaching of the Apostles; they are under the Laws of the Kingdom, the essential feature of which is a law of Love. Their present territory is the world, where they wage war with the forces of evil, but they are heirs of heaven.[14] "The first community of this sort was that formed in Jerusalem" with the events described in Acts 2.[15]

The aspect of church membership was the central burden of most of Campbell's study, debates, and writing, for it is in terms of membership (the subjects of the kingdom) that his doctrine of the church touches most intimately his conception of Christian unity. An explicit statement of his conception of the nature of the Church and its membership is found in the answers to a series of "questions on the church."

Q. What is *the church* of Christ?

A. The congregation of saints on earth and in heaven.

Q. What is meant by *a church* of Christ?

A. An assembly of persons meeting statedly in one place; built upon the foundation of the Apostles and Prophets, Jesus himself the chief cornerstone.

Q. Who are the members of a church of Christ?

A. Those only who voluntarily and joyfully submit to him as lawgiver, prophet, priest, and king: who assume him as their Saviour, die to sin, are buried with him, and rise to walk in new life.

Q. What is the Constitution of the Church?

A. Paul describes it in Heb. 8.

Q. Are no other articles of confederation necessary?

A. None for a Christian congregation. Jesus is king and lawgiver.

Q. How are the articles of the Christian Constitution acceded to and adopted?

A. In one's immersion into the death and Resurrection of the Lord.

Q. Does this make them members of every Christian community?

A. No: Their particular membership in any one community is an after act. It depends on location, application, and reception.

Q. Can any Christian congregation refuse to receive any citizen of the Kingdom?

A. No; unless he act in a manner unworthy of a citizen.[16]

In an "Extra" printed with the *Millennial Harbinger* Campbell speaks on the "Foundation of a Church":

> The materials of a church are regenerated men and women—disciples of Christ. By regenerated persons we mean those disciples born of water and the Spirit—those who, believing that Jesus is the Son of God on the proper evidence, the witness of the Spirit, penitent for their sins, understanding his blood as the only procuring cause of remission, and determined to obey the Lord in all things according to his word; such persons having confessed the Lord by being immersed into the name of the Father, and of the Son, and of the Holy Spirit according to his commandment, are the proper materials for the congregation of the Lord.
>
> . . . They pledge themselves to one another in the name of the Lord, that they will walk together as becometh saints in the relation of a Christian congregation.
>
> . . . It is enough that they give themselves to one another by some token or pledge— *"the right hand of fellowship,"* or some such significant action. . . .[17]

The fact that the church is a divine creation gives it its distinctive nature. Writing on the "Kingdom of Heaven" in the *Christian System* Campbell speaks as follows:

> So Jesus in the new creation, by his Spirit sent down from heaven after his glorification, did, by a positive, direct, and immediate agency, create one congregation, one mystical or spiritual body; and, according to the constitution or system of the Kingdom of Heaven, did give to that mystical body, created in Jerusalem out of the more ancient earthly Kingdom of God, the power of

reproducing and multiplying to an indefinite extent. But still this new and spiritual life is transmitted, diffused, and sustained by the Spirit of God, operating through the constitution, or system of grace, ordained in the Kingdom of Heaven.[18]

It is this divine origin that explains the wonderful display of divine power and makes appropriate the supernatural acts associated with the ministry of Jesus and the early preaching of the Apostles. That the church is divine in source of origin is made particularly prominent in speaking of the time when the church began: "The Christian Church, called the Kingdom or Reign of Heaven, was organized by the descent of the Holy Spirit on the first Pentecost after the sacrifice of Christ."[19]

From the great deal which Mr. Campbell wrote on the organization of the church three topics will be selected: the divinely given organization; this within the pattern of congregational independency; and the role of the ministry in the organization.

Alexander Campbell was not satisfied with any definition of the church which left it an amorphous, or mystical, concept. The very idea of "church" meant an organized body.

> Either there is, or there is not, a Christian system of church organization. If there be no Divinely instituted system of church organization, there must be a human system or there is no system at all! Has the King of the kingdom of heaven himself laid down no system of organization? Then he has no kingdom of heaven— no church on earth! He may have a people, but, without organization, he can have neither church nor kingdom, for those terms indicate organized bodies.[20]

Fairly early in the *Christian Baptist* he took sharp issue with a Baptist correspondent who felt that church government is largely left to human discretion:

> You say that "church government" is obviously left by the Bible for the exercise of much discretion. How this can be I cannot conjecture. Whatever is left for the exercise of much discretion is obviously a discretionary thing. If, therefore, church

> government be a matter obviously of human discretion, I see
> not how any form of church government, though principally of
> human contrivance, such as the Papistical or Episcopalian, can
> be condemned.... If there be no divine law enjoining any form of
> church government, if there be no divinely authorized platform
> exhibited in the Bible, then why have the Baptists contended for
> the independent form, except they suppose that they have more
> discretion than their neighbors?[21]

The reason for Campbell's strong language here is found in the fact that by
"church government" he meant the prerogative of Christ, and Christ alone,
to lay down rules for the church. There was no place for human lawmaking
in the church of Christ. In the same article he adds this statement:

> I find, therefore, that the Lord Jesus is the Governor, and the 12
> apostles under him, sitting upon 12 thrones, constitute the gov-
> ernment of the church of Jesus Christ. I know that synods and
> advisory councils have a right to govern voluntary associations,
> which owe their origin to the will of men; but in the church of
> Jesus the 12 apostles reign.[22]

The figure of a kingdom is taken by Mr. Campbell as normative for his declarations on the subject of church organization.

> That as the church, or congregation, or assembly (as it is expressed
> by all these names) is repeatedly called a *kingdom*—the kingdom
> of God, and the kingdom of heaven, it is fairly to be presumed,
> from the terms themselves, that the government under which the
> church is placed, is an *absolute monarchy*. There cannot be a king-
> dom unless there be a *king*.... On this, as a first principle, I found
> all my views of what is commonly called *church government*.
>
> In every congregation or community of Christians the per-
> sons that are appointed by the Great King to rule, act pretty
> much in the capacity of our civil magistrates; or in other words,
> they have only to see that the laws are obeyed, but have no power
> or right to legislate in any one instance for any one purpose.

> There is no democracy or aristocracy in the governmental
> arrangements of the church of Jesus Christ. . . . So that there
> is no putting the question to vote whether they shall obey any
> particular law or injunction. Their rulers or bishops have to give
> an account of their administration, and have only to see that the
> laws are known and obeyed.[23]

After reading such statements it is clear why Campbell could speak of the government of the Church as a "Christocracy."[24]

Although the preceding statements have reference to government as laying down authoritative statements of doctrine, the same principles led Mr. Campbell to insist upon a biblical basis for church organization. All figures—building and body included—point to the same government and organization.

"It was a Divine, spiritual, and neither a human nor a political organization." He disavowed any intention of placing polity over faith, but he did regard polity as essential to the carrying out of the content of faith. "I have always been a pleader for organization; still organization is not faith, nor humility nor liberality. . . .No community in America or Europe is better organized than the Roman Church."[25] Still the necessity and importance of organization are not detracted by the prior need of faith, intelligence, liberality, and zeal to accomplish anything.

The matter of actually organizing communities of his followers raised a question of the relation of these communities to the total number of Christians. Were there Christians in the sects he so roundly denounced, and if so did this not introduce the element of an invisible church into his thinking? This was treated as a purely practical problem. The fractured body of Christ must be made one; he was creating a nucleus around which that unity could form. Various questions raised on this theme are answered in the following passage, which is followed by an important declaration of the church as essentially a social institution.

Q. Do you place all the sects in the apostacy?
A. Yes, all religious sects who have any human bond of union;
   all who rally under any articles of confederation other than

the apostles' doctrine, and who refuse to yield homage to the ancient order of things.

Q. Are there no disciples of Christ in these communities?

A. There are, no doubt, many.

Q. How can the communities be in the apostacy?

A. There are republicans in England and monarchists in America. So there being Christians in any sectarian common-wealth or a sectarian in any Christian commonwealth does not change the character of such a commonwealth.

Since the very existence of sects is sinful, he states that it is the duty of sincere Christians to "come out" (Rev. 18:4). Then he continues as follows:

> Cannot a person be a Christian and live out of all Christian fellowship?
>
> If banished to a Patmos or bound in a prison. But he cannot voluntarily hold aloof because Christianity is a social religion in ordinances, duties and privileges—Heb. 10.[26]

In discussing the present administration of the kingdom of heaven on earth, organization as distinguished from government, Mr. Campbell was accustomed to lump Episcopalian, Presbyterian, and Independent forms together and reject them all. He notes that each of the three traditional systems as they developed historically were modeled after and assimilated to different forms of civil government.[27] However, it is clear that his position belongs within the Independent, or Congregational, pattern. In the proper sense, he says, the organization is Episcopal, Presbyterian, and Congregational all three.[28] He found the word *ekklēsia* used in the singular in two distinct senses— indicating a single community meeting in a single place and the congregated multitude of all these communities as existing in all ages and nations. One also reads of churches in political districts, but never of *a church in* or *of* any province or district.[29] Mr. Campbell's congregationalism is evident in the following passage:

> A church of Christ is a single society of believing men and women, statedly meeting in one place, to worship God through

the one Mediator. But a church of churches, or a church collective of all the churches in a state, or a nation, is an institution of man, and not an ordinance of God.

Nothing in the constitution of a church of Christ is more evident than its individual responsibility to the Lord Jesus Christ, for all its acts and deeds.[30]

Another statement may also be quoted:

> This body of Christ, composed of all possessed of the same faith, piety, and humanity, so far as it is found at any one time existing on this earth, is composed of many communities or congregations, each of which is in itself and to the members of which it is composed, a miniature or the individual representation of the whole body or church of Christ in the world.[31]

Since Christ is the sole Lawgiver and ultimately the Judge, the officers of the Christian communities could only perform the functions of heralds, declaring the law of the King, and administrators, seeing that His law was executed. Ephesians 4 was the *locus classicus* for Campbell's pronouncements on the subject of the ministry, and from this passage he emphasized that the ministry was a divine gift to the Church, instituted in the divine origin of the church.[32] A twofold distinction was made between the classes of ministers placed in the church. The first distinction was between extraordinary and ordinary ministers, or between those temporarily placed on the earth and those permanently identified with the church.

> The officers of the Christian Church may be arranged under two general classes—the ordinary and the extraordinary. The extraordinary officers were Apostles and Prophets; the ordinary, evangelists, bishops, and deacons.
>
> Apostles and Prophets we have in the Book as the foundation of the church—just as much as we have Christ. But while all the church of all nations and ages has apostles, prophets, miracles, gifts of healing, diversities of tongues in those once

> bestowed for its election and completion, we have evangelists, bishops, deacons, rulers, exhorters, helps.[33]

There was also a distinction made between a ministry performed on behalf of a particular church and that performed on behalf of the universal church.

> Hence we conclude that the first and second ranks—namely, apostles and prophets, officers extraordinary, were given to the whole church in the aggregate; and that *teachers*, whether called evangelists, preachers, pastors, or teachers, constitute a second class of ordinary officers, and are given to every particular congregation that places itself in circumstances favorable to the obtaining of them.[34]

In another passage on church organization he reasons that the officers or servants are of two classes—each particular community has its own bishops and deacons (presbytery and diaconate), and there are officers that belong to the whole Christian community. "Such were the Apostles, Prophets, Evangelists, and public messengers of the Apostolic Age, and such still are the missionaries and messengers belonging to the communities of any one state, nation, or province."[35]

Although the ministry is divinely given to the church, it does not constitute a distinct clergy class nor is it to arrogate titles to itself. Campbell strongly condemned the love for titles and especially the making of an ecclesiastical title a part of a person's name every time he was addressed.[36] To break with past associations he favored using "overseer" for "bishop," "senior" for "presbyter," and "servant" for "deacon." Nevertheless, he continued to bow to common designations, as in the statement, "The standing and immutable ministry of the Christian community is composed of Bishops, Deacons, and Evangelists."[37] These permanent offices in the church were not of such a nature as to raise their occupants to a peculiar status above that of the ordinary Christian. Speaking of the New Testament bishop, he makes a declaration applicable to his view of all ministers:

> But this bishop is neither priest, ambassador, minister of religion, clergyman, nor a reverend divine; but simply one that has

the oversight of one voluntary society, who, when he leaves that society, has no office in any other in consequence of his being an officer in that. . . . To suppose the contrary is to constitute different orders of men, or to divide the church into the common classes of clergy and laity, than which nothing is more essentially opposite to the genius and spirit of Christianity.[38]

Good order demands the selection of public functionaries to represent the congregation and fulfill the administrative posts left by Christ in his church. It further demands an appropriate manner for this selection. The permanent officers of bishops, deacons, and evangelists are appointed to office "by the election and appointment of the community."[39]

> Q. Is there any mode of induction into these offices?
> A. Yes; every thing in the Christian Kingdom that is done is
> to be done in some manner. Every thing is to be done in the
> name of the King, or by calling upon his name. Authority is
> always conferred by the voice and by the hands of the com-
> munity over which the supervision or presidency is to be exer-
> cised. Their own voice and their own hands, their election and
> their separation and consecration to the work, are necessary to
> the appointment of all public functionaries.[40]

On the issue "whether is the right to ordain derived directly from the Lord to the church; or indirectly through a long succession of ordained persons" Mr. Campbell turned to the realm of government, as he often did, to find an analogy to what he considered the real nature of the case:

> All the political official grace or authority vested in the present
> President of the U. S. was not transmitted to him by his offi-
> cial predecessor. It comes to him through the Constitution of
> the U. S. and his oath of allegiance to that Constitution. So is
> it in the Kingdom of Jesus Christ. The New Constitution or
> Testament, invests every officer with the grace and authority
> of his office.[41]

What then is ordination? "It is the solemn election and appointment of persons to the oversight and service of a Christian community. To ordain is to appoint; and all appointment ... was in the beginning *by an election of the whole community*." Campbell adds, "Still we must distinguish between the election or appointment and the mode of consecration or induction."[42] He reasons that there must be some form of setting persons apart to the work. The choice of the community, however, is the essential consideration, without which all forms would be unavailing. In this case, *vox populi vox Dei*. "To comprehend the meaning of the form it is necessary to regard the ordination throughout in the light of a covenant, or an agreement between the congregation that elects and the persons elected."[43] The items of agreement underlying the procedure involve a recognition by the congregation of a need for leadership, so that it agrees with the men proved to be qualified by the Holy Spirit that they devote themselves to the work, in consideration of which it agrees to submit to them in the Lord and sustain them in all respects required.

> It follows that the forms themselves must in some way correspond with the thing signified, and necessarily the parties themselves, and not a distinct order, are to take part.... The corollary from these premises is, that the congregation herself elects and ordains all her officers.[44]

From the viewpoint of a covenant no person can take part in the ceremony of induction unless he is regarded as a member of the congregation and under the authority of those invested with office or is present to give directions to them as a servant of the congregation.

What are the forms of ordination? "Imposition of hands, accompanied with fasting and prayer."[45] The placing of the holy hands of an old soldier of the Cross on the head of another person possesses more spiritual power than all the ordinations of the historic episcopate. Who may or ought to lay hands on bishops, deacons, or messengers elect? "I answer, without dubiety and in few words, The Community, the whole community, or such elders of the community as may be approved in behalf of the congregation."[46] That the ordination is in the nature of a covenant is one of the reasons urged for this point.[47] If the church already has an eldership, "The presbytery or eldership of a single church, may ordain an evangelist, an elder, or a deacon,"[48] acting in the capacity of representatives of the whole congregation. Where Apostles laid on hands in the congregations where they happened to be, they did so as seniors and not as apostles.[49] The case of Titus being commanded to ordain is explained by saying what a command to an agent by those in authority does not necessarily imply that he must execute it in person or with his own hands.[50] If each congregation selects its own officers according to the suggestions of the Holy Spirit found in the New Testament, then it has its officers by divine appointment (Acts 20:28). When ordination is performed according to the manner sanctioned by the actions of the Apostles, the Apostles in a spiritual way participate and give their approval.[51]

The order of ordination is summarized in three steps: (1) After having proved the abilities and character of the men under consideration, the church appoints a day for their election; (2) Having agreed on the men, the church sets a day of consecration; (3) That day is a day of fasting; the members select representatives to impose hands; all unite in prayer; the congregation pronounces amen. [52]

The duties of evangelists, bishops, and deacons encompass the essential activities necessary to the life of the church. Although evangelists in New Testament times were often endowed with special spiritual gifts, such were not essential to the exercise of their office. "Evangelists, or preachers of the Gospel, are not only ordinary, but necessary officers."[53] Their activities and selection are stated in the following terms:

> Evangelists must of necessity do at least three works. They must preach the word, baptize, and teach converts the ways of the Lord. Where churches do not exist they plant them and set things in order. They ordain elders and officers when this is expedient. We therefore conclude that evangelists are not only one of the most necessary and useful officers of the Christian kingdom, but also that they are to be set apart to the work by prayer, fasting, and the laying on of the hands of the eldership (Acts 13:1–3).[54]

Evangelists, or, as he sometimes delighted to call them, "messengers," are separated to the work of proclaiming the word and planting churches by an individual church and are responsible to it. Nevertheless, they belong to the church universal, in behalf of which they labor. This latter principle was to be used by Campbell later to justify their being sent out by an association of churches organized in a cooperative society.[55] Evangelists should labor among a people until they are able to make a Scriptural selection of qualified bishops and deacons. "But constitutionally it is they themselves, and not he that chooses for them their officers."[56]

If a congregation comes together without the agency of a preacher, the responsibility for taking the lead in instruction, worship, and administration of the ordinances is granted and not to be assumed. The congregation selects the best it has to act in a leadership capacity; these are not bishops and are not to act as such. But since this is an infant church, it does not need learned men in its ministry. The principle that those who are most advanced are to instruct those less advanced in Christian learning is a rule of universal application. "There is no wild democracy, no despotic papacy, no self-created ministry, no lay administration of ordinances in this economy."[57] The last phrase apparently is based on the principle that all are priests.

In the New Testament the highest office in a local church is described by two designations—*episkopos* or bishop and *presbuteros* or elder. When contemplated with reference to their age, they were called elders, because they were selected from among the older men. But when regarded with respect to their official relation, they were called overseers or bishops, because their duty was to watch over the flock. There was always a plurality appointed in each New Testament congregation.[58] But Campbell recognized that it was natural for one of superior abilities to be regarded as the president of the congregational presbytery; one must distinguish influence and presidency from authority and official position. Moreover, the single congregation was the largest diocese in the New Testament.

The qualifications for bishops were those that inhered in the nature of their office. They must have the ability to teach, to govern and preside, and the reputation of piety and humanity.[59] The degree of attainment is relative to the character and attainments of the community they are called upon to serve.[60] The duties of bishops, then, are to teach (this includes all forms, but they need not do it all themselves), to rule well (this involves more than presiding but includes watching in behalf of souls), and to visit (in sense of Jas. 1:27).[61] The bishops are not lawgivers, but administrative officers in the kingdom on behalf of Jesus and representatives of the church before the world.

Not much is said by Campbell on the subject of deacons. Chiefly, their activities are set forth in terms of the temporalities of the church. The terms steward, treasurer, almoner, servant, although not perfectly synonymous, are used by Campbell to express the office and duty of the scriptural deacon. Out of the same fund the deacons set three tables: the Lord's Table, the bishop's table, and the poor's table. Certain situations may demand the presence of deaconesses in a church.[62] The essential qualification of deacon is that he be a business man of known fidelity and integrity.[63]

Mr. Campbell sums up his view of an ideal church, so far as organization goes, in the following statement: "A community with its bishops and deacons at home, and its evangelists abroad, every one faithfully at his post, performing his duties to the Lord and to the people, fully displayed the active and salutary spirit of the Christian institution."[64]

Each local church functions in the mutual edification of its members and worship unto God. All citizens should be instructed in the law of the kingdom. "Reading, teaching, and exhortation, then, are all important in the regular meetings of the brethren."[65]

> The other social ordinances inculcated upon, and practiced by, the apostolic churches are still necessary to edification, and obligatory upon us. Such are social prayer, praise, and the Lord's Supper. These are equally incumbent upon all Christian congregations in all meetings of the Lord's Day.[66]

Alexander Campbell writes movingly in describing the solemnity, devotion of feeling, and outward decorum which characterizes an assembly of the saints met for Divine worship. Among his recommendations are that prayer be performed while kneeling, the hymns sung while standing, and the Lord's Supper be eaten with the brethren sitting together in the assembly room.[67]

Discipline, as a function of the church, was treated by Campbell as a means to edification, and hence something to be attended to on the Lord's Day before the whole church. Ultimately it is the whole congregation which must act in cases of discipline, but the case is judged by the "presidents" as the organs of the community. The body concurs in their recommendations, but is not called upon to vote. That would be equivalent to asking them whether they will execute the law of Christ. Where the congregation joins with their overseers is in determining the facts.[68] The proper area for the exercise of discipline is stated in this way: "Un-Christian words and deeds, not men's private opinions, but their individual practices."[69] In matters of personal difficulties the procedure of Matthew18 is to be followed. And in such a situation the case is not to be carried beyond the local church; its decision is final.[70] In all cases, the dispute and the evidence is laid before the elders of the church. In human affairs they represent the judges in Christ's kingdom.

Mr. Campbell finds room in his congregationalism for appeals from one community to another in certain kinds of affairs.

> That every community is independent in managing its own peculiar affairs, has always been our judgment; but that in any matter affecting the conscience or character, or prosperity of other communities, no community can scripturally, prudentially, or justly decide any question in disregard of the views, feelings, and judgment of other communities. Nor can a majority oppress a weak minority without the right of appeal from its decisions.[71]

The concern of congregation for congregation means that if one is in error the other will approach it in love to correct the error. In disputes between congregations other congregations will adjudicate and join in censure or approval. In doctrinal affairs an excommunicated person may appeal to a disinterested community or communities. The following considerations are advanced as a basis for this: (1) that no community called *a* church is absolutely independent of the church of God, but amenable to the whole church for its administration of its affairs; (2) that when a church has any matter on hand which involves the peace and prosperity of other communities or the conscience of a member it is incumbent on it to await the decision of one or more disinterested communities.[72] Acts 15 is used as a precedent for appeals to other congregations for aid in reaching decisions. Mr. Campbell in so doing notes the fact that this chapter has been abused by making it the basis of all the church councils ever held, but if the chapter is not extended beyond its import such intercongregational meetings are appropriate.

The main function for the church is to preach the gospel. The church is a missionary society. It is the pillar and support of the truth. There are many by-products of the gospel, but to Campbell the church has done its work in the world, when it reproduces other churches. With the oracles and ordinances of the reign of heaven it is fully adequate to the conversion of the whole world if it does not prove negligent in its task.[73] To perform this task demands cooperation. This consideration plus the disorderly direction the restoration movement was taking in many places led Campbell to urge a strengthened church organization and the forming of an organ through which the churches could cooperate. This constituted Mr. Campbell's greatest modification of his principles of Independency. His writings resulted in the forming of the American Christian Missionary Society in 1849.[74]

Mr. Campbell's arguments on the subject of congregational cooperation are noted here because it was within the framework of the practical problem of evangelization that they took form.

> Christian communities should co-operate in all things which they cannot so well accomplish by their individual enterprise.
>
> To do this successfully, they must either occasionally meet together, by deputies, messengers, or representatives, and consult together for the better performance of their duties. These meetings, being voluntary expedients in matters of expediency, such persons have no authority to legislate in any matter of faith or moral duty, but to attend to the ways and means of successful co-operation in all objects of duty before them.[75]

But Campbell was not content with this advisory function and saw the conventions as an intermediary actually performing the work. The following rather lengthy passage represents his whole viewpoint expressed on many occasions.

We must make a broad, clear, and indelible distinction between the elements of *faith, piety,* and *morality,* and matters of temporal expediency. The former are wholly and exclusively of divine authority. . . .

Matters of prudential arrangement for the evangelizing of the world, for the better application of our means and resources according to the exigencies of society and the ever varying complexion of things around us, are left without a single law, statute, ordinance, or enactment in all the New Testament. . . .

Whatever, then, secures the independence and individual responsibility of every particular Christian community, and at the same time leaves open to covenant agreement all matters of co-operation in promoting the common cause of Christianity in the world, fully satisfies my mind as to duty and obligation. Hence the Congregational or Baptist associational form of uniting or co-operating, when divested of those appendages, against which we remonstrated 25 years ago, is now and has always been, more acceptable to my views than any other form of co-operation in Christendom. . . .

These covenants or constitutions have, of course, no other authority than the voluntary agreement of the parties or churches entering into them. But they are morally binding. . . .

These meetings should be at regular and stated intervals, but susceptible of special calls on special emergencies. As such meetings have no special control over individual churches, nor any deputed or Divine light to exercise jurisdiction over particular communities, their attention is called and their deliberations are to be devoted to general objects, such as cannot be so well dispensed or attended to by particular congregations.

They will, therefore, occasionally require agents or missionaries, and these must necessarily be under their direction and control, they must be sustained by their liberality, or that of the churches which in their associational character employ them.[76]

Although Mr. Campbell could rightly claim that his basic principles remained unaltered, it is also clear that the preceding passages represent an emphasis on the church universal in contrast to the emphasis seen earlier on the local church. Such an emphasis made logical an organizational expression of this entity on the earth. However, nothing contributed more to turning the Disciples into simply another denomination and to creating division within the ranks of his followers, contrary to his deeper desires, than the principles on which the Missionary Society were founded.

*Originally printed in *Restoration Quarterly* 2 (1958): 228–44.

Chapter 17 Endnotes

1. Since this paper was in its first draft, I read the work by D. Ray Lindley, *The Apostle of Freedom* (St. Louis: Bethany Press, 1957). This book represents the most comprehensive treatment of the subject of this paper and provides an illuminating introduction to Campbell's thought. However, I have not felt it necessary to change any points made or to revise my choice of representative quotations.

2. Hiram VanKirk, *A History of the Theology of the Disciples of Christ* (St. Louis: Christian Publishing, 1907), 111.

3. *Millennial Harbinger* 4th series, vol. 3, (Bethany, VA: Alexander Campbell), 106.

4. W. E. Garrison, *The Sources of Alexander Campbell's Theology* (St. Louis: Christian Publishing, 1900), 73–74.

5. Campbell's emphasis on unity and the methodology of achieving unity have been frequent objects of study. See, for example, J. R. Kellems, *Alexander Campbell and the Disciples* (New York: Richard R. Smith, 1930). For an application of Campbell's teaching to the modern ecumenical movement see the excellent works of William Robinson: *The Shattered Cross* (Birmingham: Berean Press, 1945); *What Churches of Christ Stand For* (Birmingham: Berean Press, 1929); *The Biblical Doctrine of the Church* (St. Louis: Bethany Press, 1948).

6. Lindley, *Apostle of Freedom*, 58ff.

7. See the contribution by W. E. Garrison in *The Nature of the Church* (London: SCM Press, 1952), edited by R. N. Flew for the World Conference on Faith and Order.

8. Garrison, *Sources*, 161.

9. Kellems, *Alexander Campbell*, 377.

10. Alexander Campbell, *The Christian System* (Cincinnati: Standard Publishing), 126.

11. Ibid., 146.

12. Ibid., 125.

13. *Millennial Harbinger,* 3rd series, vol. 2, 62.

14. Campbell, *Christian System,* 123ff.

15. *Millennial Harbinger,* 3rd series, vol. 2, 62. For the importance Campbell attached to this point, see Lindley, *Apostle of Freedom,* 82ff.

16. *Millennial Harbinger,* 1st series, vol. 3, 351ff.

17. Ibid., vol. 6, 192.

18. Campbell, *Christian System*, 150.

19. *Millennial Harbinger*, 4th series, vol. 5, 373.

20. Ibid., 380.

21. *Christian Baptist*, vol. 5, 239.

22. Ibid., 240.

23. Ibid., 199f.

24. *Millennial Harbinger*, 4th series, vol. 2, 123. Cf. Lindley, *Apostle of Freedom*, 75–89.

25. Ibid., 3rd series, vol. 6, 92.

26. Ibid., 1st series, vol. 3, 360ff.

27. *Christian Baptist*, vol. 2, 71. For Campbell's strong feeling against a union of church and state see Lindley, *Apostle of Freedom*, 24–25, 28ff., 155–56.

28. *Millennial Harbinger*, 4th series, vol. 2, 123.

29. Ibid., 3rd series, vol. 6, 221. Later, in arguing for cooperative associations of churches, he stated: "There may be no more scriptural or rational impropriety in calling all the churches in England, Macedonia, . . ., the church in England, the church in Macedonia, . . ., inasmuch as all the particular churches in the world are, collectively the church of Christ." Ibid., 4th series, vol. 3, 304. A harmonization is possible if a distinction is made between a title and a descriptive term.

30. *Millennial Harbinger*, 3rd series, vol. 6, 223.

31. Ibid., vol. 2, 62.

32. Ibid., 4th series, vol. 5, 373.

33. Ibid., 3rd series, vol. 2, 63.

34. Ibid.

35. Ibid., vol. 6, 269.

36. Ibid., 1st series, vol. 1, 427–28. Despite Campbell's protest there was a fondness in the Restoration for "Elder" as such a title.

37. Campbell, *Christian System*, 60.

38. *Christian Baptist*, vol. 1, 55.

39. *Millennial Harbinger*, 1st series, vol. 2, 351.

40. Ibid., 351.

41. Ibid., 4th series, vol. 2, 482.

42. Ibid., 1st series, vol. 6, 497.

43. Ibid.

44. Ibid., 497–98.

45. Ibid., 498.

46. Ibid.

47. Ibid. The passage elaborates other reasons for this procedure.

48. Ibid., 4th series, vol. 3, 482.

49. Campbell, *Christian System*, 65.

50. *Millennial Harbinger*, 4th series, vol. 3, 482. A passage in the same volume seems to contradict the general tenor of the other remarks, which are to the effect that the congregation both elects and installs. Having stressed the congregational element in Acts 6, he says, "But they did not actually invest them with the office. The people's voice and suffrage went no farther [than electing]" (184). Campbell's later writings always speak of apostles and evangelists ordaining, but without comment. If, however, it is understood that these men ordain as representatives of the congregation, there is no necessary contradiction. Still, although Campbell had clearer principles about ordination than most who have followed in his steps, a question may be raised about the role of evangelists in providing for the organization of a church (see below).

51. *Millennial Harbinger*, 1st series, vol. 6, 500.

52. Ibid., 502.

53. Ibid., 3rd series, vol. 2, 64.

54. Ibid.

55. However, service to the universal church was hardly incompatible with responsibility to a local church.

56. *Millennial Harbinger*, 1st series, vol. 6, 496. Campbell warns that an itinerant preacher may be like the ostrich in laying an egg but not caring for it. Ibid., 527.

57. Ibid., 495.

58. Kellems, *Alexander Campbell*, 384ff.

59. *Millennial Harbinger*, 1st series, vol. 3, 351.

60. Ibid., 4th series, vol. 3, 247.

61. Ibid., 1st series, vol. 6, 504.

62. *Christian Baptist*, vol. 6, 210.

63. *Millennial Harbinger*, 1st series, vol. 3, 351.

64. Ibid., vol. 6, 520.

65. Ibid., 3rd series, vol 2, 65.

66. Ibid.

67. Ibid.

68. Ibid., 66.

69. Ibid.1st series, vol. 3, 351.

70. Ibid., 4th series, vol. 3, 491.

71. Ibid., new series, vol. 4, 504.

72. Ibid., 503.

73. Kellems, *Alexander Campbell*, 377ff.

74. E. I. West, *The Search for the Ancient Order* (Nashville: Gospel Advocate, 1949), vol. 1, 166ff. Campbell's position on Societies, whether he changed, and if so, how much, is discussed, 181–195.

75. *Millennial Harbinger*, 3rd series, vol. 2, 66.

76. Ibid., vol. 6, 270ff.

18

The Validity of the Restoration Principle

There is considerable uncertainty whether the traditional restoration approach is viable in these times. The validity of the restoration concept is the crucial question of the raison d'être of churches of Christ. Perhaps we as a people are not ready to undertake an inquiry concerning our fundamental assumptions, but it seems to me vitally important in these days to explore our foundation and determine what is built on rock and what is built on sand. This article offers the writer's understanding of what is valid restoration and some considerations in support of this approach. This is a preliminary enterprise designed to elicit discussion, and the writer welcomes replies.

Alexander Campbell and his associates spoke of their movement as "the current reformation." Later the terminology of "restoration" was developed in order to emphasize the need for a radical approach to remedying the ills of Christendom: not just a reformation of existing churches but a thoroughgoing return to the faith and practice of the New Testament church.

Confusing Term

The word "restoration" in the sense in which it is ordinarily employed is not really a biblical word, and its meaning unfortunately is not always immediately obvious. At least it sometimes does not communicate too well. "Restoration" to an inhabitant of the British Isles means the "Restoration of the Monarchy" after the Cromwellian Commonwealth in the seventeenth century. A Harvard professor responded to the attempt of some students to explain their Restoration heritage with the comment, "Oh, so you want to be first-century Semites!" And then there was the Lutheran teacher of church history who, after hearing me mention the *Restoration Quarterly,* referred to my connection with a renewal journal.

It is not evident that every current attempt to present the restoration plea gives attention to what was at the heart of the original movement to restore New Testament Christianity. A defense of the restoration plea, therefore, calls for some clarification as to what is meant by that plea. My reading from leaders in what is called "The Restoration Movement" has identified three significant emphases. I should like to propose what I consider to be the proper intention of each of these points.

The Biblical Ideal

(1) *To be the New Testament church today.* This point will require further discussion, but immediately a negative clarification may be made. The earliest proponents did not understand the goal of restoring the New Testament church in a historical sense. The church in the first century had as many problems as anybody—false teaching, personal rivalries and misunderstandings, division. No one—not even contemporary charismatics, I presume—wants to restore exactly the church at Corinth. The plea to be the New Testament church today meant to take the apostolic teaching about the church as found in the New Testament as a guide and model. This apostolic teaching is wrapped up in history and cannot be separated from it. The biblical message was always spoken into a historical situation to meet a human need and not into a vacuum. It is thus difficult to sift the eternal from the temporal, and the historical setting participates in the revelation. Indeed there are many features in the actual first-century churches which are commendable, but this is not for

their own sake but insofar as they reflect apostolic instructions. Determining those instructions is what must be accomplished in order to proceed to be the apostolic church in another time. It may be true that, as someone has observed, taking the New Testament teaching seriously will mean restoring some of the problems of the New Testament church as well. That would not, of course, be for their own sake, but as a by-product of trying to follow the apostles' teaching. At any rate, the appeal was to the biblical ideal rather than to the first-century church as it actually was with all its marks of imperfection involved in historical existence.

Neither Union Nor Uniformity

(2) *To practice the undenominational unity of the church.* This unity was understood as neither union nor uniformity. Union would be a federation in which there is an agreement to disagree. Uniformity would be an agreement in opinions and all details. The unity envisioned was to be a solidarity in fellowship, an organic brotherhood. It was to be not just any kind of unity, but unity in Christ, yet a refusal to recognize the present denominational divisions as the proper condition of the church. Failure to achieve this unity has been one of the principal criticisms of the Restoration Movement. Without entering into a major response at this point, I may observe that failure to implement an ideal does not invalidate that ideal—the purpose of an ideal is to hold out a goal that has not been grasped. Imperfections in the implementation of the program of restoration may say more about human weakness and sinfulness than about something basically erroneous in the program itself. Even if not, the way the program has been attempted may be at fault rather than the concept of unity by restoration.

Restoring Humanity

(3) *To restore human beings to the image of God.* Alexander Campbell saw this as the aim of the plea and the grand design of the Christian system. Restoration was not the goal but the means to the goal. The ultimate goal was the restoration of humanity to fellowship with God. Restoration, therefore, involved more than just forms, institutions, externals. These things had their place, and in their place were important, but had to be kept in perspective.

They served a larger design and purpose. Persons must be redeemed; they must be brought into a right relationship with God. One was to mature spiritually for eternal fellowship with God. Unless these things were achieved, all else was in vain.

Point one is the most controversial of the three. It is here that many of those who have been part of the Restoration heritage have concluded that modern historical, biblical, and theological studies have invalidated the restoration approach. Lessing's "ugly ditch" ("accidental truths of history can never become the proof of necessary truths of reason") has been cogently presented by F. G. Downing in his book *The Church and Jesus* (Studies in Biblical Theology Second Series, 10). If we understand the restoration of the New Testament church in the way suggested above, we may bypass many of the problems of historicity raised by Downing. That is, the restoration plea properly understood means to take the canon (as enshrining apostolic teaching and authority) as authority; it takes not the churches described but the church revealed in the New Testament as the pattern for church life today. (There is the subsequent question of what kind of pattern the New Testament provides, but this must await another study—some unfortunately think "pattern authority" is being rejected when it is only their understanding of the kind of pattern that is being questioned.) One, of course, cannot remove the canon from history in such a way as to make it an abstract ideal. There was an interaction between history and the formation of those books into a canon. My other work has demonstrated that I take history seriously in the context of canon. History has had a great deal to do with what we have received as the Scriptures and provides the proper way to determine their meaning. Nonetheless, if we take the canon as our authority, our norm is not settled by determining historically what the "early church" was and what its members believed and practiced. The concern becomes rather the following: we in our history, which has its problems, struggle to be what the apostles tried to help the early churches in their history to be. History is important for this task, but it does not say the only or the determinative word.

The first century fell short of the apostolic standard. So will we, no doubt; but that is no excuse for ignoring or not trying to follow that standard. The question here is whether it is valid to make the effort. Is it legitimate to attempt to construct a church from the biblical materials alone? This is primarily a question of theology and not of history.

It may indeed be pointed out that the approach presented thus far is begging some other, very hard questions. So be it. The attempt here will be to justify the concerns of the Restoration Movement, given its premises of canon and authority. With the clarifications offered concerning what is meant by the restoration plea, some arguments in its defense will now be presented.

Restoration Is Reasonable

The idea of restoration is *reasonable.* It is a common-sense kind of approach which, as will be seen below, is by no means unique to a small group of men of the American frontier of the nineteenth century. The inherent reasonableness of the restoration approach may be illustrated from J. G. Machen's book *Christianity and Liberalism.* An early twentieth-century Presbyterian fighting against the liberalism of his day which advanced religious naturalism under the guise of Christianity, Machen made the following argument:

> Christianity is an historical phenomenon, like the Roman Empire, or the Kingdom of Prussia, or the United States of America. And as an historical phenomenon it must be investigated on the basis of historical evidence.
>
> Is it true, then, that Christianity is not a doctrine but a life? The question can be settled only by an examination of the beginnings of Christianity. Recognition of that fact does not involve any acceptance of Christian belief; it is merely a matter of common sense and common honesty. At the foundation of the life of every corporation is the incorporation paper, in which the objects of the corporation are set forth. Other objects may be vastly more desirable than those objects, but if the directors use the name and the resources of the corporation to pursue the other objects they are acting *ultra vires* of the corporation. So it is with Christianity. It is perfectly conceivable that the originators of the Christian movement had no right to legislate for subsequent generations; but at any rate they did have an inalienable right to legislate for all generations that should choose to bear

The Early Church and Today

the name "Christian." It is conceivable that Christianity may now have to be abandoned, and another religion substituted for it; but at any rate the question what Christianity is can be determined only by an examination of the beginnings of Christianity.

The beginnings of Christianity constitute a fairly definite historical phenomenon. . . .

But if any one fact is clear, on the basis of this evidence, it is that the Christian movement at its inception was not just a way of life in the modern sense, but a way of life founded upon a message. It was based, not upon mere feeling, not upon a mere program of work, but upon an account of facts. In other words it was based upon doctrine. (20, 21)

Machen's argument included what I consider to be the valid appeal to early Christian history but which I have chosen not to defend at the moment. His illustration of incorporation paper exactly fits the appeal to the Bible as the charter of Christianity. Machen's argument does exemplify the reasonableness of the restoration plea and demonstrates that one does not have to come from a restoration heritage to think in such terms. A great part of the appeal of the Campbell-Stone movements was that their preachers offered a rational, practical, no foolishness approach to religious problems.

Revelatory Religion

The idea of restoration has a *theological* basis. It is inherent in Christianity as a historical religion and is grounded in the doctrine of revelation. There are various types of religion. There are nature religions, such as most primitive religions and the Canaanite religion of Old Testament times. In nature religions the recurring cycles of nature determine the outlook and the religious practices. There is a great concern with the natural processes which sustain and propagate life. Then there are culture religions such as the religions of classical Greece and Rome and modern Hinduism. In culture religions the ceremonies are tied to the civilization; the religion is shaped by the culture, and itself exemplifies the culture. There are philosophic religions, such as Buddhism. A philosophic religion is founded on some timeless, universal principle. Finally, there are historical religions, such as Judaism, Christianity and Islam. They are sometimes called prophetic religions, because they look back to a prophet-founder whose word of revelation is authoritative. The historical religions came into existence as a result of a significant historical event viewed as revelatory and creating a community: Israel's exodus from Egypt, Jesus' death and resurrection, Mohammed's call. In historical religions these decisive events and prophetic messages have been written in authoritative books—the Old Testament, New Testament, or the Quran. The point is that in a historical religion something decisive happened in the past which is normative for that faith. Thus there is always a pull to the past, a looking back to the sources, a concern with the way things were at the beginning of the religion. Jews, Christians, and Muslims may get rather far away from their origins, but they never do so completely without severing their religious ties, and they always include in their numbers "Orthodox" advocates of the contemporary authority of their Scriptures. This goes with being the type of religion which they are. Thus in Christian history when in the later Middle Ages the church appeared to have become a "folk religion" or a culture religion, the Renaissance arose with its slogan of "back to the sources."

A doctrine of revelation also accords with the "restoration" mentality. If God has spoken to human beings, this is religious authority for them. There is inherent in the idea of an authoritative revelation from God a concern for the sources. The nature, extent, and application of that authority are legitimate points for consideration. But the very reason they are is the premise that revelation occurred. The restoration plea is grounded theologically in the doctrine of revelation. Whether its advocates have always understood the revelation properly is another question, but the plea arises whenever the concept of revelation is present. I would ascribe primary importance to this theological argument for the idea of restoration.

Historical Expressions

The restoration idea has *historical* justification or support. The restoration or restitution of the New Testament church has been a recurring motif in church history. A. T. DeGroot assembled an astonishing number of religious groups having a wide variety of types of restoration emphasis in his book *The Restoration Principle*. Donald Durnbaugh's better focused study,

The Believer's Church, has identified a particular church type that can be traced in later medieval movements, the Anabaptists, Puritans, Pietists, and Restorationists. Common emphases include, besides the motif of restitution, believers' membership, separation from the world, discipline, the Great Commission, religious liberty, and mutual aid. The restoration theme can be traced earlier in Christian history, as for example in monasticism. One does not have to make the claims of Broadbent's *The Pilgrim Church* to assert that a certain understanding of the nature of the church, its organization, its style of life, and its worship very similar to the Campbell-Stone movements have been recurring features of Christian history. There seems indeed to be something about the nature of Christianity that nurtures the restitution motif among its adherents and something about the nature of the biblical record that produces churches of the same general type when the effort is made to take it as normative for church life. This is not to say that these movements have agreed on all major points with the Campbells or that there is some sort of apostolic succession of dissent in Christian history. But it does say that the idea of restoration is not peculiar or unique. Its validity would be under considerable suspicion to my mind if it were. As the facts stand, restoration answers to a recurring urge, I would say an urge inherent in the nature of the Christian revelation.

Contemporary Interest

The idea of restoration has a *contemporary* interest. Modern biblical theology has shown a renewed respect for the biblical message and has opened up new insights into the meaning of that message. This concern for the meaning of the text is often accompanied by a lack of sympathy or even scorn for a "restoration" position, but many frankly look to the text for theological insights. Impatience with the limitations and failures of those who have championed restoration should not lead to a disregard for the biblical message at this time when respect for it is growing. Not only is contemporary biblical theology more favorable to the restoration position than the theologies current a few years ago, but there is interest in biblical renewal in old-line Protestant denominations, a massive awakening of biblical studies within Roman Catholicism and new youth movements which in their biblical literalism should convince even the most narrow restorationist that his movement is not really a part of fundamentalism. To be relevant is not to be right. But it would be surpassingly strange for members of a movement which has stressed biblical authority to depart from their restoration moorings just when the climate offers greater receptivity for this kind of message than has been available for a number of years.

Practical Implementation

The idea of restoration is *practical*. The preceding points have argued for the general validity of the principle of restoration. There are two further points which I would make on behalf of the particular expression of restorationism to be found among the churches of Christ. This plea has been found capable of practical application all over the world. It has been implemented independently by people around the world without knowledge of the American Restoration Movement. Both isolated individuals and whole groups have been involved. They have not come to conclusions on the peculiarities that have conditioned the American historical development—for instance, they have not had controversies over Bible classes or methods of cooperation—but on the nature of biblical message, human response to it, how to organize the church, and how to worship there has been a basic similarity. By way of contrast, no one has ever adopted Lutheran theology, to take one example out of many, without reading Luther's books or being taught by a Lutheran missionary. Yet many have taken only the New Testament and reached a common understanding of what it teaches. The *20th Century Christian* had a special issue, January, 1966, on some of these cases. That was not complete, but even the cases described there are an impressive demonstration of the practicality of taking the New Testament alone as a guide in church life.

Ecumenical

The restoration plea occupies ecumenical ground. Sometimes the plea has been presented in terms of distinction from others. Not so with the early advocates. It was presented as a uniting concept. And so it can be. The churches of the restoration in their basic positions stand on the undivided ground of historic Christianity. Even the "distinctives" that are most characteristic of the movement are not really distinctive. Take the practice of immersion—virtually all Christians agree that immersion is valid baptism; none regard it as wrong. The position of those who practice sprinkling or pouring is that some use of water other than immersion is equally acceptable for valid baptism. But immersion is not a divisive concept; it is the only action that everyone agrees is acceptable. Or, consider vocal music in worship. No one has said a cappella singing is wrong; the contention is that instrumental music may acceptably be added. The common ground, universally accepted, is vocal music. The weekly communion is not considered wrong in Christendom. Many religious leaders (Calvin to name one) favored it but were not able to secure its practice. It is once more ecumenical ground in contrast to other practices (daily, monthly, quarterly, annually) which are not universally acceptable. Instead of stressing such practices as divisive, the "distinctives" are more properly uniting concepts. This approach is not an argument for what is right (which can be decided neither by the majority nor by a least common denominator), nor is it applicable to issues invented in modern times and not part of the historic practices of Christendom. But this approach is of importance for how one's position is presented.

These considerations argue for the validity of the general restoration approach. They are not all equally cogent, and their own validity will be differently assessed by different readers. The writer expects to learn from his readers.

*Originally printed in *Mission* (August, 1973), 5–10.

19

The Meaning and Significance of the Restitution Motif

I have the double assignment of conducting a Bible study and summarizing the concerns of a church history conference. These two responsibilities, in this case, are not so far apart as might be thought. The history conference has been concerned with the theme of restitution, and restitution is concerned with the Bible.

The Scripture text for our lesson is 1 Peter 1:18–2:3. I want us to focus on the statement, "The word of the Lord abides forever," a quotation from Isaiah 40:8, and the comment, "That word is the good news which was preached to you" (1 Pet. 1:25).

I

We may give an exposition of this passage in terms of a key word for 1 Peter, *salvation*. Notice the sequence of ideas.

First, salvation is through the *death and resurrection of Jesus Christ*. The text says, "You were ransomed . . . with the precious blood of Christ"

(1:18–19) whom God "raised from the dead" (1:21). Those addressed had received "sprinkling with his blood" (1:2) and knew his sufferings (1:11). They had been "born anew . . . through the resurrection of Jesus Christ" (1:3).

The second point to notice is that this salvation *was preached to them*. Good news had been preached (1:23). Verses 10–12 elaborate on this: "This salvation" has "now been announced to you by those who preached the good news to you through the Holy Spirit."

The third point is that on the basis of this message of salvation *they had believed*. "Your faith and hope are in God" (1:21). First Peter is addressed to those "who believe" (2:7). Chapter 1 verses 8 and 9 say, "Though you do not now see him you believe in him. . . . As the outcome of your faith you obtain the salvation of your souls." Directly preceding that, verse 7 speaks of the "genuineness of your faith," and verse 5 says you "are guarded through faith for a salvation ready to be revealed in the last time."

Fourth in the sequence, *they had been baptized* for salvation. Baptism is explicitly mentioned only at 3:21, "Baptism . . . now saves you, not as a removal of dirt from the body but as an appeal to God for a clear conscience." The language of our text, however, is baptismal in other passages: the idea of "obedience to the truth" (1:22) occurs in the discussion of the meaning of baptism in Romans 6:16–17; "born anew" reminds us of John 3:5, "born of water and the spirit"; for the baptismal associations of "born anew" we may further compare the statement of 1 Peter 3:21, "Baptism . . . saves you . . . through the resurrection of Jesus Christ" with the statement of 1:3, "born anew . . . through the resurrection of Jesus Christ."

Fifth in the sequence is the exhortation to *grow up to salvation* (2:3). This concern was already announced in 1:14. "As obedient children, do not be conformed to the passions of your former ignorance." Believers are exhorted to continue faithful, because final salvation remains future. The kind of conduct which is required is the theme of the rest of 1 Peter.

This five-fold sequence may be compared with the "great commission." The great commission comes at the close and climax of the Gospels. It contains the last words of Jesus, his final instructions to his disciples.

The great commission follows the *death and resurrection*. Luke brings these events into the commission itself. He has the risen Jesus say in Luke

24:46, "Thus it is written, that the Christ should suffer and on the third day rise from the dead."

The commission itself was to *preach the gospel*. Luke 24:47 continues, "That repentance and forgiveness of sins should be preached in his name to all nations." Matthew's account of the charge is that they should "make disciples of all nations" (Matt. 28:19).

The response called for was *faith*. This is implied in Matthew's "make disciples." It becomes explicit in the long ending of Mark, "He who believes and is baptized will be saved" (Mark 16:16).

Baptism is included in the response also in Matthew's account, "Baptizing them in the name of the Father and of the Son and of the Holy Spirit" (Matt. 28:19). The *Christian life* is referred to in the command. "Teaching them to observe all that I have commanded you" (Matt. 28:20). Futhermore, the promise, "I am with you always, to the close of the age," reminds us of the promise, the "word of the Lord abides" throughout the *age*. It is the same Greek word in both passages.

So we have a complete correspondence between 1 Peter and the great commission: the death and resurrection of Christ; preaching the message of salvation; believing it; being baptized; and living accordingly.

Professor Franklin Littell has taught us that those groups who have followed the restitution motif have taken the great commission seriously. They have had a distinctive doctrine of the church, and that doctrine is very similar in each group. For them the great commission has determined the nature of the church. The great commission gives the church its mission and tells how one becomes a member of it. It serves as a key to the interpretation of Acts and the rest of the New Testament. People who have followed this have been concerned with the life and practice as well as with the faith of the New Testament church. With the great commission we may find our meeting point between our Bible study and the concerns of church history.

II

Christians with the restitution emphasis have been concerned with *mission*, with preaching the Lord's salvation. They have done so even in the face of persecution. The gospel requires taking up the cross of suffering (Matt. 16:24), and there is a considerable theology of suffering in 1 Peter. The church is the suffering people of God.

And Christians who have taken the great commission seriously have emphasized the *brotherhood of believers,* the visible church. "Make disciples" implies gathering a people, and there is a great deal in 1 Peter about believers as a community, a people, a church. Our text spoke about "love for the brethren" (1:22), but compare especially 2:5, 9—the spiritual house, a holy priesthood, a chosen race, a royal priesthood, a holy nation, God's own people who declare his wonderful deeds.

As Christians have preached the gospel to all nations and as the centuries have passed, they have sought a continuity with the New Testament church in various ways. Consider some of these ways of establishing continuity:

1   Through a *papal head.* Through communion with the bishop of Rome people have claimed a connection through the succession of popes back to Peter and the apostolic church.

2   Through *episcopal succession.* Through communion with a clergy ordained by bishops in the apostolic succession some have claimed a connection with the early church.

3   Through *conciliar creeds.* Through confessing the creeds of the ecumenical councils some have claimed a connection through patristic theology with the ancient church. Accepting the ecumenical creeds and councils gives a theological continuity.

4   Through *family connections.* Being born into a Christian family or a Christian society is thought by others to bring one into the covenant relationship with God. The view is not usually stated in this way, but essentially it comes down to family ties establishing continuity for God's church.

5   Through reviving *accidental features of New Testament times.* Repetition of cultural practices of the first century, such as foot washing, may be taken as a mark of continuity with the primitive church.

6   Through efforts to reproduce the *supernatural phenomena of apostolic times.* Such things as faith healing and speaking in

tongues may be considered as guaranteeing a continuity with the apostolic church.

Whatever values these positions may have, I would affirm that continuity with the New Testament church depends on no such things. It depends on no historical connections—whether of linear succession or of repeated phenomena. To illustrate what I mean, there are churches in New England that can trace their descent back to the seventeenth-century Puritans. Their church covenants are still preserved; their buildings occupy the same plots of ground; their membership rolls contain lineal descendants of founding families. But no one would make the mistake of calling these churches Puritan—in doctrine (some are Unitarian) or in life.

On what then does continuity depend? It depends on what 1 Peter and the great commission made central: *preaching the same gospel* of Christ crucified and raised, and *making the same response* of faith and obedience. New Testament Christianity is to be found wherever people preach and live by the same gospel as in New Testament times. Continuity depends on doctrine and life.

My inclusion of "life" here distinguished restitution churches from churches of the Reformation. The churches of the restitution in the sixteenth century said of the classical reformers in that century that they sought to reform the church by a return to doctrinal purity ("justification by faith") but left life where it had been. Whatever misunderstanding this criticism reflects, it does show where the restitutionists put their emphasis. And restoration movements of every age have said that it is not only right doctrine, but right response to that doctrine that is important in defining the church. Continuity involves more than right doctrine, more than correct administration of the sacraments, more even than the exercise of discipline.

The New Testament church exists where the same gospel is preached (the death and resurrection of Jesus) and persons make the same response to it (in faith, baptism, and Christian living). The idea of restitution is a return to the lifestyle as well as to the doctrine of the apostolic church. It is the conviction that in the doctrine inheres the nature of the response. Restitution, therefore, is concerned with the nature of the church, the kind of worship, the style of life, as well as with a recognition of the central priority of the gospel.

Since the word of God converts, restorationists turn to it for guidance in worship, organization, discipline, and Christian living. These are practical needs which follow on one's conversion to Christ. There is no choice about whether to do them; the only choice is how. Saved men will worship the God who saved them; they will seek to please him in their lives; they must be related to one another in some way. It is natural to let the same Bible which brought the message of salvation guide in these matters too. The Reformers stressed doctrine; the modern church has stressed life (moral and social); restitution would hold these together. The restitution conviction is that the New Testament church exists where the same gospel is preached and the same response is made to it.

III

Programs of restitution have been subject to various dangers. Each theological approach has its peculiar difficulties. That restorationism has problems associated with it is no argument in itself against it as a theological method. Whatever approach one takes will have its own peculiar difficulties. I will mention three of the special dangers involved in a restitution emphasis. In each instance the danger can be avoided.

One danger is *emphasizing minor or peripheral points*. We can all supply horrible examples from our experience. The answer to this problem is to keep things in perspective by emphasizing the central matters (which the great commission gives us): the gospel and the nature of human response to it. Where it is found necessary to affirm other items, their secondary nature will be clearly seen. A true restitution carries its own corrective here.

Another danger is *schism*. Loyalty to restitution has been the occasion for much of the dissent studied in this conference. Nevertheless, I see no reason why the concerns of restitution may not be presented in such a way as to be uniting concepts. In these days of ecumenical scholarship restitution has a contribution to make to the "unity of the Spirit." The Bible, the gospel, Christian living are things all Christians share. The trumpet call to go back to the New Testament church can be sounded not as a retreat into schism, but as a signal for regrouping around the standard, which for the Christian is the cross.

The concern with restitution carries the risk of *substituting orthodoxy or orthopraxy for trust in the Lord.* Restoration implies that we should seek to be right in doctrine and practice. That is important. But its very importance within the restoration perspective may lead one to trust in his being right for his salvation rather than to trust in the One who saves. My salvation does not depend on my being right, but it depends on Christ. As Ron Durham has said, "I believe *that* I should be right; but I believe *in* the rightness [or righteousness] of Christ."

On the other side, there are *advantages to the restoration approach.* Restoration *emphasizes the embodiment of salvation.* The emphasis on life as well as doctrine means the doctrine must be lived. Eric Fromm in *The Revolution of Hope* says: "Ideas become powerful only if they appear in the flesh; an idea which does not lead to action by the individual and by groups remains at best a paragraph or a footnote in a book." To *have* the truth is important: more important is to *be* the truth. As the word of God became incarnate in Jesus, so salvation or the new creation must be embodied in the church. Restitution, better than other theological models, so it seems to me, witnesses to this truth.

Restitution *gives dynamic for continual renewal among God's people.* It is when the concepts of restoration are lost, codified in slogans, or not applied that the church becomes narrow, cold, and rigid. The theme of this conference has rightly united "Restitution, Dissent, and Renewal." Restoration has not only caused division; it has also produced renewal. And the papers have demonstrated the power of the New Testament teaching and example to spark revival in the religious life. A church committed to its own tradition and teaching office as authority or to human creeds is hard to reform. A church *under* the Bible has the basis for continual renewal.

Restitution *provides a point of reference* and a pattern *within which meaningful change can occur.* It is the patterns in life that give identity. This is clearly seen in the human body. It is constantly in a state of flux and change. In the midst of the flux patterns are discernible which are the touchstone of personality identity. In medicine this is called homeostasis. Perhaps the identity crisis in individuals and churches of our time is due to a loss of the idea of a divine pattern. However much the pattern idea has been abused, it is still important, and the restitution motif is a reminder that there are patterns which establish who and what we are. A pattern concept is not antithetical to all change: the blueprint or architectural understanding of pattern may be, but the biological, psychological, and sociological understandings of patterns are not. Indeed, when we think of human life, living, it is change that makes the pattern essential. Without a pattern as a point of reference, change is destructive, not creative.

Let us revert to our biblical text for our conclusion. The abiding word is the gospel preached to you. Human beings need the same gospel today. Sin is still the human problem: "all have sinned" (Rom. 3:23). Christ is still the Lord: "at the name of Jesus every knee should bow . . . and every tongue confess that Jesus Christ is Lord" (Phil. 2:9–11).

Christ is God's answer to the human problem. He is the final definitive revelation of God: God speaks now through his Son (Heb. 1:2). He is the way of salvation: "in none other is there salvation" (Acts 4:12). He is with us "always" (Matt. 28:20) as long as we are carrying out his work—making disciples, baptizing, and teaching.

The word of the Lord abides forever. That, I submit, is the meaning and significance of the restitution motif: preaching the same gospel of Christ, and calling for the same response of faith and obedience—as we do now for a faith commitment by you, for baptism into Christ if you have not received it, and for a life of Christian growth, which is the need of us all.

*Originally printed in Mission (June, 1976), 13–15.

Dr. Everett Ferguson, professor of church history at Abilene Christian University, preached this sermon at the Malibu Church of Christ at the conclusion of Pepperdine University's Conference on "Restitution, Dissent, and Renewal" (see Mission, August and September-October, 1975).

Part V

Religious Liberty

Voices of Religious Liberty in the Early Church

This Bicentennial year of America's Declaration of Independence has directed attention to freedom. The most important freedom is freedom of religion.

Religious freedom received a boost when the Roman Catholic Church endorsed the principle in the "Declaration on Religious Freedom" (*Dignitatis Humanae*) promulgated by Vatican Council II on December 7, 1965. Some of the document's central affirmations are the following:

> The truth cannot impose itself except by virtue of its own truth, as it makes its entrance into the mind at once quietly and with power. Religious freedom, in turn, which men demand as necessary to fulfill their duty to worship God, had to do with immunity from coercion in society. . . .
>
> This freedom [religious] means that all men are to be immune from coercion on the part of individuals or of social

groups and of any human power, in such wise that in matters religious no one is to be forced to act in a manner contrary to his own beliefs. Nor is anyone to be restrained from acting in accordance with his own beliefs. . . .

It follows that a wrong is done when government imposes upon its people, by force or fear or other means, the profession or repudiation of any religion, or when it hinders men from joining or leaving a religious body. All the more is it a violation of the will of God and of the sacred rights of the person and the family of nations, when force is brought to bear in any way in order to destroy or repress religion.[1]

These contemporary developments may serve to encourage consideration of the historical and theological roots of Christian thought on religious liberty. This article will present some of the pertinent statements on the subject from the early patristic period.

The context of the early Christian declarations on religious liberty was persecution by the Roman state. The legal basis for the persecutions has been much debated in scholarly circles.[2] Without entering this debate, some explanation must be given in order to make the arguments of the Christian apologists understandable.

In the book of Acts the Roman authorities did not distinguish Christians from Jews (note especially Acts 18:12–17) and so gave Christianity the protection and favor which Judaism as the national religion of a subject people enjoyed. Acts does show the background for later problems with the government in the popular turmoil, often stirred up by Jews, provoked by Christian preaching (Acts 13:50; 14:19; 16:19; 17:5–9; 19:23ff.). The major change in Christianity's status occurred under Nero, when he placed the blame for the great fire of Rome in AD 64 on the Christians.[3] Christians were now recognized as distinct from Jews, and the populace regarded them with hostility as "haters of mankind." The governing classes looked upon Christianity as a "superstition" (i.e., "credulity"), used for emotional personal religion in contrast to the official state cult. Nero's action applied only to Rome and any proscription issued by him would have died with him. But it established a precedent which could be followed in the provinces, and apparently from this "the name" was a sufficient indicator of guilt (cf. 1 Peter 4:16).

The fundamental surviving text on the legal position of Christianity is the letter of Pliny the Younger, governor of Bithynia, about AD 112 to the emperor Trajan.

> In investigations of Christians I have never taken part; hence I do not know what is the crime usually punished or investigated, or what allowances are made. So I have had no little uncertainty whether there is any distinction of age, or whether the very weakest offenders are treated exactly like the stronger; whether pardon is given to those who repent, or whether a man who has once been a Christian gains nothing by having ceased to be such; whether punishment attaches to the mere name apart from secret crimes, or to the secret crimes connected with the name. Meantime this is the course I have taken with those who were accused before me as Christians. I asked them whether they were Christians, and if they confessed, I asked them a second and third time with threats of punishment. If they kept to it, I ordered them for execution; for I held no question that whatever it was that they admitted, in any case obstinacy and unbending perversity deserve to be punished. There were others of the like insanity; but as these were Roman citizens, I noted them down to be sent to Rome.
>
> Before long, as is often the case, the mere fact that the charge was taken notice of made it commoner, and several distinct cases arose. An unsigned paper was presented, which gave the names of many. As for those who said that they neither were nor ever had been Christians, I thought it right to let them go, since they recited a prayer to the gods at my dictation, made supplication with incense and wine to your statue, which I had ordered to be brought into court for the purpose together with the images of the gods, and moreover cursed Christ—things which (so it is said) those who are really Christians cannot be made to do.

Others who were named by the informer said that they were Christians and then denied it, explaining that they had been, but had ceased to be such, some three years ago, some a good many years, and a few even twenty. All these too both worshipped your statue and the images of the gods, and cursed Christ.

Trajan's reply was as follows:

You have adopted the proper course, my dear Secundus, in your examination of the cases of those who were accused to you as Christians, for indeed nothing can be laid down as a general ruling involving something like a set form of procedure. They are not to be sought out; but if they are accused and convicted, they must be punished—yet on this condition, that whoso denies himself to be a Christian, and makes the fact plain by his action, that is, by worshipping our gods, shall obtain pardon on his repentance, however suspicious his past conduct may be. Papers, however, which are presented unsigned ought not to be admitted in any charge, for they are a very bad example and unworthy of our time.[4]

From this correspondence it is clear that the standard charge against Christians was already "the name."[5] Pliny found three classes among the accused:

1 Those who confessed to being Christians and persisted in the confession. Roman citizens Pliny sent to Rome; others he executed. Whatever else their crime, their stubborn disobedience (*contumacia*) he viewed seriously. No one was under normal obligation to sacrifice (any more than a policeman's order to "move on" implies an intrinsic duty of perpetual motion), but refusal to perform such an act when commanded by a magistrate constituted a serious challenge that governmental authority could not condone. The command itself appears to have been an improvised test as a way of determining who was a Christian and of establishing loyalty (in view of the Neronian charge against Christians).

2   Those who denied ever being Christians. They were released on the performance of a cult act proving they were not Christians. It had been learned that Christians would not perform an act of worship before an image of the emperor, which was idolatry in Christian eyes.

3   Those who had once been Christians but had become apostates. They did what the deniers did. In their case Pliny investigated the nature of the Christian cult (not included in the above quotation).[6]

He found only a "perverse superstition." Their cases he referred to Trajan with the three questions of the opening paragraph: (a) Is any distinction in treatment to be made for age and physical condition? Trajan ignored this question in his reply, for it was within a governor's discretion. (b) Are apostates to be pardoned? (c) Is it the name (*nomen*) or the crimes (*flagitia*) supposedly associated with the name which is to be punished? The last two questions are interrelated. If the punishment was for the name, the apostates could be pardoned as no longer belonging to the group. But if the punishment is for the crimes, inquisition must proceed and the guilty be punished no matter how long ago the crimes occurred. Steadfast Christians would prefer the latter course, because they contended that Christians were not guilty of any crimes. Deniers and apostates preferred the former, for this released them immediately. Pliny wanted to encourage apostates, for he felt that many could be reclaimed from Christianity if apostasy were made easy.

Trajan made three provisos in his reply: (1) Christians are not to be sought out by the authorities; (2) accusations are to be formally made according to the legal process and no anonymous accusations are to be received; and (3) the deniers are to be pardoned, i.e., the punishment is for the name only. This policy was reaffirmed by Hadrian.[7] It remained the legal situation for Christians throughout the second and first half of the third century with minor changes.

There was no empire-wide requirement to offer sacrifice until Decius (AD 250), and so no empirewide persecution of Christianity before his reign. The major challenges to Christianity under Decius, Valerian, and later under Diocletian and Galerius came too late. The church was too large and firmly entrenched for the policy of persecution to succeed. Before that time the persecutions had been local and sporadic. The *threat* of persecution was ever present, but persecution was not a constant experience. Everything depended on the general circumstances of the empire, the attitude of the populace, and the policy of the provincial governors.[8]

The Christian apologists made much of the apparent contradiction between a policy of not searching out Christians, but trying them when formal charges were brought before a governor. (This, however, accorded with normal Roman legal procedures.) They also attacked the policy of condemning for the name without investigation of the truth about crimes which were supposed to attach to the name. (Again, there were parallels in the Roman treatment of other proscribed cults—the Bacchanalia and Druidism.) Increasingly, sacrifice to the Roman gods and emperor became the test case of Christian loyalty to the empire and became obligatory on certain occasions.

Justin Martyr is representative of the second-century apologists:

> By the mere application of a name, nothing is decided, either good or evil, apart from the actions implied in the name. . . . If any of the accused deny the name and say that he is not a Christian, you acquit him, as having no evidence against him as a wrong-doer; but if any one acknowledge that he is a Christian, you punish him on account of this acknowledgement. Justice requires that you inquire into the life both of him who confesses and of him who denies, that by his deeds it may be apparent what kind of man each is. (*Apology* I, 4)

> Wherefore we demand that the deeds of all those who are accused to you be judged, in order that each one who is convicted may be punished as an evildoer, and not as a Christian; and if it is clear that any one is blameless, that he may be acquitted, as a Christian who has done no wrong. (ibid., 7)

Justin's case is both positive and negative. Positively he argues from the teachings and conduct of Christians that they are blameless of anything deserving punishment. Negatively he argues that in paganism (inspired by demons) others have their own deities and are allowed to practice their religion. "And this is the sole accusation you bring against us, that we do not reverence the same gods as you do" (ibid., 24). Athenagoras (*Plea* l) elaborated on the way Rome allowed liberty to a great variety of cults, while Christians were persecuted. There was a crucial difference, however, which the Apologists did not mention: These cults did not challenge the official state cult, for polytheism could allow a variety of cults. Christianity made an exclusive claim.

Justin goes beyond a plea for tolerance. He argues from fulfilled prophecy for the divine truth of Christianity. Moreover, he connects it with the rational order of the universe. Tying in with the Greek philosophical tradition, Justin claims that Christians worship God in accord with reason. In developing this point, Justin anticipates a line of argument on behalf of religious liberty which was to be more explicitly stated by his successors and was to have a long history in Western thought.

> For as in the beginning he created us when we were not, so do we consider that, in like manner, those who choose what is pleasing to him are, on account of their choice, deemed worthy of incorruption and of fellowship with him. For the coming into being at first was not in our own power; and in order that we may follow those things which please him, choosing them by means of the rational faculties he has himself endowed us with, he both persuades us and leads us to faith. And we think it for the advantage of all men that they are not restrained from learning these things but are even urged thereto. For the restraint which human laws could not effect, the word inasmuch as he is divine would have effected, had not the wicked demons scattered many false and profane accusations. (ibid., ch. 10)

Hence, Justin offers this appeal to the emperors:

> Not only does sound reason direct us to refuse the guidance of those who did or taught anything wrong, but it is incumbent on the lover of truth, by all means, even if death be threatened, before his own life to choose to do and say what is right. (ibid., 2)

Tertullian in his Apology makes merry with the contradiction (from the Christian standpoint) of the Roman policy toward the name (chapters 1–3). He further makes the plea for the same liberty that was granted to others:

> For see that you do not give a further ground for the charge of irreligion, by taking away religious liberty, and forbidding free choice of deity, so that I may no longer worship according to my inclination, but am compelled to worship against it. Not even a human being would care to have unwilling homage rendered him. . . . In fact, we alone are prevented having a religion of our own. We give offence to the Romans, we are excluded from the rights and privileges of Romans, because we do not worship the gods of Rome. . . . But with you liberty is given to worship any god but the true God, as though he were not rather the God all should worship, to whom all belong.
>
> But as it was easily seen to be unjust to compel freemen against their will to offer sacrifice (for even in other acts of religious service a willing mind is required), it should be counted quite absurd for one man to compel another to do honor to the gods, when he ought ever voluntarily, and in the sense of his own need, to seek their favor. (*Apol.* 24; 28)

Here Tertullian has proceeded to state another principle, namely that religion in its very essence must be a free choice. He states the principle, on the same basis as the "Declaration on Religious Liberty," most effectively and pointedly in writing to Scapula, the governor of Africa:

> It is a fundamental human right, a privilege of nature, that every man should worship according to his own convictions: one man's religion neither harms nor helps another man. It is assuredly no part of religion to compel religion—to which free will and not force should lead us—the sacrificial victims being required of a willing mind. You will render no real service to your gods by compelling us to sacrifice. For they can have no desire of offerings from the unwilling. (*To Scapula* 2)

Lactantius, writing on the threshhold of the Constantinian era, gave eloquent and forceful expression to the principle so sharply stated by Tertullian. He calls the pagans to a debate:

> It is befitting that they should undertake the defence of their gods, lest, if our affairs should increase (as they do increase daily), theirs should be deserted . . . and since they can effect nothing by violence (for the religion of God is increased the more it is oppressed), let them rather act by the use of reason and exhortations. . . .
>
> There is no occasion for violence and injury, for religion cannot be imposed by force; the matter must be carried on by words rather than by blows, that the will may be affected. . . . Let them imitate us in setting forth the system of the whole matter: for we do not entice, as they say; but we teach, we prove, we show. And thus no one is detained by us against his will, for he is unserviceable to God who is destitute of faith and devotedness. . . .
>
> Religion is to be defended, not by putting to death, but by dying; not by cruelty, but by patient endurance; not by guilt, but by good faith. . . . For if you wish to defend religion by bloodshed, and by tortures, and by guilt, it will no longer be defended, but will be polluted and profaned. For nothing is so much a matter of free-will as religion. . . .
>
> I wish therefore to ask them to whom especially they think that they are doing a service in compelling them to sacrifice against their will. . . . We, on the contrary, do not require that any one should be compelled, whether he is willing or unwilling, to worship our God, who is the God of all men. (*Divine Institutes* V. 20–21)

In his *Epitome of the Divine Institutes* 54 Lactantius makes an important claim for the connection of religion with freedom:

> Who will hear, when men of furious and unbridled spirit think that their authority is diminished if there is any freedom in the affairs of man? But it is religion alone in which freedom has

placed its dwelling. For it is a matter which is voluntary above all others, nor can necessity be imposed upon any, so as to worship that which he does not wish to worship.

Lactantius was one of the authors to preserve the text of the so-called "Edict of Milan" in 313, by which Constantine and Licinius granted toleration to Christianity equal to that which had been enjoyed by other worships.

> It seemed to us that, amongst those things that are profitable to mankind in general, the reverence paid to the Divinity merited our first and chief attention, and that it was proper that the Christians and all others should have liberty to follow that mode of religion which to each of them appeared best; so that the God, who is seated in heaven, might be benign and propitious to us, and to every one under our government. And therefore we judged it a salutary measure, and one highly consonant to right reason, that no man should be denied leave of attaching himself to the rites of the Christians, or to whatever other religion his mind directed him, that thus the supreme Divinity, to whose worship we freely devote ourselves, might continue to vouchsafe his favor and beneficence to us. . . . The open and free exercise of their respective religions is granted to all others, as well as the Christians. For it befits the well-ordered state and the tranquility of our times that each individual be allowed, according to his own choice, to worship the Divinity; and we mean not to derogate aught from the honor due to any religion or its votaries. (*On the Deaths of the Persecutors* 48)

This ideal of equal toleration for all was not long to be implemented. Constantine and his sons were increasingly drawn into Christian doctrinal and disciplinary disputes. The power of the state was turned against Christian heretics and schismatics. In the pre-Constantinian period Christians had been able to say that they had no disciplinary powers except spiritual, culminating in the withdrawal of fellowship. Thus Cyprian contrasted discipline in Israel under the Mosaic Law with Christian discipline:

In those days, indeed, they killed with the sword, while the regime of carnal circumcision held sway; but now that the servants of God live under a spiritual circumcision, the proud and rebellious are killed with the spiritual sword, by exclusion from the church. (*Ep.* IV [LXI]. 4)

Origen made the same distinction:

For Christians could not slay their enemies, or condemn to be burned or stoned, as Moses commands, those who had broken the law. (*Against Celsus* VII. 26)

Rather Christians practiced spiritual exclusion and use of peaceful means (ibid., V. 63). The reason being that "Christ conquers no one who is unwilling but he persuades" *(Sel. in Ps.* 4:1). Christian emperors in the fourth century changed that situation when Constantius exerted the powers of the state in support of Arianism against the supporters of the Nicene Creed. Athanasius saw a parallel with the earlier days of the church. "Persecution is a device of the Devil" (*Apology for his Flight* 23).

The truth is not preached with swords or with darts, nor by means of soldiers; but by persuasion and counsel. But what persuasion is there where fear of the Emperor prevails? or what counsel is there, when he who withstands them receives at last banishment and death?

This modern and accursed heresy [Arianism], when it is cast down and covered with shame by the very truth, forthwith endeavors to coerce by violence and stripes and imprisonment those who it has been unable to persuade by argument, thereby acknowledging itself to be anything other than godly. For it is the part of true godliness not to compel, but to persuade. (*History of the Arians* 33; 67)

Toward the end of the fourth century, when orthodoxy had triumphed in the state as well as the church, the spiritually-minded John Chrysostom restated the position against coercion, applying it to the treatment of the erring:

> It ill befits Christians of all men to correct the mistakes of the erring by constraint. Judges without the Christian fold may exercise coercion against those who are legally convicted, but in our case such men must be brought to a better fruit, by persuasion rather than compulsion. The laws do not confer upon us authority of this sort for coercing the delinquent, nor if they did could we use it, because God crowns those who refrain from evil by choice and not by necessity. . . . The priest has much to do also in gathering up the scattered members of the church. The shepherd can recall a wandering sheep with a shout, but if a man errs from the true faith, the pastor has need of great effort, perseverance, and patience. The wanderer cannot be dragged by force or constrained by fear. Only persuasion can restore him to the truth from which he has fallen away. (*On the Priesthood* II. 3, 4)[9]

Chrysostom himself experienced the power of the secular arm when his ecclesiastical enemies secured his banishment, and he died in exile. Theodosius I had already made orthodox Christianity the state religion. Thus Chrysostom lived in the time when Christianity's involvement with the state meant increasing repression of pagans, heretics, and unpopular preachers. For the coming centuries it was primarily among the sects that witness to the principle of religious liberty was to be found. In the modern era, in new circumstances, the principles of the early Christians have come into practice. The United States led the way in writing the principle into its constitutional structure. Pragmatic and secular considerations, however, sometimes obscure the essential philosophical and theological basis of the principle of religious liberty, to which these quotations testify.[10]

*Originally printed in *Restoration Quarterly* 19 (1976): 13–22.

Chapter 20 Endnotes

1. From the translation in *The Documents of Vatican II*, ed. Walter M. Abbott (New York, 1966), 677, 679, 685.

2. A. N. Sherwin-White, "The Early Persecutions and Roman Law Again," *Journal of Theological Studies,* New Series 3 (1952), 199–213. See also the collection of articles, including this one, in Everett Ferguson, ed., *Church and State in the Early Church,* Studies in Early Christianity 7 (New York: Garland/Taylor and Francis, 1993).

3. Tacitus, *Annals. X* V. 44. 2–8.

4. J. Stevenson, *A New Eusebius* (London: SPCK, 1957), 13–16.

5. In this paragraph I follow G. E. M. de Ste. Croix, "The Persecutions," *The Crucible of Christianity,* ed. Arnold Toynbee (London: Thames and Hudson, 1969), 345–46.

6. Given some discussion in Everett Ferguson, *Early Christians Speak* (Austin: Sweet, 1971), 81–84.

7. Text in Stevenson, *New Eusebius,* 16–17.

8. For a full-scale history of the theme see W. H. C. Frend, *Martyrdom and Persecution in the Early Church* (Oxford: Blackwell, 1957); cf. also R. M. Grant, *The Sword and the Cross* (New York: Macmillan, 1955) and Stuart Perowne, *Caesars and the Saints: the Evolution of the Christian State A.D. 180–313* (London: Hodder and Stoughton, 1972); and the collection of official documents in R. P. Coleman-Norton, *Roman State and the Christian Church,* vol. 1 (London: SPCK, 1966).

9. Cf. to the same effect in *Matt. Hom.* 29:3: But *Hom.* 46:1 says the Lord only forbids killing heretics, not taking away their freedom of speech and breaking up their assemblies.

10. For a general historical survey of the theme with special reference to the American scene see Wilhelm Pauck, "The Christian Faith and Religious Tolerance," *Church History* 15 (Sept. 1946), 220–34.

Roger Williams on Religious Liberty

Roger Williams was banished from the Massachusetts Bay Colony in 1635. The leadership in the Commonwealth of Massachusetts was held by Congregationalist Puritans who took a position of nonseparation from the Church of England.[1] Although Congregationalist in church polity, they still believed in a national church and continued state support of the church as practiced in England and church direction of the state as practiced in the Reformed tradition of Zwingli and Calvin. Roger Williams listed the following positions as the reasons for his banishment:

> First. That we have not our land by patent from the King, but that the natives are the true owners of it, and that we ought to repent of such receiving it by patent. Secondly. That it is not lawful to call a wicked person to swear, to pray, as being action of God's worship. Thirdly. That it is not lawful to hear any of

the ministers of the parish assemblies in England. Fourthly. That civil magistrates' power extends only to the bodies and goods and outward state of men, etc.[2]

John Cotton, who became the principal spokesman for the "New England Way,"[3] took strong exception to this statement of the situation and put the emphasis for the civil banishment on the manner in which Roger Williams contended for his positions and on those positions which threatened the civil order of the colony:

> Two things there were, which caused the sentence of his banishment: and two others fell in, that hastened it. 1. His violent and tumultuous carriage against the patent . . . 2. The second offence, which procured his banishment, was occasioned as I touched before . . . He vehemently withstood [the oath], and dissuaded sundry from it. . . . Two other things fell in upon these that hastened the sentence [and there follows an account of episodes related to Williams' association with the church at Salem].[4]

Despite the participants' preferences for their own way of explaining the events, the sources are in substantial agreement:[5] Williams withdrew from Massachusetts and founded the colony of Rhode Island on the principles of religious and civil liberty.

Roger Williams shared many presuppositions with his Massachusetts antagonists. He was, however, more consistent than they in drawing conclusions from his principles, and he was single-mindedly determined in their application. Moreover, he possessed a disruptive personality. His controversy with the Bay Colony had three aspects: the purity of the New England churches (which Williams questioned), the justice of his own banishment, and the broader question of a policy of religious intolerance.[6] Williams's writings steadily broadened the issue and gave the controversy a lasting significance in American and Christian history.

John Cotton addressed a letter to Williams shortly after his banishment urging him to reconsider his demand that the New England churches have absolute purity. This letter dealt with the ecclesiastical aspect of the dispute and pointed out that Williams had banished himself from the churches. The letter was published in England in 1643 and initiated the literary phase of the controversy. Williams published a reply the following year, *Mr. Cotton's Letter Lately Printed, Examined and Answered*.[7] John Cotton composed *A Reply . . .* (published 1647 and included in *The Complete Writings of Roger Williams,* vol. 2). About the same time as Williams was working on the answer to the first letter, 1644 (while in England to secure a charter for Rhode Island), he also wrote a more ambitious work, using Cotton as his point of departure. About 1634 or 1635 an Anabaptist prisoner in Newgate had collected arguments against "persecution for cause of conscience," a copy of which was forwarded to Cotton for his reply. (One of these arguments was that "persecution for cause of conscience is condemned by the ancient and later writers" including Tertullian, *Scapula* 2; Hilary, *Against the Arians* I. 3, 4; and Jerome, *In Jeremiah,* Book IV, introduction). Cotton's *Answer* had not been published, but Williams now incorporated the prisoner's piece and Cotton's *Answer* in his *Tenent, of Persecution, for cause of Conscience, discussed, in a Conference betweene Truth and Peace* (1644, vol. 3 of *Complete Writings*). John Cotton came back in 1646 with *The Controversy Concerning Liberty of Conscience* and in 1647 with an explicit reply, *The Bloudy Tenent Washed and Made White in the Bloud of the Lambe*.[8] The contents of the latter are taken up point by point in *The Bloody Tenent Yet More Bloody*, published while Williams was back in England (1652, *Complete Writings,* vol. 4). John Cotton died in 1652 before receiving the last treatise, so no more literary blood was let. A later treatise by Williams, *The Hireling Ministry None of Christ's* (1652, *Complete Writings,* vol. 7, 152–91) is a cogent statement of Williams's principles applied to the state-enforced collection of tithes in England to support the clergy.[9]

No effort will be made here to present the position of Cotton[10] nor to review the total case made out by Williams.[11] These matters will be touched on only as supplying a context for quotations from Williams which demonstrate the importance of his thinking for religious liberty.[12]

Cotton shared so many presuppositions with Williams that he was at a disadvantage before the latter's rigid consistency. He leaves the impression of defending something which in other circumstances he would not defend in order to protect the New England experiment against the "radical" ideas of Williams. His exegesis of the New Testament does not distinguish between instructions to the state and to the church, between persecution and excommunication. The kernel of Cotton's defense of the New England practice is a distinction between persecution for cause of conscience and what he calls persecution for sinning against one's own conscience:

> For an erroneous and blind conscience ... it is not lawful to persecute any, till after admonition once or twice: and so the apostle directs, Titus 3:10, and gives the reason, that in fundamental and principal points of doctrine or worship, the word of God in such things is so clear, that he cannot but be convinced in conscience of the dangerous error of his way, after once or twice admonition, wisely and faithfully dispensed. And then if any one persist, it is not out of conscience, but against his conscience, as the apostle says, verse 11. He is subverted and sins, being condemned of himself, that is, of his own conscience. So that if such a man after such admonition shall still persist in the error of his way and be therefore punished; he is not persecuted for cause of conscience, but for sinning against his own conscience. (3, 42, quoting Cotton)

Williams argued that there were many inconsistencies in the case advanced in behalf of the New England position. The magistrate was supposed to enforce the first table of the law (religious duties) as well as the second (moral duties), but was denied spiritual competence (only the church can decide in these matters):

> How can he determine what the true church and ordinances are, and then set them up with the power of the sword? How can he give judgment of a false church, a false ministry, a false doctrine, false ordinances, and with a civil sword pull them down, if he have no spiritual power, authority, or commission from Christ Jesus for these ends and purposes? (3, 227; cf. 374ff.)

If rulers have authority to enforce religion, then all rulers may do so (3, 187–88). But the Massachusetts position denied to magistrates the right to enforce false ceremonies, ministries, and doctrines (3, 312–13). Thus there was introduced the crucial matter of partiality: God's people, in the Massachusetts view, could act against the magistrates' consent, but others could not (3, 395). Liberty of conscience belonged only to God's people. But that raised another problem: "Who shall judge whether they are God's people or no?" (ibid.).

> Since there is so much controversy in the world, where the name of Christ is taken up, concerning the true Church, the ministry, and worship, and who are those that truly fear God; I ask who shall judge in this case, who be they that fear God? (3, 214)

Everyone thinks that he is right. All those who persecuted had the same conviction:

> Compel them to mass (say the Papists): compel them to church and common prayer, say the Protestants: compel them to the meeting, say the New English. In all these compulsions they disagree amongst themselves: but in this, viz. Compel them to pay; in this they all agree. (2, 300; cf. 304)

These were ad hominem strikes at his New England opponents. Williams saw the whole arrangement as resting on fundamental errors. In *The Bloody Tenent Yet More Bloody* he stated them this way:

> There are two opinions which have bewitched the nations professing the name of Christ. First, that a national church or state is of Christ's appointing. Secondly, that such a national church or state must be maintained pure by the power of the sword. (4, 481–82)

In the address "To the General Courts" of New England introducing that treatise he said:

> I have therefore in all these agitations humbly presented (amongst others) two fundamental hints or considerations. First that the people (the original of all free power and government) are not invested with power from Christ Jesus, to rule his wife or church, to keep it pure, to punish opposites by force of arms,

etc. Secondly, that the pattern of the national church of Israel, was a none-such, unimitable by any civil state, in all or any of the nations of the world beside. (4, 28–29)

The contention that the state is the people and therefore has no power over the church rests on Williams's larger political theory, from which a few points will be selected below. A national church, he claimed, was contradictory to John Cotton's advocacy of a congregational church (e.g., 4, 43). Much of Williams's content was concerned with scriptural argumentation to show that Christ had not instituted a national church and that his teaching opposed the use of physical coercion. The parable of the tares (Matt. 13:24–30, 38) played a central role.[13] The Old Testament precedent of Israel was a cornerstone of Puritan political theory, so much of Williams's time was spent arguing that the Old Testament was for the Jews alone (3, 358, 360) and that the Jewish state was typical of spiritual aspects of Christ and the church but not a precedent for civil governments (3, 316ff., 353–54; 4, 456). Williams made a sharper distinction between the Old Testament and the New Testament than Puritans normally did.[14]

On the specific matter of persecution Williams contended that it fails of its purpose. Persecution, instead of converting people, either makes hypocrites of them (4, 209) or confirms them in their views (3, 272). Since most governments have not been Christian, persecution would more often coerce consciences in the wrong way. Indeed persecution destroys conscience:

> This binding and rebinding of conscience, contrary or without its own persuasion, so weakens and denies it, that it (as all other faculties) loses its strength, and the very nature of a common honest conscience. (4, 209)

Persecution, he said,

> . . . corrupts and spoils the very civil honesty and natural conscience of a nation. Since conscience to God violated, proves (without repentance) ever after, a very jade, a drug, loose and unconscionable in all converse with men. (4, 498–99)

Persecution might bring an outward improvement, he stressed,

> . . . but the misapplication of ordinances to unregenerate and
> unrepentant persons hardens up their souls in a dreadful sleep
> and dream of their own blessed estate and sends millions of
> souls to hell in a secure expectation of a false salvation. (3, 225)

Besides its effects on the conscience, persecution is bad for the state itself.
Persecution disturbs the civil peace, does not preserve it (4, 70). The principle of persecution is actually a threat to magistrates, because Papists and
Protestants alike want a government favorable to them and will depose and
kill "heretical, apostate, blaspheming magistrates" (4, 205). Those states that
prospered, like the Dutch (4, 9), practiced toleration, but persecuting states
forced good citizens to flee and so stunted their own growth (4, 498).

Roger Williams had definite ideas about the limits and functions of civil
government. He made a sharp distinction between church and state (4, 410):

> It is true, I do absolutely deny it (against all comers) to be the
> burden of the civil state to take cognizance of any spiritual cause;
> and I do positively assert it, to be the proper and alone work of
> the holy Son and Spirit of God in the hands of his Saints and
> Prophets, to manage heavenly and spiritual causes (and that only
> with spiritual weapons against spiritual oppositions). (7, 152)

The purpose of the state is "preservation of mankind in civil order and peace"
(3, 398). Magistrates owe protection to the persons and goods of their subjects,
whether they be of true or false religion (3, 354, 372–73). This would mean
a plurality of creeds (7, 174, 181; and compare the remarkable metaphor of a
ship's crew in 6, 278–79). The power of magistrates "is not *religious, Christian,*
etc., but natural, human, and civil" (3, 398). Hence a Christian magistrate
(or merchant, physician, lawyer, etc.)—although called by Christianity to act
for a higher end, from higher principles, and in a more heavenly manner—is
no more a magistrate than a person of any other religion. Every government
draws its power and commission from the people (4, 187), and God has not
given to the people rule over Christ's spouse. Magistrates do contribute to
spiritual ends when by preserving freedom of worship they secure freedom
to the word of God: the civil state by removing its restrictions will promote
the propagation of the gospel of Jesus Christ (7, 178–79).

Williams goes beyond political and pragmatic considerations to ground liberty of conscience in theology. He was primarily a religious thinker, and his distinctive contribution to soul liberty was in his religious arguments. As an instance, his plea for liberty of conscience was made for the religious conscience, not conscience in the absolute. The state could punish offenders against the moral order of society. Indeed, even religious conscience was not warrant for transgressing *civil* law (3, 171). The state could not legislate in purely religious matters. This principle was rooted in the sovereignty of God. The limitation of the state allowed for the freedom of God to act on the human soul and conscience.

Conscience is "a *persuasion* fixed in the mind and heart of a man, which enforces him to judge . . . and to do so and so, with respect to *God,* his worship, etc." ("Letter to Major Endicot, Governor of Massachusetts," 4, 508). The conscience might very well be wrong, but this was no reason for coercing it. As a "persuasion" it could only be corrected by persuasion. Persecution is any molestation of a person for what he holds or fails to hold in religion (3, 63; cf. 4, 7). Liberty, on the other hand, is not toleration. The latter is based on "state policy and necessity of affairs" and so can be withdrawn as well as granted ("To Parliament," 4, 6). "It is the duty of the civil magistrate to suppress all violence to the bodies and goods of men for their souls' beliefs and to provide that no one person in the land be restrained from or constrained to any worship, ministry, or maintenance" (7, 190). Williams found good political arguments for religious liberty, and these have attracted the interest of historians of American political thought,[15] but the essential thing is that religious liberty is rooted in the will of God, the relation of the conscience to its creator.

The distinction between church and state included the distinction in their respective weapons.

> An arm of flesh and sword of steel cannot reach to cut the darkness of the mind, the hardness and unbelief of the heart, and kindly operate upon the soul's affections to forsake a long continued Father's worship, and to embrace a new, though the best and truest. This work performs alone that sword out of the mouth of Christ with two edges, Rev. 1 and 3. (3, 354)

The distinction between the sword of steel and the sword of the word occurs frequently. "Men repose more *confidence* (however they deceive themselves to the contrary) in the *sword* of *steel* that hangs by the side of the *civil officer,* than in the two-edged sword proceeding out of the mouth of *Christ Jesus*" (4, 261). Yet, to persecute is to charge Christ's ordinances for spiritual censure with insufficiency (3, 385), when in reality the sword of the Spirit is sufficient for all needs (4, 380).

> It is not the purpose of God, that the spiritual battles of his Son shall be fought by carnal weapons and persons. It is not his pleasure that the world shall flame on fire with civil combustions for his Son's sake. It is directly contrary to the nature of Christ Jesus, his saints and truths, that throats of men . . . shall be torn out for his sake, who most delighted to converse with the greatest sinners. It is the counsel of God that his servants shall overcome by 3 weapons, of a spiritual nature, Revel. 12:11. And that all that take the sword of steel shall perish. (3, 421)

Christ's purpose (Luke 9:56) is not "to save *souls* by destroying *bodies,* but to save *soul* and *body*" (4, 256). It is "impossible for any man or men to maintain their *Christ* by their *sword,* and to worship a true *Christ!* to fight against all *consciences* opposite to theirs, and not to fight against *God* in some of them" ("Letter to Major Endicot . . ." 4, 515). Christ's church "are so far from smiting, killing, and wounding the opposites of their profession and worship, that they resolve themselves patiently to bear and carry the cross and *gallows* of their *Lord* and *Master,* and patiently to suffer with him" (4, 48). The church is the persecuted, not those who persecute.

The essential principle is vividly but pointedly stated in the affirmation that the tenet of persecution "puts out the very *eye* of all true *faith,* which cannot but be as free and voluntary as any *virgin* in the *world,* in *refusing* or *embracing* any *spiritual offer* or *object* (4, 495). Williams "wanted freedom because it was the only way to reach the true God."[16]

As a consequence, liberty of conscience must be the right of all men. As an example of his position, pertinent to his contemporaries, Williams stated:

> I confess in this plea for freedom to all consciences in matters (merely) of worship, I have impartially pleaded for the freedom of the consciences of the Papists themselves, the greatest enemies and persecutors (in Europe) of the saints and truths of Jesus: Yet I have pleaded for no more than is their due and right, and (whatever else shall be the consequent) it shall stand for a monument and testimony against them, and be an aggravation of their former, present, or future cruelties. (4, 47)

To the suggestion that he favored the Romish party in England, he said: "All that [he] pleaded for, is an impartial *liberty* to their *consciences* in *worshipping God* as well as to the *consciences* and *worships* of other their fellow-subjects" (4, 255).

Williams concluded his summary of *The Hireling Ministry* with this proposition:

> The free permitting of the consciences and meetings of conscionable and faithful people throughout the Nation, and the free permission of the Nation to frequent such assemblies, will be one of the principal means and expedients (as the present state of Christianity stands) for the propagating and spreading of the Gospel of the Son of God. (7, 150)

That was the goal and concern of Roger Williams.

*Originally printed in *Restoration Quarterly* 19 (1976): 155–64.

Chapter 21 Endnotes

1. Perry Miller, *Orthodoxy in Massachusetts, 1630–1650* (Cambridge, MA: Harvard University Press, 1933), gives a classical delineation of their position.

2. *The Complete Writings of Roger Williams*, vol. 1 (New York: Russell & Russell, 1963 [a reprint of the original Narragansett Club Publications edition with an additional volume]), 40. Citations in parentheses in the text will be to volume and page numbers of this edition. Spelling has been modernized in all the quotations.

3. Among his works may be mentioned *The Way of the Churches of Christ in New England* (London: Matthew Simons, 1645) and its sequel, *The Way of the Congregational Churches Cleared* (London: Matthew Simons, 1648).

4. Reprinted in *The Complete Writings of Roger Williams,* vol. 2, 44.

5. Conveniently collected in T. P. Greene, ed., *Roger Williams and the Massachusetts Magistrates,* Problems in American Civilization (Boston: Heath, 1964), 1–21.

6. E. H. Emerson, *John Cotton* (New York: Twayne, 1965), 136.

7. Both published in *The Complete Writings of Roger Williams,* vol. 1.

8. London: 1647. Never reprinted, but several copies are available.

9. E. F. Hirsch ("John Cotton and Roger Williams: Their Controversy Concerning Religious Liberty," *Church History* 10 [1941], 38–51) misunderstands Williams in important respects, but she does point rightly to the relation of this controversy to events under Cromwell in England.

10. See Larzer Ziff, *The Career of John Cotton* (Princeton: Princeton University Press, 1962). Conrad Wright, "John Cotton Washed and Made White," in F. F. Church and T. George, eds., *Continuity and Discontinuity in Church History* (Leiden: Brill, 1979), 338–50.

11. For the whole structure of Williams's thought see Edmund S. Morgan, *Roger Williams: The Church and the State* (New York, Harcourt, Brace & World, 1967); for its relation to his contemporaries' political theory see James E. Ernst, *The Political Thought of Roger Williams* (Port Washington, NY: Kennikat Press, 1966 reprint), who makes him out a democratic political philosopher. A recent study emphasizing the social forces of the time is John Garrett, *Roger Williams: Witness beyond Christendom, 1603–1683* (New York: Macmillan, 1970).

12. That his political thinking was derived from theology and that Williams remained a Puritan Biblicist is stressed by Mauro Calamandrei, "Neglected Aspects of Roger Williams' Thought," *Church History* 21 (1952), 239–58. See LeRoy Moore, "Roger Williams and the Historians," *Church History* 32 (1963), 432–51, for the history of the interpretation of Williams, and Moore, "Religious Liberty: Roger Williams and the Revolutionary Era," *Church History* 34 (1965), 57–76, for the relation of his thought to theory in the time of the Revolution.

13. The historical background to this interpretation may be seen in Roland Bainton, "The Parable of the Tares as the Proof Text for Religious Liberty to the End of the Sixteenth Century," *Church History* 1 (1932), 67–89.

14. Perhaps overstressed in Perry Miller, *Roger Williams: His Contribution to the American Tradition* (Indianapolis: Bobbs-Merrill, 1953), 32ff., 149ff.

15. Ernst, *Political Thought,* 177–88.

16. Morgan, *Roger Williams,* 141.

Part VI

Biblical Eschatology

Biblical Eschatology
1. Greco-Roman and Jewish Backgrounds

Greco-Roman Views of the Afterlife

Eschatology refers to the doctrine of last things. What will happen at the end times and in the afterlife? A proper understanding of the New Testament texts requires an examination of the concepts and beliefs of the cultures at the time Christianity arose.

The common view in classical Greece was that the soul is a shadow or shade.

> And when sleep seized Achilles . . . then there came to him the spirit of hapless Patroclus, in all things like his very self, in stature and fair eyes and in voice, and in like raiment was he clad withal; and he stood above Achilles' head and spoke to him, saying: "You sleep and have forgotten me, Achilles. Not in my life were you unmindful of me, but now in my death! Bury me with all speed, and I pass within the gates of Hades. Afar do the spirits keep me aloof, and phantoms of men what have done with toils, neither suffer they me to join myself to them beyond the River, but vainly I wander through the wide-gated house of Hades. . . .

> Then in answer spoke to him Achilles . . .: "I pray you, draw nearer; though it be but for a little space let us clasp our arms one about the other, and take our fill of dire lamenting." So saying he reached forth with his hands, yet clasped him not; but the spirit like a vapor was gone beneath the earth, gibbering faintly. . . . "[T]he whole night long has the spirit of hapless Patroclus stood over me, weeping and wailing, and gave me charge concerning each thing, and was wondrously like his very self." (Homer, *Iliad* 23.62–76; 93–107)

This passage expresses some of the key features of Greek views of the afterlife. The soul looks exactly like the living self, but there is nothing to take hold of. The passage also speaks to the need for burial of the deceased; otherwise his shade wanders in a no man's land around the earth, unable to enter the underworld.

Hades was the god of the underworld, and the word came to refer to the underworld itself, the place of departed spirits. Thus the word was used for the grave and for death, which was then itself personified. Hades was a dreary place where "life" in some sense continues but what makes life worthwhile is gone.

The geography of the underworld was not well defined. There was some consideration given to Tartarus as a place of punishment for the extremely wicked. It was lower than Hades. Zeus is speaking:

> I shall take and hurl him into murky Tartarus, far, far away, where is the deepest gulf beneath the earth, the gates whereof are of iron and threshold of bronze, as far beneath Hades as heaven is above earth: then shall you know how far the mightiest am I of all gods. (*Iliad* 8.13–17)

Similarly Hesiod speaks of "dim Tartarus in the depth of wide-pathed Earth" (*Theogony* 119). Tartarus is referred to in 2 Peter 2:4.

The Greeks also occasionally spoke of Elysium (Elysian Fields) or the Islands of the Blessed for a favored few. The first mention is in the *Odyssey*:

> But you, Menelaus, son of Zeus, are not ordained to die and meet your fate in Argos . . ., but the deathless gods will convey

you to the Elysian plain and the world's end, . . . where life is easiest for men. No snow is there, nor yet great storm, nor any rain; but always ocean sends forth the breeze of the shrill West to blow cool on men. (Homer, *Odyssey* 4.563ff.)

Virgil provides a description of the common view at the beginning of the Christian era. Hermes (Mercury) led the soul of the deceased to a provisional gathering place in the underworld. Aeneas and a companion are allowed to go down into the underworld. Charon carries the buried across the River Styx; the unburied flit about the shores. Across the River there is a parting of the ways. To the left the wicked go to punishment in Tartarus. These include those who hated their brothers, or killed their father, or did not provide for their kin, or committed adultery, or did not keep their oaths, or betrayed their country, or committed incest. Various grim punishments were assigned to each. The path to the right led to Elysium. Here were those who died fighting for their fatherland, pure priests, good poets, those who ennobled life by truths, and those who by service won remembrance among men. It is possible to recognize the deceased in both places, but theirs is a shadowy existence and their form cannot be clasped.[1]

Some Greeks advanced the idea of the immortality of the soul. Orphics and Pythagoreans believed this. One view was that after three good lives in the cycle of rebirth (metempsychosis) the soul went to the tower of Cronus in the Islands of the Blessed (Pindar, *Olympian Odes* 2.56–76).

Plato was the influential figure in giving importance to the immortality of the soul. His dialogue *Phaedo* gives several arguments. The key thought is that the soul gives life; the opposite of life is death; the soul never receives the opposite of what she brings; the soul does not admit of death, therefore is immortal. Plato posited the preexistence as well as the postexistence of the soul.

Plato also described a judgment (*Phaedo* 112–114): "The souls of most of the dead go to the Acherusian lake [in the underworld]. After remaining there the appointed time, which is for some longer and for others shorter, souls are sent back to be born again into living beings" (*Phaedo* 113A–B). "Those who have lived neither well nor ill" are purified by paying a penalty for their wrongs and for their good deeds receive rewards. Those who are exceedingly wicked are thrown into Tartarus, "never to emerge," but those who are curable are cast out of Tartarus after a year (113D–114A).

> Those who are found to have excelled in holy living are freed from these regions . . . and dwell upon the earth. And of these, all who have duly purified themselves by philosophy live henceforth altogether without bodies, and pass to still more beautiful abodes which it is not easy to describe. (*Phaedo* 114B–115A)

The dialogue *Gorgias* also describes judgment according to Plato:

> Every person who has passed a just and holy life departs after his decease to the Isles of the Blest, and dwells in all happiness apart from ill; but whoever has lived unjustly and impiously goes to the dungeon of requital and penance which, you know, they call Tartarus. (*Gorgias* 523A–B)

In this context Plato gives a definition of death that became a commonplace: "Death, as it seems to me, is actually nothing but the separation of two things, the soul and the body, from each other" (*Gorgias* 524B).

By the beginning of the Christian era, there was another influential development, the idea of an astral afterlife. Cicero's "Dream of Scipio" gives expression to the new vision of the afterlife.

> But Scipio, . . . cultivate justice and the sense of duty [*pietas*], which are of great importance in relation to parents and kindred but even more in relation to one's country. Such a life [spent in the service of one's country] is a highway to the skies, to the fellowship of those who have completed their earthly lives and have been released from the body and now dwell in that place which you see yonder . . ., which you, using a term borrowed from the Greeks, call the Milky Way. (Cicero, *Republic* 6.16)

The passage continues with the Platonic distinction of body and immortal soul.

> Be sure that it is not *you* who are mortal, but only your body; nor is it *you* whom your outward form represents. Your spirit is

your true self, not that bodily form which can be pointed to with the finger. Know yourself, therefore, to be a god .... And just as that eternal God moves the universe, which is partly mortal, so an eternal spirit moves the fragile body. (*Republic* 6.26)

The place of torment for the wicked was also in the realm above the earth.

The souls of those who are given to sensual pleasures, and are, so to speak, its slaves, who follow their desires in a life devoted to pleasure, and violate the laws of gods and men—such souls, after leaving their bodies, still fly about close to the earth, and do not return to this place until after many centuries of torment. (*Republic* 6.29)

A related development in the Platonic school was that the souls (explicitly not the bodies) of the virtuous could ascend from "human beings to the status of heroes, from heroes to demi-gods, and from demi-gods, after they have been made pure and holy, ... and have freed themselves from mortality and sense, to gods, ... thus achieving the fairest and most blessed consummation" (Plutarch, *Romulus* 28.6–8).

Eventually the older view of a subterranean afterlife and the newer astral afterlife were reconciled with good persons going up and bad persons down. An intermediate "purgatory," hinted at by Plato, provided purification for those in between.

Jewish Views of the Afterlife and Eschatology

There was no uniform Jewish teaching concerning the afterlife in the New Testament period. Several options were available.

The general Old Testament view was similar to the early Greek view. *Rephaim* was the Hebrew word for the shades or ghosts of a person, like the souls of the deceased in Homer—Job 26:5; Proverbs 2:18; Isaiah 14:9; 26:14, 19. We'll come back to that later.

Sheol was the Hebrew word for the underworld, again comparable to the Greek Hades—Genesis 37:35 (where one goes at death); Numbers 16:30, 33 (Korah and his companions went down into Sheol alive). Sheol was a dark (and dry) place—Job 17:13, 16. In Sheol all are alike—Job 3:16–19. To be there was to be separated from God—Isaiah 38:18. Yet some distinction was recognized between the good and the bad—Psalms 9:17; 16:10 (quoted in Acts 2:31); 49:14–15.

This view continued in post-biblical Judaism—Sirach 17:27–28; 38:20–23. Hades is the destiny of the wicked: "The way of sinners is paved with smooth stones, but at its end is the pit of Hades" (Sirach 21:10; cf. 36:8–11).

The Sadducees maintained this perspective, in effect denying an afterlife—Luke 20:27–38; Acts 23:8. Josephus says of the Sadducees, "As for the persistence of the soul after death, penalties in the underworld, and rewards, they will have none of them" (*War* 2.165) and "The Sadducees hold that the soul perishes along with the body" (*Antiquities* 18.16).

Some Jews accepted the Greek philosophical view of immortality. This is implied in the Wisdom of Solomon's affirmation that "God created us for incorruption and made us in the image of his own eternity" (2:23) and that "the souls of the righteous are in the hand of God," so "their hope is full of immortality" (3:1, 4). This hope is for the righteous only, since the ungodly will completely perish (4:18–19; 5:14–15; 15:3). "Immortal souls" and "eternal life" are explicit in 4 Maccabees 14:5–6; 15:3; and 18:23.

Josephus attributed belief in the immortality of the soul to the Essenes: "They regard the soul as immortal and believe that they ought to strive especially to draw near to righteousness" (*Antiquities* 18.18). There is a fuller description in *War* 2.154–56, but the explicit comparison to Greek thought raises the suspicion that Josephus is accommodating their view to Greek ideas, for *War* 2.153 implies a resurrection.

Philo follows Plato:

> Souls are never colonists leaving heaven for a new home. Their way is to visit earthly nature as men who travel abroad to see and learn. So when they have stayed awhile in their bodies, and beheld through them all that sense and mortality has to show, they make their way back to the place from which they set out at the first. To them the heavenly region, where their citizenship lies, is their native land; the earthly region in which they became sojourners is a foreign country. (*Confusion of Tongues* 78)

In Judaism the immortality of the soul was the gift of God to the righteous, not a natural quality of the soul, as in Plato and as this passage from Philo implies.

A resurrection of the body is suggested in Isaiah 26:19 and affirmed in Daniel 12:2. The prospect of a resurrection for the righteous sustained the seven brothers and their mother in their martyrdom for refusal to eat swine flesh at the command of the Syrian king (2 Maccabees 7:9, 14, 23) and was a basis for prayer on behalf of the dead (12:44–45).

The *Psalms of Solomon* speaks of the "eternal destruction" of sinners, "but those who fear the Lord shall rise up to eternal life" (2.31 and 3.9–12). The inheritance of sinners "is Hades, and darkness and destruction; and they will not be found on the day of mercy for the righteous; but the devout of the Lord will inherit life in happiness" (14.9–10). The rising up to eternal life, however, may refer to the immortality of the spirit that rises to God rather than a resurrection of the body.

The Pharisees were the principal advocates of resurrection. Acts 23:8 summarizes their difference from the Sadducees. Josephus says, "Every soul, they maintain, is imperishable, but the soul of the good alone passes into another body, while the souls of the wicked suffer eternal punishment" (*War* 2.163). The fuller statement in *Antiquities* 18.14, perhaps out of deference to the Greek and Roman abhorrence of bodily resurrection, does not mention the souls returning to the body. The Mishnah (c. 200) includes among those "who have no portion in the world to come . . . he who says the resurrection of the dead is a teaching which does not derive from the Torah" (Sanhedrin 10.1).

For some this resurrection meant a repetition of this life. The *Sibylline Oracles* 4.171–92 (from the end of the first century) says that God "will raise up mortals again as they were before." *2 Baruch* 50.2 declares, "For the earth will surely give back the dead at that time; it receives them now in order to keep them, not changing anything in their form. But as it has received them so it will give them back. And as I have delivered them to it so it will raise them."[2] The Sadducees' question in Luke 20:27–38 implies this view of the resurrection, which Jesus' reply rejects.

For others the resurrected body is a transformed body (bBerakoth 17a—ca. 500, but quoting Rab [= Judah], who was ca. 200).

Judgment according to the rabbinic view had to include both body and soul because both were involved in committing a sin (bSanhedrin 911–b = *Mekilta on Exodus* 15.1).

A corollary of a bodily resurrection was an intermediate state for the soul between death and resurrection.

> When the decisive decree has gone forth from the Most High that a man shall die, as the spirit leaves the body to return again to him who gave it, first of all it adores the glory of the Most High. And if it is one of those who have shown scorn and have not kept the way of the Most High . . .—such spirits shall not enter into habitations, but shall immediately wander about in torments, ever grieving and sad. . . .
>
> Now this is the order of those who have kept the ways of the Most High, when they shall be separated from their mortal body. . . . First of all, they shall see with great joy the glory of him who receives them, for they shall have rest. . . .
>
> The day of judgment shall be the end of this age and the beginning of the immortal age to come. . . . Therefore no one will then be able to have mercy on him who has been condemned in the judgment, or to harm him who is victorious. (2 Esdras [= 4 Ezra] 7.78–80, 88–91, 112–15)

The book of *1 Enoch* has three sections in the underworld: two are for the wicked, distinguished according to whether judgment was given against them in their lifetime, and one for the righteous (chap. 22).

There were various descriptions of the postmortem abode of the righteous. One view was to be with the patriarchs (4 Maccabees 13:17; cf. Luke 16:22). The Babylonian Talmud says, "There are two ways before me, one leading to Paradise and the other to Gehinnom" (bBerakoth 28b), but the thought may refer to the final judgment. An earlier text, where the reference is to an intermediate period of time, identifies Paradise with the third heaven: "Take him up into Paradise, to the third heaven, and leave him there until that great and fearful day which I am about to establish for the world" (*Apocalypse of Moses* [= *Life of Adam and Eve*] 37.5; also 40.1). A Talmudic text speaks of the seventh heaven, where are "the souls of the righteous and the spirits and the souls which are yet to be born, and dew wherewith the Holy One, blessed be He, will hereafter revive the dead" (bHagigah 12b). This is the location where "the souls of the righteous are hidden under the Throne of Glory" (bShabbath 152b [twice]).

For some at least the righteous dead go immediately to heaven (*1 Enoch* [*Similitudes of Enoch*] 37–71). For many of the sources it is not clear whether these terms apply to the intermediate state, the final state, or both.

By New Testament times Gehenna had become the name for the place of punishment. The name derives from the Valley of Ben-hinnom (2 Kings 23:10; Jeremiah 7:31; 32:35).

The *Sibylline Oracles* speak of the different punishments on sorcerers and sorceresses, including, "They will be thrown under many terrible infernal beasts in Gehenna, where there is immeasurable darkness"; the text goes on to speak of their distressful lament below "dark, dank Tartarus," perhaps another name for Gehenna (2.283–306). The "punishments of Genennah" in the Christian *Ascension of Isaiah* 1.3 (end of the first century) are, it seems, the eternal punishments. The rabbis said God created the Garden of Eden and Gehinnom. The righteous person's portion is in the Garden of Eden; the wicked person's is in Gehinnom (bHagigah 15a). The tractate bPesachim 54a is a debate on when the fire of Gehenna was created.

Some rabbis expressed the view that Gehenna is annihilation, "nothing other than a day which will burn up the wicked"; others said, "Gehenna is neither a day nor a real place, but it is a fire that goes forth from the body of a wicked person and consumes him" (*Midrash Rabbah Genesis* 26 on 6:3).

The Second Temple period saw the development of an apocalyptic or cosmic eschatology in Judaism. Some typical features of the apocalyptic thought world are these: (1) eschatological dualism between the present evil age and the age to come; (2) spatial dualism between the transcendent God and the world; (3) ethical dualism in the struggle between good and evil; (4) pessimism and optimism, despair over the present age but hope for God's intervention; (5) determinism and freedom, for God controls history, but individual choices are not determined; (6) universalism and individualism—God's plans are universal, but he is concerned with individuals; (7) otherworldly (cosmic) language for these worldly events; (8) messianism—sometimes God uses a deliverer to accomplish his purposes.

Some examples of the apocalyptic genre of literature are the second half of Daniel and the book of Revelation in the Bible, *1 Enoch*, 2 Esdras (4 Ezra), *2 Baruch, Assumption of Moses*, and the *War Scroll* from Qumran.

Some features of apocalyptic eschatology were important for early Christianity. The combination of a subterranean intermediate state with a future temporary earthly kingdom appears most clearly in *2 Baruch* and 2 Esdras, both written at the end of the first century. Early Christian chiliasts got their schemes from this thought world, not from Revelation 20, as today. The sequence of the coming of the Messiah, setting up his kingdom, resurrection, and judgment appears in 2 Esdras 7:26–38 and *2 Baruch* 29:1–30:5. The latter text describes the marvelous productivity of the earth in the messianic age: "On one vine will be a thousand branches, and one branch will produce a thousand clusters, and one cluster will produce a thousand grapes, and one grape will produce a cor of wine"; and "manna will come down again from on high" to feed the people. The idea is repeated by Papias, but with the figures increased to ten thousand (Irenaeus, *Against Heresies* 5.33.3–4).

Various lengths were assigned to an interim messianic kingdom: forty years (Rabbi Aqiba according to *Pesiqta Rabbati* 1.7 [4a]); 400 years according to 2 Esdras 7.28 (at the end of which the Messiah dies—7:29); 1,000 years (among other options given by Rabbi Eliezer ben Hyrcanus [ca. 80–120] according to *Tanhuma* 7b; *Midrash on Psalms* 90.17).

*The four lectures that comprise this chapter were lessons brought at a church camp at Gemünden, Germany, March 12–16, 2001, not previously published.

2. New Testament Perspective

The Two Ages

The New Testament adopts the Jewish terminology of two ages, "this age and the age to come" (Matt. 12:32). This age is "the present evil age" (Gal. 1:4), but believers in Christ "have tasted . . . the powers of the age to come" (Heb. 1:5).

Jesus' coming represents an intervention from above in the present evil age. It encompasses a series of events—Jesus' ministry, death, resurrection, and outpouring of the Holy Spirit. That coming marks the beginning of the end. Believers still live in the evil age, but they have experienced the age to come and are empowered by it. The second coming will mark the end of the present evil age, and the "age to come" will continue. Here too there is a complex of events—Jesus' coming, the resurrection, and judgment.

Oscar Cullmann illustrated the relation of the two comings by D-Day and V-Day in World War II.[1] D-Day was the Allied landing on Normandy. Its success assured victory over Nazi Germany, but a lot of hard fighting still had to be done. Victory Day came with the surrender of Germany. Another illustration might be of a lame-duck president, still in office but his powers greatly diminished while the country awaits the inauguration of his successor. Satan is the lame-duck ruler of this world. The first coming of Christ dealt him a death blow, but like a mortally wounded animal he may be the more dangerous because of it.

The first coming of Christ began the overthrow of Satan. Jesus saw in the successful preaching ministry of his disciples "Satan fall from heaven" (Luke 10:17–18). Revelation describes the defeat of Satan and his angels, who are thrown down from heaven to earth, with the result that there is woe on the earth because the devil knows his time is short (12:7–12). Only at the end of the Christian age is the devil thrown into the lake of fire and sulfur (Rev. 20:10).

The resurrection of Christ began a new age. He "abolished death and brought life and immortality to light through the gospel" (2 Tim. 1:10). However, only at the end is the last enemy, death, truly destroyed (1 Cor. 15:26). Redemption is now in Christ (Eph. 1:7), and the gift of the Holy Spirit is a pledge of the yet anticipated final redemption (Eph. 1:14). This perspective on the two ages explains the New Testament language of "now" and "not yet." Christians live in two ages at once.

The Age to Come Is Now

New Testament writers often express the conviction of living in the last days, that is, the last dispensation, the last period of time. The things that happened to Israel were "an example, and they were written down to instruct us, on whom the ends of the ages have come" (1 Cor. 10:11). The God who spoke to the forefathers by the prophets "in these last days has spoken to us by a Son" (Heb. 1:1–2). Christ "was destined before the foundation of the world but was revealed at the end of the ages" (1 Pet. 1:20). "Children, it is the last hour!" (1 John 2:18), words that warn against taking "last days" too literally, or John would not have had time to write three more chapters! The emphasis in these statements is not on how long until the end, but on this being the *final* period of time. Once the end-time began, that did not necessarily imply the end itself was immediate. How long before this last age is completed is of no importance. "So if anyone is in Christ, there is a new creation: everything old has passed away; see, everything has become new!" (2 Cor. 5:17 NRSV).

In fulfillment of the messianic hopes of the Jews the Messiah brings a new age. This includes a new interpretation of the Law (Matt. 5:17–48). The first verses of the passage, Matthew 5:17–20, affirm the Law's validity. Part of the Jewish expectation of a Messiah was that he would bring the correct interpretation of the Law, or in effect a new Torah. Matthew presents Jesus as, among other things, a new Moses. Matthew 28:18–20 presents the post-resurrection situation. Jesus has all authority now, and people are to be taught "to obey everything" he commanded.

The Messiah also brings forgiveness of sins in a way and to an extent that the old covenant did not. Jeremiah's prophecy of a new covenant (Jer. 31:31–34) has at its heart the promise, "I will forgive their iniquity, and remember their sin no more" (31:34 NRSV). When Jesus came he astonished people by doing what only God can do, pronounce forgiveness of sins (Mark 2:1–12). His disciples now offer that forgiveness "in his name" (Acts 2:38).

An important part of the Jewish expectation for the new age was the manifestation of the Holy Spirit. "I will put my Spirit within you, and make you follow my statutes and be careful to observe my ordinances" (Ezek. 36:27 NRSV). Note that the Spirit will not take the place of obedience to God but will enable the people to keep the laws of God. Jesus is presented as the one who will "baptize with the Holy Spirit" (Matt. 3:11; Mark 1:7–8). After his resurrection he was proclaimed as having poured out the Spirit (Acts 2:32–33), and those baptized in his name were promised "the gift of the Holy Spirit" (Acts 2:38–39). The promises of forgiveness and of the Holy Spirit in Jeremiah and Ezekiel respectively were closely related, for only those forgiven of sin could receive the *Holy* Spirit. And indeed Paul conflated the promises in Romans 11:26–27, combining the texts promising the covenant of the Spirit (Isa. 59:20–21) and promising the covenant of the forgiveness of sins (Jer. 31:33–34).

In order to elaborate the point of the working of the Holy Spirit as representing the *now*, the present eschatological blessings, notice Paul's doctrine of the Holy Spirit. The following listing is not complete, for Paul has a lot to say about the Holy Spirit. The Holy Spirit was involved in the resurrection of Christ (Rom. 1:4).

> The Holy Spirit gives a new law (Rom. 8:2), enables the keeping of the law (Rom. 8:4–6), and gives life to the new covenant (2 Cor. 3:6).
>
> The Spirit enables one to overcome sin (Rom. 8:13) and is involved in justification (1 Cor. 6:11; 1 Tim. 3:16).
>
> The Spirit works in baptism imparting new birth and regeneration (John 3:5; Titus 3:5) and adding one to the church (1 Cor. 12:13).
>
> The Holy Spirit sanctifies (Rom. 15:16; 2 Thess. 2:13).
>
> The Spirit gives life (Rom. 8:10).
>
> The Spirit dwells in God's people (Rom. 8:9; 1 Cor. 3:16—collectively; 6:19—individually).
>
> The Spirit sets the standard for how we live, producing spiritual fruit (Gal. 5:16–18, 22, 25).
>
> The Spirit produces love (Rom. 15:30).
>
> The Spirit helps in prayer (Rom. 8:26–27, articulating our groanings; Gal. 4:6; Eph. 6:18).

The Spirit gives hope (Rom. 5:2, 5; Gal. 5:5).

The Spirit will resurrect us (Rom. 8:11).

The Spirit makes us sons of God, equal to the angels (Rom. 8:14, 16; cf. Luke 20:36).

The Spirit is connected to the kingdom of God (Rom. 14:17).

The gift of the Spirit is the firstfruits of greater blessings, a down payment guaranteeing more to come (Rom. 8:23–25; 2 Cor. 1:22; 5:5; Eph. 1:13; 4:30).

To those future blessings we now turn.

Some Things Are Reserved for the Future—The Not Yet

Paul had to oppose those with an over-realized eschatology, who put everything in the now. "Already you have all you want! Already you have become rich! Quite apart from us you have become kings! Indeed I wish that you had become kings, so that we might be kings with you!" (1 Cor. 4:8 NRSV). Particularly at issue was the resurrection. "Hymenaeus and Philetus . . . have swerved from the truth by claiming that the resurrection has already taken place. They are upsetting the faith of some" (2 Tim. 2:17–18 NRSV). Their position developed perhaps from teaching like Romans 6:4.

One motive for asceticism among early Christians was living the eschatological life now. Since there is no marriage in heaven (Luke 20:34–36), abstention from marriage is to live the angelic life now. Hence, there were some, perhaps forerunners of second-century Gnostics, who "forbid marriage and demand abstinence from foods" (1 Tim. 4:3). This would seem to be the viewpoint of those in Corinth who said it was not good to have sexual relations (1 Cor. 7:1, 12–13).

Central to the future eschatology of Christians is the promise of the second coming of Christ. When he ascended to heaven, two angels told his disciples, "This Jesus, who has been taken up from you into heaven, will come in the same way as you saw him go into heaven" (Acts 1:9–11). Against those alarmed by the teaching that "the day of the Lord is already here" (a form of the over-realized eschatology that affected many, it seems), Paul laid out some things the must happen first (2 Thess. 2:1–3). The phrase "second coming" does not occur in Scripture, but Hebrews 9:28 comes close: "Christ, having been offered once to bear the sins of many, will appear a second time, not to deal with sin, but to save those who are eagerly waiting for him." Revelation 1:7 promises, "He is coming with the clouds; every eye will see him."

The general resurrection and the judgment are yet to come. "He who raised Christ from the dead will give life to your mortal bodies also through his Spirit that dwells in you" (Rom. 8:11). "Do not pronounce judgment before the time, before the Lord comes, who will bring to light the things now hidden in darkness and will disclose the purposes of the heart" (1 Cor. 4:4–5). "God raised the Lord and will also raise us by his power" (1 Cor. 6:14). "We know that the one who raised the Lord Jesus will raise us also with Jesus, and will bring us with you into his presence" (2 Cor. 4:14). Paul makes an interesting contrast between our earthly bodies as a tent, a temporary dwelling, with a building for the heavenly abode: "For we know that if the earthly tent we live in is destroyed, we have a building from God, a house not made with hands, eternal in the heavens" (2 Cor. 5:1). "For all of us must appear before the judgment seat of Christ, so that each may receive recompense for what has been done in the body, whether good or evil" (2 Cor. 5:10). Jesus Christ "is to judge the living and the dead" (2 Tim. 4:1). "And I saw a great white throne and the one who sat on it. . . . And I saw the dead, great and small, standing before the throne, and books were opened. Also another book was opened, the book of life. And the dead were judged according to their works, as recorded in the books" (Rev. 20:11–13).

The New Testament anticipates new heavens and earth.

> The day of the Lord will come like a thief, and then the heavens will pass away with a loud noise, and the elements will be dissolved with fire, and the earth and everything that is done on it will be burned up. . . .
>
> Because the heavens will be set ablaze and disssolved, and the elements will melt with fire. But, in accordance with his promise, we wait for new heavens and a new earth, where righteousness is at home. (2 Pet. 3:10–13, NRSV modified)

Revelation 21:1 uses the singular, "I saw a new heaven and a new earth; for the first heaven and the first earth had passed away, and the sea was no more."

Do these verses speak of a renovated world? Or is a new reality described in terms (heaven and earth) we recognize?

The descriptions of heaven and hell are clearly figurative language.

In simplest terms, heaven is where God is. "See the home of God is among mortals; he will dwell with them as their God" (Rev. 21:3–4). The high wall with twelve gates of pearl, a street of gold, a river of life bright as crystal, the tree of life with twelve kinds of fruits, and so forth (Rev. 21:10–14, 18–19, 21–23; 22:1–2, 5) are not literal but are descriptions to impress readers with the beauty and splendor of the New Jerusalem.

In reverse, hell is where God is not. Jesus had more to say about hell than anyone else in the Bible. Those who should have been faithful to God "will be thrown into the outer darknesss, where there will be weeping and gnashing of teeth" (Matt. 8:12; cf. 22:13). The separation at the end of the age will result in the evil persons being thrown "into the furnace of fire, where there will be weeping and gnashing of teeth" (Matt. 13:50). To protest that hell cannot be a place of darkness and also a furnace of fire is to miss the point. These are not literal descriptions but words to convey the idea of hell as a dreadful, undesirable place. The separation at the final judgment results in the accursed ones departing "into the eternal fire prepared for the devil and his angels" (Matt. 25:41). This too is figurative language.

The Kingdom as an Illustration of Now and Not Yet

The kingdom of God was present to Jesus in his person and in his ministry. "Once Jesus was asked by the Pharisees when the kingdom of God was coming, and he answered, 'The kingdom of God is not coming with things that can be observed; nor will they say, "Look, here it is!" or "There it is!" For, in fact, the kingdom of God is among you'" (Luke 17:20–21). Yet he more often spoke of it as future. Sometimes a manifestation of the reign of God would come in the immediate future. "Truly I tell you, there are some standing here who will not taste death until they see that the kingdom of God has come with power" (Mark 9:1). More often he spoke of the kingdom in terms of the indefinite future. "I tell you, many will come from east and west and will eat with Abraham and Isaac and Jacob in the kingdom of heaven, while the heirs of the kingdom will be throw into the outer darkness" (Matt. 8:11).

In a similar way the kingdom is said to be present for Christians.

> Giving thanks to the Father, who has enabled you to share in the inheritance of the saints in the light. He has rescued us from the power of darkness and transferred us into the kingdom of his beloved Son, in whom we have redemption, the forgiveness of sins. (Col. 1:12–14)

Sin gives Satan power over human beings. When sins are forgiven, Satan has no authority over a person. Forgiveness by God rescues a person from the realm of Satan (darkness) and transfers a person into the kingdom of Christ. That deliverance does not mean we can live as we want. We are now under the rule of Christ.

Nevertheless, as was true for Jesus, the kingdom remains yet future to us. Paul near the end of his life declares, "The Lord will rescue me from every evil attack and save me for his heavenly kingdom" (2 Tim. 4:18). Peter says, "Entry into the eternal kingdom of our Lord and Savior Jesus Christ *will be* [emphasis added] richly provided for you" (2 Pet. 1:11).

Christ reigns now. He "has gone into heaven and is at the right hand of God, with angels, authorities, and powers made subject to him" (1 Pet. 3:22). This reign is associated with his resurrection (v. 21). Yet, he waits for his enemies to be made his footstool: "When Christ had offered for all time a single sacrifice for sins, 'he sat down at the right hand of God,' and since then has been waiting 'until his enemies would be made a footstool for his feet'" (Heb. 10:12–13).

Conclusion

Christians live between the times. They live in the present evil age but by another reality—the powers of the age to come. They enjoy now blessings in the Messiah (Christ)—forgiveness of sins and the presence of the Holy Spirit—but have eager expectation of the fulfillment of God's purposes in his coming again.

3. Exposition of Some New Testament Passages

Matthew 24

A version of Jesus' eschatological discourse occurs in Matthew 24, Mark 13, and Luke 21. We'll survey the contents of Matthew and Mark.

Matthew introduces the discourse with Jesus' promise of the destruction of the temple (24:1–2).[1] This statement prompts a question from the disciples: "Tell us, when will this be, and what will be the sign of your coming and of the end of the age?" (v. 3). The disciples probably thought of this as one question with two parts, but Matthew may treat it as two questions or as one question with a dual aspect that applies to both events as if one.

Jesus' reply in verses 4–8 warns against "false messiahs," a phenomenon that might have been thought to portend the end. The danger of being misled by false messiahs and false prophets is repeated in verses 11 and 24. This was a concern of Matthew's (7:15, 22). Those likely to be misled are those who "know neither the scriptures nor the power of God" (22:29 in another context). Josephus records many such false messiahs during this time.[2] What "must take place" (v. 6) refers to God's sovereignty over history and the end-time, "but the end is not yet." The troubles listed in verse 7 employ traditional biblical language found in other Jewish texts. These troubles are amply documented in the period between 30 and 70, and so for the subsequent verses, but these troubles could be documented for nearly any period of history. The "birth pangs" of the messianic age was common imagery in apocalyptic texts but is applied here to the time preceding the destruction of the temple.

The persecution of Jesus' disciples is the theme of verses 9–13. Their suffering is connected with that of Christ ("because of my name"–v. 9). Thus this passage serves as a preface to the passion narrative. Jews considered apostasy to be a sign of the end-time. Enduring "to the end" is not just survival (vv. 13 and 22) but faithfulness.

The end will not come until "the gospel of the kingdom will be proclaimed throughout the world" (v. 14). This was one factor that Jesus' disciples themselves could determine. The statement does not imply that all peoples will be converted, but all will be given an opportunity to respond.

The "desolating sacrilege" (v. 15) is one of the problematic images in the discourse. The wording comes from Daniel 8:13; 9:26–27; 11:31; 12:11. There the reference is to what was done by Antiochus IV Epiphanes in provoking the Maccabaean revolt (1 Macc. 1:44–48), specifically using the altar of burnt offering for pagan sacrifice (1 Macc. 1:54, 59; 2 Macc. 6:4–5). Josephus interpreted the desolating sacrilege as what Jews themselves did to defile the sanctuary during the siege of 66–70 (*War* 4.147–201, 343; 5.17–18). The interpretation of the desolating sacrilege in Jesus' discourse as the Roman standards set up after the temple burned does not fit, for Jesus speaks of a time when one could still flee the city. Luke 21:20 does refer to the Roman armies surrounding Jerusalem as a prelude to its desolation, but he does not use this phrase. Perhaps Jesus draws on the language of Daniel as a general description of what was happening at the temple in order to parallel the circumstances of 167 BC and AD 70.

The counsel to flee the city (vv. 16–20) reverses the normal procedure in times of occupation to flee from the countryside to find refuge in the city. Houses in Judea had flat roofs approached by outside staircases (v. 17). Workmen laid their coats at the edge of the field while working (v. 18). Women who were pregnant or nursing (v. 19) had difficulty in travel. Winter rains made swollen wadis, and gates of the city were shut on the Sabbath (v. 20); hence the reference is more to the impossibility of flight more than to its discomfort.

Even in intolerable distress, God has compassion on his servants (vv. 21–22). "All flesh" (v. 22) in Isaiah 66:16 refers to the Jewish nation.

Further warnings against false messiahs and false prophets (vv. 23–26) still concern the destruction of Jerusalem. "Great signs and omens" (v. 24) pick up on chapter 7:21–23.

The coming of the Son of Man will be public and obvious (vv. 27–28). A lightning flash is associated with theophanies—Exodus 19:16; Psalms 18:13–15; Zechariah 9:14–16. The "eagles" (v. 28) are properly "vultures" (NRSV). The statement is a proverb (Job 39:30) rather than a reference to Roman standards with eagles.

Verses 29–31 are the crux for interpretation of the chapter. The options are these: Does Jesus (1) skip from the tribulations of the fall of Jerusalem to the next important eschatological event? (2) regard the whole interim from the fall of the temple to his return as a time of tribulation? (3) blend the tribulations of 66–70 with the final ones which they prefigure? (4) begin the tribulations in 66 but postpone the rest to the end-time? or (5) intend his "coming" (v. 30) symbolically for the fall of Jerusalem?

The imagery in verse 29 draws on Isaiah 13:10; 34:4; Ezekiel 32:7; Joel 2:10, 31; 3:15; and one may compare Revelation 6:12–13. Verse 30 adds an allusion to Zechariah 12:10. This cosmic imagery in the Old Testament was used for the chaos and turmoil of earthly disasters, so it may not be referring to the final collapse of the universe.

Another difficulty has to do with the "sign of the Son of Man" (v. 30). Is the "sign" the Son of Man's appearing itself, or is it the "standard" of Isaiah 11:12; 49:22?

Christ dispatches the angels, a function of God in Jewish discourse. The "Elect" are Jesus' community.

The parable of the fig tree (vv. 32–35) indicates that the disciples will discern the meaning of the events when they occur. "Generation" (v. 34) usually means an ordinary human generation, not a "race" or the "final generation." This word would seem to be a further indication that Jesus is still talking about the events associated with the destruction of Jerusalem in 70.

Verses 36–44 are usually taken of the second coming of Christ. There are no signs given in anticipation of it. However, the destruction of Jerusalem could still be a "coming" of the Son of Man in judgment on the Jewish nation of the time.

Verses 45–51 is primarily an exhortation based on end-time motifs. The repeated exhortations of the chapter (4, 6, 13, 25, 32, 42, 44) show that the emphasis is on how to live in light of the reality of the coming tribulations and the end-time. That is the message for Jesus' disciples in every age.

Mark 13

Mark 13 is similar to Matthew 24, but there are differences.[3] The chapter contains both eschatological prediction and exhortation. Its theme of the Parousia (appearance of Christ) and watchfulness is common in early Christian teaching.

Mark 13 has two purposes: (1) to inspire faithfulness, endurance, and hope in the face of impending sufferings, and (2) to warn Christians against false teachings concerning the end. In particular, the chapter seeks to separate the destruction of the temple from the Parousia (either that the Parousia would prevent the fall of Jerusalem or that its fall was an immediate prelude to the Parousia). In this regard note verses 19 ("and never will be") and 24 ("after that suffering"). God's decree of judgment on the temple and Jerusalem is certain but is not connected with the last coming of Jesus.

Mark 13 is virtually an explication of 8:34, taking up the cross of Jesus and following him. As surely as the messiahship and suffering go together (8:29, 31), so there is a connection of proclamation of the gospel with suffering (vv. 10–11).

The introduction to the discourse (vv. 1–4) clearly indicates that the theme is the destruction of the temple. The two clauses in verse 4 are parallel, the second explaining through expansion the first. Nothing is said about Jesus' coming, but the discourse goes beyond the disciples' question.

Verses 5–8 stress the "not yet" of the end. "Watch" or "Beware" is a key word of the discourse: "that no one leads you astray" (v. 5); "they will hand you over to councils" (v. 9); "I have told you everything" (v. 23); "you do not know the time" (v. 33). The false messiahs will claim the name that belongs to Jesus (v. 6). Verses 7–8 incorporate traditional elements in the representation of the end, but the end is "not yet" (v. 7). "These things" are signs of the judging presence of God in history that is moving to an end according to his purposes.

The persecution of the disciples (vv. 9–13) uses the same word, "hand over," used for the betrayal and delivering up of Jesus. The experience of the disciples will parallel that of Jesus. "For my sake" ("because of me") and "because of my name" bracket the paragraph (vv. 9 and 13). The task of the church between the resurrection and the Parousia is to preach the good news to all nations (v. 10), an urgent task to be performed before all else.

The charge to flee Jerusalem (vv. 14–20), as much else in Mark 13, is closely parallel to Matthew 24. Verses 14 and 19 reflect Daniel and do not necessarily show a knowledge of the events of 70. "Let the reader understand" (v. 14) is a parenthesis that indicates a present application to Mark's day. Eusebius later reported that the church in Jerusalem in response to an oracle left the city and went to Pella.[4] Pella is across the Jordan and not in the mountains, so there may have been another prophetic revelation; but there need not necessarily be a literal fulfillment. We note again the indication of a time after these sufferings (v. 19). The shortening of the time is an expression of mercy (v. 20).

False messiahs would be prevalent at the time of the destruction of Jerusalem (vv. 21–23). Verse 21 may allude to the Jewish doctrine of a hidden Messiah. On verse 22 compare 2 Thessalonians 2:1–12. Jesus told them all they needed to know (v. 23) in contrast to all they wanted to know.

The "coming" of the Son of Man (vv. 24–27) is *after* the tribulation of "those days" (v. 24). The description in verses 24–25 is characteristic of God's interventions and is not about the destruction of the universe. In addition to the Old Testament verses cited on Matthew 24:29, see Judges 5:4–5; Amos 1:2; Habbakkuk 3:3–6, 10–11; Nahum 1:5; Psalms 77:14–20; 114:1–8. The elements go into confusion because he appears, not as a sign that he is about to appear. The picture of the Son of Man coming on clouds (v. 26) comes from Daniel 7:13 (cf. Mark 14:62). The language of gathering the elect from the four winds (v. 27) is drawn from Deuteronomy 30:3–4 and Zechariah 2:6. The purpose of the divine appearance is deliverance of the people of God.

The parable of the fig tree (vv. 28–31) teaches that the coming of Jesus is near ("He is at the doors"–29). No matter what happens, his words "will not pass away" (v. 31).

The time of these things is unknown (vv. 32–37). There is an imminent expectation, but the time is in God's hand. Hence, the exhortation "keep alert" is appropriate (v. 33). The meaning of the eschatological discourse for the church is the need for spiritual alertness, readiness for God at every moment. Modern experience reflects two extremes to be avoided: eschatological speculation and excitement, or apathy and comfortable acceptance of this world. Waiting for the Lord is an active pursuit.

Luke 16:19–31

Instead of retracing the eschatological discourse of Jesus according to Luke, I take another passage from the third Gospel that has been important in discussions by Christians of the afterlife.

The main point of discussion in the interpretation of Luke 16:19–31 has been, "Is it a parable?" If it is a parable, the conclusion is that it should not be taken literally, that it is not meant as an exact representation of the afterlife. I assume we should call it a parable, but I am not so sure the conclusion drawn from it being a parable is correct. The parables of Jesus were something that could happen; they were based on the realities of life. On the other hand, it is true that Jesus does not tell this story in order to give details of the geography of the other world. He tells the story in order to teach some other things. The details do correspond to common ideas of the time about the afterlife. The story is based on the existence of an intermediate state and the conviction that one's destiny is fixed at death.

I offer comments on some verses. The passage is embedded in its context. It connects with 16:1–13, especially verse 9 but note also verse 15. Verse 16 connects with verse 31. The story is part of Jesus' teaching on the right use of possessions and care for the poor.

The sharp contrasts in the circumstances of both principal characters (vv. 19–23) show a complete reversal (cf, 6:21, 25; 13:30). Lazarus was carried by angels to Abraham's bosom (v. 22). Cf. 4 Maccabees 13:17 for Abraham, Isaac, and Jacob welcoming the faithful and Luke 13:28–30 for the three patriarchs and all the prophets in the kingdom of God. This is Paradise.

The rich man is in a place of punishment in Hades (v. 23). Luke 12:5 uses Gehenna for the place of punishment. *1 Enoch* 22:8–13 has three divisions in Hades, two of which are places of punishment.

Verses 24–25 indicate the rich man is punished because of his disregard of the poor.

Verse 26 affirms that eternal destiny is fixed at death, although presumably Abraham's bosom and the place of torment are intermediate states.

According to verse 31 the testimony of Moses and the prophets is sufficient to teach righteous living. The rich man and his brothers have been sufficiently forewarned. There may be the further implication that if the Jews had really listened to Moses and the prophets they would not have denied the resurrection of Christ (cf. John 5:39, 46).

1 Corinthians 15[5]

Turning from the Gospels we consider the major treatment of the resurrection in the New Testament, 1 Corinthians 15. I offer a simplified outline of the chapter and comments on some of the verses.

A. The Resurrection of Christ—1–11.

Paul gives a basic statement of the gospel and matters of first importance (vv. 1–4). Because of the concern in the subsequent material, he elaborates on the appearances of the resurrected Christ (vv. 5–9) in support of the Scripture proof of his resurrection. The resurrection appearances are in two sets of three, a pattern perhaps already in earlier presentations of the facts of the gospel. Paul had "received" the summary of the gospel message; Galatians 1:18 is an indication of the possible source of his receiving the earliest apostolic preaching. Paul and the original apostles preached the same gospel (vv. 10–11).

B. The Resurrection of the Dead—12–19.

The resurrection of Christ demonstrates that there will be general resurrection. We may ponder what those who denied the resurrection believed. Possibilities are that either the resurrection pertains to the present newness of life (Rom. 6:4; cf. verse 19 of the chapter under discussion) or the resurrection is of the soul at death. The aversion to a physical resurrection would have had a background in Greek philosophy. Both possible explanations occur in Gnosticism later, but there is no indication of Gnosticism here, although both the opponents of resurrection here and later Gnostics drew on the same thought world.

C. The End Times—20–28.

Christ's resurrection is connected to a general resurrection as the firstfruits are to the subsequent harvest. The imagery was perhaps suggested by the offering of a sheaf of the firstfruits of the grain harvest on the first day following the Sabbath of Passover week (Lev. 23:4–5, 10–11), the day of Jesus' resurrection.

The sequence puts three things in order: the resurrection of Christ, the resurrection of those in Christ, the end. The resurrection occurs at the Parousia (v. 23). Millennialists agree on this, but contrary to their scheme Paul says that the next thing is "the end" (v. 24). The resurrection nullifies death (v. 26). But death is the last enemy to be abolished (destroyed, put to an end–26). Christ rules until all enemies are subjugated or destroyed (vv. 24–25). Therefore, his reign precedes the resurrection, rather than following it. The coming of Christ is when he turns over a kingdom to God (v. 24), not when he sets up a kingdom.

D. Practical (or ad hominem) Arguments for the Resurrection—29–34.

The most problematic part of this chapter is "baptism for the dead" (v. 29). Various interpretations have been offered. (1) The apparently straightforward meaning is "baptism on behalf of the dead," a vicarious baptism, but this seems to contradict other teaching that one's destiny is settled at death. (2) Baptism may be used metaphorically, either for the "dead" rites of paganism or being overwhelmed in suffering. Such interpretations would seem to have required some explanation by Paul. (3) The preposition *hyper* has enough variety in meaning to offer other possibilities than "on behalf of": baptism on one's deathbed, baptism over the graves of the dead, baptism because of the imminent danger of death, baptism to fill up the ranks of dead Christians, baptism on account of those now dead ("dead" is plural, which eliminates the possibility of a reference to Christ), or baptism to fulfill the request of the dead. The last is the most likely of these possibilities. (4) "Dead" may refer to dead bodies, so a baptism with a view to one's mortality, be figurative ("as one of the dead"), or refer to a newly deceased body to which a posthumous baptism is administered. None of these is obvious, although we must allow that Paul is referring to something known and done by the Corinthians and so obvious to them but not to us. (v. 5) A word to be supplied may be understood such as "resurrection," a "baptism on behalf of the [resurrection] of the dead."

Paul then refers to risking his own life for the gospel (vv. 30–32a). He draws the moral consequences of denial of the resurrection (vv. 32b–33). Belief in an eschatological resurrection should govern one's moral life. Paul concludes this section with appeal to the power of God (v. 34; cf. Matt. 22:29).

E. The Resurrection Body—35–49.

Paul offers the illustration of different kinds of bodies (vv. 35–41) in answer to the question about the nature of the resurrection body. He then introduces the idea of a "spiritual body" (vv. 42–49), still a body but "spiritualized." This teaching raises a similar question to that about the new heavens and earth: Does God give a new body, or does he do something with this one?

F. Victory of the Resurrection—50–58.

Literal "flesh and blood" will not be in the resurrection (v. 50). A transformation of the body will take place (vv. 51–54). The resurrection marks the final victory God gives over the law, sin, and death. The chapter concludes with an exhortation based on the doctrine presented (v. 58).

1 Thessalonians 4:13–5:11[6]

First Thessalonians 4:13–18 and 5:1–11 are parallel in structure. Both begin with an address to "brothers" (sisters included), a statement "about" ("concerning") the subject to be taken up, and a reference to the readers' knowledge ("not to be uninformed" and "you know accurately"). Both sections end with a statement about being with the Lord and the encouragement to exhort one another (4:17–18; 5:10–11). The common themes are hope (4:13; 5:8) and the eschatological community (4:17–18; 5:10–11). Since Paul is addressing a particular problem, the grief of his readers, he does not discuss the non-Christian dead at all (nor did 1 Cor. 15).

First Thessalonians 4:13–18 addresses concern for those who had died. Believers do not have a particular kind of grief, namely the grief of those that do not share in the eschatological blessings. Others do not have the Christian hope of being with the Lord.

The resurrection of Jesus is the basis of Christian hope (v. 14; cf. 1:10; 5:10). God will bring with Jesus at his second coming those who have died, for they are with him (Phil. 1:23). It is comforting that God has not abandoned those who had died. In the consolation literature of the time "sleep" was used as a euphemism for death, so the use of sleep for death here says nothing about the intermediate state or condition of the soul.

Is the "word of the Lord" (v. 15) a prophetic revelation to Paul or the tradition of the sayings of the Lord passed on to him? This statement echoes similar sayings in the synoptic Gospels (Mark 13:27). There is an interesting sequence of what God will do (v. 14), what the living will not do (v. 15), and what the Lord (Jesus) will do (v. 16). "Parousia" in secular usage was the ceremonial arrival of a ruler with honors, but Greek religious use was for a god coming to help people in need. Here the coming of the Lord means a positive presence for believers. For "parousia" compare 1 Thessalonians 3:13 and 2 Thessalonians 1:7 (revelation from heaven).

Three military-like sounds attend the Lord's arrival (v. 16). The latter two explain the first. "Dead in Christ" does not refer here to an intermediate state with Christ but describes their relation with Christ (1 Cor. 15:58; Rev. 14:13). Death does not sever the relationship with Christ (Rom. 8:35, 38–39).

The problem for the Thessalonian Christians was not whether the dead are raised but the relationship of the living and the dead. Notice the sequence "first" (v. 16) and "then" (v. 17). The dead are not disadvantaged. There was discussion in 2 Esd. 13:16–19, 24 and 2 Bar. 28 that at the end those alive were more blessed than those who had died.

The word "caught up" (in Latin *raptus*) gives the terminology for a "rapture." Such an idea is not in Jewish apocalyptic literature (2 Esd. 6:26; 14:9), and the rapture of modern Dispensationalists does not appear until the nineteenth century. There is nothing in the text here about the Lord returning to earth and nothing about a tribulation. These things must be read into the text in order to get a temporary rapture. Rather the text says "we will be with the Lord forever" (v. 17; compare 2 Thess. 2:1 for being gathered to him; 2 Cor. 4:14). The association with the Lord will be eternal.

First Thessalonians 5:1–11 concerns the present quality of Christians' lives in view of the day of the Lord. "Times and seasons" (v. 1) express the same idea. Paul does not write about the "when" of the Lord's coming but about the life to be lived in view of the certainty and unexpectedness of the day.

The comparison to the coming of a "thief" in the synoptic Gospels (Matt. 24:43; Luke 12:39) is a motivation for wakefulness; here (v. 2) it is connected to the ruin of those not alert to his coming. What is said of the Day of Yahweh in the Old Testament is said of the Day of the Lord Jesus by Paul.

Some false prophets spoke of "peace and security" (v. 3). Their teaching had the effect of weakening the expectation of the Parousia and causing the Thessalonians no longer to live in view of its impending arrival. Paul's correction led to the expectation of an immediate return, which had to be corrected in 2 Thessalonians. The coming of the Lord is inevitable, as in birth pains (v. 3), so there is "no escape."

Christians belong to the day, not to the night (vv. 4–5). Paul makes a play on the meaning of "day of the Lord" or gives a double meaning to it, the day of his coming and day as the character of life. Christians are to live in the light (doing the right) and not in darkness (doing evil). Verses 5 and 8 are statements of Christian identity (there is a close parallel in Romans 13:11–14).

As usual, Paul thus grounds his exhortation (v. 6) in theological affirmations. The "others" (the "rest") are non-Christians.

The nearly ubiquitous presence of the Roman military presents the image of armor (v. 8; more fully in Eph. 6:10–17), but there was an Old Testament basis for the language (Isa. 59:17). Greco-Roman literature compared a virtuous man to a soldier.

Faith, love, and hope is the natural order of this triad (1 Thess. 1:3; Col. 1:4–5), which Paul reversed in 1 Corinthians 13 for the particular reason of emphasizing the love so needed by the Corinthians. Here hope is in the prominent position, in accord with the eschatological topic.

Salvation is planned or purposed for those in Christ (v. 9). Whether "awake or asleep" (v. 10), living or dead, "we may live with him."

2 Thessalonians 1:5–2:12

Unlike 1 Corinthians 15 and 1 Thessalonians 4–5, 2 Thessalonians 1:6–8 does speak of the unrighteous. "Those who do not know God" and "those who do not obey the gospel of our Lord Jesus" are parallel statements, so they are not two classes of persons. Eternal ruin is separation from the Lord, not annihilation. Isaiah 2:10, 19, 21 are a similar call to hide from the terror threatened by God.

Second Thessalonians 2:1–12 offers many interpretive difficulties, so it is well to focus on its function rather than being overwhelmed in its uncertainties. The passage is not here for its own sake as apocalyptic description but had the practical purpose of calming eschatological excitement by mentioning what must happen before the end. It is an exhortation to live calmly and faithfully.

Three items from 1 Thessalonians 4:13–5:11 are mentioned in the same sequence in 2 Thessalonians 2:1–2: the Parousia (1 Thess. 4:15; 2 Thess. 2:1);

assembling to meet Christ (1 Thess. 4:17; 2 Thess. 2:1), and the day of the Lord, which is judgment (1 Thess. 5:2; 2 Thess. 2:2). Once more there is no place for a millennium or intermediate earthly kingdom.

The overly realized or present eschatology (v. 2) was probably derived from a teaching of Paul's that was misunderstood. That error should not unsettle believers for the paradoxical reason that things will get worse before the end.

Two things must precede the day of the Lord: rebellion or apostasy and the "man of lawlessness ["of sin" in some manuscripts], the son of destruction" (v. 3). The latter term is the basis for later elaboration of an Antichrist figure.

"What restrains" (v. 6) and "who restrains" (v. 7) have multiple interpretations. The main ones are these: (1) the Roman Empire and its emperors; (2) a divine decree by God; (3) the preaching of the gospel and Paul; (4) a supernatural force—the devil, or the Holy Spirit, or an angel. Since I do not know what and who are meant, I will only reflect on how this reference functions in the passage, that is, to show that the end is not immediate.

Verse 8 draws on Isaiah 11:4.

God does not send a "powerful delusion" (v. 11) out of a malevolent intent, but because people have first "refused to love the truth" (v. 10). Verses 11–12 are the antithesis to 1:11–12.

Revelation 19:5–20:15[7]

Revelation 19:5 begins the detailed unfolding of the theme of the seventh trumpet (11:15–19); specifically, 11:18 provides the ideas now developed: time for judging (19:11–16), for rewarding God's servants (invitation to the wedding—19:5–10), and for destroying the destroyers (19:17–21).

A. The Marriage Supper of the Lamb—19:5–10.

In response to the praise of God's judgments on Babylon (19:1–4), another voice calls for praise because God reigns (19:5–6). There are frequent references in Revelation to the reign of God and Christ (1:5; 4:10; 5:12–13; 17:14; 19:16), perhaps because of the setting of competition with the ruling power of Rome. Although the kingdom is present (1:6, 9; 5:10), persecution and martyrdom exist before its complete realization (12:10–11; 17:14).

Three Old Testament images are brought together in 19:7–8: the eschatological feast (cf. Matt. 8:11), the people of God as his bride (cf. 2 Cor. 11:2), and clean garments as a symbol of holiness (cf. Matt. 22:11–12). The marriage of the Lamb is anticipatory; it becomes actualized in 21:1–5.

John is forbidden to worship even an angel (v. 10), for that is idolatry, and the whole message of the book is not to worship anything other than God. "The testimony of Jesus" (v. 10) is the witness borne by him (1:2, 9; 12:17), and that testimony inspires prophecy and faithful witness by the martyrs.

B. War between Christ and the Beast—19:11–21.

John here, as elsewhere, uses eschatological language for events that were not literally the end. The Rider is Christ, described with phrases from chapters 1–3. He "judges" in the sense of giving evidence that convicts. Previously in the book the dragon and the beast were crowned; now it is Christ (v. 12). The only weapon needed is the proclamation of the word of God, "the sword that came from his mouth" (vv. 15, 21). The imagery of vintage is drawn from Isaiah 63:1–6. "King of kings" may mean sovereignty over earthly rulers (1:5) or over his own royal house of priests (1:6).

In contrast to the wedding feast the vultures gather to feast on the flesh of God's enemies (vv. 17–18). Compare Ezekiel 39:17–20; Matthew 24:28; Luke 17:37. There is a delayed description in 19:17–21 of the third woe, alluded to in 11:18.

C. The Thousand Years—20:1–6.

The thousand-year messianic reign is not found earlier than this passage. It is John's image for the completeness of Christ's victory or for the indefinite period in which his rule is exercised (in contrast to the limited period of persecution referred to earlier). The binding of Satan occurred with the death and resurrection of Jesus, so that he no longer rules over death and Hades (1:18; 12:7–12). The martyrs (20:4) are given special mention as enjoying the heavenly reign after their death. A "great multitude" are pictured in heaven (19:6), so that the scene is not limited to martyrs, but they are the ones specifically described here. The "first resurrection" may be figurative (11:11), but an early interpretation referred it to the souls of the righteous rising to heaven at death.

Against the pre-millennial interpretation of the passage are these considerations: (1) the persistent symbolism of Revelation argues against taking the thousand years literally; (2) elsewhere in Revelation the kingdom exists in the present era (1:5, 9; 5:10); (3) the binding of Satan is already accomplished (1:18; 12:9–11; cf. Luke 10:17–20), (4) the souls of the righteous are already in heaven, making the return to an earthly rule anticlimactic and superfluous (6:9–11; 7:9–15; 14:1–5; 16:7; 18:20; 19:1–2); (5) reinforcing the preceding point, no contemporary apocalypse combines an intermediate state in heaven with an interim earthly kingdom (the two concepts are mutually exclusive);[8] (6) this passage has none of the common features of chiliasm—luxurious abundance on earth, animals subject to human beings, increased longevity, a rebuilt Jerusalem, servitude of nations, return of the ten tribes (this passage only supplies the thousand years and all the rest of the chiliastic scheme is put together from elsewhere) and (7) some of these features (Jerusalem, fecundity of earth) are found in chapters 21–22 in the "post-millennial" description.

D. Satan Loosed—20:7–10.

Either a renewed assault by Satan will occur before the second coming of Christ, or (in spite of the apparent time reference in 20:7) Satan, although defeated, still has power to deceive (1 Pet. 5:8). Gog and Magog come from Ezekiel 38–39.

E. The Great White Throne of Judgment—20:11–15

On the ultimate sovereignty of God see 1 Corinthians 15:24–28, 54. On a final judgment see 2 Corinthians 5:10; Romans 2:16; 14:10. On the books see 3:5; 13:8; 17:8; 18:5; Jeremiah 31:34; Daniel 7:10.

Conclusion

The New Testament passages do not give a consistent and systematic account of the end times. However, certain things are repeatedly emphasized: the return of Christ, a judgment, God's care for his people, and punishment for the wicked. More on these matters will be considered in the next lesson.

4. Problems and Perspectives Related to Eschatology

A. Condition of the Soul at Death

There are several indications in the New Testament that persons after death are conscious. Jesus' story of the rich man and Lazarus (Luke 16:23–25) depends on the consciousness of the parties. Paul's desire was to depart and be with Christ (Phil. 1:23) and to be away from the body and with the Lord (2 Cor. 5:8). The wicked are kept under punishment before the judgment (2 Pet. 2:9).

An intermediate state would be consistent with a future resurrection and judgment, although an alternative would be unconsciousness and restored consciousness at the resurrection. Yet another option would be individual resurrection and judgment at death, but the passages we have looked at about resurrection and judgment associated with a future coming of Christ would not seem to allow for this option. Nonetheless, one's eternal destiny would seem to be determined at death (see D. below).

B. Nature of the Resurrection Body

The options for postmortem existence are the following: (1) a natural immortality of the soul (Plato and others); (2) created immortality of the soul (many church fathers); (3) conditional immortality of the soul, dependent on one's choices (some church fathers); (4) resurrection of the soul (at baptism, at death, or after the intermediate state of unconsciousness); (5) resurrection of a spiritual body (Origen) or being given a new body; (6) resurrection of transformed flesh (body—many church fathers); (7) resurrection of the same body (some Pharisees, some millennialists and simple Christians).[1]

The New Testament commonly speaks of the "resurrection of the dead" (Matt. 22:31; Acts 4:2; 17:32; 24:21; 26:23; Rom. 1:4; 1 Cor. 15:13, 21, 42; 1 Pet. 1:3). It also speaks of being given a new body (2 Cor. 5:1–5). Several early Christian writers use instead "resurrection of the flesh" in opposition to those (especially Gnostics) who had a negative view of the body and rejected a literal resurrection.

The main clue to the nature of the resurrection body would be that it will be like Christ's. "He will transform the body of our humiliation that it may be conformed to the body of his glory" (Phil. 3:21). The resurrected Christ is the firstfruits of those who have died (1 Cor. 15:20, 23; cf. 6:14 and Rom. 8:11). The Gospel accounts of the appearances of the resurrected Christ give some characteristics of his resurrected body. It was visible, with the appearance of any other person (Luke 24:16, 30), and bore the marks of the crucifixion, with the appearance of taking food (Luke 24:39–43). Yet it could pass through a locked door (John 20:19, 26–27) and perform familiar actions (John 21:12–13). How many of the physical manifestations were to convince the disciples that it was the same Jesus, and how much pertained to the essence of the resurrection body?

C. Will There Be an Intermediate Earthly Millennial Kingdom?

The premillennial view is that the return of Christ will precede an earthly millennial kingdom. The postmillennial view is that the return of Christ will follow a millennial kingdom in which righteousness prevails among human beings. The amillennial view rejects a literal millennium. On the last view the thousand years of Revelation 20:5, 7 is symbolic of the completeness of Christ's victory, or is the indefinite period of the Christian age, or is symbolic of the individual's interim state with Christ.

Classical millennialism (from the Latin word for one thousand, also called chiliasm, from the Greek word for one thousand) differed from dispensational millennialism that arose in the nineteenth century. Dispensationalism says that Christ came to set up a kingdom, but it was postponed when the Jews rejected him and the church was a substitute. Dispensationalism evolved a detailed scenario of end-time events including a tribulation and rapture (with debates over whether the rapture occurs before or after the tribulation).[2]

The premillennial sequence for individuals is death, a period in Hades, the second coming of Christ and resurrection of the righteous, the thousand-year reign, resurrection of others and judgment, heaven or hell. The amillennial sequence is death, the righteous with Christ, the second coming and general resurrection, judgment, heaven or hell. The view of the intermediate state is a significant clue whether an ancient author was a millennialist or not.[3] Premillennialists had the deceased in a subterranean intermediate state (some exempted the martyrs from this condition) awaiting the return of Christ whereas nonmillennialists viewed the faithful Christian as in some sense with Christ or God awaiting the second coming.[4]

One's views on the millennium are not necessarily a matter of fellowship in the church. Modern dispensational millennialism includes some serious doctrinal error, challenging the biblical doctrine of God's plan and the place of the church in that plan that potentially are salvation matters. One may compare views on the nature of the resurrection body as likewise not a matter of fellowship, except that ancient Gnosticism's denial of a bodily resurrection was part of heretical views of God and the world. Different views of end-time events in themselves need not break fellowship; preaching and teaching them in a divisive way, as anything that causes division, is a different matter.

Nevertheless, there are important arguments against the millennial interpretation (for which, see more fully the preceding lesson on Rev. 20). A literal thousand years is inconsistent with the figurative language of the book of Revelation. The millennial age is never expressly described in Scripture. It is arrived at by putting together many texts (mostly from the Old Testament) that refer to different things. There is no room for the earthly millennial kingdom in the detailed eschatological passages that should include it if there is to be such (Matt. 24; 1 Cor. 15; 1 Thess. 4–5). A millennium is inconsistent with several Scriptures. According to John 5:28–29, *all* who hear his voice will come out of their graves, not at separate times. The resurrection of believers to eternal life is on "the last day" (John 6:39–40; so also 6:44 and 54). The words of Jesus judge on "the last day" (John 12:48). The dissolution of the heavens and earth will occur on "the day of the Lord," followed by new heavens and earth (2 Pet. 3:10–13). Christ is on the throne of David now (Acts 2:29–33; 15:13–18) and is not said to return to occupy that throne.

Many modern promoters of premillennialism (not premillennialism itself) have done two disservices: they have disillusioned and disappointed their followers; and they have removed the eschatological expectation from those who have rejected their scheme. The fantasies associated with much eschatological speculation has encouraged the secularism that has weakened the eschatological hope of believers.

D. Universal Salvation

Origen, Gregory of Nyssa, and some other Greek Christian writers saw the posttemporal punishment of the wicked as disciplinary and held out the hope that all would eventually come to faith and be saved.

Universalists, who came out of Calvinistic Puritans, reasoned on the basis of Romans 5:12–21 that as Adam's sin brought condemnation to all, so Christ's obedience brings salvation to all.

Generally, the argument for universal salvation is made from the nature of God and his love that he will find a way to save all his creatures.

That does not seem to be what a number of Scriptures say (see more below), but it may be the Scriptures do not tell the whole story. Nevertheless, I do not see how we can know more than the Scriptures reveal.

E. Purgatory

In the background of the idea of purgatory were Greek ideas of a purifying punishment after death before going to a state of blessedness and the Jewish practice of prayer for the dead (2 Macc. 12:40–45). Second Timothy 1:16–18 is sometimes cited as such a prayer, and not just a wish.

Prayers for the dead are attested early in Christianity. Inscriptions from the Catacombs dated to the third century contain prayers for peace and refreshment of souls of the departed. Early church fathers such as Tertullian and Cyprian attest the practice. Such prayers came to be included in eastern and western liturgies.

Purgatory developed only in the Western church, although the Eastern church granted an intermediate state without defining it clearly and affirmed the efficacy of prayer for the dead.

Already in the *Passion of Perpetua and Felicitas* (203) there is belief that sins can be purged by suffering in the afterlife and that process speeded up by prayer. Augustine occasionally spoke of a purifying fire after death, for which he found support in 1 Corinthians 3:11–15, and of the value of the church's prayers for those who died in the communion of the church. Gregory the Great (d. 604) taught that "light" sins will be purged in purgatorial fire and it is proper to offer the Eucharist for their deliverance. "All Souls Day" (Nov. 2) was introduced in the tenth century.

The explicit doctrine was developed in the twelfth century: there is a place of punishment and purification where souls who died in a state of grace undergo punishment due for forgiven sins and expiate unforgiven venial sins before being admitted to the divine presence. Classic formulations were made by Thomas Aquinas and the Councils of Lyons (1274) and Florence (1439). The doctrine of purgatory led to the practice of indulgences, whereby a person's stay in purgatory could be shortened. In the Western church individuals move from purgatory to the divine presence one by one, but in the East the fullness of beatitude is not experienced by any until it is attained by all.

F. Everlasting Punishment or Punishing

"Eternal" (*aionios*) can refer to time (endless, or limited to an age) or to a quality (realm of eternity or age to come). When applied to acts or processes as distinct from persons or things the word describes the result of the action rather than the action itself: eternal judgment (Heb. 6:2); redemption (Heb. 9:12); salvation (Heb. 5:9); sin (Mark 3:29); destruction (2 Thess. 1:9); punishment (Matt. 25:46).

Jewish sources give a mixed picture. Judith 16:17 has weeping and feeling pain forever. Daniel 12:2 speaks of the resurrection of the wicked as well as the righteous. The Dead Sea Scrolls seem to describe "annihilation of the wicked," but they are unclear between resurrection and immortality for the righteous. Second Esdras 7:61 says that the fires extinguish the wicked. *Fourth Maccabees*, however, has them conscious of pain forever (9:9; 10:12; 12:12; 13:15).

Either view, punishing or extinction, may be accepted without weakening the reality of punishment or the seriousness of God's wrath against sin. Some passages may be quoted on both sides. I do not find the argument by "conditionalists" (those who hold that hell is real but results in annihilation) satisfactorily explaining all the passages (Matt. 13:40–43; 25:46; Mark 9:48; Jude 7; Rev. 20:10, 15; 21:8), although many of these cited by traditionalists on the subject do not say conscious suffering and many passages sound like simply destruction.[5]

Hell's fire was variously interpreted in early Christian literature, either as consuming and devouring (the conditionalist view—Arnobius), torturing (the traditionalist view—Athenagoras, Tertullian), or purifying and remedial (restorative—Origen).

G. The Doctrine That AD 70 Constituted the End

One can make a case for all of Jesus' "eschatological discourse" in Matthew 24, Mark 13, and Luke 21 referring to the destruction of Jerusalem and the temple in AD 70. That would be one "coming" of the Son of Man in judgment.

Some of the language, however, more naturally refers to the second coming. The problem is that "generation" normally means the present generation. In the preceding lesson we discussed various approaches.

The AD 70 interpretation is not conclusive enough for it to become the lens through which other eschatological statements in the New Testament are to be read.

H. Eschatological Motivation for Christian Living

The problems and uncertainties on many aspects of eschatology should not blind us to the fact that most of the eschatological passages in the Bible function to inculcate particular attitudes and conduct.

Negatively, eschatological language serves as a warning or threat. "No fornicator or impure person, or one who is greedy (that is, an idolater), has any inheritance in the kingdom of Christ and of God" (Eph. 5:5).

> The day of the Lord will come like a thief, and then the heavens will pass away with a loud noise, and the elements will be dissolved with fire, and the earth and everything that is done on it will be disclosed [or be burned up]. Since all these things are to be dissolved in this way, what sort of persons ought you to be in leading lives of holiness and godliness, waiting for and hastening the coming of the day of God, because of which the heavens will be set ablaze and dissolved, and the elements will melt with fire? (2 Pet. 3:10–12)

The implied positive is explicit in the next verse: "But, in accordance with his promise, we wait for new heavens and a new earth, where righteousness is at home" (2 Pet. 3:13).

The negative aspect of eschatology is balanced by the promise of a positive reward for righteous living. "Then the king will say to those at his right hand, 'Come, you that are blessed by my Father, inherit the kingdom prepared for you from the foundation of the world'" (Matt. 25:34). Revelation 21:1–7 and 22:1–5 describe the bliss in the new Jerusalem of the new heaven and earth. "See, I am coming soon; my reward is with me, to repay according to everyone's work. . . . Blessed are those who wash their robes, so that they will have the right to the tree of life" (Rev. 22:12, 14).

Beyond these more obvious considerations, often overlooked is the way eschatology is said to set the character of one's life. "The end of all things is near; therefore be serious and discipline yourselves for the sake of your prayers. Above all, maintain constant love for one another" (1 Pet. 4:7–8). In other words, live a life that pertains to the end-time. Since you belong to the day of the Lord, live a life of light that corresponds to the day (1 Thess. 5:2, 4–8). Christians live in the "day," not in the "night." We commented in the last lesson on the way Paul makes a play on the words day/night and awake/asleep as characteristics of two lifestyles. The day of the Lord gives identity to Christians. That day will not surprise us, because we already live in that day.

The whole passage of 1 Thessalonians 4:13–5:11 sets up a tension between imminence and indefiniteness—uncertainty as to the date and certainty of the occurrence. Given that situation, the believer lives by the enduring, permanent qualities, rather than by transient values. "Since we belong to the day, let us be sober, and put on the breastplate of faith and love, and for a helmet the hope of salvation" (1 Thess. 5:8). "Now faith, hope, and love abide, these three; and the greatest of these is love" (1 Cor. 13:13). These qualities define the way to live, whether the Lord comes soon or later, whether death comes soon or later.

We easily spend so much of our time on things that do not last. Many of these things are necessary for human life and are not wrong in themselves, but they must be kept in perspective. And we must not let them distract us from the ultimate realities.

Conclusion

Revelation (especially chapters 21–22) is a rewriting of Genesis 1–3. The end is as the beginning, only on a new level. To use the theological terms, protology and eschatology belong together. God creates a new Eden (Rev. 22:1–2). His agent for accomplishing this is Christ, the new Adam (Rom. 5:17; 1 Cor. 15:22, 45), whose obedience reversed the consequences of the first Adam's disobedience.

We may not know the what, how, or when of the end-times—what God will do (more than in broad outline), how he will do it, or when he will do it. But we do know the Who. When Christ comes, we will meet the same One whom we have known in the Gospels. Our greatest desire is to be with him.

The message of the eschatological passages of the New Testament is be watchful and be ready. We are to live as if Christ is returning today. That does not mean we quit our jobs and forget our human, earthly responsibilities. But it does mean we have our spirits ready for God.

Chapter 22 Selected Bibliography

1. Greco-Roman and Jewish Backgrounds

Selected Bibliography on Greco-Roman Views of the Afterlife

Bremmer, Jan. *The Rise and Fall of the Afterlife*. New York: Routledge, 2003.

Cullmann, Oscar. *Immortality of the Soul or Resurrection of the Dead? The Witness of the New Testament*. London: Epworth, 1958.

Cumont, Franz. *After Life in Roman Paganism*. New Haven: Yale University Press, 1922.

Davies, Jon. *Death, Burial, and Rebirth in the Religions of Antiquity*. London: Routledge, 1999.

Segal, Alan F. *Life After Death: A History of the Afterlife in Western Religion*. New York: Doubleday, 2004.

Selected Bibliography on Jewish Views of Eschatology

Avery-Peck, Alan J., and Jacob Neusner, eds., *Judaism in Late Antiquity: Part 4: Death, Life-after-Death, Resurrection and the World-to-Come in the Judaisms of Antiquity*. Leiden: Brill, 2000.

Bauckham, R. J. *The Fate of the Dead: Studies in Jewish and Christian Apocalypses*. Leiden: Brill, 1998.

Collins, J. J., ed., *The Origins of Apocalypticism in Judaism and Christianity*. Vol. 1 of *The Encyclopedia of Apocalypticism*. New York: Continuum, 2000.

Cook, Stephen L. *Apocalyptic Literature*. Nashville: Abingdon, 2003.

Nickelsburg, G. W. E. *Resurrection, Immortality, and Eternal Life in Intertestamental Judaism and Early Christianity: Expanded Edition*. Cambridge, MA: Havard University Press, 2006.

Reddish, M. G., ed., *Apocalyptic Literature: A Reader*. Nashville: Abingdon, 1990.

2. New Testament Perspective

Beasley-Murray, G. R., *Jesus and the Kingdom of God*. Grand Rapids: Eerdmans, 1986.

Bruce, F. F. *New Testament Development of Old Testament Themes*. Grand Rapids: Eerdmans, 1968.

Cullmann, Oscar. *Christ and Time*. Rev. ed. London: SCM, 1962.

Wright, N. T. *Jesus and the Victory of God*. Minneapolis: Fortress, 1996.

3. Exposition of Some New Testament Passages

Beasley-Murray, G.R. *Jesus and the Last Days: The Interpretation of the Olivet Discourse*. Peabody, MA: Hendrickson, 1993.

Caird, G. B. *The Revelation of St. John the Divine*. New York: Harper & Row, 1966.

Fee, Gordon *The First Epistle to the Corinthians*. Grand Rapids: Eerdmans, 1986.

Keener, Craig S. *A Commentary on the Gospel of Matthew*. Grand Rapids: Eerdmans, 1999.

Malherbe, Abraham J. *The Letters to the Thessalonians*. New York: Doubleday, 2000.

4. Problems and Perspectives Related to Eschatology

Allison, D. C. Jr. *The End of the Ages Has Come*. Philadelphia: Fortress, 1985.

Hill, Charles E. *Regnum Caelorum: Patterns of Future Hope in Early Christianity*. 2nd ed. Grand Rapids: Eerdmans, 2001.

Perkins, Pheme. *Resurrection: New Testament Witness and Contemporary Reflection*. Garden City: Doubleday, 1984.

Wittherington, Ben, III. *Jesus, Paul and the End of the World*. Downers Grove: InterVarsity, 1992.

Wright, N. T. *The Resurrection of the Son of God*. Minneapolis: Fortress, 2003.

Chapter 22 Endnotes

1. Greco-Roman and Jewish Backgrounds

1. Virgil, *Aeneid* 6.321–30, 417, 540–43, 608–27, 637–44, 660–64, 700–702.

2. In later rabbinic literature *Midrash Rabbah Genesis* 14.5; 95.1 (final form after 400); *Midrash Rabbah Ecclesiastes* 1.4.2 (quite late).

2. New Testament Perspective

1. Oscar Cullmann, *Christ and Time*, rev. ed. (London: SCM, 1962), 84.

3. Exposition of Some New Testament Passages

1. For this exposition I draw heavily on Craig S. Keener, *A Commentary on the Gospel of Matthew* (Grand Rapids: Eerdmans, 1999).

2. *War* 2.259–63; 2.444; 6.285–88; 7.29; *Antiquities* 18.85–87; 20.97–98; 169ff.

3. I draw heavily on G. R. Beasley-Murray, *Jesus and the Last Days: The Interpretation of the Olivet Discourse* (Peabody, MA: Hendrickson, 1993).

4. Eusebius, *Church History* 3.5.3.

5. Among the commentaries see Gordon Fee, *The First Epistle to the Corinthians* (Grand Rapids: Eerdmans, 1986).

6. For 1 and 2 Thessalonians see Abraham J. Malherbe, *The Letters to the Thessalonians*, Anchor Bible (New York: Doubleday, 2000).

7. My understanding of Revelation owes much to G. B. Caird, *The Revelation of St. John the Divine* (New York: Harper & Row, 1966), but I part company with him on the millennium.

8. More on this in the next lesson.

4. Problems and Perspectives Related to Eschatology

1. Some texts from early Christian literature on the resurrection are available in Everett Ferguson, *Early Christians Speak*, vol. 2 (Abilene: ACU Press, 2002), chapter 18.

2. Modern expressions are the "Left Behind" books and videos.

3. Charles E. Hill, *Regnum Caelorum: Patterns of Future Hope in Early Christianity*, 2nd ed. (Grand Rapids: Eerdmans, 2001) has argued this persuasively.

4. A collection of early texts on millenialism and amillennialism in Everett Ferguson, *Early Christians Speak*, vol. 2 (Abilene: ACU Press, 2002), chapter 17.

5. The arguments are presented by Edward W. Fudge and Robert A. Peterson, *Two Views of Hell* (Downers Grove: InterVarsity Press, 2000). Fudge, a conditionalist, contends hell is real but results in nonexistence; Peterson, a traditionalist, holds that hell is an eternal punishing. The analogy used by Fudge and others is that a criminal who is executed is punished but not tortured forever. In Fudge's own book on the subject, *The Fire That Consumes* (Houston: Providential Press, 1982), 425, he summarized the issue between traditionalists and conditionalists as this: "Does Scripture teach that the wicked will be made immortal for the purpose of suffering endless pain; or does it teach that the wicked, following whatever degree and duration of pain God may justly inflict, will finally and truly die, perish and become extinct forever and ever?"

"An excellent reminder of our dependence on God's gracious intervention in all our endeavors. Through the story of Moses' leadership, Weber encourages us that our highest calling as leaders is to be servants for God's purposes in every circumstance. For anyone facing challenges in leadership, this book points to our need for an encounter with God's love so that we can become obedient servants for His work. I highly recommended it."

-Dr. David W. Kim, *President, University of Valley Forge*

"**The Moses Manual** takes you on a leadership journey that brings you face to face with the largest two obstacles of effective leadership, lack of obedience and fear. I love Laverne's quote, "Obedience in spite of fears is more valuable than obedience when we know it will be ok." Laverne shares life leadership lessons woven throughout the account of Moses' journey from Egyptian prince, to shepherd to leader of the Israelites on their journey to the Promised Land. We all are on a journey and can learn some valuable lessons from this book!"

-Liz DeFrain, *PennDel Ministry Network Women's Director*

"I truly enjoyed reading **The Moses Manual.** Full of practical advice for leaders, each page of this book has treasures of wisdom and insight to help you on your journey. Drawing not just from Moses' story, but also her own experiences, Laverne has written a beautiful book that will benefit all readers. I can't tell you how many truths just jumped off the page as I read it. I loved it!"

-Adessa Holden, *Women's Minister and Author*

"This book was a page turner! I didn't want to put it down. Laverne uses relatable experiences and shares spiritual truths that speak to every leaders' dilemmas. It's well written with several aha moments."

-Pastor Gretchen Duff and the Warrior Women of Faith
Community

THE MOSES MANUAL

Wilderness Walking
For Leaders

Laverne Weber

Published by Laverne Weber Ministries

All Scripture quotations, unless otherwise indicated, are taken from the Holy Bible, New International Version®, NIV®. Copyright ©1973, 1978, 1984, 2011 by Biblica, Inc.™ Used by permission of Zondervan. All rights reserved worldwide. www.zondervan.com The "NIV" and "New International Version" are trademarks registered in the United States Patent and Trademark Office by Biblica, Inc.™

"Scripture quotations taken from the Amplified® Bible (AMP), Copyright © 2015 by The Lockman Foundation   Used by permission. www.Lockman.org"

"Scripture quotations taken from the Amplified® Bible (AMPC),
Copyright © 1954, 1958, 1962, 1964, 1965, 1987 by The Lockman Foundation Used by permission. www.Lockman.org"

Scripture taken from the New King James Version®. Copyright © 1982 by Thomas Nelson. Used by permission. All rights reserved.

Scripture verses marked KJV are from the King James Version of the Bible.

Design: James J. Holden

Subject Headings:

1. Christian Spiritual Growth   2. Christian life.   3. Bible Study

4. Leadership

ISBN **978-0-9991966-4-9** (paperback)

ISBN **978-0-9991966-5-6** (ebook)

Printed in the United States of America

DEDICATION

With special thanks to my amazing husband, Pat, and our three wonderful children, Patrick, Heidi and Gretchen. Their encouragement has carried me through many wilderness experiences.

CONTENTS

-PROLOGUE-

They were a manipulative, self-seeking, quarrelsome lot. Their history was rife with lies and betrayal. One was even named Deceiver. Although they were a close-knit family, Deceiver's sons thought nothing of deceiving their father, selling their own brother, or cheating a daughter-in-law. But God loved them and had given their ancestor, Abraham, a promise. God keeps His promises!

Now this family grew and became comfortable as they settled in Egypt. They had good land and peace. Then life in Egypt changed. A new dynasty came into power and, with it, a new Pharaoh who turned Egypt into a place of slavery, abuse, and heartache.

So often, we do not see beyond the present. God allowed the heat to be turned up in their Egypt, not

to punish, but to prepare them for His deliverance; not because He didn't care, but because He did care. He cared infinitely more than they could understand in their present. If given a choice, they might have stayed in comfortable Egypt. They may have even stayed when it wasn't so comfortable. In the end, their numbers would have diminished, and the promise given to Abraham would have failed.

Do you feel like you are content with things just as they are? Maybe you have a promise, but it seems so remote and impossible that your grip is gradually slipping. The Israelites cried out to God as the burdens of Egypt became more insufferable. They kept reminding Him of the promise. When we cry out to God, we can expect deliverance. The big question is this: *"Are we ready to be delivered from our comfort zone?"*

What promise has God given you that has yet to be fulfilled?

My father, George Hemminger, had a promise, a very definite one. When it looked impossible, he held on. When it seemed to be slipping away, he held on. And God kept that promise, and is still

keeping it, even though he has gone on to his reward. You see, I am part of that promise.

God's Time Is the Right Time

At just the right time, a woman named Jochebed conceived a man-child. She and her husband, Amran, had a daughter and a three-year-old son, but there is always something exciting about a baby. This baby would be a symbol of hope and new life in their Egypt. They prepared for the birth.

Amran and Jochebed believed in God and His promise. They cried out to a God they had only heard about, but in Whom they chose to believe. Faith is always a choice, but once made, we must expect an answer. Jochebed delivered a beautiful baby boy. Despite a new edict from Pharaoh that all Jewish boy babies must be thrown into the Nile River, Jochebed sensed that this boy baby was special. Exodus 2:2 says she hid him for three months. Daily living in the fear of discovery takes great courage. This couple had the unique ability to step out of their anxious fears and move toward God's faithfulness.

It's a familiar story. A mother who realizes she can no longer hide the cries of a three-month-old. A little papyrus ark placed in the river, a place near where crocodiles often rested, hidden in the rustling reeds, awaiting an unsuspecting prey. A little girl hides and watches over her baby brother. A princess, raised to think only of her own needs, sees a crying baby boy and feels the stirring of a mother's heart. Before long, Moses is back in Jochebed's arms, but now she is raising her son to be a grandson of Pharaoh. Now her son will live!

God's plan performed by God's people produces the promise. What if Jochebed and Amran had been too fearful to sense God's leading? What if Miriam had failed in her task? What if Pharaoh's daughter had missed the basket? *"What ifs"* can consume our thoughts and hinder our actions, but if we let God direct us, we can trust that He does have a plan, a good plan!

Have you ever felt like you were in Egypt? Did it look hopeless? What promise has God given to you and to those you lead? What is He asking you to do that is beyond your natural ability? What steps do you need to take to lead those God has called you to

lead? If you are ready to step out and into the promise of God, Moses may be just the leader to give some insights to help you in your journey.

-1-
WHO ARE YOU ANYWAY?

My frame was not hidden from you when I was made in the secret place, when I was woven together in the depths of the earth. Your eyes saw my unformed body; all the days ordained for me were written in your book before one of them came to be.
(Psalm 139:15-16, NIV)

God is not a God of coincidence; He is the God of the divine plan. The Lord spoke to the Psalmist, and He has the same message for you. God knew you and set you apart for a specific purpose even before He formed you. Before your first cells began to reproduce, God had His hand on you. You are uniquely called for this time and for His specific plan. You are a person of purpose. What is that purpose?

As I look back at my life experiences, I am amazed at the variety I see. Little seedlings of ability that I didn't consider valuable God nurtured and watered until they became a part of who I am. My

love for digging into Biblical truths, my willingness to listen and help people with broken bodies and hearts, my thrill at watching children, and now adults, *"get"* a new idea all started when I was a child. And yet, I so struggled with my value!

We have a hard time accepting our value, or we just think we are not enough. The enemy would like to rob us of all God has for us, both in this life and in eternity. I know when I am about to minister, I hear these little whispers, *"What can you tell them that they haven't heard?"* or *"Why would they want to listen to you?"* If we do not fight those thoughts with God-thoughts, we will succumb to their deceit. We need to see the truth of God's Word and accept that we are indeed of great value to the One Who created us, Who loves us, and Who will guide us as we follow His call. If we dare to seek God for Himself and for His vision, we can move into being all He created us to be.

God ordained the birth of Moses into a family of slaves. That doesn't sound right! But listen. It was obvious from his birth that this baby was an extraordinary child. His parents knew it and took great risks to preserve him. The daughter of the

wicked Pharaoh, the same despot who feared the Hebrews, the same one who decreed that all Israeli baby boys be thrown into the Nile River as crocodile food, saw this small baby boy and knew he was special. She risked her father's wrath to provide for him and finally brought him into the palace itself as her own son. I believe God enjoys seeing the enemy squirm. Only a daughter can totally wrap her father around her little finger. Only Pharaoh's daughter could have kept Moses alive, and only Pharaoh's daughter could have actually brought this child into the palace as one of Pharaoh's grandsons, possibly an heir to his throne. Only one person could have made it happen, and God put her there at the right time. He put that special love in her heart for that little Hebrew baby.

A Slave or a Prince or a Fugitive

Moses grew as a prince in Pharaoh's palace. Acts 7:22 tells us that he was educated in all the wisdom of the Egyptians and was powerful in speech and action. Here was an exemplary young man in his prime, able and ready to be a mighty leader. He had the education. He had charisma. His speech was impressive. We would look at him and say he has all

it takes to be a success. But wait. In God's perspective, there was a small matter that needed some work. Maybe just a little time or instruction. Then again, maybe it wasn't such a small matter. Maybe it would take quite a bit of time and work.

Moses knew his background. He was a Hebrew. Born a slave. Apparently, he knew his birth parents. His mother had been faithful to instruct her son in his early years in God's ways and God's promises. According to Acts 7:25, Moses believed that his own people would recognize in him the fulfillment of God's promised deliverance from Egypt.

One day Moses decided to visit his people and see their situation first hand. He stepped out of his royal box and went to where those he loved were hurting. Jesus Christ did that for us when He stepped down from Heaven's majesty into a small smelly stable. He calls us to step out of our comfortable churches into a hurting world. We are children of the King of Kings, and as such, we are now divine royalty. Like Moses, we have been adopted. Like Moses, we have potential siblings that are still slaves in Egypt.

Moses had every right to be a prince. He

belonged in the house of the king of the land. But one day, Moses stepped down to where his relatives were, and he saw their suffering. His heart responded with anger at the injustice. At this point, he faced a choice. Would he be a prince of Egypt or a Hebrew slave? Would he choose earthly comforts and pleasures or suffering for Christ? (Hebrews 11:25-26)

In a flame of passion, he killed an Egyptian to protect a Hebrew slave. He took a risk, and then he was rejected by the very ones he tried to rescue. Aware that the word was out and the Hebrews were not going to cover for him, Moses fled. What else could he do?

Sometimes we are so caught off guard when we know we are being led by God to minister to a certain group of people, only to find that they are not ready to receive us. Maybe we have been trained in the best schools. Maybe we have been lauded by our peers and praised by our instructors. We know that we have the ability. Why can't these people see that we are there for them?! Well, maybe, just maybe, we are not as ready as we thought we were.

Is it an identity crisis? Or all a part of God's preparation?

Losers Can Learn

Moses had the ability. The problem was he knew he had it. What he did not yet have was the humility and meekness necessary for God to get all the glory. Moses was ready to move out for God and God's people. There is, however, an advanced school of theology that is only found in the wilderness of personal failure. Maybe it involves sitting at the feet of one who is not as educated or as trained in the ways of this world as we are, but knows God in a simple and profound way.

My father was such a man. He had to leave school after sixth grade to help provide for his family. At the age of thirteen, God called him to the ministry while Dad was working in the blasting inferno of a steel mill furnace. He simply said, *"Yes."*

At only twenty-two, he left all he knew and went to the mission field. Dad never felt adequate for the ministry, but he poured his life and heart into it for Christ's sake. Despite many adventures and hardships for the Lord, his main focus before he passed away at the age of seventy-seven was that he had not sacrificed enough for the Christ Who died for him. I learned so much from this humble

pioneer of missions. If I ever get close to having his heart for the ministry, his powerful prayer life, his humble devotion to the Lord, or his trust, coupled with obedience, I will feel like I have begun to follow Jesus.

Moses needed to sit under the tutelage of such a man. His name was Jethro, and he was a Midianite priest. The Midianites were descendants of Abraham through his wife, Keturah, and were also God-followers. Moses, under Jethro, would have been similar to someone with a master or doctoral degree doing an internship with a simple country preacher. But that is what was good for Moses. So, God did what was needed in the life of Moses.

A proud prince became a fugitive, leaving all his hopes and ambitions behind, and going to the most isolated wasteland he could think of. It was a very low time. There he would spend forty years seemingly forgotten by God and his own people. There he would lose his Egyptian skills and style. There he would herd sheep, marry a foreign woman, and have two sons...a pretty lowly existence from that of the prince of Egypt. As Moses spent his long days tending obstinate sheep through a desolate

wilderness near a mountain called Sinai, he thought he had failed. Have you ever felt that way?

I have. I've made mistakes, ones I regret. Satan enjoys reminding us of those failures and telling us we will never be able to make a difference. God promises that He will take our weakness and use it for His glory. We must choose what voice we will believe.

Our time of personal failure is not the end. It is just the beginning of knowing our Lord in the fellowship of His suffering, His rejection, His death to self and ambition, and the new power He wants to develop within us. It is the wilderness time to be sure, but it is not a time to grieve and lose hope; rather, it is just the right time according to God's plan that was decided before we were formed in the womb of our mother.

Jesus needed to spend time in the wilderness before His earthly ministry. Paul spent some years in the wilderness preparing to be God's apostle to the Gentiles. Have you felt ready to conquer the world for Christ only to fail and find yourself in a wasteland? Then you are in good company. Lift up your head. God's promise has not changed. His

hand is still on you. It is just that you must have your own wilderness experience before you can lead a congregation through their wilderness.

Moses thought his skills as an Egyptian prince prepared him to be the deliverer of the Israelite nation. While training and skill are very important in our preparation for leadership, it is not until we fail in our natural abilities that we can say, *"God, I have nothing for You to use."* When we finally give up, God smiles and nods His approval. Now He can begin to speak to us. Now we are ready to listen. And so it was that one day while Moses was watching some self-willed and rather silly sheep, God came to where Moses was. God does that. Sometimes it is at the least expected times.

Moses struggled with his identity. Do you know who you are? Have you been broken so that you are able to let go of your plans and see what the Lord is planning?

We need to prepare for our purpose, but we also must know who we are in the now. Moses was where he was! Slave, prince, shepherd in a wilderness or the leader of several million people. He did not lament his past palace life. He just did his best in the now.

-2-

WHAT IS GOD ASKING OF YOU?

While I was speaking at a mission youth camp, a young man caught my eye and that of my interpreter. Although he looked so hardened for one so young, he came forward for prayer after the service. We prayed for him several times without seeing any change in his demeanor. Then suddenly, he fell to his knees.

That morning a part of my message, a part I'd almost left out, was on David, the shepherd boy. As a child, this young man was a shepherd boy. God had given him a dream that one of his sheep separated herself from the flock, turned to him, and he heard God calling him into the ministry. The very next day, one of the sheep separated herself from

the flock and turned and stared at him. It was exactly as in the dream. Then he heard God's call to serve Him.

But the enemy of our souls is also the enemy of our calling. One day a *"Christian"* uncle arrived and abused this little boy. He began to put up walls. That morning at the altar, he poured out his hurt and pain to Jesus and to us. Tears flowed slowly down his cheeks. In amazement, he touched the tears and looked at his wet hand. This was the first time he had cried in over ten years! In that encounter with the love of Jesus, God renewed a very *"dead"* vision.

Moses' vision was dead. He didn't think he was a failure; he knew it! He no longer had any expectations. He had buried them long ago on one of those days while he stood in the sweltering sun staring at his father-in-law's sheep. His dreams were gone, but God's call was alive.

Have you given up on your vision, that part of you that used to be so alive and hopeful? Is your vision dead? Do you feel that God and people have judged you? Maybe they have forgotten you? Maybe, you have judged yourself and passed

sentence. Do you live out your days with a sense of empty drudgery? Have you stopped expecting things to change? Pour out your hurts and disappointments to the Lord. Feel His love. Hear His call. The young man at the youth camp came to an altar. Moses traveled the distance to the Mountain of God, Mount Horeb, also called Sinai. Both left the usual, the comfortable, not really expecting, just being there.

Will You Step Into Your Purpose?

God totally knows what you have done in the past. He knows just where you are now. And He knows how to find you.

Stop right now and give your lost dream to Jesus. Choose to forgive those who have hurt you. Let the Lord carry your pain and disappointment. Let Him heal your hurting heart and ignite that little spark in your spirit.

When God Breaks Into Our Ordinary

Even at the Mountain of God, it was just another dull day for Moses. The desert heat hung in the air, and the sheep moved slowly from one tuft of scrub

grass to another. Heat makes one drowsy, but a shepherd is always alert to the sheep and the area where they feed. Moses scanned the base of the mountain. It was familiar; he'd come here often. Maybe the tranquility or the name, Mountain of God, gave him hope. Maybe here he felt there just still might be a little flicker of hope. A bush fire caught his attention.

"No wonder," he thought. *"This heat is intense."*

But the bush continued to burn, and it was not burned up. I can picture Moses rubbing his eyes and wondering if he'd been too long in the sun. Moving closer, he stared at the bush. The flame was brilliant.

> ***"I've got to get a closer look at this. I will go over and see this strange sight – why the bush does not burn up.", he said. (Exodus 3:3, NIVC)***

"Moses! Moses!"

And Moses very calmly replied, *"Here I am."*

Probably not! What was this strange sight? Who is talking? How does He know my name? I think this eighty-year-old former prince probably answered

in a hushed whisper.

What do you do when God steps out of the box of your expectations and comes to you on an ordinary day? How do you respond if your vision is dead and then your name is called?

Moses started to move closer only to be stopped by the voice of God Himself, *"Take off your shoes."*

> **Then he (God) said, "I am the God of your father, the God of Abraham, the God of Isaac and the God of Jacob." (Exodus 3:6, NIVC)**

God, the God of his father, Amram? That is personal. And the God of Abraham, and the God of Isaac, and the God of Jacob. That is eternal. This God was speaking to him. Moses hid his face.

How does one react to God? Moses reacted in awesome fear. You cannot ignore God when He comes calling your name. How will you respond?

There Are Others

God's next words were not about Moses and his suffering. Instead, the Lord's focus was His people in

Egypt. Yes, He came to Moses and called his name. God knew Moses. And God knows you. He calls your name even as you read these words. But there are others. It isn't really about us. It is about a world of people that are lost and hurting, and a God Who loved them to death, death on a cross.

I remember a time when I felt life just wasn't fair. I had my time of grumbling, and then I looked down at the coffee table where my mother-in-law had left some tracts. I picked up the one on David Livingstone. I read about his dislocated shoulder, his lack of teeth from malnutrition, the negative comments about him in England, and his passion for taking the Gospel to the Africans. As I read his comment about seeing in the distance the smoke of a thousand villages that still had not heard about Jesus, I broke. It was, and will always be, about others.

But Moses wasn't there yet. The first response he made after realizing Who was speaking was a negative one. Not only did the Pharaoh hate him, but his own people had rejected him, too. The glory and thrill of being the deliverer was in the past. This was a hard and dangerous assignment. Yet, the very Moses they had rejected was God's choice to lead

them into liberty.

Moses' first excuse is *"who am I?"* I was a mighty prince, but now I am past my prime. I am a shepherd, an old shepherd. That's all.

God must have smiled and thought to Himself, *"I know."* If God had used Moses as a prince, he would have commanded God's people, but, as a shepherd, Moses was now trained to lead God's flock. God is not looking for pompous generals; He is looking for humble, loving shepherds who will hear the call and follow the Good Shepherd. In John 21:15-17, Jesus told Simon Peter to *"Feed my lambs"* and *"Feed my sheep,"* but He also said, *"Take care of my sheep."*

Now Moses was more ready to be used from God's perspective than he had been forty years prior. God's promise that He would be with Moses was all Moses needed, but Moses did not yet know the power of his God.

I can picture God saying, *"Where are you, Moses? Take a look around. See the Mountain, my mountain?"*

And God said, "I will be with you. And this will be the sign to you that it is I who have

sent you: When you have brought the people out of Egypt, you will worship God on this mountain." (Exodus 3:12, NIVC)

What Time Is It?

God's promises may take a while to realize, but they are true for God is true. For Moses, God showed up right on time, according to eternity's clock. It was at the very end of the fortieth year. Moses would indeed bring God's people to God's Mountain to worship, and they, too, would find God's faithfulness at the very end of the fortieth year.

Where are you in God's timetable? Is it near the end of your fortieth year? When things look down, you need to look up. You are called by God, and He has a specific assignment for you. Do not allow doubts to prevent your future.

What, then, shall we say in response to these things? If God is for us, who can be against us? (Romans 8:31, NIV)

Moses hid his face from God yet dared to argue with Him. What excuses do you use to keep from stepping into the future?

What is God Asking of You?

Moses' next comment to God is a question. *"Supposing I do this?"* tells us he is not yet convinced. Humility is a good thing, but Moses had crossed from humility into fear. What held Moses back from the quick response seen in Paul on the road to Damascus or the disciples as they left all and followed Jesus? It was his fear of people's reactions, fear of his own shortcomings, fear of Egypt's power, fear of change, and fear of the cost of obedience. What are your fears?

How do Moses' fears and excuses differ from Jesus in the Garden of Gethsemane? Jesus added one little phrase that showed His true thoughts. That little phrase, *"Not My will,"* is the crux of a God-filled and focused heart. God may call us where we'd rather not go, but if we truly want His will, we will obey and trust that He will go with us and give us the power and ability we need. If God is for us, we can do all things!

-3-

EXCUSES

*If a commission by an earthly king is considered an honor,
how can a commission by a Heavenly King be considered a
sacrifice? - David Livingstone* [1]

And now ... drum roll, please ... God gives Moses a revelation of Himself. Moses asked, *"What shall I say is the name of the God of their fathers Who sent me?"* God replied by revealing not only His name but His power. The name He gave Moses, *"I AM THAT I AM,"* comes from a Hebrew phrase that denotes action. It implies all power, all presence, and all knowledge. The God of everything. He is all I need and all that I will need in the future. He is all-sufficient!

The power of a name – it declares who we are. It is our presentation to the world. It represents our

being, our character, our reputation, our value. God called Moses by name, but when He told Moses His name, it got personal.

God continued to give Moses a message. Without a Word from God, there is no hope for a nation. Jeremiah was told that God had put His Words in his mouth. It was for the benefit of the nation. God is still looking for those who will step up to the plate and deliver the words that will change the outcome of the game of life.

God's concern was His people and the promise He'd made to their fathers. He intended to keep that promise, despite all the power of Egypt. That is integrity acted out in reality.

And even though Pharaoh himself would resist to the death of his son, the people of the land would favor the Hebrews and willingly provide them with all the finances needed for the long journey ahead. The NIV Study Bible notes call this "plunder," as in a war. It was rightfully theirs in that they had been forced into slavery and had not received wages for a long period. God was going to send His people out as victors. When God steps in, we can go from victims to victors. God makes the difference, but we

must also allow Him to change our mindset so that we behave as victors.

One of the beautiful things that I've watched happen in the Victory's Journey Ministry is the change of mindset. Seeing someone who couldn't make eye contact because of their shame set free to radiate God's love is thrilling to watch! We are victorious because of Christ.

God wanted an answer, but Moses again argued. He simply didn't want to go this route, but God didn't give up. He knew, despite all of Moses' excuses, that this man was the one for the job. Is it possible that Moses' biggest struggle was with the lack of acceptance by his own people? As God answered each of the excuses Moses offered, deeper core issues were exposed.

How important is it that people believe in us? For the Israelites to be free, they must leave Egypt behind, even in their thinking. For them to leave Egypt, they must follow Moses. For us to leave our old mindset, we must leave our Egypt. For us to lead, there must be followers. It all looks so enormous....but God. God is in control, and even though there may be some tough days ahead, God

will give us what we need.

What if they do not believe? Are you trying to lead a flock that does not believe in you or even want you? This flock may look like family, friends, or even a congregation. Maybe it is a flock that, for the most part, does not know or believe in your God. Remember, it is not about you or your ability to perform; it is all about your availability and flexibility to the God Who created you and them and loves you and them.

Do Your People See a Victim Or a Victor?

In the case of Moses, the great I AM took a very ordinary part of who Moses was and transformed that thing into a visual token of His power working through His chosen vessel. It was just a shepherd's staff, a tool that was constantly in Moses' hand, a tool that identified his pathetic role in life, but it became a living moving snake when Moses did what God said to do.

The obedience factor was in *"throwing"* it down. What is God asking you to throw down that is part of your identity? And, after you have thrown it down and it becomes a living thing, will you dare to

pick it up again?

What we throw down, we may be asked to pick up again in a new form. God caused a dead stick to become a living snake. But a living snake is still a scary thing to pick up, even for a seasoned shepherd. Are you brave enough to grab hold of what God is doing, even if it is totally different than what you are familiar with? Moses obeyed because he recognized, even this early, the voice of God. Some things that God commands us to do may seem wrong because they do not follow our traditional understanding. But if God speaks, and we want to be His leaders, we must step out of tradition that is only tradition, and obey. Obedience is the beginning step. Without it, we will stay in the wilderness, and our people will stay in Egypt.

Then God got more personal. He went from *"What is in your hand?"* to Moses' own hand. God asked Moses to put his hand in his cloak. Moses obeyed, but he must have shuddered in horror as he took it back out and looked at the sight of his own flesh consumed with the dreaded incurable disease of leprosy.

For me, it was the possibility of a brain tumor.

But, God, in His faithfulness, gave me promises…
and kept them.

Fear and doubt hover so closely when God
touches our own flesh, but God took that diseased
hand, restored it, and used it as a sign of His great
power. The Book of Acts is not finished. The God
of Moses is still alive and well and able to do more
than our finite minds can imagine. *"Hide that hand,
Moses. Put it back in your cloak. Don't let anyone see."*
That part was probably the easy part, but when he
removed his hand, it was a step of faith. And God is
God. His hand was restored and as normal as the
rest of his body.

The third sign could not be demonstrated because
they were not near the source of the water God
wanted to use. Why water from the Nile River?

The Egyptians considered the Nile River to be
divine. When it was powerless and became a horror
to them, it was proof of a higher deity. This time
Moses did not have a question because he had
experienced God's power, and he believed for
himself. If God said it, that settled it.

Moses did not choose what to throw down, nor

did he choose that his hand would become a sign, nor did he choose that it would be water from the Nile River turning into blood. God chose, and God told Moses what to do. As we come near the holiness of the Almighty, we will be asked to let go of some things that are precious to us. We may see physical problems. We may have to take something in our environment and use it for God's glory. God calls, and God asks us what is in our hands. Will you *"Trust and Obey"*?

Moses' next excuse is an awareness of his personal weakness. He says he couldn't speak well in the past, and he is still slow of speech and tongue. Is this the same man referred to in Acts 7:22? There it states that **"Moses was educated in all the wisdom of the Egyptians and was powerful in speech and action."** **(NIV)**

In Jeremiah 1:6-9, we see God's prophet giving a similar excuse based on his own fear of people and his feelings of inadequacy. But, then God touches his mouth and puts His word in him. Both Moses and Jeremiah said, *"I can't"* based on their fears and their perceived limitations, but in the end, neither of them said, *"I won't"*. God did not give up. He did

not consider His called ones disposable.

I Can't or I Won't

In fact, God put His finger right on the central truth. He asked Moses, *'Who gave you your mouth?'* God gives us our physical traits, and the very ones we feel are inferior are the ones God so often uses. Why is that? It is because when we are displaying a trait people know we are weak in, God's power is apparent, and He gets the glory.

I grew up as a missionary kid in Sierra Leone, West Africa. As part of the family team, I started to teach children in Sunday School and children's services under mango trees before I was even a teenager. That was comfortable, but when we went to America on furlough and I was asked to give my testimony, I froze, choked, and spluttered. It was fear. I was afraid of people's reactions. Today I am comfortable teaching and preaching. My fears changed the day I experienced the power of the Holy Spirit as I spoke.

I was 22 years old and visiting my parents one summer. Mom and Dad were so proud of their daughter being a Bible College student, especially

since neither of them had been to high school. Dad asked me to preach. God dropped a complete message outline into my heart, but I said *"no"*. Because it was communion Sunday, I just didn't think I could speak. Imagine my surprise when my father preached my entire message, even though I was the only one who knew about it!

The next time he asked me I said, *"Yes"*. I dealt with my fears by convincing myself that since I knew the people at Bethel Temple I would be fine. That morning as I sat in the Sanctuary Sunday School class, a number of other missionaries and government folk from England began to come in, 16 of them. One was a Bible College president. I was not only frightened. I was terrified! When we had prayer time before the morning service I begged God to make a hole and let me fall in. I informed Him that I could not do this. But just like in Moses' case, God didn't listen to my fears. I finally prayed, *"God, I know I cannot do it. I am terrified. You are going to have to take over and the Holy Spirit is going to have to do the preaching through me."*

And that is just what God did. One young man testified that as I was speaking about Jesus, he saw

Jesus standing behind me.   That morning he accepted Christ as his Savior. From that moment, I realized that what God asked me to do, I probably could not do, but He could and would if I stepped out in faith.   I knew I must be dependent on the power of the Holy Spirit, and that is just where God wants us.

When your children say, *"I don't want to,"*, it is frustrating. Looking for another way is telling God that we just don't like His plan! God's anger burned against Moses when he asked God to send someone else, but God already had Aaron on his way.   God wanted to use Moses, but He already knew Moses would need an Aaron. We all need an Aaron.

And, so Moses, despite all of his excuses and the core truth that he just did not want to go, went.

It is interesting that after Moses asked his father-in-law's permission to return to Egypt, God told him the people who wanted to kill him were dead. God's timing was right because obedience in spite of fears is more valuable than obedience when we know it will be okay. God is asking for a faith that steps out into a frightening and humanly impossible situation, a situation that we really do not want to step into. Yet

it is in that stepping out that we will know the awesome power and presence of the God Who said, ***"I will never leave you nor forsake you" (Hebrews 13:5, NKJV).*** In the Amplified Version, that verse states, *"...I will not, I will not, I will not in any degree leave you helpless nor forsake nor let you down (relax my hold on you)! [Assuredly not!]"*

Moses had many excuses before he obeyed. We can read about each of his *"but, Gods,"* and be amazed at his daring to argue with God. Maybe we don't argue with the Lord so blatantly, but our excuses still come into play. We may tell God we will get to know our neighbors, but we just keep so busy we don't get around to it. We may tell God we'll do a ministry, but sometimes becomes never. We may say that we will fill a need, but our own family needs overwhelm us.

Of course, Satan will try to block us from following the call. These obstacles the enemy puts in our path are real and not things we can ignore. So what is the answer?

When we know who we are in Christ, and we know His loving care, our trust factor will overtake our fear factor. When we have really felt His love,

we will leave our Martha mentality in the kitchen and sit at His feet with Mary. As He speaks to us and infuses Himself into our spirit, we will hear His voice calling us to a higher obedience level. Then our obedience must be coupled with a determination that if I totally fall apart, I will still trust and obey the great I AM. While the enemy will try to make us turn back, if we obey the Lord's voice, God will see us through the test and give us a testimony.

-4-

SEND AARON, PLEASE!

Moses had a strong will. Anyone who opts to argue with God is pitting his will against God's, and that is daring. Moses was also filled with fear. What holds you back? What fears or feelings of inadequacy keep you from totally obeying that small, but persistent, voice of your loving Heavenly Father?

A combination of *"I don't want to"* and *"I can't"* prevents many potentially great people from accomplishing what was planned for them. On the other hand, many meek and lowly people with seemingly few abilities press in and accomplish great things for the Lord. How can that be possible?

As a teenager, I heard many messages on surrendering to the voice of God. It is that point when we acknowledge that God is God, and I am compelled to obey Him totally, even if I do not think what He is asking me to do is possible. As we do this, we release the principle of the talents. By using what is in our hands, we release God to develop new talents and abilities in us. He grows us, and things we never imagined, things we never considered, become experience. It all starts with surrender. At what point did Moses surrender? At what point did Moses give up on his perspective and decide to do what God asked of him?

God spoke to Moses. Moses knew it was God and, despite all of his excuses and downright resistance to God's call, Moses left the place of his divine encounter a different man. God was no longer the God of his fathers; God was the God of Moses.

Simple surrender, followed by taking the first step of obedience, will unlock the door to your divine destiny. And, after you have taken your first step, God will put your fears and insecurities into His perspective. He knows you can do all He asks you

to do.

And Aaron Is On the Way

Aaron, older than Moses by three years and raised by the same godly parents, seemed to already have an awareness of God and the ability to hear His voice. We so often look at the figure in the limelight and forget that for every person in the foreground, there are many behind the scenes. Aaron would not be the key leader, but, without him, Moses would have surely struggled, and possibly failed.

Aaron was going to stand by Moses in a number of difficult situations. He would help him present God's message to the people and to Pharaoh. He would also become the first High Priest, the man who went to God on behalf of the people. If you have such a person in your life, you are truly blessed!

Although not a Moses, Aaron was just as chosen and special to God and God's purpose. He would have his weaknesses and his failures, but his life would be anointed, and he and his children would make a difference. Maybe his call wasn't all that exciting (after all, a burning bush that speaks is definitely unique), but it was clear and specific. And,

most important of all, Aaron simply obeyed.

As he was going towards Moses, Moses was coming towards him. What a coincidence, or was it? How often do we see God at work and think it is just a coincidence? However, if we truly believe in an Almighty, All-knowing God, we must recognize His powerful hand at work in the smallest God-incidents! And where did Moses and Aaron "run into" each other? There at the base of the great Mountain of God, Mount Sinai, the two brothers met, kissed, and shared what God was doing. Forty years earlier, they'd thought they were ready for this assignment. Now, older and humbler, God declared they were ready.

Together they entered Egypt. Together they called for the elders of Israel. There Aaron told them everything God had spoken to Moses and also performed the miraculous signs for the people to see. This time the people believed. This time they accepted Moses as the deliverer sent from God. When God is with us, and the time is right, we can expect God to unlock the gate to hearts.

And what Moses could not do alone, he and Aaron could do together. Have you joined up with

an Aaron? I cannot begin to express the valuable role that my "Aaron" has carried in my ministry. The truth is we are not intended to be loners. We need others in the Body of Christ to help hold us up in difficult days. Aaron continued to be that person for Moses.

Aaron was able to be there for him at a time when his arms were too weak to keep holding them up...and the battle depended on it. Aaron was there when rejections came and there as they learned to worship on a higher level. Find an Aaron, or as with Paul, a Barnabas, and you will be strengthened in your ministry.

-5-

FOCUSED FAITH PRODUCES COURAGE

Did you ever get an assignment from God that looked hard, but when you realized it really was going to be hard, you were caught a bit off guard? Several years ago, the Lord impressed me that I would have to go where I did not want to go in my life's journey, but I was not to fear. He would be with me. I thanked the Lord for preparing me and for the many confirmations that this was indeed His word to me.

However, when in one year, we faced our son's two open-heart surgeries, our one daughter's two accidents, one in which we drove an hour and a half to Philadelphia not knowing what we would find when we got there, our other daughter's health

concerns, my husband's diagnosis of a heart arrhythmia and later of an esophageal disease, my mother's death, and even our cat's death, I felt stunned. *"Why, God,"* I asked, and so did Moses.

I am so glad that God understands our sorry grasp of His infinite wisdom and power in our lives. Just as we can accept it when our children ask the *"why"* questions (even though we may want to scream if we hear that word one more time!), God understands our desire to figure it all out. He made us!

Moses and Aaron arrived in Egypt. They talked to the Hebrew elders, and the people were responsive. It was a great meeting filled with joy and worship. Everyone left on a high. Things had changed. Instead of rejection, Moses was accepted. What a good feeling it is when the people God has called you to receive you with gladness! Moses must have felt so encouraged. Sometimes in a moment like this, we begin to feel that the battle is over. God knows when we need an encouraging experience, but even at these times, our focus must be on the Lord. Jesus could have been swayed by the people who saw His miracles and believed in His name, but His

reaction to them is interesting.

> *But Jesus would not entrust himself to them, for he knew all men. He did not need man's testimony about man, for he knew what was in a man. (John 2:24-25, NIVC)*

We must get to the point where we trust and obey God; understanding that people and their view of us will change. God never changes, and if He has called us to a specific ministry position, that is what we are to do. God will be with us.

It Wasn't Supposed To Be Like This

God's leaders were on track. They were walking in obedience. They were expecting an *"I will not"* from Pharaoh, and that is exactly what they got. I'm sure they thought they were prepared because God told them Pharaoh would refuse to let the people go. I'm just as sure they were not expecting it to get as bad as it did. God was still in control, but at this point, it looked like Pharaoh was in control. When we see the world's system looking so successful when things are not going as we were so sure they would, what do we do?

Moses and Aaron gave Pharaoh God's message.

But Pharaoh was furious. He gave a new command that the Israelites must not only keep up with their brick-making; they must supply their own straw. It was the last straw!

The Egyptian slave drivers beat the Israelite foremen as the quotas were not met. Human nature, being what it is, people will follow a leader as long as everything is going well, and the benefits are obvious. When trouble and hardships come, people get upset with their leaders. These Hebrew foremen found Moses and Aaron as they left Pharaoh's presence. Feeling helpless and angry, they lashed out at the two that were sent from God to bring them deliverance.

> *... they said, "May the Lord look upon you and judge you! You have made us a stench to Pharaoh and his officials and have put a sword in their hand to kill us."* *(Exodus 5:21, NIVC)*

Who were they really angry with? When we get a promise from God, it does not mean the journey from where we are to the fulfillment of that promise will be easy. Yet, when things seem to be going wrong, a common first reaction is anger and

frustration. When people feel they are helpless, there is a need to control something else. Attacking those in leadership is a form of venting personal pain. The anger was partly at Moses and Aaron as God's spokesmen, but it was primarily at God Who allowed them to feel hope and then did not prevent a worst-case scenario.

Where was their faith? Where is ours when we feel God has promised us something, and it looks like it just is not happening? In fact, it looks even worse. Maybe we are tempted to tell God we wished He'd just leave us alone. How does a shepherd handle such a flock?

Look at the reaction Moses had. He felt the pain and frustration of his new flock. He struggled, too. How could a loving, caring God do this?

Faith or Assumption

Faith that is not tested is not really faith; it is an assumption. Can we stand in the storm? Do we at least know where to run? Moses did the right thing.

When the questions come, and they will, the best place to take them is to the Lord. When the stresses, hurts, failures, and rejections are too big for us, then

we are to follow Peter's admonition and cast them on Christ. (I Peter 5:7). And Peter says very simply that we can do this because Jesus Christ cares for us.

Moses simply did not understand. It wasn't the way he expected. His frustration comes through very clearly as he demands an answer from the Lord, "Is this why You sent me?" He accuses God of not keeping His promise. Have you ever felt like Moses? Have you tried to encourage someone who was already hurting and then stood helplessly by while things got worse? It is at times like that that we are tempted to doubt the promises of God. Yet Peter also reminds us that God is not a God Who is slack concerning His promises. It is at these times when we must choose; the facts that we see or the faith in things not yet seen. When everything is going smoothly, it is an easy choice, but when we are in the middle of howling winds and crashing waves, and we cannot see over those waves, then it becomes faith, tested faith.

Think about a time when your faith was tested. How did God help you get over that hurdle?

Focused Faith; Intentional Courage

Moses knew what to do, and after he poured out his frustration and disappointment with God, he listened. Sometimes we just do the first part. We vent and walk away while God is trying to tell us something that will restore our faith and help us gain His perspective.

God reminded Moses that He had revealed Himself to Abraham, Isaac, and Jacob as the Almighty God, but now He was opening a new page in history. It was the beginning of the revelation of Himself as the Lord, or Jehovah, the redemptive name of God. He would indeed deliver His people. He had not forgotten. He would keep His promise to Moses. This would be the story of the redemption of the people of Israel, a type that would enable generations as yet unborn to better understand the redemption of all of mankind to be made possible by the Son of God Himself, Jesus Christ, our Deliverer!

This was bigger than Moses or anything Moses could comprehend. He went back to the Israelites with God's answer, but this time their response was not positive. They simply did not listen or receive the promises because they were too discouraged! In

the middle of a battle, it is hard to see ahead, but if we can remember God sees the whole picture and our obedience will affect generations to come, we can move forward with renewed courage.

Without faith showing itself in courage, we will not make it through the wilderness, but with faith in God, we can have the courage, and we can win the battles ahead.

Courage is obeying God when you know there will be negative responses. It's great to have courage, but it is not something we can carry around in our pocket, and it is not something we will know we have until we need it. Did you ever preach a message your people did not want to hear? Did you ever witness to someone who wasn't interested? Did you ever go to approach someone in love to address sin only to have them reject you and make accusations against you?

We faced that storm when we found out about someone in the church who was forcing another person to commit sin. That very Sunday, this person started a petition to remove my husband because he was not spiritually sensitive. What do you say? You go to the Lord! And you keep going.

Focused Faith Produces Courage

The plagues came. Time and again, Pharaoh resisted God's command. God gave the final warning!

So Moses said, "This is what the Lord says: 'About midnight I will go throughout Egypt.

5Every firstborn son in Egypt will die, from the firstborn son of Pharaoh, who sits on the throne, to the firstborn son of the slave girl, who is at her hand mill, and all the firstborn of the cattle as well.

6There will be loud wailing throughout Egypt--worse than there has ever been or ever will be again.

7But among the Israelites not a dog will bark at any man or animal.' Then you will know that the Lord makes a distinction between Egypt and Israel.

8All these officials of yours will come to me, bowing down before me and saying, 'Go, you and all the people who follow you!' After that I will leave."

Then Moses, hot with anger, left Pharaoh. (Exodus 11:4-8, NIVC)

The Moses Manual

Moses is no longer shaking and overcome with fear. His answer is full of authority. What changed the frightened Moses to God's man who could shrug off the king's threats? What made him the man who could tell the Egyptian king what he would do, and when? The more you are in communication with God, the more you are used of God, the more you will believe God. Faith that produces small miracles will begin to believe for larger miracles. While God was showing His power to Pharaoh, the Egyptians, and the Israelites, He was also showing Moses He could be trusted...and Moses was learning.

-6-

PEOPLE CAN BE FRIGHTENING

In Exodus 12:1, God told Moses and Aaron that the month they were in was to become the first month on their calendar. From this point on, there was to be a new agenda to life. There are seasons of life when God calls us to new beginnings. God gave Moses His instructions for a fresh start for His people, and Moses called the elders and told them what God said.

How do you think Moses felt as he called this meeting with the elders of his people? It was the first meeting since he'd faced their anger and frustration after Pharaoh made their workload even more unbearable by not providing straw for the brick making. How would they respond to him, to God,

to God's Word? There are times when God gives us a word for someone or for our flock, and after we obey, it looks like everything gets worse. It is still God's message, and our responsibility is to do what the King of Kings commands. Moses had more courage now with Pharaoh, but this was his own people. This was a challenging task. How would they react?

I remember a few years back when God gave me what I felt was a very strong word for our church membership. In the prior year, the congregation had voted against changing the church's name, something God had really impressed on my husband to do. The word God gave me to share was about loving where we were more than obeying God. If we did not obey, we were in danger of letting God pass us by.

I told God I would give the message, but He would need to have my husband ask me to say something. To that point, I had never given a business meeting devotional. As the meeting time drew closer, I felt this message becoming more intense in my spirit. I did not want God to pass our church by. I knew that would mean death to the

promises He had given us of a future revival. But I also feared people's reactions. Some might think it was a set-up. Others might think I was harsh. Maybe it would be better if I didn't have to give it. I struggled in my personal prayer times but finally realized if my husband didn't ask me, I wouldn't have to do it. After all, that had been the way I'd prayed. The business meeting day got closer. I was just getting used to the idea that I was off the hook when Pat asked me to do the devotional. How do you say *"no"* when you know God has given you something to say?

With a mixture of nerves and anointing, I obeyed God and delivered His message. No one spoke when I was finished. The change of name passed.

I don't understand why that name change was so important in God's eyes, other than it was a matter of trusting Him and the pastor God had placed in the church. Maybe it had to do with learning simple obedience. Maybe the new name, Faith Community Assembly of God, would become who we were in the future. Whatever the reason, God used me despite my lack of courage, and yet, maybe courage isn't really courage unless you are afraid.

Will People Respond or React

Would the Israelites listen to Moses and Aaron and their message from God? Would they follow through with obedience or would they choose to stay in the security of the lifestyle that was familiar? We have a message to give, but we don't know how people will respond or react. It is still our responsibility to give the message. Each individual is responsible before God for how they respond or react to that message. Some want out of *"Egypt,"* but they know it will involve changes, and change can be uncomfortable. Change takes faith and obedience. It involves moving out from the old and into the new. Some folks don't want to pay the price for those changes to happen, but the Lord says in Isaiah 43:19, ***"See, I am doing a new thing! Now it springs up; do you not perceive it? I am making a way in the desert and streams in the wasteland." (NIVC)***

"God doesn't call us to be comfortable. He calls us to trust Him so completely that we are unafraid to put ourselves in situations where we will be in trouble if He doesn't come through." – Francis Chan [2]

God will make a way for us when it looks the most impossible. He is ready to move. Are we ready

to move with Him? If we are ready to move out, He will also be our covering.

The death angel was about to pass by Egypt killing the first-born. It sounds so harsh, but God always has a way of escape. Those whose homes and hearts were covered by the blood would be spared.

By now, God's chosen people had seen Him at work, and their hearts were open to God's directives. When Moses spoke, they listened. They worshipped and acknowledged the Lord and His message. Then they obeyed. The blood of the Passover lamb, placed on the doorposts of their homes, protected the believers.

Jesus Christ is our Passover Lamb. He came in all the perfection of divine holiness and walked this earth's dusty paths as one of us, yet He did not sin. Yeast represents sin. Part of the Passover ceremony involves three pieces of unleavened (yeastless) bread. One of the ceremonial steps is that the middle piece of this bread, which has a pierced appearance, is wrapped in a white napkin and hidden for a while. Jesus, the Holy Son of God, was pierced and shed His blood for us. He was wrapped in a death shroud and buried (hidden) for three days. He took my

place and yours just as the Passover Lamb died so the first-born in the house could live. As we believe in His Name, we are covered and protected from eternal death, a very real place called Hell.

Jesus came to bring us abundant, victorious living. It is our choice. Are you ready to move out of Egypt? God has a good plan. Just because we don't see it yet is not reason to doubt. It is a time for faith!

> *"For I know the plans I have for you," declares the Lord, "plans to prosper you and not to harm you, plans to give you hope and a future. Then you will call upon me and come and pray to me, and I will listen to you. You will seek me and find me when you seek me with all your heart."*
> *(Jeremiah 29:11-13, NIVC)*

God's people obeyed, and God's deliverance came suddenly. It was night. It was dark. There was wailing in the background. So often, God's deliverance comes at the time when everything around us looks dark, and the people around us are hopeless. That deliverance comes to those who are ready and prepared.

Leaving Egypt is more than believing. It is preparation to move forward and a will to leave Egypt behind. For the congregation, it was a new beginning with a new month, highlighted by new ceremonies to help them remember all God was doing for them.

But What About Moses?

Forty years earlier, Moses fled from disgrace and rejection and fear for his very life. To obey God and bring deliverance to his people, Moses had to reenter Egypt. That involved dealing with his past fears and rejection. It meant confronting the people who represented those hard times. It meant delivering God's message to them!

Are there shadows in your past that you have tried to forget? Are there people and pains that pushed you out of your comfort zone and placed you on the backside of a wilderness? How long have you been in that wilderness?

Do you remember where Moses met God? Even in his wilderness, Moses apparently felt compelled to go to the base of the Mountain of God. There God appeared to him in a burning bush that was not

consumed. There he met the GREAT I AM. There he received his commission with God's promise of deliverance and a future. Hebrews 11:27 tells us Moses functioned as though he could see the invisible God. He had an incredible one-on-one relationship with the Lord!

If you want to be all God plans for you to be, you must seek the Mountain of God, that private place where you are open to God meeting you in a supernatural way, where you are open to His commission for your future. Then you may be told to go back and face your Egypt. That may seem overwhelming until we think about the difference in Moses when he tried to deliver his people his way, and when he did it in obedience to God's call. Also, notice that when God asked him to go back to Egypt, Moses was in a relationship with God, listening to His voice, and walking in His presence. The very things that so frightened Moses and made him feel inadequate he could face now because God was with him.

And you may have to release some old dreams to make room for some God dreams!

Victory Parade

As I have ministered to people with painful pasts, I have learned one thing; God, in His great love, will be with you when He calls you to face your past. Whatever you have to deal with, He will put you in a safe place and a safe time, lovingly watching over your every step. That very thing you have feared the most may be your doorway to a new beginning. And it isn't only about you. God called Moses to deliver God's people. Moses obeyed that call. He was just the vessel God used to set a nation free, but as he obeyed, Moses gained confidence and found his own new beginning. With each plague and with each miraculous showing of God's power working through him, Moses got bolder. As we surrender to the Lord and become His vessel to use as He sees fit, we will see more answers to prayer. We will experience the joy of being used by God in the supernatural working out of His plans. When we obey what we feel God is impressing us to do, we will grow in God ourselves and have more faith to believe for the seemingly impossible.

And God doesn't just deliver us. I believe it pleases our wonderful Heavenly Father to deliver us

in style. Satan is called the accuser of the brethren because he accuses God's people day and night (Revelation 12:10). How do you feel as a parent when you know your child is trying hard to do well, and someone accuses them of something? How do you think God feels when Satan accuses you to Him? Personally, I think God decides right then to show Satan how much He loves you!

Look at Exodus 12:35-38. In this passage, the Egyptians gave the Israelites all the gold, silver, and clothing they asked for. Without fighting a battle themselves, they totally plundered, totally stripped the Egyptians of their wealth, and the Egyptians were glad to bless them! Comparing the six hundred thousand men mentioned in Exodus 12:37 to the tally lists of future censuses, we must estimate that several million Israelites left Egypt that night. According to verse fifty-one, they moved out in order according to their divisions. Not only that, but a multitude of people also followed them out of Egypt, choosing to go with them and the God in whose power they now believed.

It is time to leave Egypt, but for Moses, who ran away, that may mean you have to dare to reenter

Egypt first. If you obey God's call to bring about His deliverance, He will bless you beyond your greatest imaginations.

Is there an area you have been afraid to face? Are there people you feel totally intimidated by? If God is for you, no man can stand against you, no power can defeat you, and no situation can stop you. You belong to God. You are a victor, not a victim. All the power of the Almighty God is available as you step out of your comfort zone to fulfill God's call on your life. As you obey God, and as you focus on ministering to people Christ loves, you will find that the Holy Spirit will enable you to be powerful in word and deed. You can be a Moses to your world!

God's Way or Mine?

Everyone knew the shortest way to Canaan, the Promised Land, was through the Philistine territory. Everyone knew that was the best way. So often, we just know the best way to do something. It is hard to accept God's plan when it just does not seem logical. It is hard to do the thing which seems to be negative. It is just hard to adjust our human thinking to God's higher perspective. But if we trust and do as we are led to do, we will eventually see the

reason and recognize God's wisdom.

Exodus 13:17 lets us know that even though the Israelites were armed for war and even though they felt confident in their ability, God knew that facing war might cause them to run back to Egypt. War is frightening.

Coming out of Egypt, we may feel we can face anything, and then we are caught off guard by seemingly small obstacles. Egypt was the biggest nation the children of God were to face, but God did that battle for them. Facing actual war, even with smaller enemies, might be too big for them so early in their new life. God knew they were just not ready.

I have, at times, told God I was ready to face something only to realize later that I was not as ready as I thought I was. What a relief to know our God knows what we can handle and does not take us on the road where those trials we cannot handle lurk. He leads us instead on paths that may seem impossible, but where we simply must trust Him to deliver us. AS we trust, we will indeed see His glory.

-7-

FAIL OR GO FORWARD

Although the shortest route to Canaan was north into Philistine territory, God chose a different route. He led them on a detour, a long one, but they were on their way! What could go wrong?

For Moses, it must have been an incredible high to watch this mighty throng of believers moving out of Egypt. Can you imagine leading a post-revival congregation of several million?! And then, to see the cloud of God's glory or the pillar of fire twenty-four-seven! There was excitement in the camp. From Moses to the youngest child, the feeling of liberty and new beginnings was intoxicating.

Then God told Moses to turn the congregation around and go back and camp right by the sea.

The Moses Manual

According to Oswald T. Allis in *"God Spake By Moses,"* [1] this put the Israelites right between the Red Sea and the mountains to the west. While we do not totally know the topography of the land, it appears that God took them from a fairly safe area to a type of cul-de-sac where they looked confused and vulnerable to the Egyptian army.

Have you been there? Have you felt that maybe God is not all that you thought He was? Have you doubted His wisdom when you felt trapped?

Have you felt confident that God was leading you only to have everything appear to go wrong (notice the word *"appear"*)? How strong is your trust factor at such a time?

But God does know what is going on, and He does have a plan, a good one. Exodus 14:1-4 is an account of God telling Moses what He plans to do. No secrets. Pharaoh will think the Israelites are confused and will pursue them, but God would be ready, and He would get the glory and be acknowledged by the Egyptians who had so resisted Him. God doesn't always tell us exactly what He is going to do, but the outcome is the same. The enemy may try his best to frighten and discomfort

us, but if we follow our God, we will see His salvation, and He will get the glory.

Pharaoh did just as God said. More concerned with the loss of workers than God or the welfare of his country, Pharaoh prepared his chariots. He took six hundred of the best chariots, and all the other chariots, all his horsemen and troops, and pursued this multitude of former slaves.

True, they were former slaves, but now they were marching in confidence into a new life. The enemy hates it when God sets someone free. That part we can understand, but why does God allow people who have been set free to get caught in a cul-de-sac with no possible way of escape? Why did he let the Israelites get into such a situation? Have you ever prayed about something, seen what looked like a wonderful answer to prayer, expected God to lead you into more great things, only to be faced with a dead end that looked hopeless?

My life preparation was to be a missionary nurse. God called me into the ministry when I was fifteen. I assumed that meant missions because it was what I knew and because I felt such a love for the people of Sierra Leone. Nursing was always a desire. I did all I

knew to do to prepare, and then I applied for a missionary appointment. I was turned down.

To say I was in shock was an understatement. I felt like my life was turned upside down. At the time, I was the 3-11 nursing supervisor of a large hospital. I had several career opportunities open to me, but my heart cried for ministry. I knew I'd never be happy unless I was where God led me. The next summer, I was able to speak with David Womack, a missionary leader. He helped me to release my dreams to God and trust Him to guide me on a daily basis. (I was able to return to Sierra Leone in 2009 to minister☺.)

Up to this point, the Israelites were *"marching out boldly"* (Exodus 14:8). Their expectations were high, and their faith was great. It was a wonderful life!

Then they looked around at their surroundings and spotted the massive Egyptian army bearing down on them in an enormous cloud of dust. Terror replaced bold faith; panic ruled instead of joy. The slave mentality returned. They felt the old sense of being vulnerable again. Egypt was so large. Pharaoh was so powerful. They cried out to God in their

anguish.

> *"Was it because there were no graves in Egypt that you brought us to the desert to die? What have you done to us by bringing us out of Egypt? Didn't we say to you in Egypt, 'Leave us alone; let us serve the Egyptians'? It would have been better for us to serve the Egyptians than to die in the desert!" (Exodus 14:11-12, NIVC)*

Scared people can do hurtful things. Just hours before, Moses was their wonderful leader, a mighty man of God, but now faced with difficulties bigger than their faith, Moses was the source of their troubles. What do you do when you are the Moses-person? How do you face these people? What do you believe about God as you look at the destructive forces around you, tearing you down and threatening the future of those you lead?

We need to fight against fear as people and as leaders. God's Word is filled with the admonition, *"do not fear."* I have heard that the phrase, *"do not fear"* appears three hundred and sixty-six times in the Bible: one for every day of the year plus a spare for leap years.

Fear Defeats Purpose

Why are we not to fear? Fear defeats purpose. It paralyzes bold believers and reduces them to trembling slaves. Focusing on the situation causes us to cry out in terror, and as soon as we do, hopelessness creeps into our spirits and fills us with a chilling dread. We are unable to lift our heads. We are unable to speak out or move out.

Moses answered in Exodus 14:13 and 14:

> *"Do not be afraid. Stand firm and you will see the deliverance the Lord will bring you today. The Egyptians you see today you will never see again. The Lord will fight for you; you need only to be still." (NIVC)*

Live In Forward Gear

Despite his brave words, Moses apparently cried out to God because God responded to him, *"Why are you crying out to me? Tell the Israelites to move on"*. Those are power-filled words. When there is no place to go, move on. When the enemy is coming up behind you and the sea is in front of you, move on. When it is humanly impossible, God is ready to

do a miracle, and He says, *"Move on"!* Can you dare to do what God says to do?

I've learned that the enemy often attacks me physically as I am about to preach or share God's Word. I could ask someone else to take my place and go curl up in my bed, but I have learned if I pray and go forward, the symptoms will be gone almost as soon as I start to speak. As we grow in the Lord, we begin to recognize certain enemy strategies. We also learn how to pray and keep moving.

The children of Israel and their leader needed to pull their gaze away from the terror thundering down upon them. Even though they couldn't see a way out of their predicament, God had a plan, and it was powerful!

Moses, Stretch Out Your Hand...and Your Faith

God told Moses to raise his staff and stretch out his hand over the Red Sea to divide it. Moses, acting on God's behalf, was faced with a choice. What if nothing happened? What if he looked like a fool? Sometimes God drops a thought in our hearts to do something unusual, and we hold back because of fear

of people and their opinions. But Moses had already seen what God could do.

Alta lived with almost constant pain. She had Tic Douloureux, or trigeminal neuralgia, a severe, stabbing pain on one side of the face. It is considered one of the most painful conditions to affect people. She was a kind, highly educated woman who was a great blessing to our family and to our church. But for thirty-eight years, she suffered much from this relentless disease.

It was a Sunday night, and as I sat at the organ, the Lord spoke into my spirit that if the pastor and elders gathered around Alta and prayed, He would heal her. Sounds great, but just that morning, a guest speaker had warned us against saying, *"God Said."* After all, we must be careful of presuming on God!

I wrestled with this. What if it was my imagination? What if I wasn't really hearing from God, but I sensed God was saying, *"Now!"*. I blurted out the message, and the leaders gathered around Alta. And God did the healing!!! Every week for months, that precious lady approached us to tell us how many days she had been pain-free.

Will we dare stretch beyond the explainable into that place where we can hear and see His hand at work?

At this point, the Angel of the Lord moved. Instead of the pillar of cloud being in front of them, it was now behind them, giving light to the children of God and dense darkness to the children of the enemy. Our God is a protecting wall that the enemy cannot penetrate without permission. While God gives His own people light to see the way to blessing, the enemy will be confused by a darkness that will affect their ability to see and understand what is happening. God's people were definitely not in the dark.

Notice the time sequence. All night long, the Lord drove the water back into walls and kept it there. The several million Israelites walked through carrying their belongings. That would take some time. The Egyptians pursued them right into this highway.

Then God looked down from the pillar of fire and cloud, His very present presence, and said, *"That's the end of the road, Enemy!"* During the last watch of the same night, God caused the Egyptian

chariot wheels to get clogged in the sand and come off. The Egyptians realized God was against them again and turned to flee, but it was too late. In obedience to God, Moses looked back and stretched his hand over the divided sea. With a mighty crash, the two walls of water collided, totally covering all of the Egyptian army that had followed the Israelites into the sea. It was only just daybreak.

Moses, once again their trusted shepherd, led his congregation in a song of praise to the Lord. Can you imagine the sound of that choir filling the crisp morning air? The remnant of the Egyptian army still on the far side of the Red Sea, heard in stunned amazement. Moses' sister, Miriam, took her tambourine and sang the refrain. The women followed her, shaking their tambourines and dancing. What a service!

Leader, caught in the spirit of discouragement and defeat, God has a boulevard through the briny sea. That very area that you haven't noticed because you *"know"* even God cannot work there, look again. As the Lord speaks to your spirit, stretch your hand out, and move forward. Tell your people it is time to refocus. Tell them it is time to move out of Egypt's

territory into total dependence on the Almighty. God did not bring you into your cul-de-sac to destroy you. He is so much bigger than that. He will indeed open the waters for you as you put your trust in Him.

-8-
HANDLING COMPLAINTS

Moses and his congregation saw God's mighty hand of deliverance at the Red Sea, and in that situation, God introduced them to one of His key principles. That principle was very simple: when your back is against the wall and your situation looks hopeless, when you can only see disaster, God has a plan, and it is awesome.

Singing, shouting, and waving tambourines, they turned their back on the land of Egypt. As they began their journey to the Promised Land the wilderness stretched hot and dry, but when you have just crossed a sea on dry land and seen your enemies destroyed by that same sea, you feel you can face anything. After all, if God is for us, we must be pretty special! The journey may be hard, but soon

they would be in the Land of Promise! They did not know that God was about to teach them another principle. When you are in the wilderness, it can get worse.

Three days in a wilderness can make you or break you. How do we react when faced with hunger and thirst? We might cry, *"Bring it on!"* and think, *"I can do this,"* but are we really ready to face the horrors of the wilderness? Incredible winds, dust in your eyes and mouth, snakes and scorpions, and, all the time, the relentless heat is beating down on you. Goshen in Egypt was pastureland, green, and lush. What a contrast! Can it get any worse?

For the children of Israel, it got worse. Three days into the wilderness, with thirst an incredible factor, they came to water. Relief and rest, or so they thought. This lovely oasis was named Marah, or Bitter, because that is just what the water was. As thirsty as they were, this water was undrinkable. Yes, the wilderness can get worse.

Earlier I mentioned that our son had open-heart surgery for a bad aortic valve in 2003. We were only expecting one surgery. He came through it, although the surgeon told us it was a very hard operation. All

was going well, and so he was transferred to the intermediate unit. We left to go back to the motel to get some lunch while he was getting settled in his new room.

Then came that nudge that I knew was from the Lord. I needed to get back to the hospital at once. As I walked into my son's room, my heart dropped. The nurse in me kicked in, and I ran out and shouted to the nurse to get the doctor. She looked at me and said I have a call in for him. I remember saying, *"STAT!"* She jumped into action. The doctor was interrupted in surgery, and Patrick was on his way to OR again.

It seems that the valve leaflet had torn and the valve was unable to pump the blood. In a few minutes, my son would have been gone.

Whether in our personal lives or in our leadership, wilderness experiences will happen. But God is faithful! In the wilderness situations, He makes a way.

Exodus 15:24 says simply, *"**so the people grumbled against Moses.**"* When you minister to people, and things get worse, they may turn on you.

How do you handle that? You are presenting godly principles that you know are true. You are praying and in communication with God for them. Yet their wilderness gets worse. You may be as stunned as they are by the situations that come against them at every turn. Your own faith may be a little shaky.

In times like this, God is still God. God had healing for those bitter waters. It was just a little miracle compared to the many He'd already done. Just a certain wood, a natural resource, nearby that changed the bitter to sweet and palatable. Just God's man crying out in prayer. When faced with grumblers and worse-than-wilderness experiences, God is listening for our cry. He is waiting to give us the directions that will help us help our people.

Note that the instruction God gave Moses did not make sense. It was not logical. It had never been done before. It was not tried and proven by someone else in ministry. But the key to the miracle was in Moses' obedience. Do you want God's answers? Expect them to be out of your normal experience range. One of the secrets to Moses' success as a pastor of such a congregation was his willingness to do what God said to do. God did the

rest!

Are you facing a test in the wilderness? How should you react? What should you do? Remember, tests produce testimonies.

While people can mutter and complain, so can leaders. We must guard our lips, for when we lead others, a higher set of requirements is put upon us. As Moses sought God and saw a miracle, he also received a new revelation of God as Healer.

God's Rest Stop

After the experience of the bitter water becoming sweet, the Bible simply says, *"Then they came to Elim, where there were twelve springs and seventy palm trees, and they camped there near the water." (Exodus 15:27, NIVC)*

We would like to just come to Elim, the place of twelve springs and seventy palm trees, but God knows that it is at Marah that we are developed. But when Marah is over, God in mercy leads us to places of rest and refreshment. Elim was such a place.

There are times when we need to sit and relax; times when our bodies and our spirits need to be

refreshed. One of the greatest temptations in leadership is to keep going towards the goal without caring for our personal needs. Moses and the congregation needed a break from the wilderness experience, and God graciously gave them that.

The whole Israelite congregation moved again. This time directly towards the Mountain of God. They had a divine appointment.

But, as the traveling grew harder, their memories of the horrors of slavery faded in the background. They remembered pots of meat, fresh vegetables, and delicious bread. It seemed glorious compared to this dusty desert with its howling winds and wild creatures.

The people murmured again...and again...and again. In researching these events, I find that there were at least thirteen times when they turned on Moses! They were thirsty. They were hungry. He wasn't feeding them!

Even at God's mountain, they turned and, in total rebellion, chose to worship a creature instead of the Creator. They wanted their own leader. They made accusations. And, in one situation, even his

most trusted co-workers turned against him.

When the Complaints Get Worse

They thought Moses was wonderful, until they didn't.

How do you react when the whole congregation is against you? How do you handle it when those you trusted listen to the *"complainers"* and then join them?

"If your identity is found in Christ, then it matters less and less what people think of you." – Leonard I Sweet[1]

They had their own agenda, sometimes fueled by jealousy. The Israelites were just not that mature in their *"God-walk."* Each of them had a "better idea." They were very concerned with their own needs and wants, to the point that God calls it a craving, or lust, in Psalm 78:18.

God's people were dysfunctional. Is this possible? The truth is that many Christians need help in *"Laying aside every weight"* (Hebrews 12:1, KJV). Even after we accept Jesus Christ as our Savior and become His followers, we may have baggage that we need God to deal with. Unless we allow God to

grow us, we will continue to act out our dysfunctional behavior. The Christian walk is the daily taking off of the old self and its attitudes and habits and putting on the new.

One of the things the ladies in Victory's Journey came up with was that in order to deal with an issue, they needed to:

- Face it

- Trace it (find where it started)

- Embrace it (admit it)

- Erase it

And God gives the grace to help us unload our junk so that we can be a blessing.

Do God's leaders always do logical things? Think of Joshua leading the army around the city of Jericho. Because the people followed him, they saw a victorious miracle. Do God's leaders always do things that are familiar? Usually not. Are God's leaders perfect? Absolutely not! Only God is perfect. It does mean that God sees the person He puts into leadership as His choice to fulfill His plan.

Handling Complaints

What a contrast between Moses and his congregation. Moses did not talk about life in the palace with its servants and fine dining. He didn't moan about the hardships of desert life. He simply followed the cloud of God's Presence, and as he did, he knew where he was headed. The congregation complained to each other at every discomfort. They forgot the pain and sorrow of babies thrown into the Nile River as crocodile food. They forgot the lashes on their backs when they were unable to meet the quota of bricks to build Pharaoh's great cities. All they remembered were onions and garlic. I like garlic, but that is a little extreme!

How can you be a Moses? What is God asking you to do to get your focus aimed correctly? What is God asking you to forget?

I can imagine Moses' reaction as he asks, *"God, what am I to do with these people?"* (Exodus 17:4, NIVC) In crying out to God, Moses went to the right Person. He asked the right question. He needed an answer, and as he listened, God directed him.

Get Away From the Shouts To Hear God's Whisper

God's first command was to get away from the people; Moses with just a few of the elders. Get away from the negative attitudes. Get away from the lack of faith. Get away from the complaining and the rebellion.

There are times when we must move away from the wrong environments if we would see the right answers. God gently led a tired and frustrated Moses to a quieter place where Moses could think clearly again.

As we get away from negative voices, we must get close to God. Repeatedly, Moses falls on his face before God. He even climbed a mountain to have that personal conversation! God spoke to Moses. Sometimes Moses interceded for the people and their sin. He reminded God of His past promises and of His reputation. On one occasion, he asked God to erase his own name from the Book if He did not forgive the people.

Moses was God's man of choice, and God trusted Moses. Moses wanted God. He wanted God to

receive glory. Moses cared about the people God cared about. He was focused on following His instructions. And Moses was humble.

Now Moses was a very humble man, more humble than anyone else on the face of the earth. (Numbers 12:3, NIVC)

A principle of the kingdom of God is that He will exalt the humble, those who are not looking for recognition, to positions of leadership. When this happens there will be those who ask, *"Why wasn't I given recognition?"* Jealousy is one of those traits that will destroy us if we do not deal with it. The solution is so simple many people miss it. God created each of us with a purpose in mind. We are not all created for the same purpose. That would be boring!

If we find our purpose and serve wholeheartedly in that area we will be fulfilled and joyful, and, it will not matter where God positions others. Sadly, there will always be someone who wants the role of honor that is not given to them. As a result, attacks will come to those who God puts into leadership roles.

Jesus tells us that if they persecuted Him, they

will also persecute us. In this passage in John 15:20, what promise do we have?

> *Remember the word that I said unto you, the servant is not greater than his lord. If they have persecuted me, they will also persecute you; if they have kept my saying, they will keep yours also. (KJV)*

God chose to work through Moses. He chooses to work through leaders today. The role of a leader is not a glamorous role. It is a hard role because leaders must hear from God and also minister to the congregation. Their life is constantly being observed. Satan's goal is to discredit them and accuse them. Regardless of how careful they are, the enemy will stir up situations to try to make their ministry ineffective. It sounds discouraging, and sometimes it is very discouraging, but if God calls you to come up to the mountain of His Presence to receive His directives, there is only one answer that will bring joy and fulfillment. That answer is, *"Yes, Lord."*

The comfort given Moses in this very hard time with the congregation he loved was that he was not alone. The Angel of the Lord was there and would lead him and his people into God's promises.

God Hunger in the Trial

Moses became bold: not just a little courageous, but incredibly brazen! He was so hungry for more of God that he dared to ask the impossible of God. Earlier, we saw that Moses, Aaron, Aaron's sons, and seventy elders saw God and lived (Exodus 24:9-11). They were not supposed to be able to see God and live, but, in His mercy, God showed them a glimpse of Himself and then allowed them to live with this knowledge.   For most of them, it was a special spiritual experience, but, for one man, a man who'd first met God in a personal way at a burning bush, it was more than that.   For that one man, sparks of holy fire burned.   Moses wanted more.   He wanted something that was not available to mere mortals. With all of his heart and mind, Moses wanted to see the full glory of God!

In a rash outburst, Moses cried out to the Creator of the Universe, *"Show me Your Glory."* Moses didn't want a manifestation or a miracle; he wanted God. And because God was pleased with Moses and saw the pure desire for relationship, God made an impossible dream come true.

I think that God's heart must have thrilled at the

very idea that a human longed so passionately for an encounter with Him. After all, that is why He created man in the first place. Since that unique relationship was destroyed in the Garden of Eden, there had been precious few who even came close to communing with their God. Not only was God pleased with Moses, Moses wanted to experience God. Do you? Or are you satisfied with the *"normal"* Christian experiences?

No man could see all of the awesome glory of God and live. (His heart probably could not tolerate the adrenaline rush!) But there is something about a hungry heart that God must move to meet, and God did.

We can know God because of Jesus Christ. How deeply we know Him is our choice. Do we want to know Him a little bit, or do we really long for His presence in our lives? Mount Sinai was the mountain of experiencing God in His promises, power, and precepts. We can experience God on a daily basis. His promises are true, but we must embrace them with a faith that holds on until we receive what has been promised. His power is available to all who would give themselves

completely to knowing God. His precepts, or commandments, are given to protect us from the consequences of sin and to allow us to enjoy a relationship with this awesome God. Seek Him and His Presence, and you will step into a new dimension of promise, power, and precept. Seek Him and He will let you experience His glory!

If we are truly hungry for God, we will go to Him. It is when we take the time to go to God's Mountain, the place of prayer, and His presence, that He gives us a word to give His people. God's messages are meant to be specific and powerful. We cannot possibly know the hearts of those we lead, but God does. He knows just what will break the hardest heart and give courage to the most timid soldier in His service. Moses did not have a promise or a pattern for the people to follow. God did. And so, Moses went to where he knew he would find God. He was not disappointed!

When the I AM THAT I AM met with Moses on Mount Sinai at the burning bush, He gave Moses a prophetic promise. Sometimes God speaks a promise through His Word and sometimes through other people, but it is an awesome thing when God

Himself speaks into us His plan.

There are certain times in my life when God has used Scripture to show me a piece of His plan for me. He has put desires in my heart for ministry and promised me that He would lead me into certain areas. A number of people have confirmed those promises as they spoke over my life in the power of the Holy Spirit, people who did not know me at all, or did not know the specific Scriptures or promises God gave me. At such times, I have felt overwhelmed by the almighty power of God to use people to verify the truth of His promises.

But God didn't confirm His promise through anyone else to Moses. He gave the promise, Moses held onto the promise, and God fulfilled the promise.

> *And God said, "I will be with you. And this will be the sign to you that it is I who have sent you: When you have brought the people out of Egypt, you will worship God on this mountain." (Exodus 3:12, NIVC)*

-9-

WHEN YOU JUST CAN'T

It's Saturday evening, and you still need to do more work on Sunday's message. On Monday, there was a pile-up on your desk that demanded your attention. On Tuesday, you had a severe migraine and couldn't focus your eyes. That evening a close friend called, and since you had not spoken for quite a while, you couldn't cut the conversation off. Besides, you wanted to chat with this friend. You also needed to talk with one of your kids about a negative report card.

Wednesday was church, and that involved extra preparation. Your desk still had urgent items covering more than one corner, and several calls came in that were emergencies. After church, you

felt achy all over.

Thursday, you woke up with a horrible cold and, try as you might, you could not concentrate on that message. Bed won.

Friday was going to be the solution, but an hour into working on your outline, the phone rang. A church leader was in a family crisis and needed you right away. Of course, you said, *"Yes."* Right after that, the song leader called and had such a sore throat he couldn't sing. His normal back-up was out of town. You swallowed hard; your throat was getting pretty scratchy, too. Several more serious calls came in, and by then, it was time to get home. Dinner and the family needed your attention. Still achy, you went to bed early, intending to rise at dawn. The alarm did not go off, and you were awakened by the children fighting and the phone ringing. Company was coming to dinner on Sunday, and there were some major household projects that must be done.

Now you sit slumped over a message that sounded so powerful on Monday morning. Somewhere in the week, you lost your passion, and now you wonder if you really heard from God. After

a few moments with the Lord, you dig in. For almost an hour, you work. God's Word grips your heart, and you are getting some of the enthusiasm back.

Suddenly the phone rings. One of the ladies you've been counseling has decided to try suicide. She is being rushed to the hospital. *"Can you meet her in the Emergency Room?"* You wonder as you pull on your coat if the hospital has an extra room, a nice one with padded walls.

Stress - Stress - Stress

Stress is a factor in our society, but it has really been around for a long time. Moses experienced stress with the children of Israel. It has been said that the more people you have in your congregation, the more problems there are to take care of. Can you imagine having a congregation or ministry group of two to three million people that loved you in the good times and were ready to stone you in the bad times?

Moses had another source of stress. He was trying to settle disputes and do all of the pastoral counseling himself. Some of his stress was his own

fault. Lack of planning, taking on more than God intended, being consumed with the job are all going to take a toll on us emotionally, physically, and spiritually.

One day Moses had a visitor. His father-in-law, Jethro, the priest from Midian, arrived, bringing Moses' wife and sons. It was a great reunion as Moses shared all the wonderful things the Lord had and was doing for His people. Jethro was thrilled and offered up sacrifices to Jehovah.

The next day Jethro noticed Moses sitting from morning to evening as a judge before the people. Can you imagine the stress of a crowd standing around you all day, every day, waiting for your answers from the Lord?

How does that thought make you feel?

Moses had good motives. He heard from God, so he felt he needed to be there for his people. But just when we think we know how to do something, God sends someone along with a better idea. Of course, we must be sure it is a God-idea, but if it is, it may just be the incredible answer that we didn't even know to ask for.

When You Just Can't

I remember years ago when my children were young, and I was carrying quite a load at the church. At the time, my mother was very needy and called me every time she thought of something to say. I'd asked her to limit her calls to three a day, but she just didn't get it. One day I received eighteen phone calls by one o'clock in the afternoon. Some were church-related and needed attention, but many of them were from my mom. When my husband walked in the door for lunch, he found one stressed woman! I hated that telephone!

Well, God had an answer. That morning Pat was picking something up for the church and saw a great sale on answering machines. I'd always felt I had to answer every call in case it was someone needing ministry...probably the way Moses felt. But on that particular day, I realized it was my sanity or my availability. It could not be both. God cared enough about my needs and well-being to lead my husband to a great sale!

Today you may be swamped with direct messages or texts. People don't mean to overwhelm you, but the enemy does. If they know you love them and will get back when you can, they will be alright.

Maybe just a short note that says, "I can't talk right now. Is three o'clock alright?" A counselor once shared with me that people don't need an immediate answer; they need to know there will be one.

While Moses Was Reaching Out To The Congregation God Was Reaching Out To Moses

Read Jethro's advice.

> *Listen now to me and I will give you some advice, and may God be with you. You must be the people's representative before God and bring their disputes to him. ... Teach them .... select capable men ... Have them serve as judges for the people at all times, but have them bring every difficult case to you; the simple cases they can decide themselves. (Exodus 18:19-22, NIVC)*

Some areas of stress are our own doing. When his father-in-law came to see him in the wilderness, Jethro noticed Moses was trying to do it all himself. Some people do this because they feel a strong sense of obligation to God and people. Some have a need to feel important or do not trust others to do a good

job. They may feel they are the only ones who will do it well. That may be true, but if we never develop our leaders, we will always have to do it all. Other people do it all because they just do not know how to delegate. Jethro, Moses' father-in-law, had a good plan.

As I get older, I am really glad for the time I took years ago to begin developing lay leaders. God has people ready and waiting to take on more responsibility. They may need some of your time in ministry, some teaching, and some hands-on demonstration, but they are also called to fulfill the work of the ministry. If you neglect them, there will be something unfulfilled in their lives. There will be people they were meant to touch that will never be reached. If, on the other hand, you take the time to develop others, you will be incredibly blessed! You cannot do it alone. Remember, it is God Who is building His church. It is His work, and He has given a variety of gifts to a variety of people to get the job done. His plan involves using the whole Body of Christ, not just one person. Ministry life involves teamwork, as every member does his or her part. A good leader must recognize that it is not just about getting a job done; it is about discipling others

to disciple others.

Stress is the result of striving to carry God's load alone. It is very individualized. It can be good when our body goes into a fight or flight mode for the purpose of protection. Stress can be a signal to find new and better solutions to certain issues. Short-term stress hormonal response is normal and part of life. It helps us develop wisdom and faith and maturity and should be followed by a relaxation response as the threat passes.

On the other hand, chronic stress develops if we cannot manage our issues. Psychologists say that some people have a lower tolerance for frustration than others; others have never learned how to handle normal daily difficulties, and so everything becomes a major issue. Obviously, this can create problems if not dealt with in a healthy way. More severe problems include anxiety disorders, depression, and post-traumatic stress disorder.

There are hot reactors that blow up at the slightest problem, there are pressure cookers who just hold it all in until there is a major explosion or until they turn the stress inward and become depressed, and there are those who just become negative people

with negative attitudes.

We cannot control certain stressors – the key is how we react. If Satan can overwhelm us, we will not be or do what the Lord Jesus desires us to be or do. Eventually, we will become totally inward in our focus, and God and others will not be important.

Attitudes affect how our body handles stress. If you believe it will all work together for good, you will be healthier than if you feel that things are out of control. Satan is our enemy, and he wants to have us give up. Faith in God is the bottom line that directs our reactions. Even when things have not gone as we planned them, even when it looks like our world is falling apart, God is still in charge, and He knows right where to find you. Feeling Him there is not necessary; knowing that His Word says He will never leave us is!

-10-
OVERCOMING CRITICISM

In ministry, we cannot be God! We need people to come alongside us. We need others to help carry the load and to support us in our prayers and ministry.

They tested God at Rephidim. The Amalekites attacked them at Rephidim. When we let our attitudes become negative and rebellious, we become vulnerable to attack. But God never changes.

The battle with the Amalekites is a lesson in teamwork. As Moses stood on the mountain, holding the staff of God aloft, Joshua and his army won the battle in the valley. When Moses became tired, and his arms could no longer hold their position, the enemy won.

Not all of the men were in Joshua's army, only some of them. The majority apparently stayed in the camp. In contrast, there were only two men with Moses, Aaron, and Hur. This is a picture of the battles in today's spiritual arena. Even when it seems the world is gaining ground, there are many people in God's camp, the Church of Jesus Christ. Where the battle rages, some people are heavily involved. They are doing the work that keeps the church alive; they are fighting hard, and sometimes they see victories, and sometimes the enemy strikes hard blows. It is tough out there in the middle of the fight. Some will die, some will receive injuries that leave scars, and some will survive to deal with the memories. But they are the kind of people that are so committed they will not retreat in defeat, whatever the cost.

But something more than soldiers was needed here. There are times when the battle-weary cannot do it alone. There was one that stood in the gap between God's victory and the soldiers in the valley below.

Remember, they are still camped at Rephidim, the place of testing God and murmuring against

their leader. Note the humble and loving spirit of Moses. The people rejected his leadership and wanted to stone him. Yet when the attack came, Moses gave all he had to stand as an intercessor between these very people and God Almighty. Are you like Moses?

Moses stood on the mountain of intercession, and there he held up his hands and the staff of God over God's army. He was God's man, but he was only a man. The weight he carried was enormous. His hands grew heavier and heavier.

I remember seeking the baptism of the Holy Spirit and thinking I had to keep my hands straight up in order to receive God's gift. As my arms got tired, they felt heavier and heavier. Eventually, they started to go numb. Instead of worshipping God, at that point, I found myself asking God to help my arms! The focus of my attention left the Presence of God and moved to my physical discomfort.

Moses, a picture of frail humanity, could not keep his arms up. They started to fall to his sides. As his hands, and thus God's staff, dropped, the enemy prevailed. So Moses would gather all the strength he had and push his arms up again, only to find them

sinking after a period of time. He could not physically carry on. True intercession is very hard work!

Better Together

God didn't send Aaron and Hur up the mountain with Moses to enjoy the scenery or watch the battle. He sent them up there to get involved with a matter of life and death for His people. Moses heard from God and went to intercede. Aaron and Hur heard from Moses and were observant enough to see a need they could help with. And they did. They were not the soldiers; they were not Moses; but without these two, the battle would have been lost. Vital to victory, they stood on each side of Moses, agreeing with him in the ministry of intercession until sunset when the enemy in the valley was defeated. They literally came alongside God's leader and picked up the load that he could not carry alone. They also looked out for a very tired Moses and provided him with a stone to sit on. Leaders need godly helpers like Aaron and Hur if they are going to truly see the victory God has promised.

I cannot thank God enough for the intercessors He has given me over the years. People I can trust.

Friends who will take the prayer call seriously. They are a vital part of the victory God gives. These people are gifts to be treasured!

We know about Aaron, but who was Hur? Josephus, the Jewish historian, says that Hur was the husband of Miriam, sister of Moses and Aaron. He's seen again when Moses goes up Mount Sinai to meet with God and leaves Aaron and Hur in charge of the Israelite congregation.

In obedience to God's directives, Moses records the event and then builds an altar. This is a place of victory, and as such, God introduces a new aspect of His character to His people. Here the Lord is called *Jehovah-nissi, The Lord is my Banner*, for here hands were lifted up to God's throne, and here under the banner of God's staff victory prevailed.

Under God, Our banner, we are winners. The battle may be fierce. The attack may be prolonged. The soldiers and intercessors may be exhausted. But we stand as one. God is our Banner, and the battle belongs to the Lord!

-11-

LOSING IT ...AND ... LOSING IT

The Israelites had been wandering in the wilderness, and they came again to the Desert of Zin to the place known as Kadesh. Here Miriam died and was buried, and the entire congregation mourned for her. Moses and Aaron were still grieving the death of their sister and partner in the ministry. Their hearts were focused on their personal pain when the enemy blind-sided them with an angry attack. In other situations, the people grumbled and were upset, but in this situation, they were angry.

And the people contended with Moses, and said, Would that we had died when our brethren died [in the plague] before the

Lord! (Numbers 20:3 – Amplified Classic)

Moses and Aaron again went on their faces before the Lord. This was the right thing to do. As they sought God, His glory appeared, and He gave Moses the directions for providing water.

> *"Take the staff, and you and your brother Aaron gather the assembly together. Speak to that rock before their eyes and it will pour out its water. You will bring water out of the rock for the community so they and their livestock can drink." (Numbers 20:8 – NIVC)*

God wanted to show His power and also to show truth regarding Himself.

> *So Moses took the staff from the Lord's presence, just as he commanded him. He and Aaron gathered the assembly together in front of the rock and Moses said to them, "Listen, you rebels, must we bring you water out of this rock?" Then Moses raised his arm and struck the rock twice with his staff. Water gushed out, and the community and their livestock drank. (Numbers 20:9-11, NIVC)*

Notice what Moses said and the tone with which he spoke. We've seen Moses stressed before, but this seems to be the proverbial final straw. Instead of crying out to God for them, he calls them rebels. Obviously, the burden he felt at this moment was a size extra-large, but he forgot that it was not his burden. For the first time, he claims that he and Aaron are the ones who must meet the people's needs. Psalm 106 tells us that he spoke rashly.

When we are emotionally exhausted, we should be on guard against acting in our own strength. Moses again would have benefited from getting away and spending time with God. He was tired and sad and stressed and made a fatal blunder that would keep him from seeing the fruit of his life's work.

Then what?

God tells Moses his sins. Faith was the missing ingredient. Although Moses was a man of faith, he did not trust God to do the necessary miracle with just a spoken word. That was outside of his comfort zone. It was new and untested. When God uses us, it is wonderful, but there is a danger in depending on a method and not on the I AM THAT I AM.

The rod was a tried and true miracle-producer. Even though God said, *"Speak to the rock,"* Moses used the rod to hit it, not once, but twice. In so doing, he reacted in anger and did not honor God as holy and sanctified in the eyes of the congregation. Yet God came through, and water did indeed gush from the rock, flowing like a river to meet the needs. God will sometimes do that type of thing just because He loves His people.

There was a bigger problem with the striking of the rock than first meets the eye. This was not just one of the rocks strewn through the wasteland. Read these verses and note the identity of this rock

> *He abandoned the God who made him and rejected the Rock his Savior.*
> *(Deuteronomy 32:15, NIVC)*

> *...and that rock was Christ.*
> *(1 Cor. 10:4, NIVC)*

All Moses had to do was speak to the rock. All we have to do is to speak the Name Jesus.

We so often miss great concepts in Scripture because we do not understand the culture. When I was a little girl, and we sang, *"Jesus is a Rock in a*

weary land," I thought of a giant rock that stood out as a symbol of strength. Yes, Jesus is our Source of strength, but He is so much more!

The weary land, or wilderness, is a dry, hot place. It is a lonely place because so often the enemy convinces us that no one cares, and if they do care, they can't help us anyway. It is a place where the sun beats without mercy, where the wind whips sand and dust in your eyes, where you are thirsty for a spiritual refreshing and hungry for a Word from the Lord, but none come. Even when you do all the right things, you feel lacking and weak. It is a place of poisonous vipers aiming to destroy you and fidgety jackals anxiously pacing in anticipation of the moment you fall. It is a place where the spiritual battle rages, but your strength is almost gone. You stagger and wipe your brow. The wilderness stretches before you as an endless sea. Squinting against the glare, you whisper the Name.

Suddenly in the midst of barrenness, something catches your eye. It is large and rugged. You take a deep breath and look again. It is still there. With great effort, you begin to move in the direction of a great Rock. Shadows play around the edges of the

Rock, and you can see a hollowed out place just your size. Water trickles over its jagged edges, and at its base are the soft shades of green grass.

That Rock is Jesus. He was there all the time, but when you whispered His Name, you saw Him. He is stronger than any fortress and stands against the enemies that long to destroy you. The cleft in the Rock is a hiding place, a shelter from enemies, protection from the heat, and whipping wind; it is a quiet place where you can lay your head against the cool surface and rest. There the Living Water flows, and the very Presence of God fills your heart with peace. It doesn't matter that the storm is still raging or the sun still beating down on the already scorched earth. It doesn't matter that the enemies are still waiting or that just a short time ago, you didn't know if you could survive. You have arrived, and in the shelter of that Rock, you are safe!

God calls us to an oasis of His peace and protection in the middle of turbulence. He wants us to have the joy of drinking the Living Water poured out for us. Will you speak to the Rock in faith, or will you keep striking the Rock in your frustration and anger? Will you obey and see the Promised

Land in your own life?

Now What

But, what if you missed God's directive? What if there is a call you did not chase after? What if you failed?!

Keep going.

God's response to the anger and disobedience was clear. Moses would not lead God's people into the Promised Land. All the testings, all the dealing with this rebellious group, all the conversations with God on the mountain could not change the fact that he'd failed and, at that moment, had lost the privilege of leading his congregation into the Promised Land.

But Moses never stopped being the best Moses he could be. He kept on putting one foot in front of the other. He kept leading God's people.

Satan wants us to give up when we fall down, but God reaches out, steadies our feet, and helps us move forward. The children of Israel still needed Moses; Joshua still needed him.

Moses was an amazing man of God. He met

God. He argued with God. He agreed with God. He was focused. And, no matter what happened, he just kept moving forward in his obedience to the call. Because his heart was focused on God's purpose, he could keep going despite the personal loss. It wasn't about Moses; it was about God and God's people.

There are times when we cannot undo what has been done, but God forgives. He still loves us. He will still use us for His glory – if we keep moving on in His purpose!

-12-

PASSING THE MANTLE

It was his birthday! Moses was a hundred and twenty years old, but his eyes were not weak nor his strength gone. Yet, it was time! We must know when it is that time.

The journey was over. Forty years of traveling through the wilderness. It had truly been an impossible dream. You can't take millions of slaves out of a country, and you can't lead that many people through a wilderness without food and water. But Moses did his part, and God did His part, and the rest is history!

Years of seeing God and Moses and years of serving as Moses' aide prepared Joshua to step into those big sandals. But Moses needed to present God's new man to the congregation. He needed to

affirm him as God's choice for the new season.

As far as you could see, they gathered to hear Moses give his farewell. As he proclaimed God's commandments and challenged the people to serve the Lord, he reminded them that success was theirs.

> *This day I call heaven and earth as witnesses against you that I have set before you life and death, blessings and curses. Now choose life, so that you and your children may live and that you may love the Lord your God, listen to his voice, and hold fast to him. For the Lord is your life, and he will give you many years in the land he swore to give to your fathers, Abraham, Isaac and Jacob. (Deuteronomy 30:19-20, NIVC)*

Moses passed his commission on to Joshua, encouraging him to be strong and courageous. God would be with him. Then this great old shepherd of God's flock sang a song of praise proclaiming the greatness of the God Who had led him these many years. He blessed that great multitude, the congregation for which he had given his whole life, the people whom he had loved and served.

Following the God he had come to trust completely, he walked up Mount Nebo. Moses was not alone. He walked with his tried and true Friend of forty years. I feel certain that they continued their conversation as they walked that final lap, remembering the journey, and looking ahead to the future.

For Moses, this climb would be his last. Although, because of his disobedience, he could not enter the Promised Land in his natural lifetime, the Lord gave His friend and servant Moses a special panoramic view of that Holy Land.

God, Himself, gives us the last chapter of the life of Moses, this incredible leader who knew God and who allowed himself to be used to do mighty deeds for the glory of the Lord.

> *And Moses the servant of the Lord died there in Moab, as the Lord had said.*

> *He (God) buried him in Moab, in the valley opposite Beth Peor, but to this day no one knows where his grave is. (Deuteronomy 34:5-6, NIVC)*

Moses did not enjoy the natural blessings of the Promised Land, but God did allow him to enter it

many centuries later for a very special occasion.

About eight days after Jesus said this, he took Peter, John and James with him and went up onto a mountain to pray. As he was praying, the appearance of his face changed, and his clothes became as bright as a flash of lightning. Two men, Moses and Elijah, appeared in glorious splendor, talking with Jesus. They spoke about his departure, which he was about to bring to fulfillment at Jerusalem. Peter and his companions were very sleepy, but when they became fully awake, they saw his glory and the two men standing with him. As the men were leaving Jesus, Peter said to him, "Master, it is good for us to be here. Let us put up three shelters--one for you, one for Moses and one for Elijah." (He did not know what he was saying.)

While he was speaking, a cloud appeared and enveloped them, and they were afraid as they entered the cloud. A voice came from the cloud, saying, "This is my Son, whom I have chosen; listen to him." (Luke 9:28-35, NIVC)

Passing The Mantle

Moses had seen the Lord's glory and His provision, but in the life to come, he would see Him and speak with Him on the Mount of Transfiguration. We serve our Lord here by faith. There are times when we see a glimpse of His great glory and power, but someday we shall see Him face to face in all of His majesty. It is our hope. There is a Promised Land, and it is for all of us who refuse to quit but choose to follow our beloved Lord and Savior until He calls us to walk up the mountain into His very presence.

About The Author

 Laverne Weber is a speaker, teacher, nurse, and author of Victory's Journey and Moving On for Men. In 1993 she founded Victory's Journey Ministries as a small group healing ministry. Through the years many have found the freedom to move out of the shadows of their past into a vibrant life in Christ.

Laverne and her husband, Pat, are retired pastors and live in Pennsylvania. They have three children and four grandchildren.

Bibliography

Chapter 1

1. Livingstone, David, retrieved from
azquotes.com/quote/531164

Chapter 6

1. Chan, Francis, retrieved from azquotes.com,
Preston Sprinkle (2014). *"The Francis Chan
Collection: Crazy Love, Forgotten God, Erasing Hell,
and Multiply"*, p. 88, David Cook

Chapter 7

1. Allis, Oswald T, *"God Spake By Moses: An
Exposition of the Pentateuch"* (Nutley, New Jersey: The
Presbyterian and Reformed Publishing Company,
1972) p. 68.

Chapter 8

1. Sweet, Leonard I (2014), retrieved from
azquotes.com, *"The Well-Played Life: Why Pleasing
God Doesn't Have to Be Such Hard Work"*, p. 116,
Tyndale House Publishers, Inc.

Made in the USA
Middletown, DE
15 October 2022

12827556R00076

CPSIA information can be obtained at www.ICGtesting.com
Printed in the USA
BVOW02s1911231113

337061BV00004B/8/P